Statistics for Social and Behavioral Sciences

Advisors:
S.E. Fienberg W.J. van der Linden

Statistics for Social and Behavioral Sciences

Wim J. van der Linden

Linear Models for Optimal Test Design

Foreword by Ronald K. Hambleton

With 44 Figures

 Springer

Wim J. van der Linden
Department of Measurement
    and Data Analysis
Faculty of Behavioral Sciences
University of Twente
7500 AE Enschede
The Netherlands
w.j.vanderlinden@utwente.nl

Advisors:
Stephen E. Fienberg
Department of Statistics
Carnegie Mellon University
Pittsburgh, PA 15213-3890
USA

Wim J. van der Linden
Department of Measurement
    and Data Analysis
Faculty of Behavioral Sciences
University of Twente
7500 AE Enschede
The Netherlands

Library of Congress Control Number: 2005923810

ISBN-10: 0-387-20272-2
ISBN-13: 978-0387-20272-3

Printed on acid-free paper.

Printed in the United States of America.   (EB)

9 8 7 6 5 4 3 2 1

springeronline.com

Voor mijn lieve Tonneke

Foreword

Over my nearly forty years of teaching and conducting research in the field of psychometric methods, I have seen a number of major technical advances that respond to pressing educational and psychological measurement problems. The development of criterion-referenced assessment was the first, beginning in the late 1960s with the important work of Robert Glaser and Jim Popham, in response to the need for assessments that considered candidate performance in relation to a well-defined body of knowledge and skills rather than in relation to a norm group. The development of criterion-referenced testing methodology with a focus on decision-theoretic concepts and methods, content validity, standard-setting, and the recognition of the merits of both criterion-norm-referenced and criterion-referenced assessments has tremendously influenced current test theory and testing .

The second major advance was the introduction of item response-theory (IRT) and associated models and their applications to replace classical test theory (CTT) and related practices. Beginning slowly in the 1940s and 1950s with the pioneering work of Frederic Lord, Allan Birnbaum, and Georg Rasch, by the 1970s the measurement journals were full of important research studies describing new IRT models, technical advances in model parameter estimation and model fit, and research on applications of IRT models to equating, test development, the detection of potentially biased test items, and adaptive testing. The overall goal has been to improve and expand measurement practices by overcoming several shortcomings of classical test theory: dependence of test-item statistics and reliability estimates on examinee samples, dependence of examinee true score estimates on the particular choices of test items, and the limitation in CTT of modeling examinee performance at the test level rather than at the item level. The last two shortcomings are especially problematic for adaptive testing, where it is important to be able to assess ability independently of particular test items and closely link item statistics to examinee ability or proficiency for the optimal selection of test items to shorten testing time and improve measurement precision on a per item basis. Today, the teaching of item-response theory is common in graduate training programs in psychometric methods, and IRT models and applications dominate the field of assessment.

The third major advance was the transition of testing practices from the administration of tests via paper and pencil to administration via the computer. This transition, which began in the late 1970s in the United States with considerable research funding from the armed services and with the leadership of such important scholars as Frederic Lord, Mark Reckase, Howard Wainer, and David Weiss, is widespread, with hundreds of credentialing exams (e.g., the Uniform Certified Public Accountancy Exams, the nursing exams, and securities industry exams in the United States), admissions tests (e.g., the Graduate Record Exam, the Graduate Management Admissions Test, and the Test of English as a Foreign Language), and achievement tests (e.g., high-school graduation tests in Virginia) being administered to candidates via computers, with more tests being added every month. The computer has added flexibility (with many testing programs, candidates can now take tests when they feel they are ready or when they need to take the tests), immediate scoring capabilities (thus removing what can often be months of waiting time for candidates), and the capability of assessing knowledge and skills that could not be easily assessed with paper-and-pencil tests. On this latter point, higher-level thinking skills, complex problem-solving, conducting research using reference materials, and much more are now being included in assessments because of the power of the computer.

Assessing candidates at a computer is becoming routine, and now a number of very important lines of research have been initiated. Research on automated scoring of constructed responses will ensure that computer-based testing can include the free-response test-item format, and thus the construct validity of many assessments will be enhanced. Research on automated item generation represents the next stage in test-item development and should expedite item writing, expand item pools, and lower the costs of item development. Automated item generation also responds to one of the main threats to the validity of computer-based testing with flexible candidate scheduling, and that is the overexposure of test items. With more test items available, the problem of overexposure of test items will be reduced.

Perhaps the most researched aspect of computer-based testing concerns the choice of test design. Initially, the focus was on fully adaptive tests. How should the first test item be selected? How should the second and third items and so on, be selected? When should testing be discontinued? How should ability or proficiency following the administration of each item be estimated? Other test designs have been studied, too: multistage computer-based test designs (instead of selecting one optimal item after another, a block of test items, sometimes called "testlets" or "modules" are selected in some optimal fashion), and linear on-the-fly test designs (random or adaptive selection of tests subject to a variety of content and statistical constraints). Even the conventional linear test has been popular with one of a number of parallel forms being selected at random for administration to a candidate at a computer. But when computer-based testing research was initiated in the late 1970s, aptitude testing was the focus (e.g., the Armed Services Vocational Aptitude Battery), and detailed content-validity considerations were not a central concern. As the focus shifted to the study of computer-based achievement tests and credentialing exams (i.e., criterion-referenced tests) and the use of test scores became more important (e.g., credentialing exams are used to determine who is qualified to obtain a license or certificate to practice in a profession), content considerations became absolutely central to test defensibility and validity, and balancing tests from one examinee to the next for the length of item stems, the balance of constructed and selected response items, minimizing the overuse of test items, meeting detailed content specifications, building tests to match target information functions, and more, considerably more sophisticated methods for item selection were needed. It was in this computer-based testing environment that automated test assembly was born.

I have probably known about automated test assembly since 1983 (Wendy Yen wrote about it in one of her many papers), but the first paper I recall reading that was dedicated to the topic, and it is a classic in the psychometric methods field today, was the paper by Professor Wim van der Linden and Ellen Boekkooi-Timminga published in *Psychometrika* in 1989. In this paper, the authors introduced the concepts underlying automated test assembly and provided some very useful examples. I was fascinated that just about any content and statistical criteria that a test developer might want to impose on a test could be specified by them in the form of linear (in)equalities. Also, a test developer could choose an "objective function" to serve as the goal for test development. With a goal for test development reflected in an "objective function," such as with respect to a target test-information function (and perhaps even several goals), and both content and statistical specifications described in the form of linear constraints, the computer could find a set of test items that maximally met the needs of the test developer. What a breakthrough! I might add that initially there was concern by some test developers that they might be losing control of their tests, but later it became clear that the computer could be used to produce, when desired, first drafts of tests that could then be reviewed and revised by committees.

The 1989 van der Linden and Boekkooi-Timminga paper was the first that I recall that brought together three immensely important technologies, two that I have already highlighted as major advances in the psychometric methods field—item-response theory and the use of the computer—and also operations research. But what impresses me today is that automated test assembly impacts or capitalizes on all of the major advances in the last 40 years of my career: criterion-referenced and norm-referenced assessments, item-response theory, computer-based testing, and new computer-based test designs, as well as emerging new assessment formats.

By 2004, I had accumulated a hundred papers (and probably more) on the topic. Most are by Professor Wim van der Linden and his colleagues in the Netherlands, but many other researchers have joined in and are producing important work and advancing the field. These papers overflow my files on item-response theory, test design, computerized adaptive testing, item selection, item-bank inventory, item-exposure controls, and many more topics. My filing system today is simply not capable of organizing and sequencing all of the contributions on the topic of automated test assembly since 1989, and I have lost track of the many lines of research, the most important advances, and so on. Perhaps if I were closely working in the field, the lines of research would be clearer to me, but like many measurement specialists, I have a number of research interests, and it is not possible today to be fully conversant with all of them. But from a distance, it was clear to me that automated test assembly, or optimal test design, or automated test construction, all terms that I have seen used in the field, was going to provide the next generation of test-design methods—interestingly whether or not a test was actually going to be administered at a computer! Now, with one book, van der Linden's *Linear Models for Optimal Test Design*, order in my world has been restored with respect to this immensely important topic, and future generations of assessment specialists and researchers will benefit from Professor Wim van der Linden's technical advances and succinct writing skills.

I believe *Linear Models for Optimal Test Design* should be required reading for anyone seriously interested in the psychometric methods field. Computers have brought about major changes in the way we think about tests, construct tests, administer tests, and report scores. Professor van der Linden has written a book that organizes, clarifies, and expands what is known about test design for the next generation of tests, and test design is the base or centerpiece for all future testing. He has done a superb job of organizing and synthesizing the topic of automated test assembly for readers, providing a step-by-step introduction to the topic, and offering lots of examples to support the relevant theory and practices. The field is much richer for Professor van der Linden's contribution, and I expect this book will both improve the practice of test development in the future and spur others to carry out additional research.

Ronald K. Hambleton
University of Massachusetts at Amherst

Preface

The publication of Spearman's paper "The proof and measurement of association between two things" in the *American Journal of Psychology* in 1904 was the very tentative start of a new field now known as test theory. This book appears almost exactly a century later. During this period, test theory has developed from a timid fledgling to a mature discipline, with numerous results that nowadays support item and test analysis and test scoring at nearly every testing organization around the world.

This preface is not an appropriate place to evaluate a hundred years of test theory. But two observations may help me to explain my motives for writing this book. The first is that test theory has developed by careful modeling of response processes on test items and by using sophisticated statistical tools for estimating model parameters and evaluating model fit. In doing so, it has reached a current level of perfection that no one ever thought possible, say, two or three decades ago. Second, in spite of its enormous progress, although test theory is omnipresent, its results are used in a peculiar way. Any outsider entering the testing industry would expect to find a spin-off in the form of a well-developed technology that enables us to engineer tests rigorously to our specifications. Instead, test theory is mainly used for post hoc quality control, to weed out unsuccessful items, sometimes after they have been pretested, but sometimes after they have already been in operational use. Apparently, our primary mode of operation is not to create good tests, but only to prevent bad tests. To draw a parallel with the natural sciences, it seems as if testing has led to the development of a new science, but the spin-off in the form of a technology for engineering the test has not yet been realized.

Part of the explanation for our lack of technology may be a deeply in-grained belief among some in the industry that test items are unique and that test development should be treated as an art rather than a technol-ogy. I certainly believe that test items are unique. In fact, I even hope they will remain so; testing would suffer from serious security problems if they ceased to be so. Also, as a friend of the arts, I am sensitive to the aesthetic dimension of human artifacts. The point is, however, that these qualities do not relieve testing professionals of their duty to develop a technology. To draw another parallel, architecture has a deep artistic quality to it, and good architects are true artists. But if they were to give up their technology, we would have no place to live or work.

The use of design principles is an essential difference between technology-based approaches and the approaches with post hoc quality control hinted at above. Another difference is the use of techniques to guarantee that products will operate according to our specifications. These principles and techniques are to be used in a process that goes through four different stages: (1) establishing a set of specifications for the new testing program, (2) designing an item pool to support the program, (3) developing the item pool, and (4) assembling tests from the pool to meet the specifications. Although it is essential that the first stage be completed before the others are, the three other stages are more continuous and are typically planned to optimize the use of the resources in the testing organization. But it is important to distinguish between them because each involves the use of different principles and techniques.

At a slightly more formal level, test design is not unique at all; some of its stages have much in common with entirely different areas, where pro-fessionals also develop products, have certain goals in mind, struggle with constraints, and want optimal results. In fact, in this book I borrow heavily from the techniques of linear programming, widely used in industry, busi-ness, and commerce to optimize processes and products. These techniques have been around for a long time, and to implement them, we can resort to commercial computer software not yet discovered by the testing industry. In a sense, this book does not offer anything new. Then, to demonstrate the techniques's applicability, we had to reconceptualize the process of test design, introduce a new language to deal with it, integrate the treatment of content and statistical requirements for tests, and formulate typical test-design goals and requirements as simple linear models. More importantly, we also had to demonstrate the power and nearly universal applicability of these models through a wide range of empirical examples dealing with several test-design problems.

Although the topic of this book is *test design*, the term is somewhat ambiguous. The only stage in the design process at which something is actually designed is the second stage, item-pool design. From that point on, the production of a test only involves its assembly to certain specifications from a given item pool. The stages of item-pool design and test assembly can be based on the same techniques from linear programming. But these techniques are much more easily understood as tools of test assembly, and for didactic reasons, I first treat the problem of test assembly and return to the problem of item-pool design as one of the last topics in this book.

In particular, the book is organized as follows. Chapter 1 introduces the current practice of test development and explains some elementary concepts from test theory, such as reliability and validity, and item and test information. Chapter 2 introduces a standard language for formulating test specifications. In Chapter 3, I show how this language can be used to model test assembly problems as simple linear models. Chapter 4 discusses general approaches available in mathematical programming, more specifically integer or combinatorial programming, to solve these models. A variety of empirical examples of the applications of the techniques to test-assembly problems, including such problems as IRT-based and classical test assembly, assembling multiple test forms, assembling tests with item sets, multidimensional test assembly, and adaptive test assembly, are presented in Chapters 5–9. The topic of item-pool design for programs with fixed and adaptive tests is treated in Chapter 10 and 11, respectively. The book concludes with a few more reflective observations on the topic of test design.

My goal has been to write a book that will become a helpful resource on the desk of any test specialist. Therefore, I have done my utmost to keep the level of technical sophistication in this book at a minimum. Instead, I emphasize such aspects as problem analysis, nature of assumptions, and applicability of results. In principle, the mathematical knowledge required to understand this book comprises linear equalities and inequalities from high-school algebra and a familiarity with set theory notation. The few formulas from test theory used in this book are discussed in Chapter 1. In addition, a few concepts from linear programming that are required to understand our modeling approaches are reviewed in Appendix 1. Nevertheless, Chapter 4 had to be somewhat more technical because it deals with methods for solving optimization problems. Readers with no previous experience with this material may find the brief introductions to the various algorithms and heuristics in this chapter abstract. If they have no affinity for the subject, they should read this chapter only cursorily, skipping the details they do not understand. They can do so without losing anything needed to understand the rest of the book. Also, it is my experience that the subject of multidimensional test assembly in Chapter 8 and, for that matter, the extension of adaptive test assembly to a multidimensional item pool in the last sections of Chapter 9, is more difficult to understand, mainly because the generalization of the notion of information in a unidimensional test to the case of multidimensionality is not entirely intuitive. Readers with no interest in this subject can skip this portion of the book and go directly to Chapter 10, where we begin our treatment of the subject of item-pool design.

Although this book presents principles and techniques that can be used in the three stages of test specification, item-pool design, and test assembly, the stage of item-pool development is hardly touched. The steps of item pretesting and calibration executed in this stage are treated well in several other books and papers (e.g., Hambleton & Swaminathan, 1985; Lord, 1980; Lord & Novick, 1968), and it is not necessary to repeat this material here. As for the preceding step of writing items for a pool, I do go as far as to show how blueprints for items can be calculated at the level of specific item writers and offer suggestions on how to manage the item-writing process (Chapter 10). But I do not deal with the actual process of item writing. Current item-writing practices are challenged by rapid developments in techniques for algorithmic item writing (e.g., Irvine & Kyllonen, 2002). I find these developments, which are in the same spirit as the "engineering approach" to test design advocated in this book, most promising, and I hope that, before too long, the two technologies will meet and integrate. This integration would reserve the intellectually more challenging parts of test design for our test specialists and allow them to assign their more boring daily operations to computer algorithms.

Several of the themes in this book were addressed in earlier research projects at the Department of Research Methodology, Measurement, and Data Analysis at the University of Twente. Over a period of more than 15 years, I have had the privilege of supervising dissertations on problems in test assembly and item-pool design by Jos J. Adema, Ellen Timminga, Bernard P. Veldkamp, and, currently, Adelaide Ariel. Their cooperation, creativity, and technical skills have been greatly appreciated. Special mention is deserved by Wim M.M. Tielen, who as a software specialist has provided continuous support in numerous test-assembly projects.

The majority of the research projects in this book were done with financial support from the Law School Admissions Council (LSAC), Newtown, Pennsylvania. Its continuous belief in what I have been doing has been an important stimulus to me, for which I am much indebted to Peter J. Pashley, Lynda M. Reese, Stephen T. Schreiber, and Philip D. Shelton. My main contact with the test specialists at the LSAC was Stephen E. Luebke, who provided all of the information about the item pools and test specifications that I needed for the projects in this book.

This book was written while I was a Fellow of the Center for Advanced Study in the Behavioral Sciences, Stanford, California. My fellowship was supported by a grant to the Center from the Spencer Foundation, for which I am most grateful. The tranquil location of the Center, on the top of a hill just above the Stanford campus, and the possession of a study overlooking a beautiful portion of the Santa Cruz Mountains, enabled me to view things in a wide perspective. I thank Doug McAdam, Director, and Mark Turner, Associate Director, as well as their entire staff, for their outstanding support during my fellowship. I am indebted to Kathleen Much for her editorial comments on a portion of this book as well as on several other papers I wrote while at the Center.

Seven chapters of this book were tried out in a course on advanced topics in educational measurement at Michigan State University by Mark D. Reckase. His critical comments and those of his students led to many improvements in the original text. Bernard P. Veldkamp read several earlier versions of the manuscript and checked all exercises, while Adelaide Ariel went far beyond her call of duty with her help with the preparation of the graphs in this book. I am also grateful to Krista Breithaupt, Simon Bussman, Britta Colver, Alexander Freund, Heiko Grossman, Donovan Hare, Heinz Holling and Tobias Kuhn, whose comments helped me tremendously to polish the final version of the manuscript. The last chapter was completed while I enjoyed a fellowship from the Invitational Fellowship Program for Research in Japan at the University of Tokyo. I am indebted to the Japan Society for the Promotion of Science (JSPS) for the fellowship and to Kazuo Shigemasu for having been such a charming host.

Last but not least, I would like to thank John Kimmel, Executive Editor, Statistics, at Springer for being a quick and helpful source of information during the production of this book.

Each of the people whose support I acknowledge here have made my task as an author much more pleasant than I anticipated when I began working on the book.

Wim J. van der Linden
University of Twente

Acknowledgment of Copyrights

Several of the figures and tables in this book are (slightly re-edited) versions of figures and tables in earlier journal articles by the author. He is grateful to *Applied Psychological Measurement* for the right to reproduce Figures 5.6, 7.1, and 7.2 and Tables 5.3, 6.2, 6.3, 7.2, 10.1, and 11.1, to the *Journal of Educational and Behavioral Statistics* for the right to reproduce Figures 9.1, 11.1, and 11.2, and to the *Journal of Educational Measurement* for the right to reproduce Figures 11.3 and 11.4 and Table 5.1.

Contents

1
Brief History of Test Theory and Design

Standardized testing was common practice in some ancient cultures long before western civilization developed—a well-known example is nationwide testing for civil service in ancient China. But we had to wait until the early twentieth century before it was introduced in western psychology. In 1905, Binet and Simon developed their intelligence test to identify students with mental retardation in Paris schools (Binet & Simon, 1905). Remarkably, this test already had most of the features characteristic of modern adaptive testing. The test was meant for individualized administration with a human proctor who scored the students during the test and selected the items. Standardization was obtained through the use of the same item pool and the application of the same detailed rules of item selection and scoring for all test takers.

The idea of standardized testing was extended from individualized testing to group-based, paper-and-pencil testing later in the twentieth century. The main stimuli for this transition were the necessities of placing large numbers of conscripts in the U.S. army during World Wars I and II and of fair admission methods to regulate the huge increase in student inflow into higher education in the second half of the twentieth century. These developments led to the large-scale use of multiple-choice tests—the ultimate format with objective, machine-based scoring of the test takers' responses to the test items.

In the early 1970s, a different type of testing emerged, first exclusively in education but later also in psychology. This new development was motivated by attempts to improve student learning in schools through frequent feedback on their achievements by tests embedded in the instruction. The first idea was to offer students self-paced routes through series of small instructional modules, each finishing with a mastery test. Later, this idea was extended with choices between alternative modes of learning and students working more freely on series of assignments. A natural consequence of this development for individualized instruction was the need for item banking to support testing on demand (also referred to as "walk-in testing"). As a result, the earlier notion of a standardized test as the same paper-and-pencil form for each test taker evolved into the idea of testing from item pools defined by extensive lists of specifications and algorithmic item writing and test assembly. The advent of cheap personal computers with plentiful computational power in the early 1990s stimulated these changes enormously. When a few years later the technology of item banking and individualized testing matured and eventually led to the large-scale introduction of computerized adaptive testing in education, it began to find applications in psychological testing as well.

It is remarkable how these developments have their parallels in two different periods in the history of testing. The first period covers the first half of the twentieth century, when classical test theory (CTT) was developed. This theory mainly supports standardized testing with a group-based paper-and-pencil test for a fixed population of test takers. In the 1950s, ideas for a new test theory were explored and a second period began, in which item-response theory (IRT) was developed. It received its first comprehensive formalization in the late 1960s, a more thorough statistical treatment in the 1970s–1980s, and began to be applied widely in the 1990s. As a matter of fact, it is still in the process of being extended, particularly into the direction of models for more complicated response formats, models with more comprehensive parameterization (for instance, to deal with background variables of the test takers, sophisticated sampling designs, and multidimensional abilities), and models for response times. The introduction of IRT has been critical to the development of the new technology of item banking and individualized testing. Also, IRT allows for item formats that are closer to the current instructional requirements and relies heavily on the (real-time) use of the computational power provided by modern computers.

In the next sections of this chapter, we review these two stages in somewhat more detail and introduce the basic concepts in test development and test theory on which this book relies.

1.1   Classical Test Design

1.1.1   Standardized Testing in Psychology

Classical test design has been strongly dominated by the idea of a standardized test developed in psychology. Psychological tests are typically produced as an *encore* to a development in psychological theory. The result of such a development is a theoretical network around one or more new constructs, for example, certain special abilities, personality traits, or psychodiagnostic dimensions. Test development begins if more systematic empirical research is needed to test hypotheses on these constructs against empirical reality.

As a result, psychological tests are seldom developed by test specialists but mostly by psychologists familiar with the research on the constructs for which they are to be used as a measurement instrument. These researchers use their knowledge to design the tasks or items in the test and to choose the rules for scoring them. Usually, the items are written together as a set that is assumed to cover the construct best. Typically this set is somewhat larger than actually needed, to allow for a possible failure of some of the items during pretesting.

This developmental process can be characterized as a one-shot approach based on the best theories and insights available at the time. New items are written and tried out only if a new version of the test has to be developed, which happens if new insights and progress in psychological theory make the current version obsolete. The same psychological test can be easily used for over a decade before the need for a subsequent version is felt.

Empirical pretesting of items usually serves a threefold purpose. First, it allows for a screening of estimates of the item parameters and the possible removal of items with estimates suggesting undesirable behavior. The parameters used in a classical item analysis are briefly reviewed in the next section. Second, predictions following from the theory underlying the constructs are confronted with empirical data. These predictions may be on the correlational structure of the test scores with other measures in the study (for example, in a multitrait-multimethod study) or on differences between the score distributions of certain groups of persons. The results from this part of the study are used both to test the psychological theory and validate the test. Third, the test is normed for its intended population of persons. This part of the tryout involves extensive sampling of the population and the estimation of a norm table for it. If a new version of an existing test is pretested, the data are used for score equating. The goal then is to estimate the transformation that maps the score scale of the new version of the test to the scale of the old version. This transformation generates the same norm table for both versions. To the knowledge of the author, the first large-scale study with this type of score equating ever was for the new version of *Wechsler-Bellevue Intelligence Scale* in 1939.

This process of development of a standardized test has a more than superficial relation with CTT. In the next section, we review a few basic concepts from CTT. These concepts will be used later in this book and will also help us to discuss the close relation between test theory and design in a subsequent section.

1.1.2 Classical Test Theory

The core of classical test theory (CTT) is a two-level model that decomposes the observed test scores into so-called true scores and errors. The presence of two levels in the model is due to the fact that CTT addresses both the case of a fixed test taker and a random person sampled from a population. At either level, the test is considered as fixed; for instance, the case of testing with random samples of items is not addressed.

Fixed Person

Let X_{jt} be the observed score of fixed person j on test t. A basic assumption in CTT is that this observed score, which can be any quantity defined on the item scores of the person, is a *random variable*. The assumption reflects the belief that if we replicated the test several times, a distribution of outcomes would be observed. This experiment can actually be done for tests of stable physical abilities, for which memory and learning do not play a role, but is hypothetical for the more mental and cognitive abilities. Although X_{jt} is random, the shape of its distribution is unknown. In fact, the goal of test theory is to provide models that help us make inferences of the properties of this distribution from actual observed scores of the person.

Observed score X_{jt} can be used to define two new quantities:

$$\tau_{jt} = \mathcal{E} X_{jt}, \tag{1.1}$$

$$E_{jt} = X_{jt} - \tau_{jt}. \tag{1.2}$$

The first quantity is the *true score* for person j on test t, τ_{jt}, which is defined as the expected value or mean of the observed-score distribution. The second is the *error* in the observed score, E_{jt}, which is defined as the difference between the person's observed score and true score. Both definitions are motivated by practical considerations only; if we have to summarize the distribution of the observed score by a single fixed parameter, and the distribution is not known to be skewed, it makes sense to choose its mean, and if an actual observation of X_{jt} is used to estimate this mean, we make an error equal to E_{jt}.

The definitions in (1.1) and (1.2) imply the following model for the score of a fixed person:

$$X_{jt} = \tau_{jt} + E_{jt}. \tag{1.3}$$

This model is nothing but a convenient summary of the preceding introduction. The only assumption underlying it is the randomness of the observed score X_{jt}; the fact that the true score and error are combined additively does not involve anything new above or beyond the definition of these two quantities.

Random Person

If the persons are sampled randomly from a population, the true score also becomes random. In addition, the observed score and error contain two levels of randomness, one level because we sample a person from the population and another because we sample an observed score from the person's distribution. Let J represent the random person sampled from the population and T_{Jt} the random true score. The model in (1.3) becomes:

$$X_{Jt} = T_{Jt} + E_{Jt}. \tag{1.4}$$

Again, the only new assumption underlying this extension of the model is on the random status of a variable—this time the true score; no assumption of linearity whatsoever has been made.

Item and Test Parameters

One of the major roles of CTT is as a producer of meaningful parameters for item and test analysis. All parameters reviewed in this section are at the level of the population model in (1.4).

A key parameter is the *reliability coefficient* of the observed score X_{Jt}, usually (but incorrectly) referred to as the reliability of the test instead of a score. This parameter is defined as the squared (linear) correlation coefficient between the observed and true scores on the test, ρ_{TX}^2. (Because the level of modeling is now well understood, we henceforth omit the indices of the scores where possible.)

The choice of the correlation between X and T is intuitively clear: If $X = T$ for the population of persons, (1.4) shows that X does not contain any error for each of them, and the correlation between X and T is equal to 1. Likewise, it is easy to show that if $X = E$ (that is, X contains only error for each person), the correlation is equal to 0.

The fact that we do not define reliability as the correlation coefficient between X and T but as the square of it is to treat ourselves to another useful interpretation. A standard interpretation of a squared correlation coefficient is as a proportion of the explained variance. Analogously, in CTT, the reliability coefficient can be shown to be equal to

$$\rho_{TX}^2 = \frac{\text{Var}(T_{Jt})}{\text{Var}(X_{Jt})}, \tag{1.5}$$

which is the proportion of of the true-score variance relative to the observed-score variance in the population of persons. This equality thus shows that the true-score variance in a population of persons can be conceived of as the proportion of observed-score variance explained by the differences in true scores between the persons.

If test scores are used to predict a future variable, Y (for example, success in a therapy or training program), the reliability coefficient remains a key parameter, but the correlation of observed score X with Y, instead of with its true score T, becomes the ultimate criterion of success for the test. For this reason, we define the *validity coefficient* of a test score X as its (linear) correlation with criterion Y, ρ_{XY}.

Observe that, unlike the reliability coefficient, the validity coefficient is not a squared correlation coefficient. The reason for this lies in the following two results for the reliability coefficient that can be derived from the model in (1.4). First, using well-known rules for variances and covariances, it can be shown that if X and X' are the observed scores on two replications of the test for the same persons, it holds that

$$\rho_{XT}^2 = \rho_{XX'}. \tag{1.6}$$

This result is most remarkable in that it shows that the reliability coefficient, which is the squared correlation between the observed scores and their unobservable true scores, is equal to the correlation between two replications of the observed scores. Likewise, it can be shown that

$$\rho_{XT} \geq \rho_{XY} \tag{1.7}$$

for any score Y. The result (1.7) tells us that the predictive validity coefficient of a test can never exceed the correlation between its observed score and true scores; or, the other way around, the observed score on a test is always the best "predictor" of its true score. Observe that (1.7) also relates the correlation of an unobservable score to the correlation between two observed scores.

An important item parameter in CTT is the *item difficulty* or π *value*. Let U_i be the score on item i in the test, with $U_i = 1$ the value for a correct response and $U_i = 0$ the value for an incorrect response. The classical difficulty parameter of item i is defined as the expected value or mean of U_i in the population of persons

$$\pi_i = \mathcal{E}U_i. \tag{1.8}$$

CTT also has an *item-discrimination parameter,* which is defined as the correlation between the item score and the observed test score

$$\rho_{iX} = \text{Cor}(U_i, X) = \frac{\sigma_{iX}}{\sigma_i \sigma_X}, \tag{1.9}$$

where σ_{iX}, σ_i, and σ_X are the covariance between U_i and X, and the standard deviations of U_i and X, respectively. Obviously, a large value for ρ_{iX} implies a score on item i that discriminates well between persons with a high and a low total score on the test; hence the name "discrimination parameter." Recall, however, that X is composed of the scores on all items in the test; it is therefore somewhat misleading to view a correlation between U_i and X as an exclusive property of item i.

Analogously to (1.9), we define the correlation between the score on item i and the observed score Y on a success criterion,

$$\rho_{iY} = \mathrm{Cor}(U_i, Y) = \frac{\sigma_{iY}}{\sigma_i \sigma_Y}, \tag{1.10}$$

as the *item validity* or the item-criterion correlation for item i. It represents how well score U_i discriminates between persons with high and low scores on criterion Y in a predictive validity study.

All the parameters above were defined as population quantities. They can be estimated directly by their sample equivalents, with the exception of the reliability coefficient, which is based on the correlation with an unobservable true score. The equality in (1.6) suggests estimating the reliability coefficient by the sample correlation between observed scores X and X' on two replicated administrations of the test. But, in practice, due to learning and memory effects, it is seldom possible to realize two exact replications.

An alternative is to use the inequality

$$\rho_{XT}^2 \geq \alpha, \tag{1.11}$$

which can be derived from the model in (1.4), where *coefficient* α is defined as

$$\alpha = \frac{n}{n-1} \left[1 - \frac{\sum\limits_{i=1}^{n} \sigma_i^2}{\sigma_X^2} \right] \tag{1.12}$$

and n is the length of the test. Coefficient α is a coefficient for the internal consistency of a test; that is, the degree to which all item scores in a test correlate positively with one another. The relation in (1.11) thus shows that the reliability of an observed score can never be smaller than the internal consistency of the item scores on which it is calculated. Coefficient α can be estimated in a single administration of the test; it only contains the item variances, σ_i^2, and the total observed-score variance, σ_X^2, which can be estimated directly by their sample equivalents. If the test approximates the ideal of a unidimensional test, the error involved in the estimation of ρ_{XT}^2 through α tends to be small.

It is helpful to know that the following relation holds for the standard deviation of observed score X:

$$\sigma_X = \sum_{i=1}^{n} \sigma_i \rho_{iX}. \tag{1.13}$$

Replacing σ_X^2 in (1.12) by the square of this sum of products of item parameters leads to:

$$\alpha = \frac{n}{n-1}\left[1 - \frac{\sum\limits_{i=1}^{n}\sigma_i^2}{\left(\sum\limits_{i=1}^{n}\sigma_i\rho_{iX}\right)^2}\right] \tag{1.14}$$

Except for the (known) test length n, this expression for α is entirely based on two item parameters, σ_i and ρ_{iX}. It allows us to calculate how the removal or addition of an item to the test changes the value of α.

For the validity coefficient, we are also able to derive an expression based entirely on sums of item parameters. The expression is

$$\rho_{XY} = \frac{\sum\limits_{i=1}^{n}\sigma_i\rho_{iY}}{\sum\limits_{i=1}^{n}\sigma_i\rho_{iX}}. \tag{1.15}$$

It shows us how the predictive validity of a test is composed of the item variances, item-discrimination parameters, and item validities.

We will rely heavily on the expressions in (1.14) and (1.15) when we discuss models for classical test assembly in Section 5.2.

1.1.3 Discussion

Classical test design and classical test theory are different sides of the same coin. Both are based on identical methodological ideas, of which the notion of standardization is the core.

When a test is designed, the conditions in the testing procedure that determine the ability to be tested are standardized. Standardization implies the same conditions over replications. The definition of the observed score in CTT as random over replications of the test is entirely consistent with this idea of standardization. The mean of the distribution of this score is a fixed parameter that summarizes the effects of all standardized conditions. It seems natural to call this mean the true score. The error score summarizes the effects of conditions that have been left free. Because these effects are random across replications, the error score is random.

At approximately the same time as the introduction of classical test theory, similar notions were developed in the methodology of experimental design, with its emphasis on manipulation and randomization. In fact, just as CTT is the statistical analog of standardized testing, the analog of experimental design is analysis of variance. It is therefore not surprising that strong parallels exist between the linear models in (1.3) and (1.4) and some models in analysis of variance.

The assumption of sampling from a fixed population is another common characteristic of classical test design and CTT. For example, one of the main goals of psychological testing is to estimate the test taker's relative standing in this population, often with the intention of seeing if this person belongs to the "normal" portion of the population distribution or an "abnormal" tail. The interest in norm tables is a logical consequence of this goal. In CTT, this interest finds its parallel in the assumption of random sampling of persons from a fixed population.

To get an accurate estimate of the true scores of a population of test takers, the test should be designed to discriminate maximally between as many persons in the population as possible. Statistically, this goal is realized best by a test with its π values close to .50 and values for the item-discrimination parameter ρ_{iX} as large as possible. This choice of parameter values has been the standard of the testing industry for a long time. The fact that these parameters can be interpreted only for a population of persons was not observed to be a hindrance but was a prerequisite according to the prevalent conception of testing (Exercise 1.1).

The classical conception of test development involved no stimulus to item banking whatsoever. If the test items are the best given the current state of psychological theory and have been shown to meet the statistical requirements for the intended population, there is no need whatsoever to write more items. Producing more can only lead to an increase in quality. The only reason to write new items is if the test becomes obsolete due to new developments in psychological theory.

It is not our intention to suggest that this classical complex is wrong. On the contrary, it is coherent, well-developed, and statistically correct. If a single test for a fixed population has to be developed, and the interest is exclusively in estimating score differences in a population of persons, the combination of classical test design and classical test theory is still a powerful choice. The methodology offered in this book can also be applied to classical test design (see Section 5.2).

But if testing has to serve a different goal, another choice of test-design principles and theory has to be made. As discussed in the next section, this was precisely what happened when testing was applied to instructional purposes.

1.2   Modern Test Design

1.2.1   New Notion of Standardization

The first large-scale use of educational tests was for admission to higher education. For this application, the assumption of a fixed population still made sense, but the assumption of a fixed test involved going through the whole cycle of test development on an annual basis. This requirement put a serious claim on the resources of the testing organizations. They soon discovered that it was more efficient to use item banking. In *item banking,* test items are written and pretested on a more continuous basis, and tests are assembled from the pool of items currently present in the item-banking system.

The need for a new test theory was felt more seriously when the use of tests for instructional purposes was explored, particularly when the ideas moved into the direction of individualized instruction. The assumption that students are sampled from a fixed population does not make much sense if individual students take different instructional routes. In fact, it is even inconsistent with the notion of learning at all. A score distribution of a population of students can only remain fixed if their abilities are—not if they develop as a result of learning and forgetting. Likewise, the idea of a single best test soon had to be killed. If students are tested individually and at different levels of development, larger numbers of tests with measurement qualities geared to the individual student's level are necessary.

If the assumptions of a fixed population and a single best test have to be dropped, other features of the classical complex become problematic, too. For example, classical item and test parameters, such as the π value, item-discrimination parameter, and reliability coefficient, are based on the assumption of a fixed population and lose their meaning if no such population exists. Likewise, the definition of the true score in CTT is based on the assumption of a single fixed test. If different students take different tests, their number-correct scores are no longer comparable. Also, if the same student is retested using different tests, it is impossible to use this score for monitoring what this person has learned.

It is obvious that with the emergence of these newer types of testing, a new test theory was required. Item-response theory (IRT), of which the key concepts are introduced in the next section, has filled the void. It is not for a fixed test for a fixed population but for a pool of items measuring the same ability and for individual persons demonstrating the ability in their responses to these items. It also offers us the tools for calibrating items taken by different persons on a fixed scale. In addition, item parameters in IRT describe the properties of the items relative to this scale instead of a population of persons. Therefore, these parameters can be used to assemble a test that is locally best (i.e., has optimal accuracy at the person's ability level). They can also be used to score persons on the same scale, no matter what test they take from the pool.

In fact, the emergence of these newer types of testing and the simultaneous development of IRT have led to the replacement of the "classical complex" in testing in Section 1.1.3 by a new paradigm. The core of this paradigm is a changed notion of standardization. To standardize a test, it is no longer necessary to give each person an identical set of items (or, for that matter, test them under identical conditions). It is sufficient that the items be written to explicit content specifications and that the remaining differences between them be adequately parameterized (that is, represented by parameters) in the test-theory model. A parallel exists between this notion of standardization and that of model-based inference elsewhere in statistics. In fact, whereas CTT and (one-way) analysis of variance have much in common, IRT is more in the spirit of the tradition of correcting for nuisance factors by introducing separate parameters for them in the model, which has analysis of covariance as its prime example. But it is beyond the scope of this book to elaborate on these observations.

As a result of this change, IRT enables us to design tests to different sets of specifications and delegate their actual assembly to computer algorithms. These two possibilities constitute the main theme of this book. A few basic notions from IRT that are required to understand its role in modern test design and test assembly are introduced in the next section.

1.2.2 Item-Response Theory

The focus of IRT is on the responses by a single person to a single test item. These responses are modeled as the outcome of a random process with probabilities that depend on a number of parameters. If the responses are scored dichotomously (for instance, as correct or incorrect), only the probability of a correct response needs to be modeled. This probability also fixes the probability of an incorrect response.

Typically, the parameters can be classified as item and person parameters. In more complex models, we may also have parameters for the conditions under which the person interacts with the items, raters who evaluate the responses, and the like. Person parameters represent the ability, level of knowledge, skill, or whatever property of the person the items measure, while item parameters stand for such properties of an item as its difficulty and discriminating power.

It is customary to present the probability of a response as a function of the person parameter. In this book, we use the term ability parameter as a generic name for the person property measured by the items and denote this parameter as θ. Mathematical functions used for the description of the probability of a response on an item as a function of θ are known as *item-response functions*. For dichotomous models, the focus is thus always on response functions for the correct response. Although the test-design principles and algorithms in this book hold for any of the IRT models currently known, our presentation will mostly be based on the three-parameter logistic (3PL) model for dichotomous responses.

The 3PL model is flexible and has been shown to fit large pools of items written for the same content domain in educational testing; in fact, it has become the industry standard for such applications. An example of a set of response functions from the 3PL model estimated for a test of English as a foreign language in a school-leaving exam in the Netherlands is given in Figure 1.1. Each of these curves represents the probability of a correct

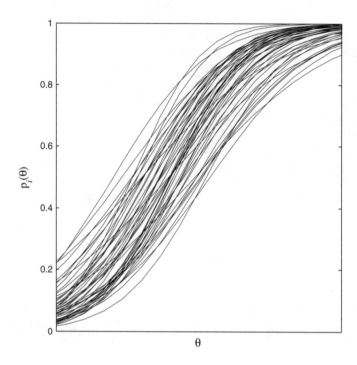

FIGURE 1.1. Set of response functions for a test of English as a foreign language.

response of a single item. Observe that all functions run smoothly from a lower asymptote to the upper asymptote at one. They do so at different rates. Also, they are located at different positions along the θ scale. As will be discussed later, the scale for θ for the 3PL model is arbitrary in the sense that it has no fixed origin or unit.

The 3PL model has three item parameters, which are explained in Figure 1.2. The height of the lower asymptote of the response function for item i is parameter c_i. This parameter can be interpreted as the minimum probability of a correct response on the item reached at an "infinitely low" ability level. Because nearly all items allow for some form of guessing if the person does not know the correct answer, c_i is known as the *guessing parameter* of item i. Parameter b_i can be interpreted as the *difficulty parameter* of item i. Its value represents the location of the item along the θ scale. A more difficult item is located more to the right on the scale, and to produce a correct response with a given probability of success on this item, a higher level of ability is required. Under the 3PL model, b_i is the value of θ at which the probability of a correct response is equal to the middle between the height of the lower and upper asymptotes, that is, b_i is the value of θ at

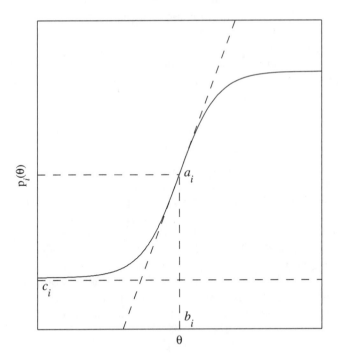

FIGURE 1.2. Graphical meaning of the item parameters in the three-parameter logistic response model in (1.16).

which the probability is equal to $(c_i + 1)/2$. Parameter a_i is proportional to the slope of the response function of the item at this point. A larger value means a steeper slope, and hence an item that discriminates better between the success probabilities for the persons just to the left and right of $\theta = b_i$. Parameter a_i is therefore known as the *discrimination parameter* of item i.

Each of the response functions in Figure 1.1 is a member of the family described by the mathematical function

$$p_i(\theta) = \Pr(U_i = 1 \mid \theta) = c_i + (1 - c_i)\frac{e^{a_i(\theta - b_i)}}{1 + e^{a_i(\theta - b_i)}}, \qquad (1.16)$$

where U_i is the response variable for item i and $\Pr(U_i = 1 \mid \theta)$ is the probability of a correct response on this item by a person with ability level θ. Because the response curves represent this probability as a function of θ, we denote it as $p_i(\theta)$. The scale of θ runs from $-\infty$ to ∞. Parameter b_i represents the location of item i on the same scale; it therefore has the same range of possible values. From the definition of c_i as a lower asymptote for a probability, it follows that c_i takes values in the interval $[0, 1]$. Finally, though items with a negative value for a_i are conceivable, such items have a direction opposite to θ and are usually ignored or reformulated. We therefore focus only on items with values for a_i running from 0 to ∞. Finally, the powers in the numerator and denominator in (1.16) have the number $e = 2.718...$ as their base. This choice of base is arbitrary but has become standard because it leads to some convenience in the statistical treatment of the model (Exercise 1.5).

Multidimensional Response Model

Sometimes the items in the pool measure multiple abilities, and the necessity of multidimensional test assembly arises. A familiar example is the case of a pool with mathematics items with a substantial verbal component. Such items measure the mathematical abilities of the persons but may also be sensitive to their verbal abilities. If so, we need to replace the model in (1.16) with one that has more than one ability parameter. In Chapter 8, which is devoted to the case of test assembly from a pool with multiple abilities, we use a logistic model with two ability parameters, θ_1 and θ_2. For this model, the probability of a correct response defines a function that describes a *response surface* over a two-dimensional ability space. An example of this surface is given in Figure 1.3.

The logistic model for this surface that will be used in Chapter 8 is

$$p_i(\theta_1, \theta_2) = \frac{e^{a_{1i}\theta_1 + a_{2i}\theta_2 - b_i}}{1 + e^{a_{1i}\theta_1 + a_{2i}\theta_2 - b_i}}. \tag{1.17}$$

This function has two discrimination parameters, a_{1i} and a_{2i}, which control the slope of the surface along θ_1 and θ_2, respectively, and a parameter b_i that represents its generalized difficulty. The model in (1.17) does not yet have a guessing parameter but the extension to a model with such a parameter, which has a structure identical to that of (1.16), is straightforward (Exercise 1.6).

1.2.3 Item Calibration and Ability Measurement

Applications of IRT typically consist of two different stages. The first stage is item calibration and the second stage ability measurement.

During *item calibration*, response data for a sample of persons on a set of items are collected and the values of the item parameters are estimated from the data. Standard statistical methods for parameter estimation, such as maximum-likelihood (ML) and Bayesian methods, are available for the estimation of these values.

The stage of item calibration also encompasses an empirical test of the goodness of fit of the IRT model to the response data. This fit replaces the evaluation of the estimates of the CTT item parameters in traditional item

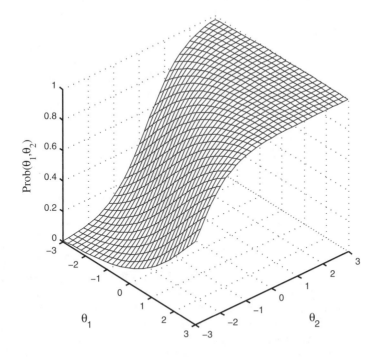

FIGURE 1.3. Example of the response surface of an item for the two-dimensional logistic response model in (1.17).

analysis. Items that do not show a satisfactory fit are diagnosed; the reason for their misfit may run from a wording problem to sensitivity of the item to abilities other than the one measured by the majority of the items in the pool.

The goal of item calibration and goodness-of-fit analysis is to establish a pool of items measuring a common ability with known values for the item parameters. Such pools are the core of the item-banking systems discussed above. The treatment of the statistical methods of item calibration and goodness-of-fit analysis used to establish item pools are beyond the scope of this book; references to literature on these topics are given at the end of this chapter.

The second stage in the application of IRT is that of *ability measurement*. A set of items from the pool is administered, and an estimate of the person's score (that is, a value for the ability parameter θ for the item pool) is calculated from the responses. To calculate this estimate, one of the statistical methods for parameter estimation referred to earlier can be used. If the item pool has been calibrated with enough precision, the person's value of θ can be calculated with known values for the item parameters in the estimation equations. The presence of these values automatically corrects for differences between the features of the items represented by these parameters. As a result, differences in item selection among persons do not create any (asymptotic) bias in their ability estimates. In this sense, we are thus free to choose whatever subset of items from the pool we want.

However, the *accuracy* of ability estimates depends directly on the values of the item parameters in the test relative to the ability of the person. For an operational item pool, it is not unusual to be able to create two tests of equal length and find that for some ability levels one of them is several times as accurate as the other. In the next section, we discuss the notion of an information function used in IRT to analyze the accuracy of ability estimates.

1.2.4 Test and Item Information Functions

Let $\widehat{\theta}$ denote the estimated value of the ability parameter for a person with true ability level θ. Obviously, the variance of $\widehat{\theta}$ over replications of the test for this person is an appropriate measure for the accuracy of the ability estimates. This variance can be denoted as $\mathrm{Var}(\widehat{\theta} \mid \theta)$.

Instead of this variance, it is more convenient to use a measure known as the *test information function* (TIF) in item-response theory. This measure, which we denote as $I(\theta)$, is an instance of a more general measure, known as Fisher's information, in statistics, which reflects the information in a sample about an unknown parameter. In the application of this measure to IRT, the responses to the test items constitute the sample, and the person's ability θ is the unknown parameter. Fisher's information measure has several properties, of which the following two are particularly useful. First, the test information function is asymptotically equal to the inverse of the variance function of the ML estimator of θ:

$$I(\theta) = \frac{1}{\mathrm{Var}(\widehat{\theta} \mid \theta)}. \qquad (1.18)$$

(By "asymptotic" we mean that the equality holds approximately for short tests but that the approximation improves with increasing test length.) This property thus suggests that the two measures can be used interchangeably.

We prefer the information function because of the second property. Information functions can also be defined at the item level as an *item information function* (IIF). We use $I_i(\theta)$ to denote the information function of item i. An IIF reflects the contribution of the response on an item to the information on θ in the test. An attractive property of information functions is that they are additive. For example, for the TIF it holds that

$$I(\theta) = \sum_{i=1}^{n} I_i(\theta). \tag{1.19}$$

Item and test information functions are easy to calculate. For a dichotomous response model, the IIF is equal to

$$I_i(\theta) = \frac{(p'_i(\theta))^2}{p_i(\theta)[1 - p_i(\theta)]}, \tag{1.20}$$

where $p'_i(\theta)$ is the first derivative of the response function with respect to θ. For the 3PL model in (1.16), this derivative is a simple expression, and (1.20) can we written as

$$I_i(\theta) = a_i^2 \frac{1 - p_i(\theta)}{p_i(\theta)} \left(\frac{p_i(\theta) - c_i}{1 - c_i} \right)^2, \tag{1.21}$$

which depends only on the item parameters. Thus, for a calibrated item pool, all IIFs are automatically known, and, because of the additivity in (1.18), we also know the TIF for any test assembled from the pool.

Graphical examples of IIFs for five different items are given in Figure 1.4. The functions of the more difficult items in this figure are located more to the right. This is as it ought to be because more difficult items are appropriate for the measurement of more able students. Also, a higher value for the guessing parameter means a function more skewed to the left. The reason for this effect is a relatively larger loss of information for less able persons because they guess more frequently than more able persons.

The most dramatic impact on the shape of the IIF has the discrimination parameter. For a larger value of this parameter, the function becomes more peaked, indicating better measurement near the location of the item. The price we pay is relatively lower information farther away from this location, where the response function tapers off to c_i or 1 and the item hardly discriminates. But the general effect of a larger value for the discrimination parameter is always positive. For example, if $c_i = 0$, the area under the IIF can be shown to be equal to a_i; hence, a larger value for this parameter means higher average information in the item score across the ability scale.

Figure 1.4 also shows the TIF associated with these five items. This function is the sum of the IIFs. Its shape is therefore entirely determined by the values of the item parameters.

1.2.5   Test Characteristic Function

In addition to the test information function, we will occasionally use one more function to characterize a test. Like the TIF in (1.19), this function,

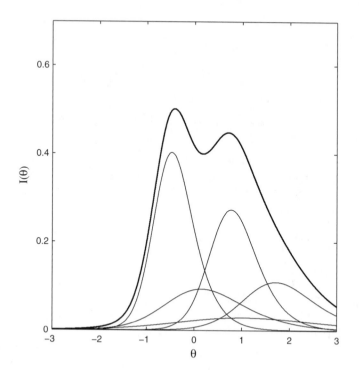

FIGURE 1.4. Graphical examples of five item information functions and their associated test information function (bold line).

known as the *test characteristic function* (TCF), is also additive in the items in the test. It is defined as the sum of the response functions:

$$\tau(\theta) = \sum_{i=1}^{n} p_i(\theta). \tag{1.22}$$

The TCF links the ability parameter θ to the classical true score τ for the observed number-correct score on the test. This interpretation follows if we note that the expected value of the score U_i on item i for a person with ability level θ is equal to

$$\mathcal{E}(U_i \mid \theta) = 1.p_i(\theta) + 0.[1 - p_i(\theta)] = p_i(\theta). \tag{1.23}$$

Therefore, $\tau(\theta)$ is the expected sum of the item scores, or, according to (1.1), the true number-correct score.

1.2.6 Comparison Between Classical and IRT Parameters

It is interesting to compare the relation between the test and item information functions in (1.19) with the one between coefficient α and the classical item parameters in (1.14). Three differences should be observed.

First, the relation between the information functions is additive, whereas that between α and the classical item parameters is not. As will be discussed later in this chapter, the additivity of the information functions simplifies the process of test assembly enormously.

Second, the item parameters in (1.14) do not only miss this additivity but are even dependent on each other. Although ρ_{iX} is generally referred to as an item parameter, it is a correlation with the observed test score. Consequently, it depends on the covariances between all items. Because of these dependencies, the effects of the removal or addition of an item to the test are unpredictable; the addition of an item even leads to an occasional decrease of the reliability of the test instead of an intended increase. The IIFs in (1.19) are entirely independent of each other; if an item is added to the test, we know beforehand what will happen to the TIF.

Third, information functions are *local* measures of measurement accuracy; they show how accurate the ability estimate will be for a person with a given θ value. On the other hand, classical item and test parameters are *global* measures; they implicitly average the local accuracy given θ over the population of persons.

It is easy to misinterpret the meaning of a global measure. For instance, a high value for the classical reliability coefficient seems to suggest a test that is uniformly accurate for all possible applications. But this impression is misleading. This test cannot be accurate for persons who are too able for it; that is, it cannot discriminate between the finer differences in ability level among such persons and tends to make large errors in their ability estimates. Local measures of accuracy, however, do enable us to tailor the accuracy of a test optimally to the ability levels for which it is intended.

1.2.7 Ability Scale and Item Mapping

The scale of θ in the response model in (1.16) has an arbitrary origin and unit. This is immediately clear from the portion of the model in the argument of the logistic function in (1.16), $a_i(\theta - b_i)$. If we change the origin of the scale (that is, replace θ by $\theta + d$, where d is the new origin), we also have to replace b_i, the location of the item on the old scale, by $b_i + d$. But then the two values of d cancel, and the model predicts the same response probability for each person. The same occurs if we introduce a new unit d. We then not only have to replace θ by θd but also b_i by $b_i d$, and, because this parameter is proportional to the slope of the response function, a_i by a_i/d. These three values of d also cancel.

This indeterminacy of origin and unit is not much of a problem. During item calibration, we just fix the scale at an arbitrary origin and unit. But the arbitrariness of the scale of θ has consequences for the shape of the item and test information functions. For instance, if we increase the unit of the scale of θ by a factor d, the values of the information function are reduced by the same factor. Likewise, if we change the origin of the scale, the point at which an information function reaches its maximum also changes. Information functions thus have no absolute meaning; by using an appropriately chosen unit and origin, they can be given any desired height and location for their maximum. (As a matter of fact, by choosing an appropriate monotone transformation of θ, an information function can even be given any desired shape. This conclusion follows from the presence of the square of the derivative, $p_i'(\theta)$, in the definition of the information function in (1.20). If a monotone transformation is applied to θ, the chain rule in differential calculus tells us that the new information function differs from the old function by a factor equal to the square of this derivative. We can therefore manipulate the shape of a TIF just by choosing the transformation with the desired effect.)

Although a mathematical truth, this fact should not be taken to imply that the same arbitrary test can be made optimal for any goal we have in mind simply by transforming its information function into a target. In practice, we always work with information functions and targets on a scale that is "fixed by interpretation." If a testing program is developed, one of the first steps is to fix the scale for its scores. Over time, those involved in the program become familiar with the item parameters in the pool and the scores of the persons on this fixed scale. If old items in the pool are replaced by new ones, they are always calibrated on the same scale. As a result, though the composition of the pool changes continuously, the scale keeps its empirical interpretation in the form of a stable distribution of item content. It therefore remains possible to interpret scores on this scale and set meaningful targets for information functions on it.

A graphical technique that is useful for understanding the empirical meaning of a θ scale is *item mapping*. In this technique, we place a sample of the items along the θ scale in the form of labels with brief descriptions of their content. The items are placed at the points at which a person would have a fixed probability of a correct response to them, say, .80. Item maps help us to infer how item content is distributed over the θ scale and to set meaningful targets for test information functions on it. An example of the use of item mapping for a domain of elementary arithmetic items is given in Figure 1.5.

Multidimensional Model

The ability space of the multidimensional response model in (1.17) is not only arbitrary with respect to its origin and units but also to the direction

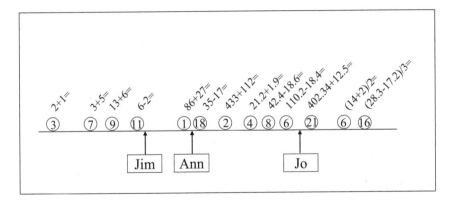

FIGURE 1.5. Example of an item map for the domain of elementary arithmetic, with the location of the ability levels of three ficticious test takers.

of its dimensions. If we rotate the space to another direction, the values of the parameters change because of the transformation we apply, but the response probabilities for the new set of parameter values remain the same. This arbitrariness allows us to rotate the ability space to dimensions that are more convenient to interpret (Exercise 8.3). We will use this opportunity in Section 8.4.3 when we treat the case of multidimensional test assembly with an interest in scores for a combination of abilities.

1.2.8   Birnbaum Approach to Test Design

In 1968, Birnbaum introduced a new approach to test design that capitalized on the additive relation between the item and test information functions in (1.19). The approach, which forms the foundation of our current view of test assembly, consists of the following three steps:

1. The goal of the test is formulated. Examples of possible goals are placement of students in courses, diagnosis of the intelligence of children in the lower tail of a given distribution, selection of applicants for a job, and assembly of a new version of a test that has to be parallel to the current version.

2. The goal is translated into a target for the TIF. If the goal is to diagnose the intelligence of children in the lower tail of a distribution, it makes sense to choose a target that is high over this tail and does not impose any constraint on the TIF everywhere else. If the goal is selection of applicants, the most important point on the ability scale is the cutoff score used in the decision, and a target with high values in a small interval about this score seems an obvious choice. The result of this step is a function $\mathcal{T}(\theta)$ that serves as the target for

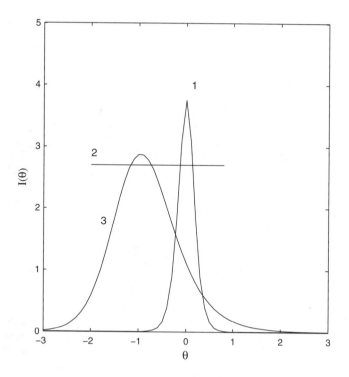

FIGURE 1.6. Examples of three possible targets for a test information function: (1) a test used for admission decisions with cutoff score $\theta = 0$; (2) a diagnostic test over lower range of abilities; and (3) a test with an information function that follows a given population distribution.

the information function of the new test. Examples of a few possible targets are given in Figure 1.6.

3. A test is assembled from the pool such that its information function approximates $\mathcal{T}(\theta)$ best. During the selection process, the additive relation between the IIFs and the TIF helps us to predict what happens to the latter if an item is added to or removed from the test.

The power of Birnbaum's approach lies in the fact that it forces the test assembler to reflect both on the goal of the test and the combination of items in the pool that guarantees the best results. Although Birnbaum's proposal underlies all modern approaches to test assembly, his original formulation has served only as a point of departure for our current, more practical methods of test assembly.

For one thing, Birnbaum's proposal did not offer any suggestion of an algorithm for finding the best combination of items in the pool. At first sight, it may seem straightforward to use a trial-and-error method in which we move from one possible combination of items to another, each time checking the match between the TIF and the target. Obviously, to check the results, we would need a computer program for plotting a TIF against a target or calculating a numerical criterion for their match. A fatal difficulty of this approach, however, is that to identify an optimal solution in the pool, all possible combinations of items have to be checked. If the pool consists of N items and a test of length n is needed, the number of possible combinations is equal to $\binom{N}{n}$. For realistic values of N and n, this number is of an astronomical order of magnitude, and in practice we are unable to find a test that is close to optimal by trial and error. (See Exercise 1.10.)

Another shortcoming of Birnbaum's approach is that it overlooks the fact that tests are always assembled to meet an (often elaborate) set of specifications. These specifications formulate requirements with respect to their content, item format, the total time available to take the test, the length of the test form in print, and so forth. Each specification implies a constraint that has to be imposed on the selection of the items. Although such constraints lead to a reduction in the number of feasible combinations of items in the pool, typically the remaining set of combinations is still much too large for all of its members to be checked. As a matter of fact, we are even bound to meet a new problem: For a realistic set of constraints, it easily becomes too difficult to find any feasible combination of items in the pool by trial and error (Exercise 1.12).

Finally, Birnbaum's approach was for the simple case of a single test from a pool of discrete items with an optimal match between the TIF and its target, whereas the practice of test assembly involves a large variety of different problems. For example, we may have to assemble a test from a pool with item sets organized around common stimuli, a set of tests that have to be parallel to a reference test, a set of subtests for use in a multistage testing system, a test with maximum predictive validity, or a test from a pool measuring more than one ability. It is not immediately obvious how Birnbaum's approach could be generalized to deal with such problems.

1.3   Test Design in This Book

In this book, we view the design of a testing program as a process consisting of the following stages:

1. For each of the tests in the program, a set of specifications is established. These specifications address all desired attributes the tests should have, such as the content categories of their items, their values for certain statistical parameters, word counts, and the degree of item overlap between them.

2. An item pool to support the program is designed. The goal of this stage is a blueprint that details the number of items with the various combinations of attributes needed in the pool. The blueprint is calculated to support the assembly of the required number of tests within a chosen planning horizon.

3. The item pool is developed. This stage consists of such activities as item writing, item review, pretesting of the items, item calibration, and analysis of the goodness of fit of the response model.

4. The assembly of the tests from the item pool according to their specifications.

The process does not need to go through these stages of test specification, item-pool design, item-pool development, and test assembly exactly in the order in which they have been presented here. It is essential that the first two stages be completed before the development of the item pool and assembly of the tests begins. But the last two stages are often interwoven because of restrictions in the resources with which the testing organization has to cope. The result is a continuous mismatch between the blueprint of the item pool and the operational pool. Consequently, the projections of the number of items to be added to the pool change frequently, and item pool-design and item-pool management become essentially the same process.

Our use of the term "test design" may seem misleading in that the only product actually designed during the four stages above is the item pool; the tests themselves are just assembled from the item pool. But because the pool should be designed to support the assembly of these tests, use of the term "test design" for the entire process is nonetheless appropriate.

The fact that nearly all chapters in this book are on test assembly might even further obscure the relation between item-pool design and test assembly. However, as we will be able to illustrate later, the techniques for the optimal assembly of tests are essentially the same as those for calculating an optimal blueprint of the pool. Because these techniques are much easier to explain using test-assembly problems, and we have to deal with a large variety of them, the subject of item-pool design is not treated until the end of the book.

1.3.1   Four Modes of Test Assembly

Four different modes of test assembly from an item pool are discussed in this section. The first two modes were popular when the interest in individualized testing emerged but the computational power needed for the application of IRT was still lacking. When personal computers became more powerful, the last two modes became prevalent.

Random Sampling of Tests

In this mode of test assembly, a test of fixed length is randomly sampled from the item pool for each individual person. The test model used to control measurement error is the binomial-error model, which is the classical test-theory model for a fixed person in (1.1) with the additional assumption of a binomial distribution for the observed number-correct score X_{jt}. Under this assumption, the classical true score is equal to the binomial success parameter, π_j. For a large pool, this parameter can be interpreted as the proportion of items in the pool "mastered" by the person.

This mode of test assembly has two disadvantages: First, any change in the item pool also changes the value of π_j for a person and therefore leads to incomparable test scores. Second, unless complicated stratified sampling techniques are used, tests cannot be assembled to specifications.

Sequential Sampling of Tests

For the binomial model to realize the same error of estimation for $\hat{\pi}_j$, smaller samples of items are necessary for values of π_j closer to .50. Therefore, it is more efficient to sample tests sequentially. In this mode, after each new item sampled from the pool, the standard error of estimation in $\hat{\pi}_j$ is estimated from the person's updated proportion of correct answers, and the test is stopped as soon as a predetermined level of error is realized.

Sequential testing was particularly popular for mastery testing. In this application, sampling is stopped as soon as a mastery decision with a fixed cutoff score for π_j can be made with a predetermined level of error.

Optimal Test Assembly

Optimal test assembly is a generalization of the Birnbaum approach that deals with the various realistic aspects of test-assembly problems discussed at the end of Section 1.2.8. Methods of optimal test assembly allow us to assemble a test or set of tests with a potentially elaborated list of specifications, from a large variety of item pools, with a result that is optimal with respect to an objective chosen from a large set of alternative by the test assembler.

The first attempts at optimal test assembly resulted in heuristic methods for the problem of assembling a single test from a pool of discrete items with a target for the information function addressed by Birnbaum. These methods were heuristic in that they based their search for the best combination of items on a plausible principle but no optimal results were guaranteed. The next developments were generalizations of these heuristics for use with several of the other problems discussed in Section 1.2.8.

In the mid 1980s, Birnbaum's problem was redefined as a problem of *combinatorial optimization* or 0-1 *integer programming*. During the next two decades, it appeared possible to formalize nearly every conceivable test assembly problem as an optimization problem in this class. At the same time, the algorithms needed to solve such optimization problems were improved, and nowadays powerful implementations of them are available as commercial software.

Adaptive Test Assembly

Adaptive test assembly resembles sequential sampling of items in that one item is picked from the pool at a time. However, the items are not picked at random but optimally: The person's ability estimate is updated during the test, and each next item is chosen to be maximally informative at the last update. Because the ability estimates converge to the person's true ability level, item selection improves during the test and the ideal of a test with maximum information at the person's true ability level is approached.

Adaptive test assembly assumes real-time ability estimation and item selection. This became possible when PCs became both more powerful and cheaper in the early 1990s. Shortly thereafter, computerized adaptive testing (CAT) was implemented in large-scale testing programs, and nowadays large numbers of persons are tested worldwide using this type of test assembly.

1.3.2   Choice of Test Assembly Modes

The test-assembly modes dealt with in this book are optimal and adaptive test assembly. In Chapter 9, we will show how adaptive test assembly can be optimized using the same techniques from integer programming as for the optimal assembly of a fixed test. A few of the basic ideas underlying the use of integer programming for assembling a fixed test are illustrated in the next section.

1.4   An Application of Integer Programming to Test Assembly

Suppose we want to assemble a fixed test from a pool of 100 calibrated items. The items in the pool are at two different cognitive levels: (1) knowledge of facts and rules and (2) application of knowledge to real-life problems. The pool has 50 items on knowledge and 50 on applications. The information function of the test has to meet a given target, $\mathcal{T}(\theta)$. Finally, we want the test to be as short as possible, but it should contain at least ten knowledge items and ten application items.

The requirement of the shortest test possible involves a minimization problem. The three other requirements are constraints to be imposed on the selection of the items. The problem can be formulated more compactly as minimize test length

subject to

1. TIF everywhere above target;
2. At least ten knowledge items;
3. At least ten application items.

In an optimal test-assembly approach to this problem, we first reformulate it as a mathematical optimization problem using decision variables. Decision variables are variables defined such that the solution of the optimization problem (i.e., the set of values for which the objective function is optimal and all constraints are satisfied) identifies the best decision that can be made. General rules for the choice of decision variables in test-assembly problems will be introduced in Section 3.1.

The current problem can be solved by the following choice of variables. Let $i = 1, ..., 100$ denote the individual items in the pool. We assume that the pool is organized such that items $i = 1, ..., 50$ are knowledge items and items $i = 51, ..., 100$ are application items. The decision variables we choose are binary variables, one for each item, which take the value $x_i = 1$ if the item i is selected for the test and the value $x_i = 0$ if item i is not selected.

The sum of the decision variables for the entire item pool is

$$\sum_{i=1}^{100} x_i.$$

As $x_i = 1$ only for the items selected, this sum is equal to the number of items in the test. Likewise, the sum of variables for the first 50 items in the pool is equal to the number of knowledge items in the test, while the sum for the last 50 items is the number of application items.

We also need the weighted sum

$$\sum_{i=1}^{100} I_i(\theta)x_i,$$

where $I_i(\theta)$ still denotes the information function of item i. Again, as $x_i = 1$ only for the items selected, this expression is the sum of the IIFs in the test; that is, its TIF. We will control the TIF at a number of points θ_k, $k = 1, ..., K$, where we require it to take a value at least equal to a target value $\mathcal{T}_k$. The number and the spacing of these points are supposed to be chosen by the test assembler.

The solution to the following minimization problem is the best possible test from the pool:

$$\text{minimize} \sum_{i=1}^{I} x_i \tag{1.24}$$

subject to

$$\sum_{i=1}^{100} I_i(\theta_k)x_i \geq \mathcal{T}_k, \quad \text{for all } k, \tag{1.25}$$

$$\sum_{i=1}^{50} x_i \geq 10, \tag{1.26}$$

$$\sum_{i=51}^{100} x_i \geq 10, \tag{1.27}$$

$$x_i \in \{0, 1\}, \quad \text{for } i=1,...,100. \tag{1.28}$$

The objective function in (1.24) minimizes the length of the test. The constraints in (1.25) impose the target values as lower bounds on the TIF at $\theta_1, ..., \theta_K$. Because the test length is minimized, the TIF is approximated from above. The constraints in (1.26) and (1.27) guarantee the required minimum number of items on knowledge and applications (Exercise 1.13).

Both the objective function and the constraints in (1.24)–(1.27) are linear in the variables. The model is therefore an example of a linear 0-1 integer programming problem. This fact simplifies the calculation of its solution enormously. The solution is an array of 0-1 values for $x_1, ..., x_{100}$ for which the objective function is minimal and all constraints are satisfied. This array identifies the best test in the pool.

The test-assembly problem in this example was unrealistically small. In later chapters, we will meet models with larger and more complicated item pools, different objective functions, and a huge range of possible constraints. To solve these models, we will often need different types of variables, and sometimes even combinations of different types of variables in the same problem. The common feature of all of these models is that they are linear in variables that, except for a few possible variables added to the model for technical reasons, take integer values. In addition, we will demonstrate that the same type of modeling can be used to optimize adaptive test assembly and to calculate optimal blueprints of item pools.

Before discussing all of these models, we will show how test specifications can be formulated as objective functions or constraints (Chapter 2), how a test-assembly problem can be modeled using such objective functions and constraints (Chapter 3), and what algorithms are available to solve our models (Chapter 4).

1.5 Literature

The standard text on the history of testing is Dubois' (1970) *History of Psychological Testing*. This book does not treat any of the modern developments in Section 1.2, and its selection of topics shows a bias against large-scale educational testing, but it should be consulted by anyone with an interest in this topic. Another classic is Cronbach's (1970) *Essentials of Psychological Testing*, which treats both the development and analysis of tests from a CTT point of view. A few more recent examples of the development of psychological tests can be found in Butterfield, Nielsen, Tangen, and Richardson (1985), Pellegrino, Mumaw, and Shute (1985), and Sternberg and McNamara (1985). The transition from classical standardized testing to item banking and its parallel development in test theory is discussed in van der Linden (1986).

The first comprehensive text on CTT was Gulliksen's (1950). A key reference in test theory is Lord and Novick (1968), which contains an advanced, precise treatment of CTT, the first comprehensive introduction to IRT (at the time mainly known as latent-trait theory), and Birnbaum's (1968) proposal to assemble a test to a target for its information function. Examples of introductions to IRT at a more intermediate level are Hambleton and Swaminathan (1985) and Lord (1980), while an elementary introduction is given in Hambleton, Swaminathan, and Rogers (1991). A comprehensive review of a large number of response models is offered in van der Linden and Hambleton (1997). The multidimensional logistic response model in (1.17) was introduced in McKinley and Reckase (1983) and further developed in Béguin and Glas (2001), Reckase (1985, 1997), and Segall (1996). For more concise introductions to CTT and IRT, see van der Linden (2005b, 2005c).

This book deals with the formulation of test specifications, item-pool design, and test assembly, but not with the topic of item-pool development, with its steps of item writing, calibration, and goodness-of-fit testing. Excellent examples of modern developments in algorithmic item writing are discussed in Haladyna (1994) and Irvine and Kyllonen (2002), whereas introductions to the topics of item-parameter estimation and goodness-of-fit testing are provided in the earlier references to the introductory texts on IRT.

A brief review of the four different modes of test assembly in Section 1.3.1 (random sampling, sequential sampling, optimal test assembly, and adaptive test assembly) is given in van der Linden (2001b). The first applications of 0-1 mathematical programming to optimal test-assembly problems can be found in Feuerman and Weiss (1973) and Votaw (1952). The idea of applying this technique to IRT-based test assembly was suggested in Yen (1983). The first to show how the technique could be applied to assemble a test to a target for its information function was Theunissen (1985). The model he suggested was the one for test-length minimization discussed in Section 1.4. Theunissen's paper stimulated several others, including the author of this book, to further explore the power of mathematical programming for solving a large variety of problems in test design. Introductions to the various types of mathematical programming and its algorithms are given in Chapter 4 and in Appendix 1 of this book.

1.6 Summary

1. The history of testing shows two different types of test development: a period of classical test design in which testing was mainly modeled after the ideal of a standardized test for a fixed population developed in psychology, and a period of development toward individualized testing using item banking and algorithmic test design.

2. The first period has its parallel in classical test theory (CTT). This theory assumes random sampling of persons from a fixed population, a true score defined by the standardized conditions in the testing procedure, and random error to represent the effects of the remaining conditions.

3. The second period has its parallel in item-response theory (IRT). This theory has been developed to explain the response probabilities of single persons on single test items. It supports testing from calibrated item pools, optimal test assembly, and scoring of persons on a scale defined independently of a single test.

4. Item and test information functions are local measures of the accuracy of an ability estimate. These functions are additive. This feature is used in the Birnbaum approach to test design, which consists of the following steps: (i) analysis of the goal of the test, (ii) translation of this goal into a target for the information function of the test, and (iii) assembly of a test from the pool with an information function that best approximates this target.

5. Birnbaum introduced his approach for the simple problem of assembling a single test from a pool of discrete items, with no other specifications than a target for the information function, and trial-and-error selection of the items. Optimal test assembly generalizes this approach to problems with a variety of types of item pools, elaborated sets of test specifications, and the use of algorithms for optimal selection of the items from the pool.

6. A key feature of optimal test assembly is its modeling of the problem as a linear constrained optimization problem using integer-valued decision variables. A solution to this problem is an array of values for the variables that optimizes its objective function and satisfies all constraints. Solutions to integer programming problems can be calculated using standard commercial software.

7. In this book, optimal test assembly is treated as part of the larger problem of test design, which runs through the following stages: (i) formulating the specifications for the tests that the program has to support, (ii) designing an item pool, (iii) developing the item pool

(that is, writing, pretesting, and calibrating the items), and (iv) assembling the tests from the pool according to their specifications.

8. The design of an item pool is documented in the form of a blueprint that details the number of items with the various combinations of attributes needed in the pool. Optimal blueprints can be calculated using the same techniques of integer programming as for optimal test assembly.

9. Besides optimal test assembly, the following three modes of assembling tests from an item pool have been used: (i) random sampling of tests, (ii) sequential sampling of tests, and (iii) adaptive test assembly. The first two modes were popular when not enough computational power was available to implement an optimal test-assembly approach. Adaptive test assembly is treated as a special case of optimal test assembly in this book.

1.7   Exercises

1.1 The classical goal in psychological testing is a test with item difficulties equal to .50 and item discrimination as large as possible. Suppose we have been successful in creating a test of n items each with $\pi_i = .50$ and $\rho_{iX} = 1$. How would the distribution of the number-correct score X for the population of test takers look? What would happen if a test with these properties was used to evaluate learning in school or for selection or admission?

1.2 Assume the 3PL model in (1.16) holds for item i with parameter values $a_i = .9$, $b_i = 1.0$, and $c_i = 0$. For what value of θ does a test taker have a probability of a correct response equal to .50? What happens to this value of θ if c_i increases?

1.3 What are the probabilities of a correct response on the item in Exercise 1.2 for test takers at $\theta = .8$ and $\theta = 1.2$? What happens to these probabilities if a_i increases?

1.4 Show that the structure of the 3PL model in (1.16) can be derived from the assumption that the person knows the correct answer with probability $e^{a_i(\theta-b_i)}/[1+e^{a_i(\theta-b_i)}]$ or guesses at random with a probability of success equal to c_i.

1.5 What happens to the model in (1.16) if the base of the powers in the denominator and numerator is changed to a number other than e—for instance, 10?

1.6 Extend the multidimensional logistic model in (1.17) with a guessing parameter c_i, using the same argument as in Exercise 1.4. Why do we need a single guessing parameter c_i for this model and no separate parameters c_{1i} and c_{2i}? Why does this multidimensional model have a single difficulty parameter b_i?

1.7 Calculate the values of the IIF for the item in Exercise 1.2 at $\theta = .8$, 1.0, and 1.2. What happens to these values if a_i increases to 1.8? What happens if c_i increases to .2? Explain the results.

1.8 Assume the 3PL model in (1.16) holds with $c_i = 0$. Derive a general expression for the maximum value for the IIF.

1.9 Assume again that the 3PL model in (1.16) holds with $c_i = 0$. Derive a general lower bound on the number of items needed for the TIF in (1.19) to reach a target value $T(\theta)$. What happens to this bound if a_i increases? What if c_i increases? Which of the two parameter has the largest effect on the required test length?

1.10 Use trial values to find the minimum size of the item pool required to give each living person a different test of ten items. (Hint: The current world population is over 6.4 billion.)

1.11 Suppose an item pool contains I items, half of which are multiple-choice and half have a constructed-response format. How many different tests of length n with n_{MC} multiple-choice items and n_{CR} constructed-response items are possible?

1.12 Suppose we want to assemble a test of ten items from a pool of 48 items. An analysis of the pool shows that it has approximately 13,000 different tests that satisfy the set of content specifications. What is the probability that a random selection of ten items from the pool satisfies the test specifications?

1.13 Find a useful lower bound for the length of the test produced by the test-assembly model in (1.24)–(1.28). What quantities in the model have an impact on the actual length of the solution? Suppose the TIF is controlled only by a lower bound T_k at $\theta_k = 0$. Use the general expression derived in Exercise 1.9 to suggest a better lower bound for the length of the test, assuming the average value for the discrimination parameter in the item pool is equal to 1.5.

2

Formulating Test Specifications

As discussed in the previous chapter, a new testing program begins with the formulation of a set of specifications for the tests it has to support. These specifications are used to design an item pool for the program. Once the item pool has been realized, they are also used to guide the assembly of the tests from the pool.

Although test specifications are key to the design of a testing program, we lack a standard language for them. It is not uncommon, even within the same organization, to find different traditions of formulating test specifications. Sometimes they are formulated verbally as a set of learning objectives or a list of dos and don'ts for the test developers. But they can also be in the form of one or more classification tables for the items, with numbers that indicate their desired distribution in the test. Also, occasionally test specifications are not available in explicit form at all but exist simply as part of the history of the program shared by its test developers.

It is the goal of this chapter to introduce a universal language for discussing test specifications, review possible types of specifications formulated in this language, and discuss a standard format for a set of specifications. Our treatment of these topics should not be viewed as an attempt to introduce another set of personal preferences into a field that has already shown little standardization. Instead, it is motivated by a formal analogy between problems of test design and problems in other industries that are known to belong to the class of constrained combinatorial optimization problems. This analogy will be explained more precisely in Chapter 4. Until then, we define *constrained combinatorial optimization* loosely as the process of searching a set of entities for the best subset meeting a number of constraints. Problems of optimal test assembly fit this general description because they imply the search for a best test in an item pool that has to satisfy a given set of test specifications.

2.1 Examples of Test Specifications

The examples of test specifications in Table 2.1 are entirely fictitious, and the set does not have any coherent structure. Also, it is much smaller than the sets of test specifications typically found in real-life testing programs, which can easily contain hundreds of them. The only purpose in giving these examples is to show a sample of the large range of verbal statements of test specifications that can be met in practice.

The following observations are made about these examples. First, each of them addresses one or more properties of the items or the test. Examples of such properties are: content (nos. 7, 14, and 17), word count (no. 15), reliability (no. 3), presence of certain stimulus material (no. 4), response format (no. 5), response time (no. 12), and in a stimulus common with other items (no. 11).

We will use *attribute* as a generic term for any property relevant for the design of a test. Below, we will classify attributes both by level (e.g., item or test attribute) and by type (e.g., quantitative attribute). The notion of an attribute enables us to give a useful definition of the term test specification. Throughout this book, the following definition is adhered to:

> A test specification *is a statement that formulates a requirement for an attribute of a test or its items.*

Second, some of the specifications in Table 2.1 are simple (that is, they formulate one requirement), whereas others are composites, involving more than one requirement. An example of a composite specification is the one on test length (no. 1), which can be split into two simple requirements: one that the test length be greater than 60 and another that it be smaller than 75.

Third, some specifications are formulated in an unnecessarily complicated way. For example, the specification on item bias (no. 8) can easily be reduced to: "The numbers of items biased against males and females should be equal." Likewise, it is unnecessary that the specification on the minimization of test length (no. 16) refers to all other specifications; a shorter but equally effective form would be: "The test length should be minimal."

Fourth, specifications can also be incomplete. An example of an incomplete specification is the one with respect to the time available to take the test (no. 12), which does not refer to any explicit item or test attribute. A complete version of it could be: "The sum of the expected response times on the items should be smaller than 60 minutes."

1. Test length between 60 and 75 items
2. Number of items on applications equal to 24
3. Reliability of the test should be as high as possible
4. At most ten items with graphics
5. No more than half of the items can have a multiple-choice format
6. Items with explicit gender/minority orientation should be avoided
7. Number of items on nervous system smaller than five
8. For an item biased against males, there should be one against females
9. Item p-values between .40 and .60
10. Test information function as close as possible to the target
11. Size of sets of items with a common reading passage between 4 and 6
12. Total time available to take the test is 60 minutes
13. Items 17 and 103 never in the same test
14. Number of items on nervous system and blood vessels between 10 and 15
15. No item should have more than 150 words
16. Test should meet all specifications, with a minimum number of items
17. As many items on addition as on subtraction

TABLE 2.1. Examples of test specifications.

Fifth, some of these specifications use different wordings but express essentially the same kind of requirement with respect to an attribute. For example, expressions such as "smaller than," "no more than," "at most," and "total time available" all impose an upper bound on an attribute. Likewise, expressions such as "should be avoided," "smallest," "minimum number," and "as close as possible" point at minimization of an attribute. In Section 2.3, we will show that all test specifications basically fall into two different categories: They either formulate a constraint that imposes a bound on an attribute or formulate an objective that involves minimization or maximization of an attribute.

To avoid ambiguities and possible complications in test design, particularly with larger sets of test specifications, an important principle in formulating test specifications is the following:

> *Each test specification should be (1) simple, (2) concise, but (3) complete.*

If a test specification does not satisfy this principle, it might not only be hard to determine whether it implies a constraint or an objective but may also cause uncertainty in the design of the test and hence lead to unpredictable results.

2.2   Classification of Attributes

Two classifications of item and test attributes are presented, one by type and the other by level. Being able to identify the correct type and level of an attribute is important because, as will be shown in Chapter 3, this identification helps us to model test-assembly problems correctly.

2.2.1   Type of Attribute

The following types of attributes can be distinguished:

1. *Quantitative attributes.* Examples of quantitative attributes are word counts, expected response times, frequency of previous item or stimulus usage, reliability, statistics such as the item p-value and test information, indices for gender or minority orientation of items, and readability indices. The common feature of all quantitative attributes is that they take numerical values. These values can be real (e.g., response times or item information) or integer (e.g., word counts), but this distinction plays no further role in the formulation of a specification with a quantitative attribute.

2. *Categorical attributes.* Examples of categorical attributes are content category, response format of items (e.g., constructed response, multiple-choice, or completion), cognitive level (e.g., knowledge, analysis, or application), use of auxiliary material (e.g., graph or table), mental operation required to solve an item, and the author of the item. The common feature of all categorical attributes is that they divide or partition the item pool into subsets of items with the same attribute (e.g., subsets of items on certain biological topics or containing the same type of graphical material).

3. *Logical attributes.* These attributes differ from quantitative and categorical attributes in that they are not properties of single items or tests but of pairs, triples, and so forth of them. The logical attributes used in this book mainly involve relations of exclusion and inclusion between items or tests. For example, a relation of exclusion between items exists if they cannot be selected for the same test because one has a clue to the solution of the other (so-called "enemy items"). A relation of inclusion exists if items belong to a set with a common stimulus and the selection of any item implies the selection of more than one. Specifications no. 11 and no. 13 in Table 2.1 involve logical attributes.

It is sometimes possible to reduce a quantitative attribute to a categorical attribute by pooling items with values close to one another. To be able to deal with quantitative attributes, some of the heuristics for test assembly in Chapter 4 use this option. We are not in favor of this practice. It is rarely necessary to follow it and often leads to errors of a size that is hard to determine.

If a test-assembly problem has more than one categorical attribute, each separate attribute introduces a partition of the item pool. The same holds for any possible combination of attributes (for example, when item content is classified along multiple dimensions or using a hierarchy of topics). Which partitions are relevant should follow from the set of test specifications. Specification no. 14 in Table 2.1, which refers to items that are on both the nervous system and blood pressure, is an example of a specification that involves a partitioning of the item pool by a combination of two attributes.

2.2.2   Level of Attribute

Attributes exist at the following levels:

1. *Item level.* Several examples of attributes at the item level have already been met in the previous pages. Item attributes are fundamental in the sense that several higher-level attributes are actually aggregates of them. In Chapter 1, we already pointed out that, for instance, coefficient α and the TIF are defined as aggregates of item attributes; see (1.14) and (1.19).

2. *Stimulus level.* This level of attribute is met when an item pool consists of sets of items organized around a common stimulus, as is a usual format, for example, in testing reading comprehension. Basically, stimuli can have the same types of attributes as items. Although they often have quantitative attributes (e.g., a word count), it is unlikely for them to have psychometric attributes.

3. *Item-set level.* In addition to attributes of a stimulus, we need to allow for the attributes of the set of items associated with it. Except for an obvious attribute such as the number of items in the set, attributes at this level are mostly aggregates of item attributes, such as the average p-value in the set, the number of items with a certain response format, and the distribution of item content.

4. *Test level.* Examples of test attributes are test length, TIF, classical reliability coefficient, a distribution of item content, number of item sets, and total word count. Attributes at this level are invariably quantitative and, like item-set attributes, often aggregate toward lower-level attributes.

5. *Multiple-test level.* If the problem consists of the assembly of a set of tests, we need additional attributes at this level to specify the required result. Examples of multiple-test attributes are item overlap between a pair of tests in a set, the degree to which tests are statistically parallel, and shifts in the distribution of item content between tests.

This classification of attributes by level is not exhaustive. For instance, sometimes tests consist of sections or subtests, each dealing with a different type of knowledge or ability, and we may be able to identify relevant attributes of these sections or subtests. Because their existence does not involve any new technical difficulties, we skip the treatment of such levels in this book. An exception is Section 8.4.3, however, where the problem of assembling a multidimensional test with different sections measuring different ability dimensions is addressed (Exercise 2.1).

2.3   Constraints and Objectives

As already noted, in spite of seemingly large differences in wording, test specifications often express identical requirements. Provided they are written in a simple, concise, and complete form, each specification has the basic format of a constraint on a test or an objective for an attribute of it:

1. A test specification is a *constraint* if it requires an attribute to satisfy an upper or lower bound.

2. A test specification is an *objective* if it requires an attribute to take a minimum or maximum value possible for the item pool.

In Table 2.1, specification no. 4 is a constraint because it requires the number of items with graphics in the test (the test attribute) to be less than or equal to 10 (the upper bound), whereas no. 1 can be rewritten as two constraints, one with an upper bound of 75 and the other with a lower bound of 60 on the length of the test (the test attribute). In Chapter 3, we will show that constraints can always be modeled as mathematical (in)equalities.

On the other hand, specifications nos. 3, 6, 10, and 16 are objectives because each of them requires an attribute (such as the test reliability, number of items with gender or minority orientation, "distance" to a target information function, and test length) to be maximal or minimal. In Chapter 3, we will show that objectives can be modeled as mathematical functions that have to be minimized or maximized. The function that is minimized or maximized is known as the *objective function* of the problem (Exercise 2.2).

For brevity, throughout this book we will refer to constraints by the type and level of attribute they address. That is, if a constraint is on a categorical, quantitative, or logical attribute, we will refer to it as a *categorical, quantitative,* or *logical constraint.* Likewise, if a constraint is at the item or test level, we will refer to it as an *item-level* or *test-level constraint.* The same practice will be followed for objectives.

Although some types and levels are met more frequently than others, it is possible to have meaningful constraints and objectives with nearly all possible combinations of type and level of attribute. In Chapter 3, we will formalize the full range of possible constraints and objectives for each possible combination of type and level (Exercise 2.12). Following are a few verbal examples:

1. All items with a certain combination of topics should be excluded from the test (a set of categorical constraints at the item level).

2. Minimize item overlap between alternative tests at the second stage of a multistage testing system (a logical objective at the multiple-test level).

3. Maximize item information at ability estimates in an adaptive test (a set of quantitative objectives at the item level).

4. Two given passages for a reading comprehension test exclude one another (a logical constraint at the stimulus level).

When formulating a set of test specifications, we may have the choice between formulating a specification as an objective or a constraint. Such choices are possible particularly when we are familiar with the item pool and know that either option leads to approximately the same result. For example, if an item pool is known to have only ten items with graphics and the distribution of attributes in the pool shows no dependencies between them, a constraint imposing a lower bound equal to nine or ten, say, on the number of items with graphics and the objective of maximizing this number can be expected to produce approximately the same result.

Although the term "objective" suggests something of primary importance, in test assembly *constraints actually are more useful than objectives.* The critical difference between the two is the degree of control over the composition of the test they offer. If we want to have absolute control over attributes, the best strategy is to formulate constraints with tight bounds on them. If we formulate an objective for one of them, the only thing we know in advance is that it will get a maximum or minimum value possible for the pool given all constraints, but its actual value may be much higher or lower than anticipated.

---

optimize *Objective Function*

subject to

    Constraint 1
    Constraint 2
    ...
    Constraint N

TABLE 2.2. Standard form of a set of test specifications.

2.4 Standard Form of the Set of Test Specifications

If a set of test specifications is in a simple, concise, and complete form, it can always be presented in the standard form in Table 2.2. In Section 4.1, we will introduce a few more conventions for this standard form, such as conventions to present the types and levels of constraints in a fixed order, include one of the more standard technical constraints, and add descriptive labels to the objective and constraints.

2.4.1 Number of Objective Functions

Only one objective function can be optimized at a time. If we tried to optimize two functions simultaneously, each of them would draw the results into a different direction, and a gain for one would necessarily mean a loss for the other. A good example of this trade-off is offered by the objectives with respect to test reliability (no. 3) and test length (no. 16) in Table 2.1. It is a well-known result from test theory that, under mild assumptions, reliability increases monotonically with the number of items. Maximizing the reliability of a test and minimizing its length are thus entirely antagonistic objectives.

Nevertheless, sometimes we may have a test-assembly problem with more than one attribute that, ideally, has to take the largest or smallest value possible for the item pool, while these attributes are not entirely as antagonistic as reliability and test length. One valid reason for this problem to happen is uncertainty about the bounds on the attributes that are realistic for a given item pool. Another example is a test measuring a multidimensional ability structure that we want to be as efficient as possible along each of the dimensions. For such problems of *multiobjective test assembly*, several strategies for reformulating them as an optimization problem with one technical objective function exist, such as optimizing a weighted average of the attributes, prioritizing the objectives and optimizing them sequentially, and minimaxing over the objectives (i.e., optimizing a common bound to them). These strategies will be discussed in more detail in Section 3.3.4.

An interesting question is how to proceed if all existing test specifications imply constraints and there appears to be no objective. This problem is not realistic because for a testing program it should always be possible to identify a new attribute that, however secondary its importance, could be optimized, and it would be a loss of opportunity to ignore this possibility. But if the case were to arise, it is actually one in which a test assembler is only interested in selecting a test from the subset of tests from the pool that meet the constraints (called a feasible subset; see Section 2.4.2). Because the test assembler is actually indifferent as to the differences between the tests in this subset, a simple strategy for this case is to choose an arbitrary objective function (for instance, one based on a dummy variable added to the model) and use one of the algorithms in this book to find a test. This strategy is recommended because, as already indicated at the end of Section 1.2.8, for a realistic set of constraints, the task of finding a test in this subset is certainly not trivial.

2.4.2   Number of Constraints

Although unlikely to happen, a test-assembly problem need not have any constraint at all. In this case, we would just have an unconstrained optimization problem, and all we have to do to solve it is find a test with the best value for the objective function among the set of all possible tests from the pool.

On the other hand, we have no upper limit on the number of constraints. To explain this lack of limit, we need a few new notions. A *feasible* test is a test that meets all constraints. The *feasible set* of solutions for a test-assembly problem is the set of all possible feasible tests. An objective function helps us to identify a best test in the feasible set, which is known as an *optimal feasible solution*. If the set of feasible solutions is empty, the problem is known as *infeasible*.

If an extra constraint is added to a test-assembly problem, its only effect on the set of feasible solutions is a possible decrease in its size. If a size decrease happens, we have to select the test from a smaller subset and, consequently, the solution may deteriorate (that is, have a less favorable value for the objective function). Both effects do not need to happen, however. If the new constraint is redundant (i.e., already implied by the old constraints), nothing happens at all. But if it is stringent and becomes active in the solution, the set of feasible solutions becomes smaller and the solution deteriorates. Adding too many such constraints can lead to overconstraining the problem (that is, to an infeasible problem). Thus, *it is the nature of the constraints and not their number that determines when we have too many of them.* The notions in this section are graphically illustrated for a two-variable linear optimization problem in Section A1.2.2.

In practice, infeasibility is rarely a problem in test assembly. Several of the empirical examples of test assembly later in this book had hundreds, or even thousands, of constraints and still have a solution. Two caveats are necessary, however. First, it is always recommended *to avoid constraints that take the form of a mathematical equality*. Such constraints imply an enormous reduction of the set of feasible solutions, and the presence of one or two of them easily overconstrains the problem, particularly if they are quantitative. The only exception we will make is an equality constraint on the length of the test. The issue of test assembly with equality constraints will be picked up again in the discussion of (3.50) in Section 3.2.4. Second, the item pool should be large enough and on-target. If the pool is small, it may be depleted quickly, and certainly will be if it is supposed to support a series of tests. An item pool is off-target if (1) it is short on certain attributes or (2) has a correlational structure among the attributes that makes it impossible to select items with some attributes without running short on items with others.

2.5 Literature

Although several introductory textbooks deal with the topic of item writing and test construction, specialized literature with rules for formulating test specifications is hardly available. This omission may be due to the fact that psychological tests are typically developed as the direct result of research on the constructs they are assumed to measure (Section 1.1.1), whereas educational testing has had a long tradition of test development based on instructional objectives (e.g., Popham, 1978).

There are a few exceptions, however. A textbook that has provided generations of testing specialists with their first introduction to test design is Bloom, Hastings and Madaus's (1971), *Handbook on Formative and Summative Evaluation of Student Learning*. The tradition of specifying a test by a two-way table, with a content classification defining one dimension and a behavioral taxonomy the other, was introduced in this text. The notion of a behavioral taxonomy has been developed further, for example, in Fleishman and Quaintance (1984), whereas Wigdor and Green (1991) investigate the possibilities of test specification based on task analysis.

The distinction between constraints and objectives is standard in the field of mathematical programming. A few introductory textbooks on mathematical programming are discussed at the end of Appendix 1. The classification of attributes, constraints, and objectives into different types and levels has been developed over the history of the author's work on test design. The three basic types of attributes, constraints, and objectives were introduced in van der Linden (1998a), whereas the distinction between the different levels of attributes, constraints, and objectives in this chapter was formulated in van der Linden (2000b).

2.6 Summary

1. The first step in the design of a new test program is the formulation of a set of specifications for its tests.

2. A test specification is a statement that formulates a requirement for an attribute of a test or its items.

3. Attributes are substantive or statistical properties of a test. Attributes can be (i) quantitative, (ii) categorical, or (iii) logical. In addition, they can be formulated at the level of (i) individual items, (ii) stimuli, (iii) item sets in a test, (iv) individual tests, or (v) sets of tests that are to be assembled.

4. A test specification can be formulated as (i) a constraint that requires an attribute to satisfy an upper or lower bound or (ii) an objective that requires it to take a minimum or maximum value possible for the item pool. For brevity, constraints and objectives are referred to by the type and level of attribute they address.

5. Each specification should be (i) simple, (ii) concise, but (iii) complete. This principle allows us to determine whether a specification is a constraint or an objective. Also, if some of the specifications do not obey this principle, the desired composition of the tests becomes ambiguous and the control of the quality of the tests in the program becomes less than optimal.

6. The standard form of a test-assembly problem is as an objective function to be optimized subject to a number of constraints. Although a problem always has a single objective function, there exists no upper limit on its number of constraints.

7. Constraints define the set of feasible tests for a given item pool. The objective function expresses our preferences for the tests in this feasible set. An optimal feasible test is one in the set of feasible tests with an optimal value for the objective function.

8. Unless redundant, the addition of a constraint to a test-assembly problem leads to a smaller set of feasible tests. If the set of feasible tests becomes smaller, the optimal value of the objective function for the item pool can deteriorate but never improve.

9. Although the number of constraints is unlimited, depending on their nature, a test-assembly problem can be infeasible for a small number of them. But, in practice, infeasibility is no problem, provided the set of constraints is well formulated and the item pool is on-target.

10. Equality constraints should be avoided because they easily overconstrain the test-assembly problem, particularly if they are quantitative.

2.7   Exercises

2.1 Identify the attributes in each of the specifications in Table 2.1, and determine their type and level.

2.2 Which of the specifications in Table 2.1 imply a constraint? Which imply an objective?

2.3 Reformulate the specifications in Table 2.1 as explicit constraints with upper or lower bounds or objectives with minimization or maximization.

2.4 There always exists a trade-off between objectives for test assembly problems. Which pairs of objectives in Table 2.1 can be expected to have the strongest trade-offs? Which will have the weakest?

2.5 Why should we relax specification no. 2 in Table 2.1? How could it be relaxed if it occurred in a problem with minimization of the length of the test? How could it be relaxed in a problem with maximization of the reliability of the test?

2.6 Specification no. 4 in Table 2.1 implies a constraint with an upper bound equal to 10. Why might it be less meaningful to reformulate this specification as an objective with minimization of the distance between the number of items on graphics in the test and a goal value equal to 10?

2.7 Specification no. 5 in Table 2.1 is somewhat unusual in that it does seem to imply a constraint but has no explicit bound. Reformulate this specification as a constraint with an explicit bound. What bound should be used?

2.8 Specification no. 9 in Table 2.1 implies two different constraints. Reformulate this specification as an objective with about the same effect as the two constraints. For which other specifications in this table is this reformulation possible?

2.9 Specification no. 10 in Table 2.1 requires an entire TIF to approximate a target. In Section 1.4, we dealt with this type of problem by constraining the TIF to target values at points θ_k, $k = 1, ..., K$. The objective of minimal test length in (1.24) forces the TIF to approximate the target values $\mathcal{T}_k$ from above. Formulate an alternative objective function with the same effect.

2.10 Specification no. 13 in Table 2.1 is somewhat unusual in that it seems to imply neither a constraint nor an objective. Choose 0-1 variables x_{17} and x_{103} and formulate the specification as a constraint. Suppose this constraint makes the problem infeasible. Can this constraint be relaxed (that is, its upper bound made less tight)? Can it be replaced by an objective function with approximately the same effect?

2.11 Specification no. 15 in Table 2.1 implies an item-level constraint for each item in the pool. Reformulate this set of constraints as a single constraint. What strategy would allow us to drop these constraints at all?

2.12 Section 2.3 gives an example of a logical objective at the multiple-test level and a quantitative objective at the item level. Formulate a meaningful example of:

(a) quantitative and categorical objectives at the multiple-test level;

(b) quantitative, categorical, and logical objectives at the test level;

(c) categorical, quantitative, and logical objectives at the stimulus level;

(d) quantitative, categorical, and logical objectives at the item-set level;

(e) categorical and logical objectives at the item level.

3
Modeling Test-Assembly Problems

Although the idea of modeling a test-assembly problem may seem far-fetched, it is actually a very effective way of approaching the problem. Once a problem has been modeled, we can study its structure, use a standard algorithm to calculate a solution, and evaluate the impact of possible changes in the test specifications on the solution. The alternative approach would be to develop a separate algorithm for each problem. The advantages of modeling hold especially if the model turns out to have a simple structure, such as the linear structure for the test-design problems in this book.

The process of modeling a test-assembly problem goes through the following four steps:

1. identifying the decision variables;
2. modeling the constraints;
3. modeling the objective;
4. solving the model for an optimal solution.

At first sight, the more challenging steps in this process may seem to be the modeling of the constraints and the objective, but actually it is that of identifying the decision variables. This step typically involves a conceptual reorganization of the problem into a set of elementary decisions with outcomes that together define the complete set of possible solutions to the problem. Once the variables have been identified, the steps of modeling the constraints and objective become relatively straightforward. In the sections below, we will present the basic formulations for each possible type and level of constraint and objective. As a result, these two steps mostly reduce to the identification of the nature of the constraints and objective and an appropriate choice from the menu of available options in this chapter.

In the fourth step, the model is fed into a (commercial) computer program with an integer programming algorithm (commonly known as a *solver* or an *optimizer*), which calculates the solution. A discussion of these algorithms is postponed until Chapter 4.

The constraints and objectives discussed in this chapter are for the standard problem of assembling a single test from a pool of discrete items. As a consequence, we do not yet deal with constraints and objectives for problems with multiple tests and item sets. These topics will be treated in later chapters.

3.1   Identifying Decision Variables

To facilitate the task of identifying decision variables, it helps to think of test-assembly problems as *selection* or *assignment problems* in which "objects" (such as discrete items, stimuli, and sets of items) are selected from a pool and assigned to an empty test. The assignment should be such that an optimal value for the objective function is obtained and all constraints are satisfied. Another analogy, which will be discussed in more detail in section 4.3, is that of *shipping* or *transporting* items from one location to another. We use $i = 1, ..., I$ to indicate the items in the pool.

Ignoring all constraints, the number of different tests possible from a pool of I items is 2^I. As already noted in the preceding chapter, this is an astronomical number even for item pools much smaller than those typically met in practice (see Exercise 1.10). We have several ways to index the different tests that can be assembled from an item pool. One is to produce a list of them and code each test on the list using one integer variable, $y = 1, ..., 2^I$. This variable is a *decision variable* in the sense that its range represents all possible outcomes of the unconstrained version of the problem, and the decision on what test to select is equivalent to the choice of a value for this variable. Choosing y as the decision variable is not very helpful, however. The job of listing all possible tests is unrealistic for any item pool of nontrivial size. Also, there exist another choice of decision variables that allows us to formulate the test specifications as explicit objective functions and constraints.

This more effective choice of variables is based on the fact that each of the 2^I possible tests can be coded by a string of zeroes and ones. The coding scheme is given in Table 3.1. If this scheme is used, the selection of a test from the pool amounts to a series of decisions, one for the code of each item. The decision problem now has I decision variables x_i, each

Item	1	2	...	i	...	$I-1$	I
Variable	x_1	x_2	...	x_i	...	x_{I-1}	x_I
Test 1	0	0	...	...	...	0	0
Test 2	1	0	...	...	...	0	0
Test 3	1	1	...	...	...	0	0
...			...	...	...		
Test 2^I	1	1	...	...	...	1	1

TABLE 3.1. 0-1 decision variables for the items in the pool.

defined as:

$$x_i = \begin{cases} 1 & \text{if item } i \text{ is selected in the test} \\ 0 & \text{if item } i \text{ is not selected in the test.} \end{cases} \tag{3.1}$$

These variables were already used in the example in Section 1.4.

This choice of variables does allow us to introduce constraints on the selection of the test that reduce its choice from the full set of possible tests to a choice from the subset of feasible tests. For example, the constraint that the length of the test be equal to n reduces the set to the subset of tests for which the number of ones in Table 3.1 is equal to n. Because we have 0-1 variables, the same reduction is obtained if the sum of the variables x_i is set equal to n; that is, if the equality constraint

$$\sum_{i=1}^{I} x_i = n \tag{3.2}$$

is imposed on the selection of the test. A well-known rule from combinatorics tells us that this constraint reduces the size of the feasible set to $\binom{I}{n}$.

Suppose that the next constraint to be imposed on the problem is that items 11 and 14 not enter the test together. For the variables x_{11} and x_{14}, this means that either of them is allowed to have the value zero or one but the combination of two ones must be excluded. A simple way to formulate this constraint is by imposing an upper bound on the sum of their values:

$$x_{11} + x_{14} \leq 1. \tag{3.3}$$

If this constraint is added to the problem, the set of feasible tests becomes smaller again.

If more constraints are added to the problem (for real-world problems we often need several hundred of them to model all test specifications), the composition of the set of feasible tests quickly becomes difficult to track. In fact, we easily lose track of the size of this set! Even for the combination of the two constraints in (3.2) and (3.3), the combinatorics needed to calculate the size of the feasible set is not trivial. Basically, if we want an optimal test that meets a set of specifications, we have to search for the proverbial needle in the haystack, but with the additional complications that both the size and the shape of the haystack are unknown.

Fortunately, as we will see in Chapter 4, we have algorithms that allow us to search "unknown" sets of feasible solutions for a best solution. For now, the only point to note is that by choosing decision variables of the type in (3.1), we appear to be able to formulate different types of constraints on the selection of a test.

Observe that the choice of decision variable y was at the highest level in the test, whereas the choice of the variables x_i was at the lowest level possible, namely the individual items. Generally, as higher-level attributes are mostly aggregates of lower-level attributes (Section 2.2.2), a choice at a lower level is advantageous in that it gives us the flexibility to formulate constraints and objectives at the same or any higher level in the test.

Another type of decision variable is used to model the problem of item-pool design (see Chapters 10 and 11). A design for an item pool is a blueprint that shows us how many items have to be written for each possible combination of attributes. The problem of finding an optimal blueprint can also be treated as an instance of constrained combinatorial optimization, this time with integer decision variables $y_d=0$, 1, 2... defined over possible combinations of attributes, d. These variables constitute a set of decision variables for the problem because each possible array of their values corresponds to a blueprint of the pool.

The choices of 0-1 or fully integer variables do not exhaust all of our options. In later chapters, we will meet real-valued variables, introduced mainly for technical reasons, 0-1 variables defined for each possible combination of an item in the pool with an individual test in a multiple-test-assembly problem, and variables chosen at intermediate levels in the test (e.g., stimulus level). We will also meet problems that need to be modeled using combinations of different types of variables (Exercise 3.1).

The reader may still have the impression that, in spite of the formal approach to test assembly introduced in this book, formulating test-assembly problems still remains somewhat of an art. This impression is certainly correct. But the most important part of this art is to choose appropriate decision variables. A test assembler skilled in the approach in this book knows what types of variables are available, how to combine them in one problem, how to use them to formulate constraints and objectives, and what types of formulations should generally be avoided. In addition, this person keeps an eye on the total number of variables required as well as the algorithms available to calculate a solution.

3.2 Modeling Constraints

Separate sections are devoted to the formulation of quantitative, categorical, and logical constraints. In each of these sections, we show how these constraints can be formulated at the various levels distinguished in the test. After all types of constraints have been introduced, we show how to check a given set of constraints both for correctness and feasibility (Section 3.2.4).

3.2.1 Quantitative Constraints

Quantitative attributes are attributes that take numerical values. Each of the constraints in this section addresses such an attribute. We will use q_i as a generic symbol for the value of item i on a quantitative attribute.

Quantitative Constraints at the Test Level

The basic format of a quantitative test-level constraint is

$$\sum_{i=1}^{I} q_i x_i \gtreqless b_q, \tag{3.4}$$

where the relation symbol denotes the choice of a inequality or equality. The right-hand-side coefficient in this constraint, b_q, is the bound imposed on the weighted sum of variables on the left-hand side. Because $x_i = 1$ only for the items in the test, the sum in (3.2) is equal to the sum $\sum q_i$ for a test from the pool. This fact is used in the verbal interpretations of the examples of test-level constraints below, in which we refer just to "the test" and skip the reference to the decision variables.

Suppose that we want to assemble a test for which the total amount of time needed to solve the items is not larger than, say, 60 minutes. Suppose also that we have estimates of the amount of time a typical test taker needs to answer the items in the pool; for example, estimates of the 90th percentiles in the distributions of the actual response times in a previous sample of test takers. If t_i denotes the estimate for item i, the constraint can be formulated as

$$\sum_{i=1}^{I} t_i x_i \leq 60. \tag{3.5}$$

This constraint should be read as, "The total amount of time needed to answer the items in the test should not be larger than 60 minutes."

To make a set of tests look equally fair, it is often important that their lengths in print do not differ too much. Let l_i denote the number of lines needed to print item i. Suppose a printed page consists of 25 lines and we need test forms that are close to six pages in print; say, not shorter than

five lines below this limit, but certainly not longer. This requirement is met
if the following two constraints are imposed on the selection of the items:

$$\sum_{i=1}^{I} l_i x_i \leq 150, \tag{3.6}$$

$$\sum_{i=1}^{I} l_i x_i \geq 145. \tag{3.7}$$

This set of constraints should be read as, "The total number of lines needed
to print the test should not be larger than 150 or smaller than 145."

Quantitative attributes regularly met in IRT-based test-assembly problems are the item and test information functions (Section 1.2.4). Suppose
a test is assembled for admission decisions with a cutoff score at θ_c. Let
$I_i(\theta_c)$ denote the value of the information function of item i at this point.
The test is only considered adequate for the admission decisions if its information function has a minimum value of eight at the cutoff score. The
required constraint is

$$\sum_{i=1}^{I} I_i(\theta_c) x_i \geq 8. \tag{3.8}$$

This constraint should be read as, "The value of the test information
function at θ_c should be larger than or equal to eight."

After some practice, the reader will be able to immediately interpret
constraints presented as mathematical (in)equalities. Also, the reverse step
of writing verbal constraints as mathematical (in)equalities will quickly
become routine.

Quantitative Constraints at the Item-Set Level

All previous examples of constraints were at the test level because their
sums ranged over the variables of all items in the pool. This observation
immediately suggests how to formulate quantitative constraints at lower
levels in the test.

If a pool has item sets with common stimuli, the sets are often larger
than required for the test. If so, it may make sense not only to constrain
the size of the sets in the tests but also to impose certain bounds on some
of their quantitative attributes. Let V_s be the set of indices of the items
for stimulus s available in the pool. Item $i \in V_s$ is thus an arbitrary item
in the set in the pool associated with stimulus s. Suppose that the sum of
the π values of the items for stimulus s has to be between the values 2 and
3. The following constraints force the sum of π values to be between these
bounds:

$$\sum_{i \in V_s} \pi_i x_i \leq 3, \tag{3.9}$$

$$\sum_{i \in V_s} \pi_i x_i \geq 2. \tag{3.10}$$

These constraints should be read as, "The sum of π values of the set of items for stimulus s in the test should not be larger than 3 or smaller than 2."

Observe that the sums in these two constraints are no longer over the variables of all items in the pool but only over those in the item set for stimulus s. An alternative formulation of the constraints is possible if the items in each set are indexed using adjacent values for i. For example, if the range for stimulus s runs from $i = 23$ to $i = 35$, the sum in (3.9) and (3.10) can be formulated as $\sum_{i=23}^{35} \pi_i x_i$. However, the notation with the sum over a set of item indices is more general and works for any type of pool.

If the constraints hold for multiple stimuli $s = 1, ..., S$, each with possibly different upper and lower bounds $b_s^{\max}$ and $b_s^{\min}$, respectively, they can be written more compactly as the following two sets of inequalities:

$$\sum_{i \in V_s} \pi_i x_i \leq b_s^{\max}, \text{ for all } s, \tag{3.11}$$

$$\sum_{i \in V_s} \pi_i x_i \geq b_s^{\min}, \text{ for all } s. \tag{3.12}$$

Observe that (3.9)–(3.12) constrain the sums of π values as desired but have an undesirable effect on the selection of the item sets: Their presence in a test-assembly model leads to the selection of each item set that meets the bounds, no matter how many sets there are in the pool. This unconditional selection of item sets is usually undesirable. Besides, if the model also has a constraint fixing the number of sets in the test, the problem is bound to become infeasible. To avoid such complications, we need logical constraints that allow us to constrain the attributes of an item set *conditional* on its selection. If we use such constraints, the required number of item sets can be specified independently by another constraint. The introduction to logical constraints is postponed until Section 3.2.3.

Quantitative Constraints at the Item Level

As the variables x_i are at the item level, we are able to introduce constraints on the selection of individual items. Suppose we wish to be more stringent than the constraints in (3.9)–(3.12) and require *each* item in the test to have a π value between .40 and .60.

The upper bound of .60 is imposed on each item in the test by the following set of constraints:

$$\pi_i x_i \leq .60, \text{ for all } i. \tag{3.13}$$

These constraints work because x_i can be equal to 1 only for items with π values not larger than .60, whereas the constraint is still true for any π value if $x_i = 0$.

It may seem natural to impose the lower bound of .40 by reversing the inequality in (3.13), that is, imposing $\pi_i x_i \geq .40$ for all items. But this type of constraint does not work. For items in the pool with a π value smaller than .40, the inequality is always false: for both $x_i = 0$ and $x_i = 1$, the left-hand side is always smaller than the lower bound of .40 on the right-hand side. (A more general treatment of the notions of true and false constraints and their role in a check on the correctness of constraints is given in Section 3.2.4.)

The following set of constraints, however, does work well:

$$.40x_i \leq \pi_i, \text{ for all } i. \tag{3.14}$$

These constraints restrict the selection of items to those that have a π value larger than .40 but do not impose anything on the π values of the items that are not selected (that is, if $x_i = 0$).

The constraints in (3.13) and (3.14) have no summation sign. A more coherent way of looking at them, however, is as the limiting case of a constraint with a sum over one individual item. The constraints in (3.13) and (3.14) were formulated for all items in the pool. If we need to constrain the π values of a certain subset of items, they should be formulated for the indices in this subset only.

Discussion

If quantitative attributes are constrained at the test or item-set level and the same is done for their number of items, we in fact constrain *average values* of the attributes. Direct constraints on averages are also possible. For a test-level constraint, the only thing we need to do is adapt the basic format in (3.2) to

$$n^{-1} \sum_{i=1}^{I} q_i x_i \gtrless \mu_q, \tag{3.15}$$

where μ_q is the required bound on the average of attribute q, and the test length is assumed to be fixed to n. This constraint is also linear in the decision variables. Generally, we try to avoid such composite constraints, however. According to the principle of formulating test specifications discussed in Section 2.1, it is safer to formulate simple constraints for separate attributes. Possible shortcuts should be introduced only when the complete set of constraints has been checked (see Section 3.2.4) and combining constraints into a new one is known not to introduce any problems.

It is possible to have specifications that seem to constrain two different quantitative attributes. If this occurs, they should be modeled as a bound on the difference or sum of two of the weighted sums $\sum_{i=1}^{I} q_i x_i$ in (3.2).

The result is again a linear (in)equality in the decision variables and does not present any problem for the optimization techniques used in this book (Exercise 3.5).

Sometimes, however, a closer look reveals a different type of constraint. A case in point is specification no. 8 in Table 2.1. Measures of gender and minority orientation can be defined in different ways. For example, one possible definition of gender orientation is as a single quantitative attribute g_i with negative and positive values for the degree of male and female orientation. For this definition, no. 8 requires the sum of the attribute values g_i over all items in the pool to be equal to zero. Because we generally avoid equality constraints on quantitative attributes, the sum should be forced to be in a small interval about zero; that is, the constraints should be formulated as

$$\sum_{i=1}^{I} g_i x_i \leq \delta, \tag{3.16}$$

$$\sum_{i=1}^{I} g_i x_i \geq -\delta, \tag{3.17}$$

with δ an arbitrary small positive number selected by the test assembler that defines an interval $(-\delta, \delta)$ about zero. As will be shown at the end of Section 3.2.2, gender orientation can also be defined as a categorical attribute. In this case, we need a single constraint that combines two different sums.

An alternative way to realize item-level constraints is to remove the items that do not meet them from the pool before the test is assembled. Any selection from the remaining pool would then automatically meet the constraints. In addition, this measure would reduce both the number of constraints and the number of decision variables. A disadvantage, however, is that we may have to recode all items and reformulate the remaining constraints to meet the new code. Fortunately, most commercial software programs for combinatorial optimization preprocess the model before a solution is calculated. During this stage, unneeded variables and constraints are removed from the model. If this occurs, the item pool is automatically recoded and the constraints are reformulated. If the program provides this option, the easiest way to proceed with item-level constraints, such as those in (3.13) and (3.14), is to insert them into the test-assembly model and let the program "clean up" the item pool and constraint set.

3.2.2 Categorical Constraints

Categorical attributes partition the item pool into subsets of items with a common attribute. We will use C to denote the class of subsets in the partition and c as a generic symbol for a subset or category. Categorical constraints are always on the number of items selected from these subsets or from combinations of them. Because the decision variables are binary, the selection of certain numbers of items from a given subset or combination of subsets can be realized by imposing bounds on simple sums of their variables; no weighting whatsoever is needed.

Categorical Constraints at the Test Level

Suppose we need to constrain the distribution of categorical attributes in the test; such as item content. We use V_c to represent the set of indices of the variables of the items in subset c. Constraints on the distribution of the items in the test can be formulated as

$$\sum_{i \in V_c} x_i \leq n_c^{\max}, \text{ for all } c, \tag{3.18}$$

$$\sum_{i \in V_c} x_i \geq n_c^{\min}, \text{ for all } c, \tag{3.19}$$

where $n_c^{\max}$ and $n_c^{\min}$ are upper and lower bounds on the number of items from set V_c, respectively. These constraints should thus be read as, "The number of items in the test with content attribute c should not be larger than $n_c^{\max}$ or smaller than $n_c^{\min}$."

The same type of constraints can be formulated with respect to any other categorical attribute, such as a behavioral taxonomy, item author, the presence of certain auxiliary material in a stimulus (graphs, tables, or mathematical equations), a cognitive operation required for the solution of the item. Because these extensions are straightforward, we skip their treatment.

The generalization to a constraint on a combination of categorical attributes is as follows. Suppose we want to assemble a test in which items with a certain content have a certain format (e.g., biology items have a multiple-choice format). In addition to the subsets V_c, we introduce subsets V_f, which contain the indices of the items for format f available in the pool. Constraints on combinations of item content and format can be formulated using the intersection $V_c \cap V_f$:

$$\sum_{i \in V_c \cap V_f} x_i \leq n_{cf}^{\max}, \text{ for all } c \text{ and } f, \tag{3.20}$$

$$\sum_{i \in V_c \cap V_f} x_i \geq n_{cf}^{\min}, \text{ for all } c \text{ and } f, \tag{3.21}$$

where $n_{cf}^{\max}$ and $n_{cf}^{\min}$ are bounds on the number of items with content c and format f.

The formal difference between the constraints in (3.18) and (3.19) and (3.20) and (3.21) is the use of a set operation in the definition of the range over which the sum in the last two constraints is taken. This operation could have been avoided by introducing a joint partition of the item pool with respect to c and f using a new single index. But we prefer the notation in (3.20) and (3.21) because it correctly suggests that any categorical constraint can be formulated by set operations on a few basic classifications of the items in the pool with a known substantive interpretation.

Each of the sets of constraints in (3.18)–(3.21) is for the entire collection of subsets. If we want to constrain the selection of items from a smaller collection, we should choose the ranges of c and f correspondingly.

Categorical Constraints at the Item-Set Level

The constraints in (3.18)–(3.21) are at the test level because they control the distribution of the items in the test; they do not necessarily impose a constraint at a lower level in the test. The only thing needed to formulate a constraint at a lower level is to choose the appropriate set of items for which the bounds must hold.

Recall that we used V_s to denote the sets of indices of the items in the pool associated with stimuli $s = 1, ..., S$. Constraints on the selection of items from these sets with respect to content attribute c can be formulated as bounds on the number of items from the intersections $V_s \cap V_c$. Let $n_{sc}^{\max}$ and $n_{sc}^{\min}$ be the upper and lower bounds on the number of items needed from these intersections. The required constraints are:

$$\sum_{i \in V_s \cap V_c} x_i \leq n_{sc}^{\max}, \text{ for all } c \text{ and } s, \tag{3.22}$$

$$\sum_{i \in V_s \cap V_c} x_i \geq n_{sc}^{\min}, \text{ for all } c \text{ and } s. \tag{3.23}$$

Again, as in (3.9)–(3.12), these constraints lead to unconditional selection of items from any set in the pool. How to make the selection of individual items from a set conditional on the selection of the entire set will be discussed in Section 3.2.3.

Categorical Constraints at the Item Level

It is also possible to formulate categorical constraints at the item level. The two most common types of constraints at this level occur if some of the items in the pool have a unique combination of attributes and the test assembler wants to include these items in the test or exclude them from it. Let i be an item with such a combination of attributes. The two constraints that include and exclude item i are

$$x_i = 1 \tag{3.24}$$

and

$$x_i = 0, \tag{3.25}$$

respectively.

If these two constraints have to be formulated for more than one item, the use of set notation makes a compact formulation possible. Let V_1 and V_0 be two sets of items that have to be constrained in and out of the test, respectively. The required constraints are

$$x_i = 1, \ i \in V_1, \tag{3.26}$$

$$x_i = 0, \ i \in V_0. \tag{3.27}$$

In fact, it is possible to go one step further and replace either set of constraints in (3.26) and (3.27) by a single constraint:

$$\sum_{i \in V_1} x_i = n_1, \tag{3.28}$$

$$\sum_{i \in V_0} x_i = 0, \tag{3.29}$$

where n_1 is the number of items in set V_1. Because the decision variables are 0-1, (3.28) and (3.29) impose the same constraints on item selection as the constraints in (3.26) and (3.27).

Discussion

A special attribute of a test is its length. The type of constraint needed to restrict the length of a test was already introduced in Section 3.1:

$$\sum_{i=1}^{I} x_i \gtrless n. \tag{3.30}$$

The same type of constraint can be formulated on the size of an item set. If we want to constrain the selection from set V_s between $n_s^{\max}$ and $n_s^{\min}$, the necessary constraints are

$$\sum_{i \in V_s} x_i \leq n_s^{\max}, \tag{3.31}$$

$$\sum_{i \in V_s} x_i \geq n_s^{\min}. \tag{3.32}$$

Test length and item-set size are in fact quantitative attributes, which in set theory are known as the cardinality of a set. Nevertheless, the format of the constraints in (3.30)—3.32) resembles that of a categorical constraint. This happens because the contributions by the items to the length of a test or the size of a set are $q_i = 1$. For convenience, however, from now on we will refer to (3.30)–(3.32) as categorical constraints. This decision allows us to describe:

1. quantitative constraints as constraints with *real-valued* bounds on *weighted* sums of variables and

2. categorical constraints as constraints with *integer* bounds on *unweighted* sums of variables.

We continue the discussion at the end of Section 3.2.1 on the type of attribute involved in gender orientation in specification no. 8 in Table 2.1. If gender orientation is defined as a categorical attribute with possible values "male orientation" and "female orientation," we need constraints on two subsets of items in the pool. Let V_m and V_f denote the sets of indices of items in the pool with a male and a female orientation, respectively. The required constraints are no longer those in (3.16) and (3.17) but

$$\sum_{i \in V_m} x_i - \sum_{i \in V_f} x_i \leq \delta, \tag{3.33}$$

$$\sum_{i \in V_m} x_i - \sum_{i \in V_f} x_i \geq -\delta, \tag{3.34}$$

where δ now has an integer value close to zero. If we know that the item pool supports an equality constraint on this attribute, we can set $\delta = 0$.

3.2.3 Logical Constraints

The types of constraints considered in this section are logical because they deal with attributes that exist as logical relations between pairs, triples, and so on of items. The most important relations imply if-then, or *conditional*, selection of items. Two different kinds of conditional constraints are discussed.

The first kind arises if a set of items has the attribute of *exclusion*; that is, if one of the items in the set is selected, we cannot select any of the others. Such items are sometimes referred to as "enemies". Let i_0 and i_1 be the indices of a pair of enemies. The constraint needed to prevent the selection of one item if the other is selected is

$$x_{i_0} + x_{i_1} \leq 1. \tag{3.35}$$

This type of constraint was already met in Section 3.1.

If larger sets of enemies exist, the following generalization of (3.35) is needed:

$$\sum_{i \in V_e} x_i \leq 1, \tag{3.36}$$

where V_e is a set of enemies. For multiple sets of enemies $e \in E$, the set of constraints can be formulated more compactly as

$$\sum_{i \in V_e} x_i \leq 1, \text{ for all } e. \tag{3.37}$$

The second kind of constraint arises if the set has the attribute of *inclusion*; that is, if one of the items in the set is selected, we need to select more than one. The foremost example of this problem is test assembly from a pool with sets of items with a common stimulus. In Chapter 7, we will introduce several strategies for dealing with such item sets. Here, we already discuss one strategy that allows us to illustrate the logical nature of the constraints needed to model the relation.

Suppose each item set in the pool has one item that can be considered as its ideal representative—for example, because it has an optimal combination of attributes for the stimulus. We call such items *pivot items*. Let i_s^* be the index of the pivot item in the set associated with stimulus s. The following adjustment of (3.31) and (3.32) makes the selection of the required number of items from the set conditional on the selection of pivot item i_s^*:

$$\sum_{i \in V_s} x_i \le n_s^{\max} x_{i_s^*}, \tag{3.38}$$

$$\sum_{i \in V_s} x_i \ge n_s^{\min} x_{i_s^*}. \tag{3.39}$$

The bounds in these constraints, which are still linear in the variables, are equal to zero if $x_{i_s^*} = 0$ but equal to $n_s^{\max}$ and $n_s^{\min}$ if $x_{i_s^*} = 1$. Thus, dependent on the selection of the pivot item, we select zero or between $n_s^{\max}$ and $n_s^{\min}$ items from the set. However, these types of constraints do not work if the only bound imposed on the set size is a lower bound, that is, if we use (3.39) without (3.38) (Exercise 3.6).

It is easy to verify that the same type of constraint can be used if the size of set s should be equal to n_s items:

$$\sum_{i \in V_s} x_i = n_s x_{i_s^*}. \tag{3.40}$$

The same adjustments to the bounds are needed for constraints on the attributes of item set V_s in the model. If the attribute is quantitative, the set of constraints in (3.11) and (3.12) needs to be adjusted as

$$\sum_{i \in V_s} q_i x_i \le b_s^{\max} x_{i_s^*}, \text{ for all } s, \tag{3.41}$$

$$\sum_{i \in V_s} q_i x_i \ge b_s^{\min} x_{i_s^*}, \text{ for all } s. \tag{3.42}$$

For categorical attribute constraints, such as those in (3.22) and (3.23), the adjustments are

$$\sum_{i \in V_s \cap V_c} x_i \le n_{sc}^{\max} x_{i_s^*}, \text{ for all } c \text{ and } s, \tag{3.43}$$

$$\sum_{i \in V_s \cap V_c} x_i \ge n_{sc}^{\min} x_{i_s^*}, \text{ for all } c \text{ and } s. \tag{3.44}$$

3.2.4 Checking Constraints

Although it was immediately clear for most of the previous constraints that they functioned as required, for some of them, such as the constraints with the upper bounds on quantitative item attributes in (3.14) and the logical constraints on item sets in (3.38)–(3.44), further analysis was required to establish their correctness. In this section, we first offer a simple rule that can be used to check whether a constraint is correct (that is, whether it represents the test specification we have in mind). We then address the issues of checking the feasibility of an individual constraint and a set of constraints.

Checking Constraints for Correctness

A well-formulated constraint is true for some combinations of values for its decision variables and false for others. Consider for example the constraint

$$x_{i_0} + x_{i_1} \leq 1, \tag{3.45}$$

which was used in (3.35) to represent the specification that items i_0 and i_1 are enemies and cannot be selected simultaneously in the test. This constraint is true for the combinations of values $(x_{i_0}, x_{i1}) = (0,0)$, $(1,0)$, and $(0,1)$ but false for $(1,1)$.

Generally, a solution to a test-assembly model is an *array of values for the decision variables for which all constraints are true*. If we insert the constraint in (3.45) into a model, the solution will thus consist of the combinations $(x_{i_0}, x_{i1}) = (0,0)$, $(1,0)$, or $(0,1)$, but never the combination $(1,1)$. This is precisely as desired because the first three combinations represent outcomes that are admissible according to our specification, whereas the last combination is an inadmissible result.

This conclusion generalizes to the following rule for checking the correctness of a constraint:

> To check whether a constraint is correct, it has to be established whether (i) it is true for all combinations of values that represent an admissible outcome according to the specification and (ii) it is false for all other combinations.

Observe that both conditions formulated in this rule have to be checked. It is tempting to check whether the true combinations are admissible and forget about the false combinations. For example, the following constraint may seem attractive as an alternative representation of the same test specification:

$$x_{i_0} + x_{i_1} = 1. \tag{3.46}$$

This alternative is true for $(x_{i_0}, x_{i_1}) = (1,0)$ and $(0,1)$, which are admissible outcomes. But it should not be chosen because it is false for $(x_{i_0}, x_{i_1}) = (0,0)$, which is also an admissible outcome.

An alternative to (3.45) is

$$x_{i_0} + x_{i_1} < 2, \tag{3.47}$$

which is also true for all combinations of values that are admissible and false for all combinations that are not. This result is trivial, of course; it follows directly from a comparison between (3.45) and (3.47). (This constraint is only given for illustration; readers should generally avoid constraints in the form of strict inequalities.)

For simple constraints such as those in (3.45)–(3.47), it is possible to check all possible combinations of values for their variables. For more complicated constraints with larger numbers of variables, it often suffices to check combinations of values for critical variables. For example, the left-hand side of (3.38) and (3.39) consists of a sum of variables with a simple direct interpretation, but $x_{i_s^*}$ on the right-hand side is a more critical variable. To establish whether these two constraints are correct, we only need to check the admissibility of the outcomes for the two possible values of $x_{i_s^*}$.

In spite of our plea for simple constraints in Section 2.1, the relation between test specifications and constraints is not always one-to-one. An exception has already been met in (3.38)–(3.42). Each of these constraints imposes a separate bound on item set V_s. But, at the same time, the entire set of these constraints is needed to realize the logical specification of a common stimulus for this item set.

If multiple constraints appear to be necessary to realize one test specification or, put the other way around, one constraint realizes multiple specifications, we should use the rule formulated in this section to check each individual relation.

Checking Individual Constraints for Feasibility

We began the previous section by stating that a well-formulated constraint is true for some combinations of values for its decision variables and false for others. It is instructive to look more closely into "constraints" that are either true or false for all possible combinations of values. Examples of such constraints are the following two inequalities for the same variables as in (3.45):

$$x_{i_0} + x_{i_1} \leq 2, \tag{3.48}$$

$$x_{i_0} - x_{i_1} > 1. \tag{3.49}$$

The first is true for all possible combinations of values. Such constraints are compatible with any solution that satisfies the other constraints in the problem; they are thus redundant (Section 2.4.2). Constraints of this type are harmless in the sense that they do not reduce the set of feasible solutions or change the value of the objective function for the solution in any way.

(Whether we want such constraints in our model formulation is an issue with technical implications that we want to avoid here.)

The second constraint is false for each possible combination of values. The presence of this type of constraint makes a test-assembly model infeasible; it becomes impossible to find a single combination of values for which all constraints are true. Infeasibility of a simple categorical constraint with a few variables, such as the one in (3.49), is easy to detect. More subtle types of constraints that easily lead to infeasibility are equality constraints, particularly if they are on quantitative attributes.

At the test level, a quantitative equality constraint has the form

$$\sum_{i=1}^{I} q_i x_i = b_q, \qquad (3.50)$$

where the attribute values $q_1, ..., q_I$ are empirical values for the items in the pool but the bound b_q is set by the test assembler. Generally, it is unlikely that a combination of values for the variables $x_1, ..., x_I$ exists for which the sum in (3.50) exactly matches the bound for the actual attribute values of the items in a given pool. It was for this reason that in Section 2.4.2 we recommended constraining quantitative attributes to small intervals, such as in (3.16) and (3.17), instead of to a single value.

Checking Constraint Sets for Feasibility

Even if each individual constraint passes the check, we have no guarantee whatsoever that the full set is feasible. A test-assembly model is also infeasible if it has an inconsistent subset of constraints. A subset of constraints is *inconsistent* if there exists no combination of values for the variables for which all its members are true.

An example of an inconsistent set of two constraints is

$$x_{i_0} + x_{i_1} < 1, \qquad (3.51)$$

$$x_{i_0} + x_{i_1} > 1. \qquad (3.52)$$

This example is trivial; more subtle forms of inconsistency typically arise for larger sets of constraints in problems with larger numbers of variables.

To detect such cases, it may seem as if we have to check all possible combinations of constraints for all possible combinations of values for their variables—a task that, for purely combinatorial reasons, is just impossible for real-life problems. A practical alternative is just to run a solver for the problem and see what happens. If no solution exists, the computer program may report so in reasonable time.

If a problem is infeasible, our first strategy for finding a solution should be to replenish the item pool or, if a multiple-test problem is to be solved, reduce the number of tests required. A more complicated strategy is to tentatively relax the bounds for the constraints expected to cause the problem.

If the removal of one constraint removes the infeasibility, we may also decide to reformulate it as an objective function and formulate the previous objective as a constraint (see Section 2.3).

In practice, test assemblers mostly avoid inconsistencies intuitively. For example, more elaborate content classifications of test items often have a tree structure, with levels of attributes nested under each other. A test assembler working with such structures is automatically aware of the fact that bounds set at one level have to be consistent with those set at another. If infeasibility does arise, it typically is the result of a capacity problem such as when a large multiple-test-assembly problem has to be solved or the pool has been depleted of some types of items.

3.3   Formulating Objective Functions

After the preceding introduction to the different types and levels of constraints possible in test assembly, the formulation of an objective function is straightforward. In principle, any attribute formulated as an expression on the left-hand side of one of the preceding constraints can serve as an objective function. The only exceptions are the logical attributes in Section 3.2.3, which involve the necessity of conditional item selection. These attributes are dealt with more conveniently as constraints.

3.3.1   Quantitative Objective Functions

The general form of a quantitative objective function at the test level is

$$\text{optimize} \sum_{i=1}^{I} q_i x_i. \tag{3.53}$$

For each choice of attribute q_i, we get a different objective function. For example, if we choose q_i to be the value of the information function of item i at a cutoff score θ_c in an admissions-testing problem, the function

$$\text{maximize} \sum_{i=1}^{I} I_i(\theta_c) x_i \tag{3.54}$$

is an alternative to the constraint in (3.8) that requires the information in the test at θ_c to satisfy a lower bound.

To show a few more examples, let t_i, f_i, and ρ_i denote the estimated time needed to answer item i, the number of times item i was selected in previous tests, and the value of item i for a classical item-discrimination index (e.g., the point-biserial correlation coefficient). The objective functions

$$\text{minimize} \sum_{i=1}^{I} t_i x_i, \tag{3.55}$$

$$\text{minimize} \sum_{i=1}^{I} f_i x_i, \tag{3.56}$$

$$\text{maximize} \sum_{i=1}^{I} \rho_i x_i \tag{3.57}$$

optimize the total time needed to answer the items in the test, the sum of the previous exposure rates of the items, and the sum of the values of the item-discrimination index.

Quantitative objective functions at a lower level in the test are possible but less common. For example, if word counts are available for the stimulus of each item set $s = 1, ..., S$ in the pool, we may want to select the sets such that the total count for their stimuli is minimal. This objective can be realized by using the decision variable for the pivot items i_s^* in Section 3.2.3 as a carrier of the word count w_s for their stimulus s. The objective function then becomes

$$\text{minimize} \sum_{s=1}^{S} w_s x_{i_s^*}. \tag{3.58}$$

Adaptive Testing

It is even possible to formulate quantitative objectives at the item level. The foremost example of test assembly with this type of objective, already alluded to in our third example of objective functions of different type and level in Section 2.3, is adaptive testing with item selection based on the objective of maximum information at the last update of the ability estimate, $\widehat{\theta}$. Let R be the set of items in the pool not yet administered to the test taker. We realize the objective by selecting a test of length one from set R using the objective function and constraint

$$\text{maximize} \sum_{i \in R} I_i(\widehat{\theta}) x_i \tag{3.59}$$

subject to

$$\sum_{i \in R} x_i = 1. \tag{3.60}$$

At first sight, this formulation may seem somewhat overdone because we can pick the item that maximizes the information at $\widehat{\theta}$ directly from the pool. The conclusion would be correct if in adaptive testing the items were selected only on the basis of their information. In real-world adaptive testing programs, they also have to be selected to satisfy a common set of content constraints for each person as well as some technical constraints specific to adaptive testing. In Chapter 9, we will show that this can be done by using a sequence of n extended versions of the basic model in (3.59) and (3.60). Item selection based on these models is known as the *shadow-test approach* to adaptive testing.

3.3.2 Categorical Objective Functions

A categorical objective function has the general form

$$\text{optimize} \sum_{i \in V} x_i, \tag{3.61}$$

where V is an appropriately chosen set of items.

For example, if items of a certain content have to be de-emphasized in the test but we cannot constrain their number directly because of the danger of infeasibility, an objective function of the type in (3.61) could do the job. If the items with the intended content are in set V_c, the objective function is

$$\text{minimize} \sum_{i \in V_c} x_i. \tag{3.62}$$

If we want to de-emphasize items from multiple sets—say, V_1, V_2, and V_3—the objective function changes to

$$\text{minimize} \sum_{i \in V_1} x_i + \sum_{i \in V_2} x_i + \sum_{i \in V_3} x_i, \tag{3.63}$$

or, equivalently,

$$\text{minimize} \sum_{i \in V_1 \cup V_2 \cup V_3} x_i. \tag{3.64}$$

Observe that the objective functions in (3.63) and (3.64) actually address multiple objectives and weigh each objective equally; approaches with differential weighting are discussed in Section 3.3.4.

To give another example, suppose that an item pool has set-based items and we want to minimize the presence of items of a certain format in the item sets in the test. As before, let V_s denote the set of items for stimulus $s = 1, ..., S$ and V_f the set of items with the format we want to de-emphasize. The objective function required is

$$\text{minimize} \sum_{s=1}^{S} \sum_{i \in V_s \cap V_f} x_i \tag{3.65}$$

(Exercise 3.3).

Analogous to the quantitative objective function in (3.59), it is possible to formulate a categorical objective function at the level of an individual item. One possible application is the presence of an item with a unique combination of attributes that we would like to select, but only if its selection keeps the problem feasible. If item i is the intended item, the following objective function should be used:

$$\text{maximize} \ x_i. \tag{3.66}$$

Likewise, if we want to avoid this item, the objective function becomes

$$\text{minimize } x_i. \tag{3.67}$$

It is instructive to compare these two objective functions with the constraints in (3.24) and (3.25), which require item i to be in and out of the test, respectively. If the item pool is poor, these constraints may cause the problem to become infeasible.

We can also choose the subset in (3.61) to be the entire pool. If so, the objective function minimizes the length of the test:

$$\text{minimize } \sum_{i=1}^{I} x_i. \tag{3.68}$$

From a measurement point of view, it only makes sense to adopt this objective function, which was already used in the introductory example in Section 1.4, if the test-assembly model has enough constraints to guarantee both the content validity of the test and the statistical precision of its scores. But even then the actual length of the test that is found may unpleasantly surprise the test assembler!

3.3.3   Objective Functions with Goal Values

It is possible to formulate an objective function that minimizes the distance between a test attribute and a goal value.

For example, a classical ideal in test assembly is to have the average π value of the items as close as possible to .50 (Section 1.1.3). Suppose the test is constrained to have n items. The same objective is then realized if we require the sum of the π values to be as close as possible to $.5n$. Observe that the sum can be on either side of the goal value of $.5n$. Thus, what we actually want is the following minimization of the absolute difference between this sum and the goal value:

$$\text{minimize } \left| \sum_{i=1}^{I} \pi_i x_i - .5n \right|. \tag{3.69}$$

The function in (3.69) is not linear. But a standard trick to get a linear representation of the same objective is to constrain the sum to a small interval about the goal value and minimize the size of the interval. Let $(.5n - y, .5n + y)$ be the interval, where y is a new, nonnegative real-valued variable that controls its size. We formulate the problem as

$$\text{minimize } y \tag{3.70}$$

subject to

$$\sum_{i=1}^{I} \pi_i x_i \le .5n + y, \tag{3.71}$$

$$\sum_{i=1}^{I} \pi_i x_i \geq .5n - y, \qquad (3.72)$$

$$y \geq 0, \qquad (3.73)$$

where the constraints define the interval and the objective function minimizes its size.

It is instructive to compare this formulation with the constraints in (3.16) and (3.17). To use the latter, we must be able to specify exact bounds on the attribute; the alternative in (3.70)–(3.73) can always be used if we have a goal value.

Variable y is a real-valued decision variable. Therefore, the optimization problem in (3.70)–(3.73) contains a mixture of integer variables (restricted to 0-1) and a real variable. Such problems are known as problems of mixed integer programming (MIP) (see Section A1.1.4).

3.3.4 Multiobjective Test Assembly

The standard format of a test-assembly problem has one objective function (Section 2.4). If a set of test specifications implies a problem with multiple objectives, the first option should always be to try reformulating all but one of them as a constraint. If this appears to be impossible, some of the methods of multiobjective test assembly in this section can be tried. Basically, these methods combine different objectives into a single function or optimize them sequentially.

Weighting Objectives

This method can be used if the test assembler is able to specify his or her preferences for the objectives by a set of weights. Suppose a problem has the objectives of minimizing both the total time needed to answer the items and the number of times the items were administered earlier. If these objectives were to be taken separately, they would lead to the objective functions formulated in (3.55) and (3.56). But if the test assembler is able to specify weights w_t and w_f for the two objectives, they can be combined into a single objective function as

$$\text{minimize } w_t \sum_{i=1}^{I} t_i x_i + w_f \sum_{i=1}^{I} f_i x_i. \qquad (3.74)$$

The choice of weights in a multiobjective test-assembly problem of this nature may be problematic, particularly if the objectives are on different scales. Also, if some of the weights are chosen close to each other, the solution becomes unpredictable because of the trade-off between the attributes. A partial remedy to the problem of choosing weights is to run the problem first for the separate objective functions. The optimal values found in these runs tell us what values would be obtained if the entire weight was put on one of the objectives and no weight on any of the others. The actual weights could then be set by compromising between these values.

Goal Programming

The notion of a goal value for an objective function was already introduced in Section 3.3.3. If we have a problem with multiple objectives with goal values for their attributes, an alternative approach becomes possible.

Suppose the sets V_1 and V_2 contain items that belong to two different content categories and we have goal values $n_1^{(g)}$ and $n_2^{(g)}$ for the number of items from the two sets in the test. The following generalization of (3.70)–(3.73) compromises between the two objectives:

$$\text{minimize } y_1 + y_2 \tag{3.75}$$

subject to

$$\sum_{i \in V_1} x_i \leq n_1^{(g)} + y_1, \tag{3.76}$$

$$\sum_{i \in V_1} x_i \geq n_1^{(g)} - y_1, \tag{3.77}$$

$$\sum_{i \in V_2} x_i \leq n_2^{(g)} + y_2, \tag{3.78}$$

$$\sum_{i \in V_2} x_i \geq n_2^{(g)} - y_2, \tag{3.79}$$

$$y_1, y_2 \geq 0. \tag{3.80}$$

The constraints require the numbers to be in intervals about their goal values, $[n_1^{(g)} - y_1, n_1^{(g)} + y_1]$ and $[n_2^{(g)} - y_2, n_2^{(g)} + y_2]$, and the objective function minimizes the sum of the sizes of these two intervals.

An attractive aspect of this method relative to the previous one is that the introduction of the goal values leads to better control of the results. The objective function in (3.75) still suffers from a trade-off between the objectives, however. If the test assembler is able to choose weights for the two goals in this problem, more control is obtained if this function is replaced by a weighted sum of the decision variables, $w_1 y_1 + w_2 y_2$. A version of goal programming based on this type of weighting underlies the Swanson-Stocking heuristic for test assembly discussed in Section 4.4.3.

Maximin Approach

The idea underlying the maximin approach can be explained using the problem in (3.75)–(3.80). This time we have no goal values for the number of items from V_1 and V_2 but want to have the maximum number from each set. We follow a *maximin approach* to this problem with two objectives if we simplify the objective function and constraints in (3.75)–(3.80) to

$$\text{maximize } y \tag{3.81}$$

subject to

$$\sum_{i \in V_1} x_i \geq y, \tag{3.82}$$

$$\sum_{i \in V_2} x_i \geq y, \tag{3.83}$$

$$y \geq 0. \tag{3.84}$$

The new variable y is a common lower bound to the number of items from the two attribute sets V_1 and V_2. This bound is maximized in (3.81), hence the name maximin approach. Although y is real-valued, it will take an integer value in the solution because the left-hand sides of (3.82) and (3.83) are integer.

It is instructive to compare this approach with the previous one based on weighting of the objectives. If equal weights are chosen, as was done in (3.81)–(3.84), the objective function of weighted-objectives approach in (5.74) takes the form

$$\text{maximize } \sum_{i \in V_1} x_i + \sum_{i \in V_2} x_i. \tag{3.85}$$

But using (3.85) can easily lead to a solution with an unexpectedly large number of items from one set compensated by a small number from the other. Generally, if the objectives are on the same scale, a maximin approach gives a better safeguard against unexpected extreme values for the individual objectives than the method with the weighting of the objectives.

The same type of control of unexpected results is possible if we want to select the maximum number of items from V_1 and V_2 but these numbers have to satisfy a proportional relation. Suppose the relation is $r_1 : r_2$. The only thing to do is add the coefficients r_1 and r_2 to the right-hand sides of (3.82) and (3.83):

$$\text{maximize } y \tag{3.86}$$

subject to

$$\sum_{i \in V_1} x_i \geq r_1 y, \tag{3.87}$$

$$\sum_{i \in V_2} x_i \geq r_2 y, \tag{3.88}$$

$$y \geq 0. \tag{3.89}$$

If the test-assembly problem is a minimization problem, decision variable y can be chosen to be an upper bound that is minimized, and the approach in (3.81)–(3.84) and (3.86)–(3.89) is then known as a *minimax approach*.

Maximin and minimax approaches require all objectives to have attributes on the same scale. Otherwise, the attributes have to be rescaled. The condition is automatically satisfied in test assembly with different goal values for the test information function at different ability levels, which is one of the common multiobjective problems in IRT-based test assembly. In Chapter 5, we will show how the maximin and minimax approaches apply naturally to this class of problems. The core of our approach will be a modified version of the model in (3.86)–(3.89). In Chapters 6 and 8, the approach is generalized to the more complicated multiobjective problems of assembling a set of tests and assembling a test measuring multiple abilities.

Sequential Optimization

All previous methods combine multiple objectives into a single function, which either is a weighted sum of their attributes or a common bound on it. The method of sequential optimization is based on an entirely different idea. It assumes that the test assembler is able to rank the objectives from most to least important. The test-assembly problem is then replaced by a sequence of problems, one for each objective.

The sequence begins with the problem for the most important objective. At this step, all other objectives are ignored. The value of the objective function for the solution of this problem is recorded. The next problem addresses the second objective function, but the problem now has a constraint on the attribute in the first objective with a bound derived from the value of the objective function found in the solution to the first problem. These steps are continued until the last problem has been solved, the solution of which is the solution to the multiobjective problem.

We illustrate this approach for the problem with the objectives for the total time needed for the test and the exposure rates of the items in (3.55) and (3.56). Suppose

$$\text{minimize} \sum_{i=1}^{I} f_i x_i \qquad (3.90)$$

is the more important objective, and a solution to the problem with this objective yields the optimal value b_f^* for the objective function. The second problem is formulated as:

$$\text{minimize} \sum_{i=1}^{I} t_i x_i \qquad (3.91)$$

subject to

$$\sum_{i=1}^{I} f_i x_i < b_f^* + \delta, \qquad (3.92)$$

with δ a small tolerance added to the upper bound in (3.92) to keep the problem feasible. The solution to this problem is the one used as the solution to our original problem.

In sum, in this sequential approach, we first find an optimal solution for the most important objective. Then we search a neighborhood of this solution in the set of feasible solutions for one that has an optimal value for the second objective. The procedure is repeated until all objectives have been processed. The solution to the last problem is our overall solution.

3.3.5 Nonlinear Objectives

The examples in (3.59) and (3.60) and (3.70)–(3.73) demonstrate a trick used more frequently later in this book, namely the realization of a (possibly nonlinear) objective through a combination of a linear objective function and linear constraints. In Section 5.2, we will use this trick to deal with problems in which the classical reliability and validity coefficients are maximized. Both coefficients are nonlinear in the items. In Section 8.3.1, we will use this trick to linearize multidimensional test-assembly problems.

3.4 Literature

Several of the constraints and objective functions in this chapter have been used to solve test-assembly problems in the research papers in the bibliography at the end of this book. A first review of them appeared in van der Linden and Boekkooi-Timminga (1989) and a more comprehensive review in van der Linden (1998a). Several examples of logical constraints in test assembly are given in Theunissen (1986). For an extensive review of multiobjective decision-making approaches to test assembly, the reader should consult Veldkamp (1999).

The problem of building a mathematical programming model is dealt with more generally in Williams (1990). This textbook is a rich source of suggestions for those with a deeper interest in modeling test-assembly problems.

3.5 Summary

1. The process of solving a test-assembly problem consists of four steps: (i) identifying the decision variables; (ii) modeling the constraints;

(iii) modeling the objective; and (iv) using an algorithm to solve the model for an optimal solution.

2. A set of decision variables for the problem of assembling a single test from a pool of discrete items is a set of variables whose combinations of values identify all possible tests from the pool.

3. To find good decision variables for a problem, it helps to think of a test-assembly problem as a selection or assignment problem in which "objects" (items, stimuli, or sets of items) are selected from a pool and assigned to an empty test.

4. Choosing variables at a lower level in the test gives us more flexibility to model constraints and objective functions at the same and higher levels in the test.

5. A quantitative constraint has the form of an inequality that imposes a real-valued bound on a weighted sum of decision variables. The weights are the values of the items for a quantitative attribute.

6. A quantitative constraint is at the test level if its sum ranges over the entire item pool, at the item-set level if it ranges over an item set, and at the item level if it ranges over an individual item.

7. A categorical constraint has the form of an inequality that imposes an integer bound on an unweighted sum of decision variables. The level of a categorical constraint is also determined by the range of this sum.

8. Logical constraints are on attributes defined on pairs, triples, and so on, of items. They are typically necessary to perform conditional item selection. Two common types of logical constraints are for the selection of items from sets of "enemies" and from sets with a common stimulus.

9. Constraints can be checked for correctness by determining if they are true or false for those combinations of values that are admissible and not admissible according to the test specifications they represent.

10. A single constraint leads to an infeasible test-assembly problem if it is false for each combination of values for its variables. We generally avoid equality constraints on attributes because they are most likely to create an infeasible problem, particularly if they are formulated for quantitative attributes.

11. A test-assembly problem also becomes infeasible if it has a subset of constraints that cannot be true simultaneously; that is, a subset that is inconsistent.

12. A quantitative objective function consists of a weighted sum of decision variables, where the weights are the values of the items for a quantitative attribute. A categorical objective function consists of an unweighted sum of decision variables.

13. The level of the objective function is determined by the range of the variables over which its sum is defined.

14. Objective functions can be used to minimize the distance between an attribute and a goal value for it.

15. If a test-assembly problem has more than one objective, they should be (i) combined into a single objective function that is a weighted sum of their attributes (ii) used in a maximin or minimax approach in which a common bound on their attributes is optimized or (iii) optimized sequentially.

3.6 Exercises

3.1 Suppose an item pool consists of item sets for stimuli $s = 1, ..., S$. Let n_{cs} be the number of items with categorical attribute c in the set for stimulus s, and let q_s be the sum of the values of the items in the set for s on quantitative attribute q. Use 0-1 variables x_s to formulate a test-level constraint on the categorical and the quantitative attributes. Use these variables to formulate a stimulus-level constraint on the two attributes. Why is it impossible to formulate constraints at the item-set and item level using these variables?

3.2 Use 0-1 variables for the selection of the (pivot) items to formulate the following constraints:

(a) The number of multiple-choice items on vocabulary should not be smaller than 15.

(b) The sum of π values of items with a short-answer format on biology should be larger than eight.

(c) The item sets on geography should have a stimulus with a map.

(d) The number of printed lines for each stimulus should be larger than or equal to then.

(e) The number of printed lines for each item set should be larger than or equal to 35.

(f) Stimuli 18 and 27 should not be in the same test.

3.3 Use 0-1 variables for the selection of (pivot) items to formulate the following objectives:

(a) Minimize the absolute difference between the number of items biased against and in favor of second-language test takers.

(b) Minimize the number of items on algebra or geometry.

(c) Minimize the number of items on spelling and vocabulary.

(d) Maximize the number of items on social studies that refer to social tension.

(e) Minimize the absolute difference between the expected total time on the test and the available time of 60 minutes.

3.4 Use 0-1 variables for the selection of (pivot) items to formulate the following conditional constraints:

(a) If item 8 is in the test, the expected time on the other items in the test should be less than 105 minutes.

(b) Item 39 can be in the test only if it has at least one item that does not involve a computation. (What happens to the constraint if item 39 involves a computation itself?)

(c) If stimulus 11 and 12 are in the test, the total number of item sets should not be larger than five.

(d) There should be no item overlap between two tests if both of them have a length smaller than 30. (Hint: Use different sets of variables for the selection of items for the two tests.)

3.5 Minimize the absolute difference between the average item difficulty parameter b_i of two different tests, assuming the lengths of the tests are constrained to n_1 and n_2.

3.6 What happens if the decision variables for the pivot items are added to the right-hand sides of (3.38) and (3.39) but not to the right-hand sides of (3.41)–(3.44)? Show why the constraint in (3.39) does not work if (3.38) is not present. How can this problem be fixed if we have to model the specifications of a test from a set-based pool with only a lower bound on the size of a set or on its attributes?

3.7 Suppose all items have been coded using a readability index r. A test assembler wants both to maximize the readability of the items in the test and to minimize the difference between the average π value of the items and a goal value of .50. How should the strategies for combining multiple objectives in the test-assembly problem in Section 3.3.4 be applied? Which strategy seems best? (Assume that the test length is constrained to be equal to a known value for n.)

3.8 A pool with items on mathematical ability has the following content categories: items 1–5: arithmetic; items 26–50: graphs; items 51–75:

use of pocket calculator. The values of the IIFs at $\theta = -1$ and 1 for each item are known. Furthermore, each item requires about the same amount of time from the test takers. A test assembled from the pool should have a TIF between 7 and 8 at both θ values. The number of items on arithmetic should not be larger than the total number of items on graphs or the use of a pocket calculator. If one of items 61–65 is in the test, all other items should be in the test as well. The test should have a minimal administration time. Formulate these specifications in standard form. Which of the constraints is not likely to be active in the solution?

4

Solving Test-Assembly Problems

Now that we know how to model objective functions and constraints for test-assembly problems, we are able to formulate the standard model for the problem of assembling a single test from a pool of discrete items. This will be done in (4.1)–(4.10) in Section 4.1.

A solution to this model is a vector of values for the 0-1 variables $(x_1..., x_I)$ that satisfies all of its constraints and optimizes its objective function. A basic feature of the model is its linearity in the decision variables. Because of it, the model can be solved using one of the algorithms developed in the field of integer linear programming. A few such algorithms are discussed in Sections 4.2 and 4.3. Due to continuous optimization of implementations of these algorithms, virtually all test-assembly problems met in practice can now be solved in a routine fashion using commercial software. Before the current level of performance was reached, larger problems often had to be solved by an approximation algorithm or a heuristic technique developed for it. A selection of heuristic techniques for test assembly is presented in Sections 4.4 and 4.5. A critical difference between exact algorithms and these techniques is discussed in Section 4.6. Optimal design methods are methods of sample optimization for parameter estimation developed in statistics. These methods have also been applied to test-design problems. Because our approach to the problem of item-pool design in Chapters 10 and 11 can be viewed as a generalization of the optimal design method in statistics, its basic ideas are introduced in Section 4.7.

Readers can go through the rest of this chapter in two different ways. If they trust the algorithms and their major goal is only to get familiar with the various applications of the test-design methodology in this book, the rest of this chapter can be read cursorily. In fact, it is even possible to skip everything after Section 4.1 and go directly to Chapters 5 through 12 without missing anything needed to understand them. Readers who first want to know how solutions to test-design problems are obtained should read the rest of this chapter more carefully. In Sections 4.2 and 4.3, we assume familiarity with a few basic notions from linear programming (LP). Appendix 1 gives a brief introduction to these notions.

4.1   Standard Model for a Single Test

The standard model for the assembly of a single test with a quantitative objective from a pool of discrete items is

$$\text{optimize } \sum_{i=1}^{I} q_i x_i \quad \text{(objective)} \tag{4.1}$$

subject to possible constraints at the following levels:

Test Level

$$\sum_{i=1}^{I} x_i \gtreqless n, \quad \text{(test length)} \tag{4.2}$$

$$\sum_{i \in V_c} x_i \gtreqless n_c, \quad \text{for all } c, \quad \text{(categorical attributes)} \tag{4.3}$$

$$\sum_{i=1}^{I} q_i x_i \gtreqless b_q; \quad \text{(quantitative attributes)} \tag{4.4}$$

Item Level

$$\sum_{i \in V_1} x_i = n_1, \quad \text{(categorical attributes)} \tag{4.5}$$

$$\sum_{i \in V_0} x_i = 0, \quad \text{(categorical attributes)} \tag{4.6}$$

$$q_i x_i \leq b_q^{\max}, \quad \text{for all } i, \quad \text{(quantitative attributes)} \tag{4.7}$$

$$b_q^{\min} x_i \leq q_i, \quad \text{for all } i, \quad \text{(quantitative attributes)} \tag{4.8}$$

$$\sum_{i \in V_e} x_i \leq 1, \quad \text{for all } e; \quad \text{(enemies)} \tag{4.9}$$

Definition of Variables

$$x_i \in \{0, 1\}, \quad \text{for all } i, \quad \text{(range of variables)} \tag{4.10}$$

In this model, q_i, V_c, V_0, and V_1 are the same generic symbols for quantitative and categorical attributes as in the preceding chapter, V_e denotes a set of enemy items, and $\gtrless$ indicates the choice of an equality or an inequality sign.

In specific applications, the basic model in (4.1)–(4.10) will have to be extended and/or reduced in several possible ways. For instance, the objective function needed can be a categorical function rather than a quantitative function, or a function defined at a different level in the test. To deal with the entire set of test specifications in a real-world problem, we also typically need more than one constraint of the types in (4.2)–(4.9). Finally, several of the extensions addressed in subsequent chapters, such as multiple-test-assembly problems or test assembly from pools with item sets, are ignored here. We will present updates of (4.1)–(4.10) when we deal with these extensions in later chapters.

Any test-assembly model presented in this book will have its constraints presented in the same order as in (4.1)–(4.10). The principles that govern this order are:

1. Higher-level constraints precede lower-level constraints.

2. Categorical constraints precede quantitative constraints.

3. Quantitative constraints precede logical constraints.

4. Constraints on the ranges of the variables are presented last.

Another convention we will follow is to add labels to constraints with the names of the attributes they address wherever this is meaningful and the typographical space allows us to do so.

Exceptions to these conventions are sometimes necessary, however. For example, if an objective is formulated as a combination of an objective function and one or more definitional constraints, such as in (3.81)–(3.84) and (3.86)–(3.89), we will present these constraints directly after the objective function.

It is customary in mathematical programming to write constraints with all variables on the left-hand side of the (in)equality and a known constant on the right-hand side. We will abandon this convention in favor of representations that further a more direct interpretation.

4.1.1 Checking Interactions Between the Objective Function and Constraints

In Section 3.2.4, we pointed out the necessity of checking constraint sets both for correctness and feasibility before calculating solutions to test-assembly models. Here we add the recommendation to check the interactions between the objective function and the constraints. This check is not necessary to guarantee the existence of a solution but helps us understand the nature of the solution and may lead to an occasional last-minute simplification of the model.

The check should be for possible patterns of correlation between the attributes in the constraints and the objective function over the items in the pool. If positive correlations exist and the attribute in the objective function is maximized, the constraints tend to be realized at larger values between their bounds. Likewise, if the objective function is minimized, the constraints tend to be realized at smaller values. For negative correlations, the opposite tendencies are observed. If no correlation exists, the results become less predictable.

Attributes that always correlate positively are categorical attributes and quantitative attributes with positive values q_i. If a quantitative attribute of this type is maximized, the solution tends (i) to promote values $x_i = 1$ for the items with the largest values for q_i (ii) for as many items as possible. The second tendency implies a test with larger values for its categorical attributes. The opposite tendencies are observed if an attribute of this type is minimized.

An example of a categorical attribute that correlates with several other attributes is test length. For instance, if the objective is to maximize the value of the TIF at one or more θ values, the test length will show a tendency to go to its upper bound. The same occurs if we maximize the sum of the classical item-discrimination indices. The opposite occurs, for example, if we minimize the total word count for the test.

In Section 2.4.2, the notion of an *active constraint* was introduced as a constraint that is realized at a bound in the solution (see also Section A1.2.2). We can conclude that active constraints tend to be found among those attributes that correlate strongly with the attribute that is optimized.

The result of a check on the interactions between the objective function and constraints can lead to useful changes in the model. For example, if the model involves maximization, typically, for a well-designed item pool, it makes no sense to have constraints with lower bounds on attributes that correlate positively with the objective function. For the same reason, we can often replace an equality constraint in a set of original specifications for a maximization problem by a larger-than-or-equal constraint and expect a solution close to the original bound. This trick helps us avoid infeasibility due to equality constraints.

Observe, however, that all of these relations are only tendencies. Whether a constraint will be realized close to its upper or lower bound ultimately depends on the joint distribution of the item attributes in the pool and how realistically the bounds have been chosen relative to it. As a matter of fact, one of the more difficult aspects of the combinatorial optimization problems addressed in this book is that their solutions are difficult to predict because they depend on the nature of the entire problem rather than a single feature. By the nature of a problem we mean the number and types of constraints, the values of their coefficients and bounds, the coefficients in the objective function, and the direction of optimization. (For a more formal definition, see Section A1.1.1.)

4.2   Branch-and-Bound Search

Branch-and-bound algorithms are based on implicit enumeration of all possible solutions to a problem (Section A1.5). They search the entire solution space for an optimum but do so efficiently, cutting off entire portions of the space for which an optimum appears to be impossible.

Branch-and-bound algorithms search iteratively. They begin in a point in the space of the relaxed version of the problem (i.e., with all integer constraints removed) and then jump systematically from point to point, each time checking the value of the objective function. The *incumbent* is the feasible integer point with the best value for the objective function visited so far. The algorithms stop as soon as no improvements on the incumbent are possible. This is then declared to be an optimal solution to the problem.

Branch-and-bound algorithms capitalize on two simple but important principles. Both principles deal with the effect of adding a constraint to a problem. The principles are:

> *(i) If a constraint is added to a maximization problem, the value of the objective function for the solution may decrease but cannot increase.*

> *(ii) If a problem is infeasible, adding a constraint to it cannot make it feasible.*

Branch-and-bound algorithms begin with a solution to the fully relaxed version of the original problem and then systematically restore the integer constraints on the variables. If a new integer bound on a variable yields a solution worse than the incumbent, the first principle above tells us that later problems with the same bound can never be better and should be ignored. If a new integer bound on a variable results in an infeasible problem, the second principle tells us that all later problems with the same bound are infeasible and should be ignored.

More precisely, for a 0-1 maximization problem, these algorithms are as follows:

1. The solution to the fully relaxed problem (that is, with all integer constraints removed) is calculated. The solution to this problem has a value for the objective function that is an *upper bound* to the optimal solution for the original problem.

2. The integer constraint on one variable is restored. This leads to two new problems, one with $x_i = 1$ for this variable and one with $x_i = 0$.

3. The solutions to these two problems are calculated and checked:

   (a) If the problem is infeasible or leads to a solution with a value for the objective function lower than the incumbent, it is ignored along with all possible future problems with the same value for x_i.

   (b) If a solution is already entirely integer and has a higher value for the objective function, it becomes the new incumbent.

4. Steps 2 and 3 are repeated until all possible solutions have been checked or are known to be ignorable.

The power of these algorithms thus exists in the application of the two principles of constraint addition in step 3: If a solution with a known integer value for a given variable does not beat the incumbent, any problem with additional constraints on the remaining free variables cannot beat it either and can be ignored. Likewise, if the problem becomes infeasible, adding integer constraints on the remaining free variables can never give us feasibility in return. Therefore, if the solution gives a value for the objective function lower than the incumbent, or if infeasibility occurs while branching on x_i, all future problems with the same value of x_i are ignored.

4.2.1 Tree Search

The graphical illustration of the branch-and-bound method in Figure 4.1 shows that the algorithm performs what can be called a *tree search*. The node at the root of the tree represents the fully relaxed solution. Each branch represents a variable constrained to the value one or zero. If a solution has a smaller variable for the objective function than for the incumbent, the branch is *pruned*; problems represented by nodes further along this branch can never improve on the incumbent and are ignored. The same happens if the problem is infeasible. If a branch is pruned, the algorithm moves back in the tree and begins a search along another branch. The algorithm stops if all nodes are investigated or pruned. The process

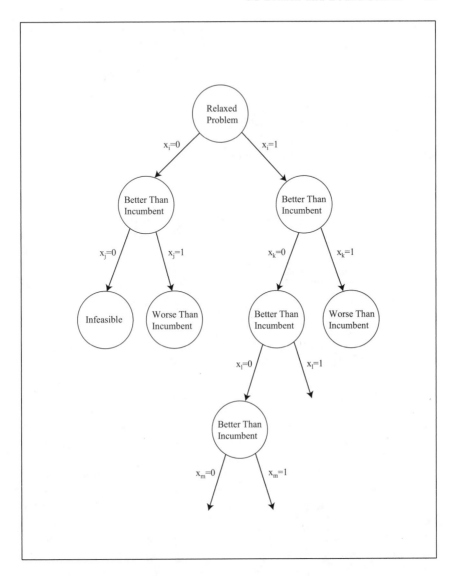

FIGURE 4.1. Graphical illustration of a tree search by a branch-and-bound algorithm.

of branching and pruning using the current bound provided by the incumbent explains why an algorithm based on this type of search has the name "branch-and-bound."

Unlike what we might have expected for an algorithm that searches for a solution to an IP problem, branch-and-bound algorithms do not jump from discrete point to discrete point in the feasible space of the problem.

They begin in the fully relaxed (i.e., real-valued) solution space and restrict themselves to "more discrete" subsets of it at subsequent steps.

Another characteristic feature of branch-and-bound algorithms is their *backtracking*; that is, their ability to move back and continue the search along another branch. These algorithms use backtracking to prevent from getting trapped in a suboptimal solution or having to violate constraints to be able to produce a "solution." This feature is absent in the constructive heuristic techniques for test assembly in Section 4.4, but a random version is present in the local search algorithms in Section 4.5.

4.2.2 Implementation Decisions

Before the branch-and-bound method can be used, several implementation decisions have to be made. For example, it has to be decided (1) how to initialize the incumbent, (2) where to start the algorithm (i.e., on which variable to branch first), (3) what priority order to follow for the branching on the remaining variables, (4) what algorithm to use to calculate the solutions at the nodes, and (5) how to backtrack if a branch is pruned. Commercial software with branch-and-bound-based solvers typically offers numerous options or settings for dealing with these decisions. The performance of an algorithm for a problem can be boosted enormously by making appropriate choices. A current trend in the software industry is to automate this step; the software then diagnoses the problem and optimizes the settings of the solver for it.

Typically, the solutions at the nodes during the search are found using a simplex algorithm. For this algorithm, implementation decisions have to be made as well (Section A1.3). As the integer values for the fixed variables at the nodes are known, the simplex algorithm is only used to calculate optimal values for the variables that are still free. If the search proceeds along the same branch, at each subsequent step, the number of fixed variables increases and the simplex algorithm is executed for an increasingly smaller set of variables.

Clever strategies for branching capitalize on the structure of the problem. For example, earlier branching on variables with a high impact on the other variables in the problem generally leads to more effective pruning (i.e., an earlier and/or larger reduction of the search tree) and therefore to a faster search. This strategy is useful for the test-assembly problems with item sets in Chapter 7, where we will use variables for both the selection of the items and the stimuli in the test. Branching on the variables for the stimuli has a higher impact than branching on the variables for the items. For example, if a variable for a stimulus is fixed at zero, the same value is implied for the variables for the entire set of items associated with it in the pool.

If a good feasible solution is known, it should be chosen as the first incumbent. This strategy, which also leads to more effective pruning, is recommended for the shadow-test approach to adaptive test assembly in

Chapter 9. In this approach, each item for the adaptive tests is selected from a shadow test assembled to the same set of specifications, fixing the variables of the items already administered to the test taker at one. Because the set of content constraints remains the same throughout the test and only the objective function changes, the previous solution provides an excellent initial solution for the next shadow test (Section 9.1.5). For more details on strategies for implementing branch-and-bound algorithms, see the technical literature at the end of this chapter.

The previous discussion was for an application of a branch-and-bound algorithm to a problem with 0-1 variables. If the problem is integer and has variables that are not 0-1, branching in step 2 occurs by imposing a series of constraints on these variables that successively split their range at an integer value into two smaller intervals. If the problem belongs to MIP, variables that are not integer are just left unconstrained.

4.2.3 Problem Size and Solution Time

It is impossible to know the actual running time of a branch-and-bound algorithm for a test-assembly problem in advance. Depending on the implementation of the algorithm, a solution can be found in a few steps, but an unfortunate implementation can also make us wait forever. Because exact predictions are impossible, we have to resort to (1) predictions based on worst-case analyses, (2) predictions based on the average for a large class of similar cases, and (3) practical experience.

As for the worst-case performance, a useful distinction exists between the computational complexity of mathematical programming problems that are solvable in polynomial time and problems that are not. A problem is solvable in *polynomial time* if there exists an algorithm that solves it with an upper bound to its running time that is a polynomial in the size of the problem, where the size of the problem is defined as, say, the number of bits required to represent the model in the computer. Problems for which this bound is not known to exist are *NP-hard* (nondeterministic polynomial-time hard). Many test-assembly and item-pool-design problems in this book are, as a class, NP-hard. These problems are currently solved only with significantly longer exponential-time algorithms.

However, practical experience shows us that for test-assembly problems of a realistic size this need not be a problem, provided some elementary implementation decisions are made. More importantly, as already indicated, the software industry has been successful in automating these decisions, and modern software programs help the user by preprocessing the problem and finding a fast implementation of the algorithm. For such programs, it becomes less and less necessary to override the default settings in the program.

The maximum number of nodes in a branch-and-bound problem with 0-1 decision variables depends on the number of variables, which is never smaller than the number of items in the pool. It follows that a basic determinant of the running time for the algorithm is the *size of the item pool*. This fact may seem somewhat counterintuitive to readers familiar with the idea of assembling a test by one of the constructive heuristics in Section 4.4. Such heuristics pick one item at a time, and, consequently, have a running time that is linear in the *size of the test*. In 0-1 test assembly, however, test length is just a bound in a constraint; see (3.30). A longer test implies a larger bound but does not imply more time.

The majority of the empirical examples in this book were for a pool of 300–800 items and had some 100–400 constraints. Typically, their solution required a handful of seconds on a PC with a Pentium II 860 MHz processor and 128 MB of memory for the integer solver in the *CPLEX* software discussed in Section 4.2.5. The only exceptions were a multiple-test-assembly problem with an extremely large number of variables (Section 11.5.4) and a severely constrained problem with a set of tests for a balanced-incomplete-block design (Section 6.6). The former was solved using the standard approximation discussed in Section 4.2.4, whereas we used a local search heuristic discussed in Section 4.5.2 to solve the latter.

In numerous simulations of the shadow-test approach to adaptive testing in Chapter 9, the assembly of shadow tests from pools of comparable size never took more than a second.

4.2.4 A Useful Approximation

The largest problems addressed in this book are in Chapter 11, where we show results for the simultaneous assembly of ten tests from a pool with 5,316 items. Each of these problems had over 53,000 variables and more than 6,000 constraints. The objective function was of the maximin type. The solution of two of these problems took 87 seconds. For the third problem, something occurred that might happen if we try stretching the limit. This problem was a version of the first two problems with a few seemingly innocent changes in a few constraints. Nevertheless, it appeared impossible to calculate an optimal solution in realistic time. We therefore resorted to an approximation that can always be used as a backup: The program was stopped as soon as an integer solution with a value for the objective function close enough to an upper bound was found.

A useful upper bound to the value of an objective function in a maximization problem is always available in the form of the value for a solution to the fully relaxed version of the problem. This follows immediately from the first principle of constraint addition in Section 2.4.2 that played a central role in our discussion of the branch-and-bound method above. This principle implies that relaxation of the integer constraints in a test-assembly problem leads to an extension of its feasible space and therefore a larger potential maximum value of the objective function in the solution.

In practice, it often occurs that the final solution is found early but the search of the entire tree has to be completed just to prove the optimality of the current solution. In such a case, the introduction of the upper bound with a reasonable tolerance does no harm at all.

For the third problem in Chapter 11, we chose a tolerance equal to 5%, and the solution was found in approximately 3 hours. This solution was thus known to be *closer than* 5% to the true optimum value of the objective function for the problem.

4.2.5 Software

A test-assembly software package based on integer programming is *Con-TEST* 2.0 (Section 4.8). This package has an interface that allows the user to specify constraints and the objectives in the natural language used in Chapter 2. All necessary mathematical modeling is done by *ConTEST* 2.0. The program runs on a DOS platform; *Windows* software with the same functionality for the larger class of test-design problems in this book has been planned. The DOS-based program *OTD* by Verschoor (1991) can be used to run the model with minimum test length in Section 1.4.

All problems in this book were solved using the integer solver from *CPLEX*, a package of solvers for linear and quadratic programming problems published by ILOG, Inc. (Section 4.8). Users with their own software for writing out the model for their test-assembly problems can directly use the appropriate solver from this package. Alternatively, *OPL Studio*, also by ILOG, Inc., can be used. This general-purpose modeling system helps users to specify their problems using an intuitive programming language and reduces the amount of programming necessary. The system also comes with *OPLScript*, a command language for dealing with sequences of models or solving models interactively. Solutions to models in *OPL Studio* are found by a solver started directly from the program. An example of a small test-assembly problem specified in *OPL Studio* that illustrates some of these options is given in Appendix 2.

For instructional purposes, it is possible to use the LP options in *Excel* in *Microsoft Office* to illustrate how to model and solve small test-assembly problems. The solvers provided in this program do not have enough power for any real-life test-assembly problem, however.

4.3 Network-Flow Approximation

Network-flow problems are integer programming problems with a special structure. Thanks to this structure, the simplex algorithm boils down to a simple and extremely fast algorithm. If all bounds in a network-flow problem are integer, the fully relaxed version of the model has an integer solution, which is always found by this fast algorithm (Section A1.4).

An approximate but nowadays less frequently needed approach to solving test assembly is to approximate the original problem by a problem with a network-flow structure. To get a satisfactory approximation, it may be necessary to remove some of the constraints in the original problem and solve a version of the model with a penalty term for them in the objective function (Lagrangian relaxation; see below). Sometimes, this approximate problem is embedded in a larger heuristic scheme that iteratively improves on the first solution.

A graphical representation of a network-flow problem is given in Figure A1.4. Suppose the supply points of this network represent the different classes of items, $i = 1, ..., m$, in a joint partition of the item pool based on the categorical item attributes. The supply of items available for class i is S_i. The demand points, $j = 1, ..., n$, represent the same partition for the test, and the minimum numbers of items needed at these points are D_j. The problem of assembling a test to meet these numbers can be represented by the following network-flow formulation (compare (A1.11)–(A1.14)):

$$\text{minimize} \sum_{i=1}^{m} \sum_{j=1}^{n} \varphi_{ij} x_{ij} \quad \text{(transportation costs)} \tag{4.11}$$

subject to

$$\sum_{j=1}^{n} x_{ij} \leq S_i, \quad \text{(supply)} \tag{4.12}$$

$$\sum_{i=1}^{m} x_{ij} \geq D_j, \quad \text{(demand)} \tag{4.13}$$

$$x_{ij} \geq 0, \quad \text{for all } i \text{ and } j, \quad \text{(range of variables)} \tag{4.14}$$

where x_{ij} is the number of items shipped from i to j and the objective function minimizes the transportation costs, φ_{ij}. The model can be extended with transshipment points, which have equal supply and demand.

To implement this approach, an adequate definition of the transportation costs has to be found. For example, if the objective is to maximize the information in the test at a cutoff score θ_0, the transportation costs should be taken to be $-\bar{I}_i(\theta_0)$, where $\bar{I}_i(.)$ is the average value of the item information functions at supply point i and the minus sign changes (4.11)–(4.14) into a maximization problem. Observe that (4.14) defines a problem with real-valued variables, but an integer solution is found because the bounds S_i and D_j are integer.

Comparing this problem with (4.1)–(4.10), it is obvious that not all real-world test-assembly problems would fit this representation. Particularly if we have quantitative constraints, enemy sets, or problems with item sets (Chapter 7), the standard network formulation has to be extended. Several strategies for dealing with such extensions are possible. An obvious strategy for quantitative attributes is to categorize them. More ingenious strategies exploit the fact that transshipment points can be added to the problem (Section A1.4) or use the technique of Lagrangian relaxation.

In *Lagrangian relaxation*, the more difficult constraints are replaced by a penalty term added to the objective function. For example, for the general model in (4.1)–(4.10), we could leave out the quantitative constraints in (4.4) and introduce penalty terms for them in the objective function, which would lead to the following expression for (4.1):

$$\sum_{i=1}^{I} q_i x_i + \sum_{q=1}^{Q} \lambda_q [\sum_{i=1}^{I} q_i x_i - b_q]. \quad \text{(Lagrange multipliers)} \quad (4.15)$$

Positive values for the Lagrange multipliers λ_q are to be selected by the test assembler. Obviously, for larger values of λ_q, minimization of this expression leads to realizations of the test attributes $\sum_{i=1}^{I} q_i x_i$ closer to b_q but also to larger values than necessary for the original objective function, $\sum_{i=1}^{I} q_i x_i$. Because solutions to this type of problem are obtained extremely fast, it is possible to embed a series of them in an iterative heuristic scheme that uses previous results to improve on values chosen for λ_q.

4.4   Constructive Heuristics

Heuristic techniques, *heuristics* for short, are procedures for finding a solution to a test-assembly problem based on a plausible intuitive idea. Heuristics are designed with the structure of a specific class of problems in mind. As a consequence, they have to be adapted or replaced by another type of heuristic if we move to a problem in another class. We resort to heuristics if the problem is too large to be solved optimally in realistic time.

Constructive heuristics are usually extremely fast. However, by definition, we have no mathematical proof of their optimality. Therefore, we have to evaluate their attractiveness against the plausibility of the ideas on which they are based or by scrutinizing the solutions they produce.

The three heuristics below were developed for the same type of problem as addressed in the Birnbaum approach in Section 1.2.8; that is, (1) IRT-based test-assembly problems in which the objective is to minimize the distance between the test information function and a target, where (2) only a few categorical constraints have to be imposed, and (3) the pool consists of discrete items. These heuristics are *constructive* in that they literally build the test one item at a time.

4.4.1   Greedy Heuristics

Heuristics of this type have been invented (and reinvented!) in almost every area of application of mathematical programming. Their basic idea is to solve the problem by taking a sequence of steps, each time doing whatever is locally best. In a maximization problem, these heuristics produce the largest increase for the objective function possible at each step. Because they ignore all future consequences of the steps, the nickname of *greedy heuristic* is appropriate.

Suppose we have target values at θ_k, $k = 1, ..., K$ for the information function of a test we want to assemble. These target values are denoted as $\mathcal{T}_k$. The value of the information function of item i at θ_k is denoted as $I_i(\theta_k)$. A greedy heuristic picks items that fill the gap between the target and current values of the information function maximally. Suppose items $i_1, ... i_{g-1}$ have already been selected, and the next item to be selected is the gth item. The information in the first $g-1$ items at θ_k is $\sum_{j=1}^{g-1} I_{i_j}(\theta_k)$.

A greedy heuristic would select this item using the following two rules:

1. Find the θ_k value with the largest positive difference,

$$\mathcal{T}_k - \sum_{j=1}^{g-1} I_{i_j}(\theta_k). \tag{4.16}$$

2. Select the item in the pool that has the largest value for its information function $I_i(\theta_k)$ at the value θ_k found in the previous step.

If constraints on categorical attributes have to be imposed, greedy heuristics typically rotate the selection of the items among the partition classes in the item pool introduced by the attributes. To deal with differences between the numbers of items needed from these classes, they visit them proportionally. Quantitative constraints can only be imposed by this method if we pool their values into a few categories first. If multiple parallel forms of a test have to be assembled, item selection is rotated both over classes of items in the pool and the individual tests. This rotation works only if the number of constraints is not too large and all constraints are equalities.

Because of the greedy nature of the heuristic, the result often is a test information function that overshoots its target values. From a measurement point of view, more is not necessarily worse. But if a sequence of tests is to be assembled and there is no interim replenishment of the pool with items of the same quality, greedy algorithms produce a first test with an information function that overshoots its target, while later tests show a quick deterioration of their quality. The phenomenon holds universally for any type of sequential selection of items or tests (Section 4.6), but the deterioration is largest for greedy algorithms. To remedy such problems, test-assembly heuristics usually have a second stage in which items are swapped between the test(s) and the pool to get more desirable results. Essentially, such stages introduce a form of backtracking, which, as we saw in Section 4.2, branch-and-bound algorithms perform in a complete and much more effective way.

4.4.2 Luecht Heuristic

The Luecht heuristic is based on the same principle of local optimization as the class of greedy heuristics in the preceding section, but it is a projection method in the sense that it looks forward and uses the differences between the target and current values for the test information function to reduce its greediness to desirable proportions.

The Luecht heuristic finds the gth item by taking the following steps:

1. Divide the remaining difference between the target values and current values of the information function in (4.16) in equal portions. If $g-1$ items have been selected, these portions are equal to

$$[\mathcal{T}_k - \sum_{j=1}^{g-1} I_{i_j}(\theta_k)]/(g - n + 1). \tag{4.17}$$

2. Select the item with an information function that matches (4.17) best over all values θ_k, $k = 1, ..., K$, using a weighted criterion that favors an item more strongly, if its information better matches the norm in (4.17) at θ_k values where this norm is larger.

The Luecht heuristic has also been extended to deal with constraints and multiple-test problems, exactly as for the previous class of heuristics. Because of its criterion of a weighted match to (4.17), this heuristic, which is also known as the *normalized weighted absolute deviation heuristic* (NWADH), does not have the tendency to overshoot target values for information functions, though its solution can still be improved by a second stage of item swapping.

4.4.3 Swanson-Stocking Heuristic

This heuristic was motivated by the idea of goal programming (Section 3.3.4). It assumes test specifications with upper and lower bounds for all of their attributes, including the test information function, but treats these bounds as goal values rather than strict bounds. In addition, it requires the specification of weights by the test assembler, one for each attribute, to reflect their relative importance.

The heuristic also selects one item at a time but does so by minimizing a criterion based on a weighted sum of deviations from all bounds, including those on the information function. Let $h = 1, ..., H$ be the constraints and a_{ih} the value of item i on the attribute in constraint h. If h is categorical, $a_{ih} \in \{0, 1\}$, whereas if h is quantitative, $a_{ih} = q_i$. In addition, we use R_g to represent the set of $I - g + 1$ items in the pool after the first $g - 1$ items, $i_1, ..., i_{g-1}$, have been selected.

The Swanson-Stocking heuristic identifies the gth item by taking the following steps:

1. Calculate the contribution of each item in the pool to each constraint h as the sum of (1) the attribute values of the $g - 1$ items already selected, (2) the attribute value of the candidate item, and (3) $n - g$ times the average attribute value of all other $I - g$ items in the pool:

$$\pi_{i_g h} = \sum_{j=1}^{g-1} a_{i_j h} + a_{i_g h} + (n - g) \frac{\sum\limits_{i \in R_g \backslash \{i_g\}} a_{ih}}{(I - g)}. \qquad (4.18)$$

2. For each constraint h, calculate the distance between contribution $\pi_{i_g h}$ and the bound as

$$\left| \pi_{i_g h} - b_h \right|. \qquad (4.19)$$

If the constraint has both an upper and a lower bound, and $\pi_{i_g h}$ is between the bounds, (4.19) is set equal to zero.

3. Select the item with the smallest weighted sum of distances; that is, according to

$$\sum_{h=1}^{H} w_h \left| \pi_{i_g h} - b_h \right|, \qquad (4.20)$$

where the weights w_h have to be specified by the test assembler.

Like the Luecht heuristic, the Swanson-Stocking heuristic is a projection method. It represents the items to be selected at later stages by the average attribute values of the remaining items in the pool (i.e., the third term of (4.18)). Also, like the preceding two heuristics, it has a second stage with backtracking in the form of item swapping between the initial solution and the pool.

4.5   Local Search Heuristics

The two heuristics for local search that we discuss in this section belong to the flourishing field of Monte Carlo optimization. Readers familiar with Bayesian methods in test theory will recognize one of these heuristics (simulated annealing) as the popular Metropolis algorithm for drawing from posterior distributions in parameter estimation in IRT.

Both heuristics are inspired by natural processes that seem to imply some form of optimization. The genetic algorithms in Section 4.5.1 model optimization as an evolutionary process in a population of candidate solutions. The terminology used to describe these algorithms borrows heavily from evolutionary theory in biology. The method of simulated annealing in Section 4.5.2 simulates the thermal process of cooling a solid physical body in a heat bath to an optimum, a well-known problem in statistical physics.

The analogy between these heuristics and the empirical processes that have inspired them makes them fancy but does not guarantee their success as an optimization method for an arbitrary mathematical problem. Rather, we should view them as schemes that are much more general than the constructive heuristics in the preceding sections and that have to be optimized for the application at hand. Their generality is both a strength and a weakness. On the one hand, these schemes are not just for IP problems, but can be applied to any constrained combinatorial optimization problem, which makes them a likely choice for problems with objective functions or constraints that are hard to represent linearly. On the other hand, to define a good local search, deep knowledge of the specific structure of the problem is required.

The basic idea underlying any local search heuristic is that of a walk through a chain of subsets of points in the feasible space of the problem. These subsets can be viewed as *neighborhoods* of the interim solutions found during the walk. The link to a new neighborhood is established by searching the neighborhood of the current solution for improvement, hence the name *local search*. An instructive analogy is that of the walk through an unknown area of a blindfolded person who uses a cane to explore his neighborhood before making a step and keeps doing so until a satisfactory destination is reached.

Important differences between local search heuristics exist in the definition of the neighborhoods (unlike the analogy with the blindfolded person above, a good neighborhood does not necessarily consist of points that are close in a physical sense!) and the way the neighborhoods are searched. Sections 4.5.1 and 4.5.2 illustrate such differences.

4.5.1 Genetic Algorithms

The class of *genetic algorithms* is diverse. Each of its algorithms is based on the idea of an entire generation of candidate solutions evaluated at one time instead of a single candidate. The candidates are allowed to produce offspring. The fittest candidates are then selected as the new generation, whereas the weaker candidates die. This step is repeated a large number of times, upon which the fittest candidate met so far is declared to be the solution. Obviously, for this process to work for an optimization problem, the fitness function should have a monotonic relation to the objective function that is optimized.

The rule for the production of offspring defines the neighborhoods in a genetic algorithm, whereas the operation of selection determines the outcome of a local search. Finding effective rules and operations is part of the problem of finding a good implementation of the algorithm.

This basic formulation of a genetic algorithm as a continuous process of *offspring generation* and *selection* is usually extended with other genetic operations, such as mutation and recombination. *Mutations* are small perturbations of candidate solutions. In a test-assembly problem, a typical perturbation is the (random) swap of an item between a candidate test and the set of remaining items in the pool. *Recombination* is the operation of combining two candidates into a new one. In a test-assembly problem, re-combination would mean combining the strings of items from two different tests into a new test (crossover). These operations can be chosen to have a random component and/or a step involving local optimization, such as finding a best mate, before recombination.

An example of a genetic algorithm for a test-assembly problem with minimization of the objective function could consist of the following steps:

1. Use the item pool to create an initial generation of tests.

2. Use the operations of mutation and recombination to expand the set of tests.

3. Calculate the values of the objective function for the tests.

4. Use these values to select a new generation of tests.

5. Repeat the previous three steps until a test with an acceptably low value for the objective function is met.

Of course, the larger the number of iterations, the better the solution expected. In fact, the current enormous power of our computers has stim-ulated the interest in local search heuristics.

A problem requiring considerable ingenuity is that of how to keep the algorithm operating within the feasible space for the optimization problem. Ideally, the initial pool should contain feasible candidates only, and this feasibility is maintained during the processes of mutation and offspring generation. Incidental operation outside this space is no problem, provided we know that the process returns to it with improved values for the fitness function. For real-life test-assembly problems, with hundreds of constraints and hence a size of the feasible space of much lower order than the full space of all possible tests, this requirement is a frequent obstacle.

One standard approach for reducing infeasibility, reminiscent of the tech-nique of Lagrangian relaxation in Section 4.3, is to use penalty terms for constraint violation. These penalty terms are combined with the objective function into a fitness function. The idea is that because of low fitness the majority of infeasible solutions sooner or later die. For test-assembly problems, the definition of effective penalties is still an area of exploration.

4.5.2 Simulated Annealing

This heuristic scheme differs from genetic algorithms in that the process moves from the search of a single candidate solution to the next. The search is performed by simulating the technique of annealing in condensed matter physics. Annealing is a thermal process for obtaining a minimum-energy arrangement of particles in a solid, such as a crystal. The arrangement is obtained by melting the solid and then carefully cooling it.

The simulation of this process is based on a Monte Carlo technique introduced in the 1950s. In this technique, the next energy state of the solid is obtained by a random perturbation of the previous state, which is then accepted with a certain probability. (If the perturbation is not accepted, the solid remains in the same state.) The process is controlled by a parameter that governs the distribution of the acceptance probabilities. A sequence of values for this control parameter systematically lowers the probability of acceptance of worse solutions during the process. This sequence is known as the cooling schedule for the process.

The analogy between the physical process of annealing and local search in a combinatorial minimization problem arises if we equate (i) each arrangement of particles in the solid to a candidate solution, (ii) its energy level to the value of the objective function, and (iii) the minimum-energy state to the solution that is sought.

The neighborhoods in a search based on simulated annealing are defined by the perturber used to generate new candidate solutions. Typically, a random mechanism is chosen that ranges over the entire solution space. The acceptance of a new candidate is also always a random event. Because of these features, simulated annealing implies a random walk through the space of solutions until one with an acceptable value for the objective function is found.

For a test-assembly problem with minimization of the objective function, simulated annealing involves the following steps:

1. Choose a test as the incumbent solution for the optimization problem.

2. Perturb the test randomly and calculate its value for the objective function.

3. If the new test has a lower value for the objective function, accept it as the new incumbent. If it has a larger value, accept it with a (small) probability that depends both on the degree of deterioration of the objective function and the control parameter.

4. Lower the value of the control parameter.

5. Repeat the previous three steps until a test with an acceptably low value for the objective function has been found.

The probability of accepting a worse solution in step 3 is often defined as

$$\Pr\{\text{acceptance} \mid t\} = \begin{cases} 1 & \text{if } o(p) < o(i) \\ \exp\left[-\frac{o(p)-o(i)}{t}\right] & \text{if } o(p) \geq o(i), \end{cases} \qquad (4.21)$$

where $o(i)$ and $o(p)$ are the values of the objective function for the incumbent and the new solution proposed by the perturber, respectively. This probability density is derived from the Boltzmann distribution in physics, which describes the distribution of energy states of a solid as a function of the temperature. Parameter t in (4.21) is the control parameter; lowering its value gives new probabilities of acceptance that are uniformly lower in the degree of deterioration of the objective function, $o(p) - o(i)$. It is not necessary to work with this density function; in principle, another function decreasing in $o(p) - o(i)$ with a parameter that can be used to lower the acceptance probabilities uniformly to zero might do as well.

The fact that the algorithm accepts worse solutions with decreasing probabilities helps it leave a local optimum and is critical to its success. The same feature is introduced by the mutation operation in a genetic algorithm and the possibility of backtracking in a branch-and-bound algorithm (see Section 4.6). Like genetic algorithms, the more challenging part of using simulated annealing for test assembly is to find a perturber that ranges over the entire feasible space of tests but does not leave it.

An empirical example of an application of the method of simulated annealing to a test-assembly problem is given in Section 6.6, where we use this method to calculate a set of test booklets that constitutes an optimal balanced-incomplete-block design for a large-scale educational assessment.

4.6   Simultaneous and Sequential Optimization

The three constructive heuristics in Section 4.4 are *sequential;* they assemble a test by selecting one item at a time. On the other hand, the branch-and-bound algorithms in Section 4.2 optimize over all decision variables *simultaneously;* at each iteration step, they evaluate an entire solution against an incumbent. The same holds for the network-flow formulation in Section 4.3 and the local search heuristics in Sections 4.5.1 and 4.5.2.

A basic problem inherent in using a sequential heuristic for solving a combinatorial optimization problem is that consequences of unfortunate earlier decisions can only be discovered later, when they can no longer be undone. As a result, sequential heuristics are bound to lead to suboptimal solutions and often have to violate constraints to find a test at all.

An example of these two tendencies is given for the following small test-assembly problem for the item pool in Table 4.1:

$$\text{maximize } \sum_{i=1}^{5} I_i(\theta_c) \quad (\text{maximum information at } \theta_c) \qquad (4.22)$$

subject to

$$\sum_{i=1}^{5} x_i = 2, \quad (\text{test length}) \qquad (4.23)$$

Item	$I_i(\theta_c)$	V_1	V_2	V_E
1	.50	+	+	+
2	.40	+	−	+
3	.30	+	+	−
4	.20	−	+	+
5	.10	−	+	−

TABLE 4.1. Example of constraint violation by a sequential heuristic.

$$\sum_{i \in V_1} x_i \geq 2, \quad \text{(attribute 1)} \tag{4.24}$$

$$\sum_{i \in V_2} x_i \leq 1, \quad \text{(attribute 2)} \tag{4.25}$$

$$\sum_{i \in V_e} x_i \leq 1, \quad \text{(enemies)} \tag{4.26}$$

$$x_i \in \{0, 1\}, \quad i = 1, ..., 5. \quad \text{(range of variables)} \tag{4.27}$$

The objective of this problem is to maximize the test information at a cutoff score θ_c. In Table 4.1, "+" and "−" are used to indicate which items have and do not have attributes 1 and 2 used in the categorical constraints in (4.24) and (4.25) and which items are in enemy set V_e in (4.26). From this table, it is immediately clear that the optimal solution is the test consisting of items 2 and 3, which has a maximum value of .70 for the objective function.

A greedy heuristic would pick item 1 as the first item for the test because it has the largest value for $I_i(\theta_c)$. It would then get stuck: Item 2 cannot be selected because its choice would lead to violation of constraint (4.26), whereas choosing item 3 would violate constraint (4.25), item 4 constraints (4.24)–(4.26), and item 5 constraint (4.25). Other heuristics may begin with another item but are bound to run into comparable problems. Heuristics therefore need strategies to compromise between constraints in such cases. For example, in the Swanson-Stocking heuristic, the weights in (4.20) set by the test assembler determine which constraints are violated.

If a heuristic has to be used, one of the local search heuristics in Section 4.5 appears to be a better choice. These heuristics are based on simultaneous optimization. It is interesting to compare the various rules and strategies used in the constructive and local search heuristics discussed earlier in this chapter. For example, a reproduction rule in a genetic algorithm is, in fact, the equivalent of an item-swapping rule in the second stage of the constructive heuristics above, but it is applied with greater sophistication and much more force to a larger set of potential solutions. Also, the critical difference between a branch-and-bound algorithm and a local search heuristic is that the former is based on complete enumeration of the space of possible solutions, whereas the latter evaluates only a (random) subset of it.

The same discussion of sequential and simultaneous optimization returns if we deal with the problems of multiple-test assembly (Chapter 6) and adaptive test assembly (Chapter 9). If more than one test has to be assembled, sequential optimization results in tests of deteriorating quality. The tests also have an increasing tendency to violate some of the constraints. Nevertheless, multiple-test problems sometimes are too large for simultaneous optimization and have to be found in a sequential fashion. In addition, item selection in adaptive testing is sequential by nature.

If sequential optimization has to be performed, the only way to avoid a sequence of solutions with deteriorating results and increasing tendency of constraint violation is by looking forward. This is exactly why in the Luecht heuristic the projection of the remaining portion of the information function in (4.17), and in the Swanson-Stocking heuristic the projection of the attribute values of the remaining items in the test in (4.18), are calculated. In Chapters 6 and 9, we introduce *shadow-test methods* for multiple-test assembly and adaptive testing, which project in a more effective way. They do so by calculating predictions of the entire test that is sought and requiring these to be both feasible and optimal.

4.7 Optimal Design Approach

Optimal design methods have been developed in statistics. Their goal is to optimize the design of a sample for parameter estimation.

A classical example is the design of a sample for estimating the regression parameters in the simple linear model

$$\mathcal{E}(Y \mid x) = \beta_0 + \beta_1 x, \tag{4.28}$$

where Y is a (random) dependent variable, x a fixed predictor, and β_0 and β_1 are the regression parameters (intercept and slope parameters). A possible design for a (fixed-size) sample for estimating these parameters is a specification of the distribution of units sampled at preselected values of the predictor variable, x. Intuitively, the necessity of optimizing a sample for this problem makes sense. For example, the stability of the estimators of β_0 and β_1 depends on the range of x values. If the range is small, the sample needs to be large for the estimators to become stable. But if the range increases, stable estimators are obtained for smaller sample sizes. Or, in graphical terms, the larger the range of x values, the more certain we are of how to draw a regression line in a bivariate scatter plot of the data.

The criterion for the optimization of the sample should be based on the (asymptotic) 2×2 covariance matrix of the estimators of these unknown parameters β_0 and β_1. A common criterion for parameter estimation problems in the optimal design literature is the determinant of these matrices (D-optimality). The determinant of the covariance matrix is a generalized variance measure for the normal approximation to the (joint) sampling distribution of the estimators. If this criterion leads to an intractable optimization problem, it is often approximated by the criterion of A-optimality (the trace of covariance or information matrix) or L-optimality (the largest eigenvalue of these matrices). Usually it is convenient to approximate the covariance by the information matrix and define the criteria on the latter. In this section, we follow this practice; for a problem with a covariance matrix, see our treatment of the topic of multidimensional test assembly in Chapter 8.

A more formal characterization of an optimal design for an estimation problem such as the one in (4.28) is as follows. The set of all possible values of x is called the *design space*. If this space is continuous or consists of a large number of discrete points, the problem is typically reduced to that of finding an optimal sample over a well-chosen selection of *design points* $d = 1, ..., D$ from it. For each point d, an integer sampling weight w_d is defined. A *sample design* for the estimation of the parameters (β_0, β_1) is a specification of the values of (d, w_d), $d = 1, ..., D$, which thus tells us how many units are to be sampled at each point. An *optimal sample design* is the set of values for (d, w_d), $d = 1, ..., D$, that minimizes one of the criteria above for the estimators $(\widehat{\beta}_0, \widehat{\beta}_1)$ of (β_0, β_1).

Suppose we want to design a test that is optimal for measuring the ability θ_p in the 3PL model in (1.16) for a test taker p. If we focus only on the item parameters (a, b, c) and ignore all other item attributes, the problem of finding an optimal test can be conceived of as an optimal design problem with optimization over possible designs (d, w_d) with design points defined as $d = (a, b, c)$. Each of these designs is a possible distribution of the item-parameter values for the test.

A natural objective function for this problem is the value of the test-information function in (1.19) at θ_p, which can be written as

$$I(\theta_p) = \sum_{d=1}^{D} w_d I_d(\theta_p), \tag{4.29}$$

with $I_d(\theta_p)$ the value of the item-information function in (1.20) at θ_p and w_d the number of items at point $d = (a, b, c)$. Observe that there is no need to choose between the criteria of D- and A-optimality for this problem. Since we optimize an estimator of a single parameter, both criteria reduce to (4.29). Obviously, the best solution is one that puts all weight on a design point with b close to θ_p and a maximal.

Since the parameter θ_p is unknown, the usual approach is to assume an array of ability values, $\theta_1, ..., \theta_P$, $P > 1$, that is representative of the population of test takers and optimize the test for their estimators $\widehat{\theta}_1, ..., \widehat{\theta}_P$. This assumption creates a *multiobjective* decision problem because the test has to be optimized jointly with respect to the accuracy of P different estimators. In Section 3.3.4, we introduced several approaches for dealing with test-assembly problems with multiple objectives.

In the optimal design literature on test assembly, it is customary to treat the array $\theta_1, ..., \theta_P$ as a P-dimensional parameter. Because the estimators $\hat{\theta}_1, ..., \hat{\theta}_P$ are independent, the criteria of D- and A-optimality simplify to the product and sum of the diagonal elements of the information matrix, respectively; that is, to

$$D = \prod_{p=1}^{P} \left[\sum_{d=1}^{D} w_d I_d(\theta_p) \right] \tag{4.30}$$

and

$$A = \sum_{p=1}^{P} \left[\sum_{d=1}^{D} w_d I_d(\theta_p) \right], \tag{4.31}$$

where the bracketed term is the value of the test information function at θ_p in (4.29). A test with maximum value for one of these criteria can be easily found using a branch-and-bound search over all design points (see Section 4.2).

We are not in favor of this approach. In statistics, the criteria of D- and A-optimality have been proposed to reduce an information matrix to a scalar that can be used as an objective function in an optimization problem. As the application does not involve a true multidimensional problem but that of estimating a set of P unidimensional parameters, it is more appropriate to use a multiobjective approach to compromise between the accuracy of the estimators. In fact, the function in (4.31) can already be viewed as an implicit choice of the weighted-objectives approach in (3.74) with all weights set equal to $w = 1$. The criterion in (4.30) also combines the P objectives into a single function but, from the perspective of multiobjective decision-making, the use of a product for this purpose is less satisfactory.

Most of the approaches for dealing with multiple objectives in test assembly problems in Section 3.3.4 give us much better control of the individual objectives than (4.30) and (4.31). Particularly, to prevent unexpectedly low accuracy for some of the P ability estimators, a maximin approach is more effective. Several applications of this approach will be discussed when we treat the problem of IRT-based test assembly directly as a multiobjective decision problem in Section 5.1.

It is certainly not our intention to claim that an optimal design approach to test assembly is never appropriate. If the ability parameter space is truly multidimensional, we need such criteria as D- and A-optimality to formulate an objective function. Chapter 8 is entirely devoted to problems of this type. Also, in Chapters 10 and 11, we will introduce methods for item-pool design that generalize the idea of a design space to include nonstatistical item attributes. They will also allow for a large number of constraints to deal with the content specifications of the tests in the program that the pool has to serve. These methods enable us to calculate a blueprint for the item pool that shows us what distribution of items over the design space is optimal for the testing program.

In sum, the most important differences between an optimal design approach and the optimal test-assembly methods in this book are:

1. In an optimal design approach, a set of values for the item-parameter values is sought that is theoretically best, whereas in an optimal test-assembly problem the search is for the best combination of items in an *existing* pool.

2. In optimal design, the focus is only on statistical parameters, whereas in optimal test assembly items are selected both for their statistical and nonstatistical attributes.

3. In optimal test assembly, the optimization of a test for a set of a unidimensional ability parameters is treated more explicitly as a multiobjective decision problem.

4. An optimal design approach typically deals with unconstrained problems, whereas in optimal test assembly we have the additional complexity of a set of content constraints that is typically large, predominantly nonstatistical, and constitutes the most important part of the problem (see Section 2.3).

4.8 Literature

Introductions to the branch-and-bound method can be found in the references to the linear programming literature at the end of Appendix 1. The question of how to optimize an implementation of this method for a test-assembly problem is addressed in Adema (1992b) and Veldkamp (2001, chapter 4). The references to the test-assembly package *ConTEST* 2.0 mentioned in Section 4.2.5 are Timminga, van der Linden, and Schweizer (1996, 1997). The current versions of the software with the integer solvers referred to in Section 4.2.5 are *CPLEX* 9.0 and *OPL Studio* 3.7 (ILOG, Inc., 2003). A trial version of *OPL Studio* with restricted capacity can be downloaded from *www.ilog.com*. An alternative package of solvers is available in *Lindo* 6.1 (LINDO Systems, Inc., 2003). A trial version of this package can be downloaded from *www.lindo.com*. Paragon Decision Technology (2004) offers an alternative modeling system called *AIMSS* 3.5 (URL: *www.aimms.com*).

A review of network-flow approximations to test-assembly problems is given in Armstrong, Jones, and Wang (1995). A more detailed treatment of network-flow approximation for the problem of assembling multiple tests meeting the same target information function is found in Armstrong, Jones, and Kunce (1998) and Armstrong, Jones, and Wu (1992). Generalizations of this approach for the problem of assembling a set of tests for use in a multistage testing system are presented in Armstrong and Little (2003) and Wu (2001). The problem of assembling classically parallel tests is addressed in Armstrong, Jones, and Wang (1994), whereas Armstrong and Jones (1992) show how a network-flow approximation can be used to solve item-matching problems. Armstrong, Jones, Li, and Wu (1996) present results from a comparative study between network-flow approximation and the Luecht heuristic.

A greedy heuristic for test assembly in this chapter is presented in Ackerman (1989; see also Wang & Ackerman, 1998). The Luecht heuristic was published in Luecht and Hirsch (1992); a more detailed treatment of it is given in Luecht (1998). For details on the Swanson-Stocking heuristic, refer to Swanson and Stocking (1993). Case studies for this heuristic are reported in Stocking, Swanson and Pearlman (1993).

A excellent reference for local search heuristics is Aarts and Lenstra (2003). This volume contains interesting introductory chapters on genetic algorithms (Mühlenbein, 2003) and simulated annealing (Aarts, Korst, & van Laarhoven, 2003), as well as on tabu search (Hertz, Taillard, & de Werra, 2003) and neural networks (Peterson & Söderberg, 2003), which are other types of heuristics with potential applicability to test assembly. Applications of genetic algorithms to test assembly are given in Verschoor (2004), whereas van der Linden, Veldkamp, and Carlson (2004) and Veldkamp (2002) should be consulted for applications of the method of simulated annealing to test-assembly problems.

Classical introductions to optimal design in statistics are Atkinson (1982) and Fedorov (1972). These texts are rather advanced. An intermediate introduction to this topic is given in Silvey (1980). Applications of optimal design techniques to item calibration and test assembly are reported in a series of papers by Berger (1994, 1997, 1998), Berger and Matthijssen (1997), Berger and van der Linden (1992, 1995), Berger and Veerkamp (1996), and van der Linden (1994a).

4.9 Summary

1. It is useful to check test-assembly models for interactions between the objective function and the constraint set. The check may help us to understand at which bounds constraints tend to be realized and may suggest simplifications of the model.

2. Branch-and-bound algorithms for solving integer programming problems are based on a tree search. The search begins with the calculation of a solution to the fully relaxed version of the problem, after

which the integer constraints on the variables are restored in an iterative fashion. If a node in the tree has a solution that does not beat the incumbent, the branch departing from the node is pruned, the algorithm backtracks, and the search is continued along another branch.

3. The class of test-assembly problems are NP-hard; it has not been proven that solutions to the problems in this class can be found by a polynomial-time algorithm. However, this property refers only to an upper bound approximated in a worst-case scenario. Due to continuous optimization of implementations of the branch-and-bound method for classes of problems, we are now able to find solutions to test-assembly problems with large numbers of variables in reasonable time.

4. Several test-assembly problems can be approximated by a network-flow formulation or solved by a heuristic with a sequence of network-flow problems embedded in it. Solutions to network-flow problems are found with small polynomial running time.

5. Heuristics are techniques for finding a solution to a test-assembly problem based on a plausible idea. The quality of their solutions has not been proven to be optimal but has to be assessed by scrutinizing their nature.

6. Constructive heuristics build a test by selecting one item at a time. Greedy heuristics select items that are locally best. Both the Luecht and Swanson-Stocking heuristics are more careful in that they select items by evaluating projections of the future consequences of local steps.

7. Local search heuristics search neighborhoods of interim solutions for improvements. They stop when an acceptable solution has been found. These heuristics should be viewed as general schemes that have to be adapted to the specific structure of test-assembly problems. Finding an implementation that restricts the search to the set of feasible tests is critical to their success.

8. Genetic algorithms are local search heuristics that simulate an evolutionary process for a pool of candidate solutions using such operations as selection, mutation, and recombination to produce a next generation of solutions. Simulated annealing is a local search technique that models the search analogously to the thermal process of a solid reaching a minimum-energy arrangement of its particles through a cooling schedule.

9. Constructive heuristics for test assembly perform sequential optimization, whereas branch-and-bound algorithms and local search heuristics optimize simultaneously (i.e., over all decision variables at the same time). Solutions obtained by sequential optimization tend to be suboptimal and to violate constraints.

10. An optimal design approach to test assembly views a test as a set of values for its statistical item parameters that has to be optimized to produce the best ability estimates for a population of persons. Our basic method of item-pool design in Chapters 10 and 11 can be viewed as a generalization of this approach that allows for the presence of nonstatistical attributes of the tests and large sets of content constraints.

5
Models for Assembling Single Tests

This chapter deals with applications of the methodology introduced in the previous chapters to four different classes of test-assembly problems. In each of these problems, the task is to assemble a single test from an item pool, but they differ in the objectives with which the tests are assembled.

The first class of problems departs from Birnbaum's (1968) problem of assembling a single test of discrete items to a target for its information function (Section 1.2.8). An important difference between absolute and relative targets is introduced. We discuss a few methods for specifying both types of targets. In addition, we show how once a target of either type is specified, the test-assembly problem can be modeled as an MIP problem.

Whereas the first class of problems assumes the fit of the item pool to an IRT model, the second class of problems is based on classical test theory only. The objectives are to assemble a test with optimal reliability or predictive validity, respectively. In principle, these objectives lead to problems with nonlinear objective functions. Because we generally want to avoid such functions, an important part of our treatment is to show how these problems can be linearized.

In the third class of problems, the objective is to assemble a test to match a prespecified observed-score distribution for a given population of test takers. The observed-score distribution may be one for a previous test in the same program, but it is also possible to specify a target distribution based on practical considerations only. This objective may seem somewhat unusual. But, as a matter of fact, an identical objective is pursued in the practice of observed-score equating, where, once a test is assembled and administered, the number-correct score is transformed to produce the same score distribution as for a reference test. We show that this form of *post hoc* equating can be avoided by imposing a set of constraints on the test-assembly problem. Surprisingly, the constraints we need have a simple linear form.

The final class consists of item-matching problems. In item matching, the objective is to assemble a new test that matches a reference test item by item. The method we discuss can be used with any combination of item attributes: classical item indices, IRT parameters, or more substantive quantitative or categorical attributes. If a test is assembled to have the same information function or reliability as a reference test, the two tests are weakly parallel. Item matching enables us to assemble a test that is parallel to a reference test in a much stronger sense.

As just noted, the critical difference between these four classes of test-assembly problems resides mainly in their objective functions. These functions may require a few technical constraints. But for any of these models it is possible to add a set of substantive constraints to the model to deal with the remaining content specifications. As numerous examples of such constraints were already presented in Chapter 3, we will omit a further discussion of this option in this chapter.

5.1   IRT-Based Test Assembly

A target for a TIF is a function $\mathcal{T}(\theta)$ that provides goal values for it along the θ scale in use for the item pool. For mainstream response models, such as the 3PL model in (1.16), TIFs are well-behaved, smooth functions. It therefore holds that if we require a TIF to meet a smooth target $\mathcal{T}(\theta)$ at one point on the θ scale, it automatically approximates the target in a neighborhood of this point. Also, target values for fewer points tend to result in much faster solutions. In practice, we therefore specify target values for TIFs at only a few points on the θ scale, which we denote as $\mathcal{T}(\theta_k)$, $k = 1, ..., K$. Extensive simulation studies and ample experience with practical test-assembly problems have shown that this number need not be larger than 3–5 points.

As already discussed in Section 1.2.7, we assume that these points are selected by a test assembler familiar with both the numerical scale and the substantive interpretation of the θ scale in use for the item pool. To give an idea of a typical choice of a set of values θ_k, we consider the case of a target for the TIF that has to provide diagnostic information on a population of persons centered at $\theta = 0$ with standard deviation $\sigma_\theta = 1$. For the 3PL model, target values that can be expected to yield excellent results are typically specified at $(\theta_1, \theta_2, \theta_3) = (-1.0, 0, 1.0)$ or $(\theta_1, \theta_2, \theta_3, \theta_4) = (-1.5, -.5, .5, 1.5)$.

The problem of assembling a test with an information function that has to meet a target is a *multiobjective* test-assembly problem. More specifically, if we intend to minimize the differences between the TIF and its target at values θ_k, $k = 1, ..., K$, we have a problem with K different objectives. General approaches to multiobjective test-assembly problems were discussed in Section 3.3.4. These approaches will be used extensively to solve our current class of problems.

5.1.1 Absolute and Relative Targets

An important distinction exists between absolute and relative targets. A target is *absolute* if it specifies a fixed number of information units at the points θ_k. This type of target was assumed when Birnbaum introduced his approach to test assembly (Section 1.2.8). To specify a meaningful absolute target, we need to be familiar not only with the θ scale but also with the unit of the information measure that the scale implies. If we are unfamiliar with it, unexpected results may occur (for example, unrealistically long or short tests if the test length is left free, or large deviations from the target if it is constrained). For this reason, absolute targets are used almost exclusively when tests are assembled to be parallel to a known reference test. We will use $\mathcal{T}_k$ as shorthand notation for the absolute target values $\mathcal{T}(\theta_k)$, $k = 1, ..., K$, for the TIF.

If an absolute target is specified, we in fact imply that more information than specified by the target is undesirable. From a measurement point of view, this implication seems peculiar, but in practice it often makes sense. An example is admissions testing, with different institutions setting their own admission scores on an observed-score scale for the test. If the information function of a new test overshot the target along a portion of the θ scale, the observed-score distribution would change in the neighborhood of some of the admission scores. As a consequence, without any change in the population of examinees, the proportion of examinees that qualify for admission may go up or down, a result that would certainly embarrass the institutions concerned.

However, in other applications more information is always better, as long as it is distributed along the θ scale in a way that reflects the objectives for the test. Examples are found in broad-range diagnostic testing and testing for licensing with a fixed minimum level of performance required for passing. The only thing we then want to control is the shape of the information function. But if we are interested only in the shape of the target but not in its height, we in fact have a relative target for the TIF. Formally, a *relative target* can be defined as a set of numbers $\mathcal{R}_k > 0$ that represent the required amount of information at θ_k relative to the other points in the set $k = 1, ..., K$. For instance, if we want the test to have twice as much information at θ_k as at θ_{k+1}, the numbers $\mathcal{R}_k$ and $\mathcal{R}_{k+1}$ need to be chosen such that $\mathcal{R}_k/\mathcal{R}_{k+1} = 2$. Because we have to specify

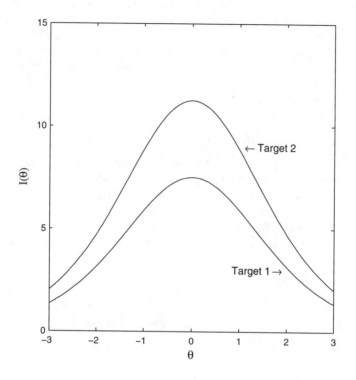

FIGURE 5.1. Example of two targets for a test information function with the same shape but heights differing by a factor of 1.5.

ratios of numbers only, fortunately to select them we need not be familiar with the unit of the information measure. Hence, as will become clear below, the choice of a relative target is less likely to result in test assembly with unexpected results.

An example of two target information functions with the same relative shape is given in Figure 5.1. The two targets have identical ratios for their values at each pair of θ values. As a consequence, their height differs only by a common factor, which is 1.5 in this example. When we model test-assembly problems with a relative target below, we introduce a new decision variable to represent this factor.

5.1.2 Methods for Specifying Targets for Information Functions

To specify an absolute target for a new testing program, we could simply follow a trial-and-error method, alternately selecting a set of values for the target function and checking the actual TIFs for the tests assembled from the pool. In principle, this method works fine because solutions are quickly obtained. The following alternative methods are more direct, however:

1. The first alternative is based on descriptive statistics of the distribution of the item parameters in the pool. From these statistics, we can choose a set of n combinations of values that are typical of the pool, where n is the intended test length. We can then calculate the information function for this set and edit it to improve its representation of the primary objectives for the testing program. For instance, if the test has to be diagnostic over a θ interval, we could replace the information function by one with a uniform shape at average height. Or if the test is for decision making at one or more cutoff scores θ_c, we may feel obliged to increase the information at these scores, taking information away from other areas along the scale.

2. A second alternative is to ask test specialists to assemble manually a specimen of the tests that should be used in the program. This specimen should meet all other specifications, except those involving the information functions of the items, and consists of items that the specialists consider typical. The actual information function of the specimen provides us with a good estimate of the general level of information possible for the test. The function can then be edited for better representation of the goals for the testing program. An advantage of the second method is that it takes all nonstatistical item attributes into account and therefore is based on a feasible test from the item pool. A disadvantage is that it is not based on the distribution of the item parameter values in the pool.

3. An interesting method is the Kelderman method, which is based on the equality in (1.18) between the information function and the inverse of the (asymptotic) variance of the ML estimator of θ

$$[I(\theta)]^{-1} = \text{Var}(\widehat{\theta} \mid \theta), \tag{5.1}$$

where our notation shows the dependence of the variance on the true value of θ. For two persons with true abilities θ_1 and θ_2, it holds for the variance of the difference between their estimators that

$$\text{Var}(\widehat{\theta}_1 - \widehat{\theta}_2 \mid \theta_1, \theta_2) = \text{Var}(\widehat{\theta}_1 \mid \theta_1) + \text{Var}(\widehat{\theta}_2 \mid \theta_2)$$
$$= [I(\theta_1)]^{-1} + [I(\theta_2)]^{-1}. \tag{5.2}$$

Because both estimators have an (asymptotic) normal distribution, it follows that

$$\Pr\{\widehat{\theta}_1 > \widehat{\theta}_2 \mid \theta_1, \theta_2\} = \Phi\left(\frac{\theta_1 - \theta_2}{\{[I(\theta_1)]^{-1} + [I(\theta_2)]^{-1}\}^{1/2}}\right), \tag{5.3}$$

where $\Phi(.)$ is the distribution function of the standard normal distribution. If $\theta_1 < \theta_2$, $\Pr\{\widehat{\theta}_1 > \widehat{\theta}_2 \mid \theta_1, \theta_2\}$ is the probability that the scores on the tests for persons at θ_1 and θ_2 are ordered erroneously. Making the information values explicit, we obtain

$$[I(\theta_1)]^{-1} + [I(\theta_2)]^{-1} = \left\{(\theta_1 - \theta_2)[\Phi^{-1}(\Pr\{\widehat{\theta}_1 > \widehat{\theta}_2 \mid \theta_1, \theta_2\})]^{-1}\right\}^2.$$
(5.4)

In the Kelderman method, a set of pairs of points (θ_1, θ_2) is presented to a panel of test specialists, who are asked to specify the probabilities with which they are willing to accept test scores for persons at these points who order them erroneously. If these probabilities are known, so is the right-hand side of (5.4), and we have a set of equations, one for each pair, that can be solved for the unknown information values on their left-hand sides, which serve as target values. Although this method also runs the risk of resulting in target values leading to unexpected test lengths, it has the advantage of translating the costs due to measurement errors directly into target values for the information function.

To specify a relative target for a TIF, the following two approaches are available:

1. Each of the three methods above can be used, but we ignore the absolute nature of the resulting numbers, using them only as relative target values in the test-assembly models we introduce below.

2. A simpler alternative is to offer test specialists an arbitrary number of chips (100, say) and ask them to distribute them over the points θ_k, $k = 1, ..., K$, in an item map (Figure 1.5) such that their distribution reflects the relative accuracy needed in the test scores for persons at these points. The number of chips at θ_k is then the relative target value $\mathcal{R}_k$. The total number of chips is arbitrary because the numbers $\mathcal{R}_k$ are unitless.

5.1.3 Assembling Tests for Absolute Targets

Before discussing several examples of objective functions that can be used to select a TIF to meet a set of target values, we discuss a set of constraints that also does the job. Let $\delta_k \geq 0$ and $\varepsilon_k \geq 0$ be small tolerances with which the TIF is allowed to be larger or smaller than the target values $\mathcal{T}_k$. Adding the following set of constraints to the model forces the TIF to be close to the target:

$$\sum_{i=1}^{I} I_i(\theta_k)x_i \leq \mathcal{T}_k + \delta_k, \quad \text{for all } k,$$
(5.5)

$$\sum_{i=1}^{I} I_i(\theta_k)x_i \geq \mathcal{T}_k - \varepsilon_k, \quad \text{for all } k. \tag{5.6}$$

The tolerances in (5.5.) and (5.6) are indexed by k to allow them to be dependent on the value of $\mathcal{T}_k$; for example, somewhat larger for the middle values of $\mathcal{T}_k$ or at values θ_k where the item pool has been relatively depleted.

An advantage of using a set of constraints to realize a target is that we still have the opportunity to formulate an objective function for another attribute. On the other hand, to avoid infeasibility, the tolerances δ_k and ε_k have to be chosen realistically for the item pool. If we follow the alternatives below, for a well-designed item pool infeasibility is no problem.

Our first approach to the multiobjective problem of matching a target at K points is the weighted-objectives approach in Section 3.3.4. Let w_k be the weight for the objective of minimizing the positive deviation of the TIF from target value $\mathcal{T}_k$. The following combination of objective function and constraints allows us to minimize a weighted sum of positive deviations from the K target values,

$$\text{minimize } \sum_{k=1}^{K} w_k \sum_{i=1}^{I} I_i(\theta_k)x_i, \tag{5.7}$$

subject to

$$\sum_{i=1}^{I} I_i(\theta_k)x_i \geq \mathcal{T}_k, \quad \text{for all } k \tag{5.8}$$

(Exercise 5.1).

If we had omitted the set of constraints in (5.8), the objective function would minimize the total weighted sum of the TIF values at the values θ_k. Because of the presence of the constraints, the objective function minimizes only positive deviations from the target values.

The objective in (5.7) and (5.8) permits compensation between individual values of the TIF, and the result may therefore show an undesirably large local deviation. This element of unpredictability is absent in the following application of the minimax principle introduced in Section 3.3.4:

$$\text{minimize } y \tag{5.9}$$

subject to

$$\sum_{i=1}^{I} I_i(\theta_k)x_i \leq \mathcal{T}_k + y, \quad \text{for all } k, \tag{5.10}$$

$$\sum_{i=1}^{I} I_i(\theta_k)x_i \geq \mathcal{T}_k, \quad \text{for all } k, \tag{5.11}$$

$$y \geq 0, \tag{5.12}$$

where y is a real-valued decision variable. The constraints in (5.11) require the TIF to be larger than the target values, while the constraints in (5.10) define decision variable y as an upper bound to all positive deviations from these values. The upper bound is minimized in (5.9). Ideally, the best possible result is obtained for $y = 0$, but typically a slightly larger value is obtained because it is hard for a sum of item-information functions from a pool to meet a set of target values exactly (Exercise 5.2).

Thus far, one of our assumptions has been that small positive deviations of the TIF from the target values are permitted but negative deviations are forbidden. If both types of deviations are considered equally undesirable, the target values become goal values for the TIF, and the following alternative to the model for the weighted-objective approach in (5.7) and (5.8) can be useful:

$$\text{minimize} \sum_{k=1}^{K} w_k(y_k^{\text{pos}} + y_k^{\text{neg}}) \tag{5.13}$$

subject to

$$\sum_{i=1}^{I} I_i(\theta_k)x_i = \mathcal{T}_k - y_k^{\text{pos}} + y_k^{\text{neg}}, \quad \text{for all } k, \tag{5.14}$$

$$y_k^{\text{pos}} \geq 0, \quad \text{for all } k, \tag{5.15}$$

$$y_k^{\text{neg}} \geq 0, \quad \text{for all } k, \tag{5.16}$$

with $w_k \geq 0$ for all k.

The constraints in (5.14)–(5.16) define the new decision variables y_k^{pos} and y_k^{neg} as possible positive and negative deviations from the target values $\mathcal{T}_k$. If the objective function takes a minimal value, at each θ_k only one of the two variables can be positive and the other is equal to zero. For example, substitution of $y_k^{\text{pos}} = 0$ in (5.14) shows that y_k^{neg} is a possible negative deviation at θ_k in the solution. Likewise, y_k^{pos} is a possible positive deviation (Exercise 5.3).

The attribute in (5.13) is the weighted sum of absolute deviations of the TIF values from $\mathcal{T}_k$; (5.13)–(5.16) is thus a linear equivalent of the following objective function, which minimizes the sum of the absolute deviations from the target values:

$$\text{minimize} \sum_{k=1}^{K} w_k \left| \sum_{i=1}^{I} I_i(\theta_k)x_i - \mathcal{T}_k \right|. \tag{5.17}$$

It is for this reason that (5.13)–(5.16) can be used as a two-sided alternative to (5.7) and (5.8).

Likewise, (5.9)–(5.12) can be replaced by a minimax approach in which the largest absolute deviation from $\mathcal{T}_k$ is minimized. The optimization problem then becomes

$$\text{minimize } y \tag{5.18}$$

subject to

$$\sum_{i=1}^{I} I_i(\theta_k)x_i \leq \mathcal{T}_k + y, \quad \text{for all } k, \tag{5.19}$$

$$\sum_{i=1}^{I} I_i(\theta_k)x_i \geq \mathcal{T}_k - y, \quad \text{for all } k, \tag{5.20}$$

$$y \geq 0. \tag{5.21}$$

The constraints in (5.19) and (5.20) enclose the differences between the TIF and target values in an interval about zero, $[-y, y]$, and the size of the interval is minimized by (5.18) (Exercise 5.4).

Our favorite approach is the minimax model in (5.18)–(5.21), particularly if the test is assembled in a program where a fixed target has to be maintained over time. In such applications, positive and negative deviations from the target values are equally undesirable. By minimizing the largest deviation from the target, the model presses the TIF as closely as possible against the target, avoiding surprises in the form of large local deviations.

5.1.4 Assembling Tests for Relative Targets

If the target for the TIF is relative, we maximize its height at each θ_k, $k = 1, ..., K$, but at the same time want to maintain its relative shape. Intuitively, the problem seems to be one with K objectives and a set of additional constraints to maintain the shape of the TIF.

We begin with the formulation of the constraints. Because the target values $\mathcal{R}_k$ have no fixed unit, one of them can be set equal to one, provided we adjust all other values correspondingly. Suppose we choose to set $\mathcal{R}_1 = 1$. The following $K - 1$ constraints require the TIF at θ_k to be $\mathcal{R}_k$ times as large as at θ_1 and therefore guarantee the desired shape of the TIF:

$$\sum_{i=1}^{I} I_i(\theta_k)x_i = \mathcal{R}_k \sum_{i=1}^{I} I_i(\theta_1)x_i, \text{ for } k \geq 2 \tag{5.22}$$

(Exercise 5.5).

By imposing these constraints, we automatically reduce the number of K objectives to one. Therefore, to maximize the TIF at the K values θ_k simultaneously, we only need to maximize the TIF value at one of these values. Suppose we choose to maximize test information at θ_1. In principle, the following objective function then seems to complete our formalization of the problem:

$$\text{maximize} \sum_{i=1}^{I} I_i(\theta_1)x_i. \tag{5.23}$$

An annoying complication, however, is that (5.22) contains equality constraints on a quantitative test attribute. Such constraints should always be avoided because of possible infeasibility; see our discussion of (3.50). A simple remedy may seem to replace them by the following inequalities:

$$\sum_{i=1}^{I} I_i(\theta_k)x_i \geq \mathcal{R}_k \sum_{i=1}^{I} I_i(\theta_1)x_i, \quad \text{for } k \geq 2. \tag{5.24}$$

A consequence of this step is that, though the solution can be expected to realize these inequalities close to equality, the information at θ_1 tends to stay somewhat behind. This effect can be remedied by lowering the target values at $\theta_2,...,\theta_K$ somewhat relative to the value at θ_1. But a more satisfactory solution is to substitute a new variable y for the common factor $\sum_{i=1}^{I} I_i(\theta_1)x_i$ in the lower bounds in (5.24) and formulate the model as

$$\text{maximize } y \tag{5.25}$$

subject to

$$\sum_{i=1}^{I} I_i(\theta_k)x_i \geq \mathcal{R}_k y, \quad \text{for all } k, \tag{5.26}$$

$$y \geq 0. \tag{5.27}$$

This argument has resulted in another application of the maximin principle. This claim becomes clear if both sides of (5.26) are divided by $\mathcal{R}_k$. Variable y then becomes an explicit common lower bound to the relative information $\mathcal{R}_k^{-1} \sum_{i=1}^{I} I_i(\theta_1)x_i$ at the points θ_k, which is maximized in (5.25).

5.1.5   Cutoff Scores

If a test is used for decisions with a cutoff score θ_c, often all we need is informative estimates $\hat{\theta}$ in the neighborhood of θ_c. If these estimates have to meet a prespecified level of information, the results in Section 5.1.3, which are for simultaneous optimization at θ_k, $k = 1, ..., K$, specialize to optimization only at θ_c.

For the same case of decision making, a relative target for the TIF boils down to simple maximization at θ_c, ignoring the information at all other values of θ; that is, to the objective function

$$\text{maximize } \sum_{i=1}^{I} I_i(\theta_c)x_i. \tag{5.28}$$

5.1.6   Empirical Examples

An empirical example of a single test assembled from a previous pool of 753 items from the *Law School Admission Test* (LSAT) is given. The total length of the test was 101 items. The items were in three different sections and measured analytic reasoning, logical reasoning, and reading comprehension. As in the LSAT, one of these sections was doubled in our example. The specifications of the LSAT were modeled as constraints dealing with such attributes as test and section length, item type and content, answer key, gender and minority orientation of the items, and word counts. The objective function was that for the maximin model in (5.18)–(5.21). All specifications were modeled except those for the stimuli and item sets in two of the sections of the test that have an item-set structure. Examples for the LSAT that do include these specifications are given in Chapter 7, which is devoted entirely to the assembly of tests with item sets.

The LSAT has an information function between two functions over the interval between $\theta = -3.0$ and $\theta = 3.0$ that serve as its lower and upper bound. To show an example with an absolute target function, we chose the function that represented the midpoints between these bounds. To show the impact of the number of θ values at which the TIF is controlled, three different tests were assembled. The TIF of the first test was controlled only at $\theta_k=0$, the TIF of the second test was controlled at $\theta_k=-1.2$, 0, and 1.2, and the TIF of the third test was controlled at $\theta_k=-2.1$, -1.2, 0, 1.2 , and 2.1. The three models had a total of 754 variables (the number of items in the pool plus minimax variable y), 114 content constraints, and 2–10 constraints used to control the TIFs.

As shown in the top panel of Figure 5.2, the TIF for the first test met the target at $\theta_k=0$, exactly as required. But it was too low for the smaller θ values and too high for the larger values. The addition of the constraints on the TIF at $\theta_k=-1.2$ and 1.2 was already sufficient to meet the target function over the entire range. In fact, the TIFs in the middle panel of Figure 5.2 obtained for this case and the one with an additional control at $\theta_k=-2.1$ and 2.1 in the bottom panel are indistinguishable for all practical purposes. These results confirm what we have found in numerous IRT-based test-assembly problems and had already formulated as a recommendation in the introduction to Section 5.1: In practice, it is sufficient to control the TIF only at 3–5 well-chosen values.

Although the results in Figure 5.2 may look impressive, the graphs do not reveal the most important result in these examples—which is the fact that each of these three tests met the entire set of the content specifications for the LSAT.

5.2   Classical Test Assembly

A classical objective in test assembly is to maximize the reliability coefficient of the test. If the test is used for prediction of an external criterion (e.g., success in a program or a job), tests are assembled to have maximum predictive validity. Both objectives are nonlinear. To apply the

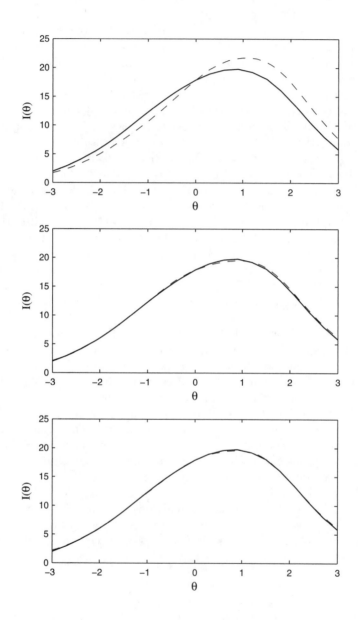

FIGURE 5.2. Information functions of three LSAT forms assembled for a common target (bold line) at $\theta_k = 0$ (top), $\theta_k = -1.2, 0, 1.2$ (middle), and $\theta_k = -2.1, -1.2, 0, 1.2, 2.1$ (bottom).

methodology in this book, we thus have to decide how to linearize these objectives.

5.2.1 Maximizing Test Reliability

Generally, it is difficult to estimate the reliability coefficient of a test. But a well-known lower bound to the reliability coefficient is Cronbach's coefficient α, which was written in (1.14) as

$$\alpha = \frac{n}{n-1}\left[1 - \frac{\sum\limits_{i=1}^{n}\sigma_i^2}{\left(\sum\limits_{i=1}^{n}\sigma_i\rho_{iX}\right)^2}\right], \tag{5.29}$$

where n is the length of the test, σ_i^2 and ρ_{iX} are the variance and discriminating power (item-test correlation) of item i, respectively, and X is the observed score on the test.

Suppose we have a pool of items, $i = 1, ..., I$, with estimates of the item parameters σ_i^2 and ρ_{iX} and want to assemble a test of n items with a maximum value for (5.29). We postpone a discussion of a problem involved in the definition of the scale of X in ρ_{iX} to Section 5.2.4.

If we use 0-1 decision variables for the selection of the items, the value of α for an arbitrary test with n items from the pool can be written as

$$\alpha = \frac{n}{n-1}\left[1 - \frac{\sum\limits_{i=1}^{I}\sigma_i^2 x_i}{\left(\sum\limits_{i=1}^{I}\sigma_i\rho_{iX}x_i\right)^2}\right]. \tag{5.30}$$

Hence, selecting a test with α as the objective function involves an optimization problem that is nonlinear in the variables.

However, as n is fixed, maximization of α is equivalent to the minimization problem

$$\text{minimize } \frac{\sum\limits_{i=1}^{I}\sigma_i^2 x_i}{\left(\sum\limits_{i=1}^{I}\sigma_i\rho_{iX}x_i\right)^2} \tag{5.31}$$

subject to

$$\sum_{i=1}^{I}x_i = n, \tag{5.32}$$

$$x_i \in \{0, 1\}, \quad \text{for all } i. \tag{5.33}$$

Although the objective function is still nonlinear, both its denominator and numerator contain expressions that are linear in the variables x_i. The problem is therefore equivalent to an optimization problem with two linear objectives: (1) minimization of $\sum_{i=1}^{I} \sigma_i^2 x_i$ and (2) maximization of $\sum_{i=1}^{I} \sigma_i \rho_{iX} x_i$.

A standard approach in multiobjective optimization is to formulate one of the objectives as the objective function and reformulate the other as a constraint (Section 3.3.4). We choose to formulate the first objective as the constraint and the second as the objective function, and we replace (5.31)–(5.33) by the problem

$$\text{maximize} \sum_{i=1}^{I} \sigma_i \rho_{iX} x_i \qquad (5.34)$$

subject to

$$\sum_{i=1}^{I} \sigma_i^2 x_i \leq \kappa, \qquad (5.35)$$

$$\sum_{i=1}^{I} x_i = n, \qquad (5.36)$$

$$x_i \in \{0,1\}, \quad \text{for all } i, \qquad (5.37)$$

where $\kappa > 0$ is a constant.

Our choice to formulate the constraint on $\sum_{i=1}^{I} \sigma_i^2 x_i$ can be motivated by the fact that further analysis of (5.31) shows that α is more sensitive to its denominator than its numerator. In addition, for dichotomous items, (5.35) constrains the sum of the item variances $\sigma_i^2 = \pi_i(1-\pi_i)$, which has a known range of possible values: Its minimum is equal to zero and its maximum equal to $.25n$. It can be shown that larger values for α tend to be obtained for κ closer to $.25n$ than to zero. Empirical results substantiating this claim are reported in Section 5.2.4. If the applications are for a new item pool and we have no idea what value to choose for κ, the best approach is to solve the model in (5.34)–(5.37) for a sequence of values of κ approaching the maximum and choose the solution with the largest values of α.

5.2.2 Maximizing Predictive Validity

A similar approach is possible for the problem of maximizing the predictive validity of a test. Let Y be the external criterion that the test has to predict; the validity coefficient is the product-moment correlation between test scores X and Y, ρ_{XY}.

As shown in (1.15), for a test of n items, the validity coefficient can be written as

$$\rho_{XY} = \frac{\sum_{i=1}^{I} \sigma_i \rho_{iY}}{\sum_{i=1}^{I} \sigma_i \rho_{iX}}, \qquad (5.38)$$

where ρ_{iY} is the item-criterion correlation or item validity. Both the numerator and denominator of the validity coefficient have expressions that are linear in the items, and the same type of linear decomposition as for coefficient α is possible.

In this case, the decision of which expression to optimize is based on the following argument: Both expressions depend on σ_i, but we can expect the item discriminations, ρ_{iX}, to show a somewhat larger variation than the item validities, ρ_{iY}. It therefore makes sense to choose the expression in the denominator for the objective function.

The following model results:

$$\text{minimize} \sum_{i=1}^{I} \sigma_i \rho_{iX} x_i \tag{5.39}$$

subject to

$$\sum_{i=1}^{I} \sigma_i \rho_{iY} x_i \leq \kappa, \tag{5.40}$$

$$\sum_{i=1}^{I} x_i = n, \tag{5.41}$$

$$x_i \in \{0,1\}, \quad \text{for all } i. \tag{5.42}$$

The minimum and maximum values possible for $\sigma_i \rho_{iY} x_i$ are equal to zero and .50, respectively. The maximum is reached if $\pi_i = .50$ and ρ_{iY} is 1.0, but it is unlikely to have values of ρ_{iY} larger than .40 in practice. For a new problem, again it is recommended to run the model with κ varying the between the minimum and maximum possible values of the sum in (5.40) for the item pool and choose the solution test with the largest value for ρ_{XY} as the solution.

5.2.3 Constraining Test Reliability

Applications of classical test theory can be met in which the intention is not to maximize the test reliability but to keep it as close as possible to a target value. This treatment of reliability is standard in a testing problem for which each next test form has to be parallel to a reference test.

A simple set of constraints to maintain the value of α in a testing program is

$$\sum_{i=1}^{I} \sigma_i \rho_{iX} x_i \leq \kappa_1 + \delta, \tag{5.43}$$

$$\sum_{i=1}^{I} \sigma_i \rho_{iX} x_i \geq \kappa_1 - \delta, \tag{5.44}$$

$$\sum_{i=1}^{I} \sigma_i^2 x_i \leq \kappa_2 + \varepsilon, \qquad (5.45)$$

$$\sum_{i=1}^{I} \sigma_i^2 x_i \geq \kappa_2 - \varepsilon, \qquad (5.46)$$

where κ_1 is the empirical value of the reference test for $\sum_{i=1}^{n} \sigma_i \rho_{iX}$, κ_2 the value for $\sum_{i=1}^{n} \sigma_i^2$, and δ and ε are small tolerances.

In principle, the same type of constraints are possible for the predictive validity coefficient in (5.38), but we are not aware of any problems in the practice of testing for which this solution would make sense.

Observe that in (5.43)–(5.46) we constrain two sums of item attributes across tests. Tests can be made parallel in a stronger sense if we constrain attributes on an item-by-item basis. This problem belongs to the topic of item matching, which will be addressed in Section 5.4.

5.2.4 Empirical Example

The model in (5.34)–(5.37) was used in a simulation study with a pool of 500 items and values for the item variances and discriminations generated for a population of test takers with a standard normal distribution of θ. The test length was set at $n = 20$. The maximum value of $\sum_{i=1}^{I} \sigma_i^2 x_i$ was 5, and the bound κ in (5.35) was varied between 3 and 5, with step size .5.

One of the problems with banking large numbers of items on empirical values for their classical indices is the definition of the item-discrimination index ρ_{iX}. Using this index makes sense only if the total scores X are comparable across items. In practice, this requirement can be met if the values of the index have been collected using tests that are (approximately) parallel. In this simulation study, we were able to calculate the values of the index using the observed scores of simulated test takers for the entire item pool, B. We first assembled the test using the item-bank correlations, ρ_{iB}. Once the test was assembled, we used simulated observed scores on it to calculate the actual item-test correlation, ρ_{iX}, and recalculated α. Because all responses were generated under the unidimensional 3PL model, the two correlations were monotonically related, and optimization using ρ_{iB} and ρ_{iX} resulted in the same test.

The results are presented in Table 5.1. The second and third columns report the values of coefficient alpha for ρ_{iB} and ρ_{iX}, denoted as α^* and α, respectively. These columns show that the values of α were always higher than those of α^*. This inequality holds because α was calculated for a total score on the best items in the (unidimensional) pool. Table 5.1 also shows better results for larger values of κ. In fact, the best results were obtained for $\kappa = 5$, which is the maximum value of $\sum_{i=1}^{I} \sigma_i^2 x_i$ possible for a test with $n = 20$ items. For this value of κ, the constraint in (5.35) was thus

κ	α^*	α
5.0	.8395	.8712
4.5	.8388	.8678
4.0	.8288	.8559
3.5	.8008	.8401
3.0	.7696	.8205

TABLE 5.1. Values of coefficient alpha for tests assembled for $\kappa=3.0$ (.5) 5.0.

redundant; the same results would have been obtained if we had selected the n items with the largest values for $\sigma_i \rho_{iX}$.

This conclusion does not generalize to test-assembly problems with empirical values for the item indices, however: If the pool is not purely unidimensional, the optimum value of α is obtained for κ somewhat lower than the maximum. More importantly, if the test has to be selected to meet a set of content specifications, we cannot pick the n items with the largest values for $\sigma_i \rho_{iX}$ but need (5.34)–(5.37) as the core of a full-fledged test-assembly model to select the best test from the set of feasible solutions.

5.3 Matching Observed-Score Distributions

Most long-running testing programs report their scores on a scale introduced before they began to use IRT for analyzing the test items and assembling their tests. These scales are typically observed-score scales; for example, number-correct scales with an additional (monotonic) transformation to give the scores a standard range. In this section, we ignore this additional transformation without any loss of generality.

The use of observed-score scales entails the necessity of score equating, and the method of equipercentile equating has been the standard of the testing industry for a long time. In an equipercentile equating study, the new test is administered along with a reference test; for example, using a sampling design with randomly equivalent groups. The data from the study are used to find the transformation that maps the new number-correct scores to the scale of the reference test.

It is possible to replace this form of *post hoc* observed score equating by a few simple constraints in the test-assembly model that guarantee the number-correct scores on the new test to be on the same scale as the number-correct scores on the reference test. The test-assembly model then automatically performs what can be called *observed-score pre-equating*.

Test assembly with these constraints has several practical advantages:

1. No resources are spent on separate equating studies.

2. Scores on the new test can be reported immediately after the test is administered.

3. The scale for the scores on the new test is not distorted by a nonlinear transformation but keeps its interpretation as a number-correct scale. In principle, a simple count of the correct answers on the new test is all that is needed to report scores.

4. Uncertainties inherent in traditional equating studies, such as those due to imperfect implementation of an equating design, an arbitrary population definition, and smoothing of the observed-score distributions, are avoided.

5. The observed scores on the new test are equitable; for any person, they have the same error distribution as the scores on the reference test.

Of course, these advantages are only realized if the items fit the response model used in the testing program. This condition is stringent. But if it is not met, the quality of the item pool may be doubtful. If the cause of misfit is a violation of the unidimensionality assumption for θ, observed-score equating becomes a meaningless operation at all.

5.3.1 Conditions on the Response Functions

Suppose we have two tests, each consisting of n items. The response functions of the items in the two tests are denoted as $p_i(\theta)$ and $p_j(\theta)$, where both i and j run over $1, ..., n$. We use X and Y to denote the number-correct scores on the two tests. The rth power of the response probabilities of item i is denoted as $p_i^r(\theta)$. For example, if $r = 2$, it thus holds that $p_i^2(\theta)$ is the square of the probability of a correct response on item i by a person with ability θ.

A general property of the distributions of the observed scores X and Y on these two tests is the following:

Proposition 5.1. For any population of persons, the distributions of the observed scores X and Y are identical if and only if

$$\sum_{i=1}^{n} p_i^r(\theta) = \sum_{j=1}^{n} p_j^r(\theta), \quad -\infty < \theta < \infty, \tag{5.47}$$

for $r = 1, ..., n$.

For $r = 1$, the sum of the response functions in (5.47) is known as the *test characteristic function*, or TCF, in (1.22). The proposition thus shows that for two observed-score distributions to be identical, not only should the characteristic functions of the two tests match, but the same should hold for the sums of the higher-order powers of their response functions. In addition, it is known that the importance of these conditions strongly decreases with the order of the power. In fact, if the test length increases, eventually all conditions for $r \geq 2$ become superfluous. For the test lengths met in practice, the conditions have to be satisfied only for, say, the first 2 or 3 powers.

The conditions in (5.47) are on expressions that are well-behaved, smooth functions of θ. For this reason, just as for the TIFs in Section 5.1, if the conditions are approximated for a few well-chosen values of θ, they are in fact approximated over the entire portion of the scale covered by these values. Also, note that, though they contain powers of response probabilities, the conditions in (5.47) are linear in the items. Both features suggest incorporating constraints into the test-assembly model that realize the conditions with respect to a reference test. The model then automatically produces a test that has the same observed-score scale as the reference test for any population of test takers.

5.3.2 Constraints in the Test-Assembly Model

Let $j = 1, ..., n$ denote the items in the reference test. The sums of the powers of the response probabilities in (5.47) for this test at a given set of values θ_k, $k = 1, ..., K$, are known constants,

$$\mathcal{T}_{rk} = \sum_{i=1}^{n} p_i^r(\theta_k), \tag{5.48}$$

which can be calculated directly from the response functions of the reference test. We use $\mathcal{T}_{rk}$ as target values for the sums of the rth powers of the response probabilities of the test that is assembled from the pool, that is, for the sums

$$\sum_{i=1}^{I} p_i^r(\theta_k) x_i \tag{5.49}$$

for all k.

The problem is another example of a multiobjective test-assembly problem. We therefore propose the following weighted minimax approach:

$$\text{minimize } y \tag{5.50}$$

subject to

$$\sum_{i=1}^{I} p_i^r(\theta_k) x_i \leq \mathcal{T}_{rk} + w_r y, \quad \text{for all } k \text{ and } r \leq R, \tag{5.51}$$

$$\sum_{i=1}^{I} p_i^r(\theta_k) x_i \geq \mathcal{T}_{rk} - w_r y, \quad \text{for all } k \text{ and } r \leq R, \tag{5.52}$$

$$\sum_{i=1}^{I} x_i = n, \tag{5.53}$$

$$x_i \in \{0, 1\}, \quad \text{for all } i, \tag{5.54}$$

$$y \geq 0, \tag{5.55}$$

where $w_r > 0$ is the weight for the rth power and R is the condition with the highest order used. The constraints in (5.51) and (5.52) enclose the differences between the sums of powers of the probabilities for the test and the target values in intervals about zero, $[-w_r y, w_r y]$, and the common factor y in the size of these intervals is minimized in (5.50). Generally, because $p_i^r(\theta_k)$ is smaller for a larger value of r, we should choose smaller values of w_r for lower values of r. However, in the empirical examples discussed in Section 5.3.4, we already got excellent results using $w_r = 1$ for all values of r.

5.3.3 Discussion

Unlike the target values $\mathcal{T}_{rk}$ in (5.48) suggest, these values need not be calculated for an actual test. They can also be derived from a typical set of item-parameter values in the item pool and then be maintained during the program. This setup guarantees the maintenaince of a fixed observed-score scale. Changes in the actual observed-score distributions are then entirely due to changes in the ability distribution of the persons, and we can directly use the former to monitor the latter.

The attentive reader may have noted that the conditions in (5.47) are in fact on the conditional distributions of X and Y given θ. If it holds that the two conditional distributions are identical over the whole range of values of θ, the marginal distributions are identical for *any* population of test takers. The method in the preceding section is thus population-independent. Another advantage of the current method of *local observed-score equating* over the practice of using marginal observed-score distributions is that the equated scores are equitable; that is, they have identical error distributions for each test taker (see point 5 in the introduction to Section 5.3). A discussion of all key differences between local and global equating is, however, beyond the scope of this book.

5.3.4 Empirical Examples

The same pool of 753 items from the LSAT and the same set of content constraints as in the examples in Section 5.1.6 was used.

A reference test was assembled from the pool to meet all the constraints using the same target information function as in Section 5.1.6. The target values $\mathcal{T}_{rk}$ in (5.48) were calculated from the response functions of this test. The remaining part of the item pool was used to assemble a test to meet these target values. The model used to assemble the test was exactly the same as for the reference test, except for the objective function and constraints on the TIF in (5.18)–(5.20), which were replaced by those on the sums of powers of the response probabilities in (5.50)–(5.55).

The tests were assembled under three different conditions: (1) constraints on the target values for the first-order sums of powers ($r = 1$), (2) on the first two orders ($r = 1, 2$), and (3) on the first three orders ($r = 1, 2, 3$). For each condition, two different tests were assembled, one with the constraints only at $\theta_k = 0$ and the other at $\theta_k = -1.2$, 0, and 1.2. For each case, the weights in the constraints were put equal to $w_r=1$. The observed-score distributions for the solutions and the target test were calculated for a population of test takers with a standard normal distribution for θ using the well-known Lord-Wingersky algorithm. (For this algorithm, see the literature section at the end of this chapter.)

The observed-score distributions for the solutions and their targets are displayed in Figures 5.3–5.5. For each of the three conditions, the best results were always obtained for the constraints at three θ values. Nevertheless, the results for one θ value in the condition with $r = 1$ were already surprisingly good. The best results in these six examples were obtained for the constraints for $r = 1, 2$ at three θ values (lower panel in Figure 5.4), with those for $r = 1$ at three θ values (lower panel in Figure 5.4) being virtually identical.

5.4   Item Matching

Several of the test-assembly problems addressed so far can be considered as problems in which we tried to optimize a match between a test attribute and a target. The test attributes were generally sums of item attributes (item-information functions and powers of item response functions). As will be demonstrated in this section, it is also possible to assemble a test with the objective of matching the attributes with those of a reference test item by item. This type of matching is much stronger: If two tests are matched at the item level, they are also matched with respect to the sums of their attributes. But the reverse is not necessarily true; if we match at the test level only, large compensation between the attributes of the individual items is possible.

Two main versions of this type of test assembly are discussed. We first show how to model the problem of matching the items in a new test to those in a reference test. Thereafter, we show how the same approach can be used to split a given test into two halves that are as parallel as possible; for example, in terms of their classical item parameters. This problem arises if we try to optimize a split-half estimate of the test reliability; split-half coefficients are estimates of a lower bound to the test reliability, and the closer the two halves are to being parallel, the sharper the bound. Our

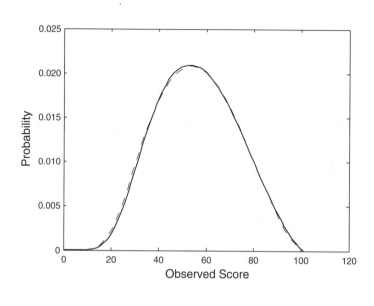

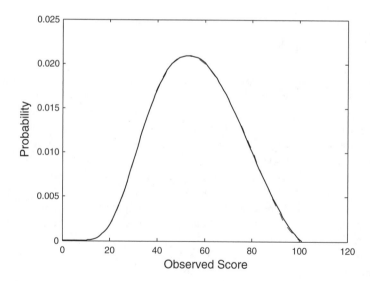

FIGURE 5.3. Observed-score distribution (dashed line) for a test assembled to a target (bold line) at $\theta_k = 0$ (top) and $\theta_k = -1.2, 0, 1.2$ (bottom) ($r = 1$).

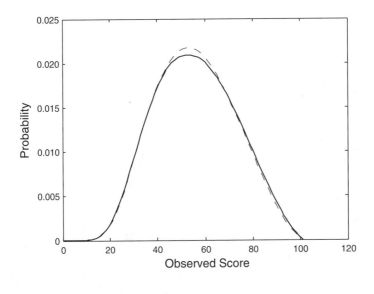

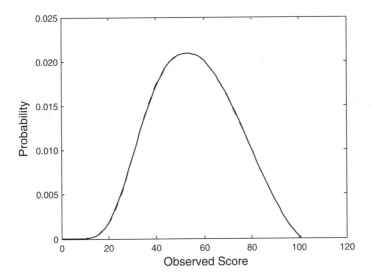

FIGURE 5.4. Observed-score distribution (dashed line) for a test assembled to a target (bold line) at $\theta_k = 0$ (top) and $\theta_k = -1.2,\ 0,\ 1.2$ (bottom) ($r = 1, 2$).

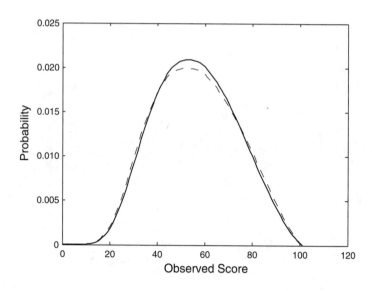

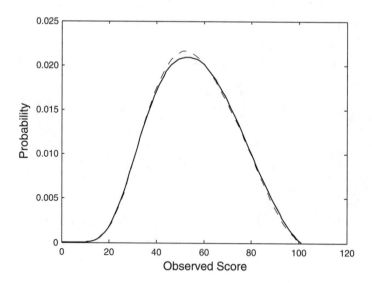

FIGURE 5.5. Observed-score distribution (dashed line) for a test assembled to a target (bold line) at $\theta_k = 0$ (top) and $\theta_k = -1.2,\ 0,\ 1.2$ (bottom) ($r = 1, 2, 3$).

method is a generalization of a graphical method for splitting a test into two halves known as Gulliksen's matched random subsets method.

In item-matching problems, the objective typically is with respect to a few quantitative item attributes, mostly statistical attributes such as the classical item parameters π_i and ρ_{iX}, the IRT parameters a_i, b_i, c_i, and the values of the item-response or item-information functions, $p_i(\theta)$ and $I_i(\theta)$, at a few well-chosen θ values. Categorical item attributes, which are usually needed to deal with the content specifications of the test, can be dealt with by imposing additional categorical constraints on the test. So far, we have used q_i as a generic symbol for a quantitative attribute of item i. Because we will now be dealing with multiple quantitative attributes, we adopt a second index and use q_{jl}, $l = 1, ..., L$, to denote the L attributes considered.

Like most of the earlier problems in this chapter, the problem of matching items on L attributes is another multiobjective problem. In fact, due to the type of decision variables needed to formalize the problem, the number of objectives is much larger than L. We deal with these objectives in two different fashions, which, by now, have become our standard treatment of such problems: by combining them into a single objective function using a weighting procedure or applying the minimax principle.

5.4.1   Matching Items in a Reference Test

Suppose we have a reference test with items to which the new test has to be matched. The items in the reference test are denoted as $j = 1, ..., n$. Their attributes are the targets for a new test assembled from a pool of items, $i = 1, ..., I$. In Section 3.1, we indicated that a fruitful way of identifying the decision variables for a new type of test-assembly problem is to view the selection of the items from the pool as an assignment problem. The current problem is one in which we need to assign n items from the pool to the n items in the reference test such that together they form a set of n pairs with optimally matching attributes. This formulation suggests the use of a separate decision variable for each possible pair of items, (i, j); that is, decision variables

$$x_{ij} = \begin{cases} 1 & \text{if item } i \text{ is matched with item } j \\ 0 & \text{otherwise.} \end{cases} \qquad (5.56)$$

The total number of variables is $n \times I$. Item matching thus involves a much larger optimization problem than the ones discussed earlier in this chapter. The choice of these variables also involves a new problem. We now have to keep the values of these variables consistent across pairs; if an item is assigned to a pair, it cannot be assigned to another pair. Finally, the choice of variables makes clear that we have a problem with $n \times L$ objectives; for each of the n pairs, the items have to be matched on L different attributes.

In each of our approaches to the current problem, we combine the item attributes into a measure for the distance between two items. A useful measure is the following weighted version of the Euclidean measure, δ_{ij}, between items i and j:

$$\delta_{ij} = \left[\sum_{l=1}^{L} w_l (q_{il} - q_{jl})^2\right]^{-1/2}, \tag{5.57}$$

with $w_l > 0$.

If all weights are set equal to $w_l = 1$, the measure is the length of the line between items i and j in a multivariate plot of their attributes. The possibility of choosing different weights w_l for each attribute q_l can be used to allow for possible differences in scale and/or importance between the item attributes.

The first model is

$$\text{minimize} \sum_{j=1}^{n}\sum_{i=1}^{I} \delta_{ij} x_{ij} \tag{5.58}$$

subject to

$$\sum_{i=1}^{I} x_{ij} = 1, \quad \text{for all } j, \tag{5.59}$$

$$\sum_{j=1}^{n} x_{ij} \leq 1, \quad \text{for all } i, \tag{5.60}$$

$$x_{ij} \in \{0, 1\}, \quad \text{for all } i \text{ and } j. \tag{5.61}$$

The objective function in (5.58) minimizes the sum of the distances between the items in the pairs. In principle, we could have chosen a weighted sum. But because all pairs are equally important, no further weighting seems necessary. The constraints in (5.59) and (5.60) are to keep the values of the variables consistent; each of the items in the reference test has exactly one item assigned to it, and each item in the pool can be assigned at most once.

For the objective function in (5.58), results are possible in which an unexpected large term is compensated by a set of smaller terms. The minimax principle deals directly with such cases. Two different applications of the principle are possible. In the first application, we replace (5.58) by

$$\text{minimize } y \tag{5.62}$$

subject to

$$\delta_{ij} x_{ij} \leq y, \quad \text{for all } i \text{ and } j, \tag{5.63}$$

$$\delta_{ij} x_{ij} \geq -y, \quad \text{for all } i \text{ and } j. \tag{5.64}$$

This combination of objective function and constraints minimizes the largest distance between the items over all pairs (Exercise 5.8).

It is also possible to apply the principle at the level of the individual attribute values of the items. We then replace the constraints in (5.63) and (5.64) by

$$(q_{il} - q_{jl})x_{ij} \leq w_l y, \quad \text{for all } i, j, \text{ and } l, \tag{5.65}$$

$$(q_{il} - q_{jl})x_{ij} \geq -w_l y, \quad \text{for all } i, j, \text{ and } l. \tag{5.66}$$

In this version of the problem, the distance measure in (5.57) is no longer needed. The weights w_l in this measure now figure in the definitions of the intervals $[-w_l y, w_l y]$ about zero, in which the differences between the attribute values $q_{il} - q_{jl}$ for the items in the pairs are enclosed. Just as in the somewhat less stringent preceding version of the problem, the objective function minimizes the common factor y in the size of these intervals.

5.4.2   Test Splitting

The previous problems can be solved for any set of quantitative item attributes. The next problem is typically formulated for the classical item indices π_i and ρ_{iX}. We now have a test consisting of the items $i = 1, ..., n$, and we want to split the test into two halves with an optimal match between their items. Upon correcting for test length, the correlation between the scores on the two test halves, known as the "split-half reliability coefficient," is a lower bound to the reliability coefficient of the test. If the two test halves are chosen to be as parallel as possible, the lower bound approximates the reliability coefficient.

A traditional graphical method for finding an optimal split is *Gulliksen's matched random subsets method*. The method is based on a bivariate scatter plot of the n items with the values π_i and ρ_{iX} as coordinates. An example of a Gulliksen plot is given in Figure 5.6 later in this chapter. Using this plot, pairs of items are formed that minimize the distances between the items in the pairs. The two test halves are formed by randomly assigning to them the two items in each pair.

To formulate this method as an MIP problem, we need the same decision variables as in (5.56) but now with both i and j running over the same items $1, ..., n$ in the test. As the measure of the distance between i and j, we use (5.57) with π_i and ρ_{iX} as attributes. Just as in the Gulliksen method, the problem is solved in two stages.

First-Stage Model

In the first stage, we form pairs of items solving the model

$$\text{minimize} \sum_{i=1}^{n} \sum_{j=1}^{n} \delta_{ij} x_{ij} \tag{5.67}$$

subject to

$$\sum_{j|j\neq i} x_{ij} = 1, \quad \text{for all } i, \tag{5.68}$$

$$x_{ij} = x_{ji}, \quad \text{for all } i \neq j, \tag{5.69}$$

$$\sum_{i,j|i=j} x_{ij} = 0, \tag{5.70}$$

$$x_{ij} \in \{0,1\}, \quad \text{for all } i \text{ and } j \tag{5.71}$$

(Exercise 5.9).

The objective function is defined as the sum of the distances over all possible pairs of items in the test, whereas the constraints in (5.68) require that each item be assigned precisely to one pair. Because i and j run over the same set of items, it holds that pair (i,j) is identical to (j,i) and that pairs can only be formed between items $i \neq j$. These conditions are imposed by the constraints in (5.69) and (5.70). A more parsimonious formulation of this model is given in Section 5.4.3 below.

Second-Stage Model

In the second stage, we have $n/2$ pairs of items, and our task is to assign the items in these pairs to the test halves $h = 1, 2$. We use $i_p = 1, 2$ to identify the items in pair p. Rather than assigning the items randomly, as in the Gulliksen method, we use this stage for further optimization. To do so, we need the variables

$$x_{i_p h} = \begin{cases} 1 & \text{if item } i_p \text{ is assigned to test half } h \\ 0 & \text{otherwise.} \end{cases} \tag{5.72}$$

The model for classical test assembly in Section 5.2.1, as well as the fact that optimal results were obtained in the empirical example in Section 5.2.4 with the constraint in (5.40) redundant, suggests to assign items to test halves such that the difference between the sums $\sum \sigma_i \rho_{iX}$ for the two halves is minimal. The following minimax model realizes this objective:

$$\text{minimize } y \tag{5.73}$$

subject to

$$\sum_{i=1}^{2} \sum_{p=1}^{n/2} \sigma_{i_p} \rho_{i_p X}(x_{i_p 1} - x_{i_p 2}) \leq y, \tag{5.74}$$

$$\sum_{i=1}^{2} \sum_{p=1}^{n/2} \sigma_{i_p} \rho_{i_p X}(x_{i_p 1} - x_{i_p 2}) \geq -y, \tag{5.75}$$

$$\sum_{i=1}^{2} x_{i_p h} = 1, \quad \text{for all } p \text{ and } h, \tag{5.76}$$

$$\sum_{p=1}^{n/2} \sum_{h=1}^{2} x_{iph} = 1, \quad \text{for all } i, \tag{5.77}$$

$$x_{iph} \in \{0,1\}, \quad \text{for all } i, p, \text{ and } h. \tag{5.78}$$

The constraints in (5.76) enforce the assignment of one item from each pair p to each test half h, whereas those in (5.77) are necessary to guarantee that each item is assigned to a test half.

5.4.3 Discussion

The formulation in (5.67)–(5.71) was chosen for didactic reasons only. A more parsimonious formulation is possible if we use the variables in (5.56) only for $i < j$; that is, in the upper off-diagonal triangle of the matrix of all possible values of (i,j). The previous model can then be replaced by

$$\text{minimize} \sum_{i=1}^{n-1} \sum_{j=i+1}^{n} \delta_{ij} x_{ij} \tag{5.79}$$

subject to

$$\sum_{i=1}^{j-1} x_{ij} + \sum_{i=j+1}^{n} x_{ji} = 1, \quad \text{for all } j, \tag{5.80}$$

$$x_{ij} \in \{0,1\}, \quad \text{for all } i < j. \tag{5.81}$$

The sum in the objective function is now only over the variables in the upper triangle, and the constraints use the same set of variables to force each item to be assigned to exactly one pair. The sets of constraints in (5.69) and (5.70) are thus no longer needed (Exercise 5.10).

Item-matching problems are instructive in that they illustrate several new definitions of decision variables. Also, the problem of splitting a test into halves that are item-by-item parallel shows that some test-assembly problems can only be solved in more than one stage.

It is easy to generalize the problem of test splitting above to the problem of splitting a set of items into three or more parallel parts. This problem arises, for example, when we assemble a set of rotating item pools for use in adaptive testing (Section 11.5.5).

5.4.4 Empirical Example

The method of splitting a test into two parallel halves was applied to a 20-item version of an achievement test from the *IEA Second Mathematics Study*. The values of the items for π_i and ρ_{iX} were estimated from a sample

Item	π_i	ρ_{iX}	Item	π_i	ρ_{iX}
1	.85	.39	11	.83	.52
2	.50	.41	12	.68	.54
3	.60	.40	13	.80	.43
4	.66	.60	14	.84	.45
5	.87	.25	15	.86	.34
6	.28	.37	16	.52	.47
7	.87	.40	17	.62	.58
8	.48	.48	18	.61	.40
9	.74	.47	19	.51	.48
10	.65	.60	20	.66	.58

TABLE 5.2. Estimated values for item difficulty and discrimination index.

Item Pair	$|\pi_i - \pi_j|$	$|\rho_{iX} - \rho_{jX}|$
1,7	.02	.01
2,6	.22	.04
3,18	.01	.00
10,4	.01	.00
5,15	.01	.09
8,19	.03	.00
9,13	.06	.04
14,11	.01	.07
20, 12	.02	.04
16, 17	.10	.11

TABLE 5.3. Optimal item pairs and test halves (first items in the same half).

of 5,418 students in the Dutch part of this study. The estimates are given in Table 5.2; the Gulliksen plot of these estimates is given in Figure 5.6. For some of the items in the plot, it is obvious how to pair them; for others, several alternatives are possible.

Table 5.3 shows the results obtained for the models in stages 1 and 2 above, with all weights w_l in (5.57) set equal to one. The item pairs in Table 5.3 are reported such that the first items in each pair were those assigned to the first test half and the second items to the second half. The table also shows the differences between the π_i and ρ_{iX} values of the items in the pairs. All differences were small except the one for π_i for the pair with items 2 and 6. Figure 5.5 shows that item 6 was an outlier in the distribution of π_i values on the horizontal axis; a solution with a small difference in π_i values was thus impossible.

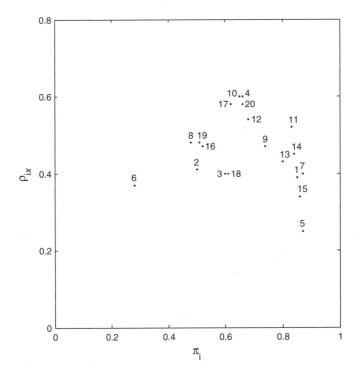

FIGURE 5.6. Gulliksen plot with estimates of π_i and ρ_{iX} for a test from the IEA Second Mathematics Study.

5.5   Literature

Kelderman's method for specifying target information functions was formulated in his 1987 paper. The maximin approaches to test assembly with absolute or relative targets for a TIF were introduced in van der Linden and Boekkooi-Timminga (1989). For a more comprehensive discussion of the differences between absolute and relative targets, see van der Linden and Adema (1998). Using extensive simulation studies, Timminga (1985) showed that controlling the test-information function at a smaller number of θ values generally resulted in faster solutions and that problems with 3–5 values already gave excellent results. Both Baker, Cohen, and Barmish (1988) and de Gruijter (1990) addressed the case of a uniform absolute target for the test-information function. They pointed to the fact that the results for this type of target can be sensitive to the composition of the item pool, particularly to the number of items available near the endpoints of the interval over which the target is specified. Test assembly with target values for the TIF at a cutoff score is discussed in Glas (1988). Reviews of IRT-based test assembly are given in Adema, Boekkooi-Timminga, and Gademan (1992), Adema, Boekkooi-Timminga, and van der Linden (1991), Armstrong, Jones, and Wang (1995), Timminga and Adema (1995), van der Linden (1994b, 1998a, 2001b, 2002), and Veldkamp (2005).

The models for classical test assembly in Sections 5.2.1 and 5.2.2 were formulated in Adema and van der Linden (1989) and van der Linden (submitted), respectively. An alternative approach to the problem of maximizing the reliability of a test was offered in Armstrong, Jones, and Wang (1998), who used network-flow programming with Lagrangian relaxation (Section 4.3) to formulate a search procedure for a solution to the nonlinear objective in (5.31).

The idea of assembling a test to meet a target for its observed-score distribution was formulated in van der Linden and Luecht (1996). These authors tried to achieve this goal by matching both the characteristic function and the information function of the test to a target. Their intuition was that the former would control the true scores and the latter the errors on the test; together they would therefore control its observed-score distribution. The fact that this job can only be done by controlling sums of (lower-order) powers of the response functions was derived in van der Linden and Luecht (1998). The differences between global and local observed-score equating discussed in Section 5.3.3 were further explored in van der Linden (2000c, 2005e). The Lord-Wingersky algorithm for calculating observed-score distributions on tests was presented in their 1984 paper.

Gulliksen introduced his matched random subsets method in his 1950 monograph on test theory. The formalization of the method in Section 5.4.2 and 5.4.3 was given in van der Linden and Boekkooi-Timminga (1988). Armstrong and Jones (1992) suggested extending the model with a set of constraints that enable solution of the model in polynomial time (see Section 4.2.3).

5.6 Summary

1. Tests can be assembled both to an absolute and a relative target for their information function. An absolute target requires the test-information function to be at a fixed height. If a relative target is used, only the shape of the test-information function is specified, but its height is optimized.

2. If the test-assembly model has a constraint that fixes the length of the test, an absolute target can easily lead to infeasibility. For a relative target, this is impossible.

3. Because information functions are smooth, the number of points at which target values for a TIF should be specified need not be larger

than 3–5 well-chosen points. If the objective is to maximize the test information at a cutoff score, the model has only one point.

4. An absolute target for a TIF can be derived from descriptive statistics of the distribution of the item parameters in the pool, a specimen of the test assembled manually, or from (asymptotic) probabilities of test scores ordering the abilities of persons erroneously specified by a panel of test specialists (Kelderman method).

5. A simple way of specifying a relative target for a TIF is by asking test specialists to distribute an arbitrary number of chips over the points θ_k in an item map such that their distribution reflects the relative accuracy of the test scores needed at these points.

6. Test-assembly problems with targets for the test-information functions are problems with multiple objectives, one for each target value. The models presented in this chapter solve them by combining the objectives as a weighted sum or applying the minimax principle.

7. In classical test assembly, we maximize the reliability or the predictive validity of the test. Both objectives involve a nonlinear function consisting of two linear expressions. We can maximize both the reliability and the validity by using one of these expressions as the objective function and constraining the other by a well-chosen upper bound.

8. A test can be assembled to have an observed-score distribution matching the distribution of a reference test for the same population of test takers. The only things required are a few constraints on the sums of the lower-order powers of the response probabilities at a few points θ_k in the test-assembly model.

9. In item-matching problems, a new test is assembled with attributes that match those in a reference test item by item. The same type of problem arises when we want to split a given test into two halves with an optimal match between their item attributes.

10. Item-matching problems lead to the definition of decision variables at the level of pairs of items or combinations of items and test halves.

5.7 Exercises

5.1 The model in (5.7) and (5.8) yields a test with a TIF approaching the target values $\mathcal{T}_k$ from above. Reformulate the model for a test with a TIF approaching the target values from below.

5.2 A run with the test-assembly model in (5.9)–(5.12) for $\mathcal{T}_1 = 10$, $\mathcal{T}_2 = 15$, and $\mathcal{T}_3 = 10$ and the test length fixed at $n = 40$ yields a solution with a value for the objective function equal to $y = .8$. Interpret the result. How reasonable is the result for a pool with an average item-discrimination parameter a_i equal to 1.3?

5.3 A run with the test-assembly model in (5.13)–(5.16) for the same target values as in Exercise 5.2 and $w_k = 1$, $k = 1, 2, 3$, gives the following results for the variables in the objective function: $y_1^{pos} = .4$ $y_2^{pos} = 0$, $y_3^{pos} = .7$, $y_1^{neg} = 0$, $y_2^{neg} = .5$, and $y_3^{neg} = 0$. Calculate the values of the TIF at $k = 1, 2, 3$.

5.4 A run with the test-assembly model in (5.18)–(5.21) yields a solution with a value for the objective function equal to $y = .8$. How do we know if this value represents a positive or a negative deviation from a target value for the TIF?

5.5 The model in (5.25)–(5.27) maximizes the TIF subject to a set of constraints on its shape. Formulate a model for maximizing the height of a TIF that accepts small positive and negative deviations from the intended shape.

5.6 Formulate a model for minimizing the difference between the reliability of a test and a reference test.

5.7 The results in Figure 5.5 show a minor deterioration of the observed-score distribution for the example with the extra constraint for $r = 3$, whereas (5.47) predicts a better approximation if this constraint is added. Explain the result.

5.8 The constraints in (5.63) and (5.64) are quantitative constraints at the item level. Why does (5.64) not need the form with the inverse inequality sign in (3.14)?

5.9 Generalize the model in (5.67)–(5.71) to the case of splitting a test into three parallel parts.

5.10 Show that (5.79)–(5.81) is identical to (5.67)–(5.71).

5.11 A five-item reference test has the following values for the difficulty parameter: $b_1 = -1$, $b_2 = -1$, $b_3 = 0$, $b_4 = .5$, and $b_5 = 1$. Formulate a model for the selection of a new test of five items from a pool of I items with values for the difficulty parameter matching those in the reference test as closely as possible. Why does the model not need a constraint on the length of the test?

6
Models for Assembling Multiple Tests

Each of the models in the preceding chapter was for the assembly of a single test. Although the notion of parallel tests has already turned up in a few places, it has always been used to describe the problem of assembling a single test to be parallel to a reference form—not a *set* of tests to be mutually parallel or to meet another attribute at the multiple-test level. (See Section 2.2.2 for the definition of attributes at this level.) In this chapter, we do address models for the assembly of such sets. The following are examples of a few applications:

1. A set of tests has to be assembled that are mutually parallel in a weaker or stronger sense of the notion. A familiar example is that of a testing program with a periodic assembly of sets of parallel forms of a paper-and-pencil test for administration at different time slots or locations. Each of these forms has to meet exactly the same content and statistical specifications. Another example is a computer-based program with a pool of parallel forms stored in the computer and random sampling of a form for each person ("linear on-the-fly testing").

2. The set of tests has to consist of tests differing systematically in difficulty or information function; otherwise each test has to meet the same content specifications. An example is a set of two tests for use in an evaluation study of a treatment or educational program with a pretest-posttest design. Typically, the posttest has to be efficient at a higher level than the pretest to allow accurate measurement of changes in the abilities of the subjects. More sophisticated examples arise in large-scale educational assessments, where the progress

of schools in achievement domains is followed. In such studies, sets of test booklets assembled from an item pool covering the domain are administered according to a stratified sampling plan. The booklets have to meet certain content specifications. Besides, we often want them to have an overlap in items, which is required to estimate correlations between scales or subscores. Designs for educational assessments with these features are known as balanced incomplete-block (BIB) designs.

3. The set of tests has to be assembled for use in a computer-based multistage adaptive testing system. In this mode of testing, each person begins with a broad-range subtest (or "routing test") after which the computer calculates an interim estimate of his or her ability level. At the next stage, the computer selects a subtest from a small set of available tests that matches the estimate best. This procedure can be repeated a few more times. The sets of subtests used in the system have to cover the ability scale systematically, and each test therefore has to be assembled to its own statistical specifications. In addition, we typically want subtests for the same stage to meet the same content specifications.

4. The last example of the assembly of multiple tests is that of the assembly of a pool of testlets for use in testlet-based adaptive testing. In this type of adaptive testing, at each step a testlet is selected to match the update of the ability estimate of the person. The pool of testlets has to be assembled to statistical specifications guaranteeing systematic coverage of the ability scale. As for the content specifications, subsets of testlets in the pool have to meet different subsets of specifications. To run a testlet-based adaptive test, we need an algorithm for constrained adaptive testing that realizes the same set of content constraints for each person (Chapter 9).

Each of the examples above involves a distinct objective for each of its tests. Therefore, we typically have problems with more objectives than those in the previous chapter. For example, if we assemble T tests and each test has to meet a target for its information function at K ability points, the problem has $K \times T$ objectives. However, these larger multiobjective test-assembly problems can be solved using a direct generalization of the approaches we have used before.

In the next sections, we will first show that sequential assembly of a set of tests is not a good idea, even if we follow up with a heuristic correction to reduce aberrations in the results. We will then present a general model for simultaneous assembly of a set of tests that always produces an optimal solution. For some real-life problems, the model may occasionally be too large to find an exact solution. If so, our recommendation is to use the "big-shadow-test method" introduced at the end of this chapter, which solves the original simultaneous problem through a sequence of smaller simultaneous problems.

6.1   Sequential Assembly

Let $t = 1, ..., T$ denote the tests in the set we want to assemble. In a sequential approach, we assemble test $t = 1$ using an appropriate choice of model from Chapter 5. After the test has been assembled, we remove the items in the test from the pool and assemble test $t = 2$. The procedure is repeated until all T tests have been assembled.

If sets of tests have to be parallel, at each step the model remains the same. If the tests have to differ systematically, the objective functions and/or some of the constraints in the model change. It is also possible to choose an entirely different model at each step; in principle, a sequential approach can be used with any combination of the models in Chapter 5.

Each time a test is assembled, the pool changes. To prevent recoding of the remaining items in the pool after each new test, we can insert the following set of constraints in the models for $t = 2, ..., T$:

$$x_i = 0, \text{ for all } i \text{ already selected.} \qquad (6.1)$$

A sequential approach to the assembly of a set of tests suffers from the same two disadvantages as sequential heuristics for the solution of a model for a single test discussed in Section 4.6. First, the value of the objective function of the solution to each subsequent model deteriorates; the best items are picked for the first test, the next best items for the second test, and so on. This process is immediately clear for the classical test-assembly model for maximization of the test reliability in (5.34)–(5.37). As the empirical example in Section 5.2.4 showed, the constraint in (5.35) needs a large value for κ and tends to be redundant. Consequently, the model tends to pick the n items with the largest values for $\sigma_i \rho_{iX}$ in the pool (subject to all content constraints). After the first test has been assembled, the best n items in the pool have been skimmed off, and the optimal value of the objective function for the second test will be lower. Generally, the deterioration is most serious for sets of parallel tests. If a combination of a pretest and posttest for an evaluation study has to be selected, both tests are less likely to compete for the same items (though they will compete if the items in some content categories are scarce). The size of the pool is also a critical factor; generally, the smaller the pool, the stronger the effect.

Second, even though the pool contains a feasible set of T tests, we can easily run into infeasibility problems before the whole set is assembled. The problem is illustrated in Table 6.1, which shows the same phenomenon as in Table 4.1 at the level of a set of tests. Suppose we want to assemble two tests from this pool with maximum contribution to the objective function.

Item	Contribution to Target	Attribute V_1	Attribute V_2
1	.30	+	−
2	.85	+	+
3	.89	+	+
4	.48	+	−

TABLE 6.1. Example of unnecessary infeasibility in sequential test assembly.

Each test has to consist of two items with attribute V_1 and at least one item with attribute V_2. The pool of four items in this example admits a solution, namely, that with the first two items in one test and the last two in the other. An attempt to assemble the two tests sequentially, however, would result in test $t = 1$ consisting of the second and third items and infeasibility for $t = 2$ (Exercise 6.1).

6.1.1   Heuristic Correction

The example in Table 6.1 shows that a sequential approach operates in fact as a greedy heuristic (Section 4.4.1) at the level of the set of tests. Just as for the case of greedy heuristics for the assembly of a single test, it is desirable to succeed with a second stage in which we try to improve on the initial result. An obvious second-stage procedure is to swap items between the T tests until results with a more satisfactory quality are obtained. This swapping enables us to improve on the values of the objective functions but does not necessarily fix the problem of infeasibility.

6.2   Simultaneous Assembly

The previous problems are absent if the tests are assembled simultaneously (that is, as a solution to a single model). This type of assembly requires a restructuring of the problem using a new type of decision variable. The variables we need remind us of those for the test-splitting problem in (5.72), which were used to assign items to test halves. These variables had double indices, one for the items in the pool and the other for the test halves.

For the current problem, the variables become

$$x_{it} = \begin{cases} 1 & \text{if item } i \text{ is assigned to test } t \\ 0 & \text{otherwise,} \end{cases} \qquad (6.2)$$

for all i and t. As before, we need to complement these variables with a set of constraints that keeps their values consistent; that is, we must prevent the assignment of an item to more than one test.

Using (6.2), any model for a single test can be reformulated as a model for multiple tests. To illustrate the claim, we reformulate the standard model for a single test in (4.1)–(4.10). The model is

$$\text{optimize } \sum_{t=1}^{T} \sum_{i=1}^{I} q_i x_{it} \quad \text{(objective)} \qquad (6.3)$$

subject to possible constraints at the following levels:

Multiple-Test Level

$$\sum_{t=1}^{T} x_{it} \leq 1, \quad \text{for all } i; \quad \text{(no overlap)} \qquad (6.4)$$

Test Level

$$\sum_{i=1}^{I} x_{it} \gtreqless n_t, \quad \text{for all } t, \quad \text{(test length)} \qquad (6.5)$$

$$\sum_{i \in V_c} x_{it} \gtreqless n_{ct}, \quad \text{for all } c \text{ and } t, \quad \text{(categorical attributes)} \qquad (6.6)$$

$$\sum_{i=1}^{I} q_i x_{it} \gtreqless b_{qt}, \quad \text{for all } t; \quad \text{(quantitative attributes)} \qquad (6.7)$$

Item Level

$$\sum_{i \in V_1} x_{it} = n_{1t}, \quad \text{for all } t, \quad \text{(categorical attributes)} \qquad (6.8)$$

$$\sum_{i \in V_0} x_{it} = 0, \quad \text{for all } t, \quad \text{(categorical attributes)} \qquad (6.9)$$

$$q_i x_{it} \leq b_{qt}^{\max}, \quad \text{for all } i \text{ and } t, \quad \text{(quantitative attributes)} \qquad (6.10)$$

$$b_{qt}^{\min} x_{it} \leq q_i, \quad \text{for all } i \text{ and } t, \quad \text{(quantitative attributes)} \qquad (6.11)$$

$$\sum_{i \in V_e} x_{it} \leq 1, \quad \text{for all } e \text{ and } t; \quad \text{(enemies)} \qquad (6.12)$$

Definition of Variables

$$x_{it} \in \{0, 1\}, \quad \text{for all } i \text{ and } t. \quad \text{(range of variables)} \qquad (6.13)$$

The changes in (6.3)–(6.13) relative to the original model in (4.1)–(4.10) are:

1. the replacement of the variables x_i by x_{it};

2. the extension of the objective function to the case of T tests;

3. the addition of the no-overlap constraints in (6.4);

4. the indexing of the bounds in the constraints by t.

The generalization of the objective function in (6.3) is simple and consists of taking an (unweighted) sum over the tests. Another example of an objective function for simultaneous test assembly is the generalization of the minimax principle in (6.14)–(6.17) below. The bounds in the constraints are indexed by t to enable us to assemble sets of tests with different specifications. If some types of constraints are not needed for some of the tests, we can simply leave them out or give them bounds that are small or large enough to make them redundant.

The objective function in (6.3) is for a generic quantitative test attribute. If the tests are assembled to meet targets for their information functions, we replace the function by a generalized version of one of the alternatives in Section 5.1. For example, if each test has to meet a set of absolute target values and we want to use the minimax principle in (5.18)–(5.21) instead of the sum in (6.3), the latter should be replaced by

$$\text{minimize } y \tag{6.14}$$

subject to

$$\sum_{i=1}^{I} I_i(\theta_{kt})x_{it} \leq \mathcal{T}_{kt} + w_t y, \quad \text{for all } k \in V_t \text{ and } t, \tag{6.15}$$

$$\sum_{i=1}^{I} I_i(\theta_{kt})x_{it} \geq \mathcal{T}_{kt} - w_t y, \quad \text{for all } k \in V_t \text{ and } t, \tag{6.16}$$

$$y \geq 0, \tag{6.17}$$

where the target values $\mathcal{T}_{kt}$ in (6.15) and (6.16) are indexed by t to allow us to set different targets for different tests. In addition, as k can be given a different set of values V_t for each test, we can specify the target values at a different set of θ values for each test. Finally, we have added weights w_t to (6.15) and (6.16) to have the option of weighing deviations from target values differently for different tests.

If the tests have to satisfy sets of relative target values $\mathcal{R}_{kt}$, we can generalize the application of the minimax principle in (5.25)–(5.27) in the same way as has been done in (6.14)–(6.17).

6.2.1 Item Overlap

Occasionally, item overlap between tests is less of a concern, or it may even be necessary to have overlap between some of the tests. Two different types of overlap control are relevant.

First, if items are allowed to be assigned to more than one test but we want to constrain the number of tests for which each item is allowed to be selected, we can simply relax (6.4), replacing its right-hand side by a number $n_o^{\max} > 1$:

$$\sum_{t=1}^{T} x_{it} \leq n_o^{\max}, \quad \text{for all } i. \tag{6.18}$$

Second, we may want to constrain the amount of overlap between some pairs of tests. Unfortunately, this problem is more complicated, the reason being that the items now have to be selected conditionally; in fact, we then require that if a certain set of items is assigned to one test, a subset of it must be assigned to the other test, and conversely.

To formulate the logical constraints necessary to deal with such problems, we need additional decision variables

$$z_{itt'} = \begin{cases} 1 & \text{if item } i \text{ is assigned to test } t \text{ and } t' \\ 0 & \text{otherwise,} \end{cases} \qquad (6.19)$$

for all i and for each pair of tests t and t' for which control is needed. If the overlap has to be between upper and lower bounds $n_{tt'}^{\max}$ and $n_{tt'}^{\min}$, respectively, the following constraints replace those in (6.4) for tests t and t':

$$\sum_{i=1}^{I} z_{itt'} \leq n_{tt'}^{\max}, \qquad (6.20)$$

$$\sum_{i=1}^{I} z_{itt'} \geq n_{tt'}^{\min}, \qquad (6.21)$$

$$2z_{itt'} \leq x_{it} + x_{it'}, \quad \text{for all } i, \qquad (6.22)$$

$$z_{itt'} \geq x_{it} + x_{it'} - 1, \quad \text{for all } i. \qquad (6.23)$$

The last two constraints are necessary to keep the values of $z_{itt'}$, x_{it}, and $x_{it'}$ consistent. The constraints in (6.22) force $x_{it} = 1$ and $x_{it'} = 1$ if $z_{itt'} = 1$, whereas those in (6.23) guarantee the opposite, namely $z_{itt'} = 1$ if $x_{it} = x_{it'} = 1$.

Problems constraints on item overlap between larger sets of tests easily run the danger of becoming prohibitively large. The number of additional variables that they require is $\binom{T}{2}I$, whereas the number of constraints needed of the type in (6.22) and (6.23) is twice as large (Exercise 6.5).

6.2.2 Controlling Targets Through Constraints

We began our discussion of the assembly of a single test for an absolute target for its information function in Section 5.1.3 by showing that information functions can also be controlled through a set of constraints. The same holds for problems with multiple tests. The following simple generalization of (5.5) and (5.6) does the job:

$$\sum_{i=1}^{I} I_i(\theta_{kt}) x_{it} \leq \mathcal{T}_{kt} + \delta_{kt}, \quad \text{for all } k \in V_t \text{ and } t, \qquad (6.24)$$

$$\sum_{i=1}^{I} I_i(\theta_{kt}) x_{it} \geq \mathcal{T}_{kt} - \varepsilon_{kt}, \quad \text{for all } k \in V_t \text{ and } t. \qquad (6.25)$$

Just as in (6.15) and (6.16), these constraints enable us to formulate a different set of target values at a different set of θ values for each test.

6.3 Big-Shadow-Test Method

Models for the assembly of multiple tests lead to problems larger than those for single tests. The number of decision variables defined in (6.2) necessary to formulate a problem of T tests from a pool of I items is equal to TI. This number increases linearly with the number of tests. Models for multiple tests also always have I more constraints than those for single tests because of the no-overlap constraints in (6.4). If we want to control the overlap between pairs of tests using (6.20)–(6.23), the increase becomes much larger. In the worst case, with overlap controlled between each pair of tests, the number of variables is equal to $TI + \binom{T}{2}I$ and the model has $\binom{T}{2}I$ more constraints to specify the required overlap, where $\binom{T}{2}$ is the binomial coefficient. As already indicated in Section 4.2.3, due to recent optimization of commercial MIP solvers, problem size is no longer the limiting factor it used to be. Nevertheless, it may be convenient to have an alternative method for problems that still appear to be too large.

A useful backup method is the *big-shadow-test method* explained in this section. A graphical presentation of this method is given in Figure 6.1. The basic idea underlying this method is *to solve a large simultaneous problem as a sequence of smaller simultaneous problems*.

For example, if we need to assemble a set of $T = 10$ tests, and the entire problem is too large but solutions to sets of three tests can be obtained in reasonable time, we can solve the problem through the following five steps. At the first step, tests $t = 1$ and 2 and a *shadow test* representing the remaining tests $t = 3, ..., 10$ are assembled simultaneously. The items for tests $t = 1$ and 2 are removed from the pool, but the items in the shadow test are replaced. At the second step, tests $t = 3$ and 4 are assembled simultaneously along with a new shadow that now represents tests $t = 5, ..., 10$. Again, the items for tests $t = 3$ and 4 are removed and those in the shadow test are replaced. The procedure is repeated until, at the last step, we assemble tests $t = 9$ and 10. It should be noted that the size of the test is only a constraint in the model and not a basic determinant of the computation time (see Section 4.2.3). This feature allows us to include a shadow test in the problem that is solved at each step.

Shadow tests are no regular tests; their items are always returned to the pool. They are only assembled to balance the selection of items between current and future tests. Because of their presence, they neutralize the greedy character inherent in sequential test-assembly methods. In doing so, they prevent the best items from being assigned only to earlier tests and keep the later test-assembly problems feasible.

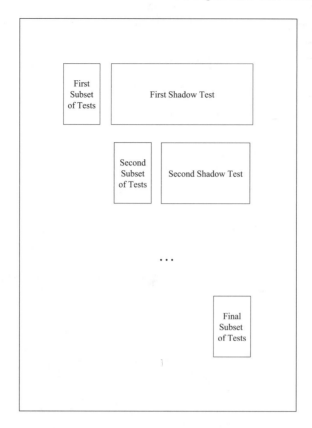

FIGURE 6.1. Graphical representation of the big-shadow-test method for assembling multiple tests.

The set of specifications for the shadow tests is the aggregate of the specifications for the regular tests they represent. Their size is thus always the sum of the sizes of these tests. We call this method the *big*-shadow-test method because in Chapter 9 we will introduce a method for item selection in adaptive testing (Chapter 9) with shadow tests that always have the size of a single fixed test.

How to aggregate the specifications of a set of tests to those for the shadow test is illustrated for the case in which at each step one regular test and one shadow test are assembled. Although the two tests are assembled simultaneously, for notational simplicity we will not use variables with double indices but separate sets of variables for the regular and the shadow tests, x_i and z_i, respectively, where $i = 1, ..., I$ now denote the current items in the pool. Suppose we have a (possibly different) relative target for each of the tests $t = 1, ..., T$, with weights $\mathcal{R}_{kt}$ for the information in test t at ability value θ_k.

The standard model for the simultaneous assembly of test t and the shadow test representing tests $t + 1, ..., T$, with the maximin principle for the relative targets proposed in (5.25) and (5.27), is

$$\text{maximize } y \quad \text{(objective function)} \tag{6.26}$$

subject to possible constraints at the following levels:

Multiple-Test Level

$$x_i + z_i \le 1, \quad \text{for all } i; \quad \text{(no overlap)} \tag{6.27}$$

Test Level

$$\sum_{i=1}^{I} I_i(\theta_k)x_i \ge \mathcal{R}_{kt}y, \quad \text{for all } k, \quad \text{(target for test } t) \tag{6.28}$$

$$\sum_{i=1}^{I} I_i(\theta_k)z_i \ge \sum_{g=t+1}^{T} \mathcal{R}_{kg}y, \quad \text{for all } k, \quad \text{(target for shadow test)} \tag{6.29}$$

$$\sum_{i=1}^{I} x_i \gtreqless n_t, \quad \text{(length of test } t) \tag{6.30}$$

$$\sum_{i=1}^{I} z_i = \sum_{g=t+1}^{T} n_g, \quad \text{(length of shadow test)} \tag{6.31}$$

$$\sum_{i \in V_c} x_i \gtreqless n_{ct}, \quad \text{for all } c, \quad \text{(categorical attributes of } t) \tag{6.32}$$

$$\sum_{i \in V_c} z_i \gtreqless \sum_{g=t+1}^{T} n_{cg}, \quad \text{for all } c, \quad \text{(categorical attributes of shadow test)} \tag{6.33}$$

$$\sum_{i=1}^{I} q_i x_i \gtreqless b_{qt}, \quad \text{(quantitative attributes of } t) \tag{6.34}$$

$$\sum_{i=1}^{I} q_i z_i \gtreqless \sum_{g=t+1}^{T} b_{qg}; \quad \text{(quantitative attributes of shadow test)} \tag{6.35}$$

Item Level

$$\sum_{i \in V_1} x_i \gtreqless n_{1t}, \quad \text{(categorical attributes of } t) \tag{6.36}$$

$$\sum_{i \in V_0} x_i = 0, \quad \text{(categorical attributes of } t) \tag{6.37}$$

$$\sum_{i \in V_1} z_i \gtreqless \sum_{g=t+1}^{T} n_{1g}, \quad \text{(categorical attributes of shadow test)} \tag{6.38}$$

$$\sum_{i \in V_0} z_i = 0, \quad \text{(categorical attributes of shadow test)} \tag{6.39}$$

$$q_i x_i \leq b_q^{\mathrm{max}}, \quad \text{for all } i, \quad \text{(quantitative attributes of } t) \qquad (6.40)$$

$$b_q^{\mathrm{min}} x_i \leq q_i, \quad \text{for all } i, \quad \text{(quantitative attributes of } t) \qquad (6.41)$$

$$q_i z_i \leq b_q^{\mathrm{max}}, \quad \text{for all } i, \quad \text{(quantitative attributes of shadow test)}$$
$$(6.42)$$
$$b_q^{\mathrm{min}} z_i \leq q_i, \quad \text{for all } i, \quad \text{(quantitative attributes of shadow test)} \quad (6.43)$$

$$\sum_{i \in V_e} x_i \leq 1, \quad \text{for all } e, \quad \text{(enemies)} \qquad (6.44)$$

$$\sum_{i \in V_e} z_i \leq 1, \quad \text{for all } e; \quad \text{(enemies)} \qquad (6.45)$$

Definition of Variables

$$x_i \in \{0, 1\}, \quad \text{for all } i, \quad \text{(range of } x_i) \qquad (6.46)$$

$$z_i \in \{0, 1\}, \quad \text{for all } i. \quad \text{(range of } z_i) \qquad (6.47)$$

All bounds in the constraints for the shadow test are obtained by summing the corresponding bounds for the tests $t+1, ..., T$. The only exceptions are the quantitative constraints at the item level in (6.42) and (6.43); these are required to hold for any item in the pool.

Observe that the model above has a set of *relative* targets for the individual tests that are maximized simultaneously. Thus, the big-shadow-test method enables us to maximize the joint height of the information functions of all individual tests—a feature that is impossible to realize through an ordinary sequential approach.

If the tests are to be assembled to absolute targets, we use the constraint set in (6.27)–(6.45) completed with the following objective function and constraints to deal with the targets:

$$\text{minimize } y \quad \text{(objective function)} \qquad (6.48)$$

$$\sum_{i=1}^{I} I_i(\theta_k) x_i \leq \mathcal{T}_{kt} + w_{kt} y, \quad \text{for all } k, \quad \text{(target for test } t) \qquad (6.49)$$

$$\sum_{i=1}^{I} I_i(\theta_k) x_i \geq \mathcal{T}_{kt} - w_{kt} y, \quad \text{for all } k, \quad \text{(target for test } t) \qquad (6.50)$$

$$\sum_{i=1}^{I} I_i(\theta_k) z_i \leq \sum_{g=t+1}^{T} \mathcal{T}_{kg} + w_{k(t+1,T)} y, \quad \text{for all } k,$$

$$\text{(target for shadow test)} \quad (6.51)$$

$$\sum_{i=1}^{I} I_i(\theta_k)z_i \geq \sum_{g=t+1}^{T} \mathcal{T}_{kg} - w_{k(t+1,T)}y, \quad \text{for all } k.$$

(target for shadow test)   (6.52)

The weights w_{kt} and $w_{k(t+1,T)}$ have been added to the model to show that it is possible to use different tolerances for the information functions of test t and the shadow test representing tests $t+1, ..., T$.

6.3.1 Discussion

In each of the implementations of the big-shadow-test method discussed above, one shadow test was assembled at each step (except the last). It is also possible to implement the method with multiple shadow tests. This choice is attractive, for example, if a set of nonparallel tests with subsets differing considerably in their specifications has to be assembled. During the assembly process, each of these subsets can then be represented by a different shadow test.

It is also possible to vary the number of tests assembled at each step. For instance, if a large number of tests have to be assembled, the size of the item pool decreases quickly and, at the later steps, we might be able to increase the number of regular tests assembled per step. To date, neither this version nor the preceding version of the big-shadow-test method have been studied in detail.

The targets for the regular test and the shadow test in (6.49)–(6.52) are formulated at the same set of values θ_k, $k = 1, ..., K$. If targets for different tests need to be controlled at different values θ_k, it is recommended to have k range over the union of sets of all values and drop the individual constraints in (6.49)–(6.52) for which no control is needed.

The big-shadow-test method is a general heuristic scheme. It has four features that distinguish it from the more specialized heuristics we reviewed earlier. First, the degree to which the method behaves as a heuristic can be controlled by the test assembler. The critical parameter is the number of steps. The model in (6.26)–(6.47), with one single test at each step, has $T - 1$ steps and illustrates one extreme of the range of possibilities. The simultaneous model in (6.3)–(6.13), with T tests and no shadow test, is the other extreme. The smaller the number of steps, the closer the result can be expected to be to the exact solution obtained by the simultaneous model. The only restriction in our attempt to get as close as possible to the exact solution is computation time.

Second, unlike the heuristics with second-stage item swapping discussed in Section 6.1.1, the big-shadow-test method looks ahead and prevents unbalanced solutions instead of fixing them after the fact.

Third, whereas other heuristics are typically formulated for a specific type of objective function and/or class of constraints, the big-shadow-test method is based on a general scheme that can be used with any type of problem for which a model for a single test can be formulated; that is, with any of the models introduced in Chapter 5.

Finally, as already indicated in our discussion of the model in (6.26)–(6.47), the big-shadow-test method enables us to assemble a set of tests for relative targets whose heights are maximized simultaneously. This feature cannot be realized by a purely sequential heuristic.

6.4   Alternative Backup Methods

Other general methods with heuristic elements have been proposed, each of them for the problem of assembling a set of parallel tests. These methods are based on the idea of splitting the item pool or other collections of items into equivalent parts. For the sake of completeness, we review them briefly here:

1. The idea underlying the first method is to split the item pool into T (randomly) equivalent subpools. The T tests are then assembled sequentially from different subpools using a single-test model. The splitting of the pool prevents the problem of solutions with a deteriorating value for the objective function inherent in sequential assembly. The price to be paid, however, is a lower value for the objective function. This can easily be seen by noting that, in fact, each individual problem is solved subject to the following set of constraints:

$$x_i = 0, \text{ for all } i \text{ in the } T - 1 \text{ other subpools.} \qquad (6.53)$$

   This set of constraints is much larger than that in (6.1), and problems with larger sets always tend to result in lower values for the objective function.

   If the pool is split at random, the addition of the *ineligibility constraints* above can lead to infeasibility of some of the T separate problems. This possibility can be prevented by splitting the total pool subject to the condition that each subpool contains at least one solution. But this choice leads to a generalization of the test-splitting problem in Section 5.4.2 that is of the same order of complexity as our original problem of assembling T parallel tests, whereas each test still has to be assembled subject to the constraint in (6.53).

2. The second alternative involves the use of network-flow programming. The problem of assembling T tests is reconceptualized as that of shipping items from the pool to demand nodes that represent combinations of the (categorical) attributes addressed in the test specifications (see Section 4.3). If each test is required to have n_j items at demand node w, the number of items shipped is equal to

n_jT. The actual selection of the items is performed by optimizing an objective function (for example, one derived from a common target for the information functions of the test or a lower bound on their reliability).

In a second stage, the collection of items at each node is split into T parallel portions, one for each test. The split can be random, with additional swapping of items to improve on the initial result, but explicit optimization is also possible.

In principle, network-flow programming applies only to tests with categorical constraints, preferably formulated as equalities. Quantitative or logical constraints have to be dealt with using the technique of Lagrangian relaxation (Section 4.3) and/or by introducing other heuristic elements. The method is fast and has been shown to produce excellent results for a number of specific problems, but it lacks the general applicability of the big-shadow-test method.

3. The last alternative is similar to the previous one. The only difference exists in the first stage, which now consists of the assembly of one big test that is required to meet specifications T times as large as for the regular tests. The test is then split into T separate tests.

The first-stage test is assembled using an appropriate choice from the models for single tests in Chapter 5. The specifications for this test are established using the same principles as for the part of the model for the shadow test in (6.26)–(6.47). Only heuristic methods for the splitting of the test into T separate tests have been investigated. But splitting one big test into T parallel tests seems possible using a generalization of the test-splitting method in Section 5.4.2. Thus, in this respect the third method seems to have important advantages over the first method, which involves an application of the test-splitting method to the entire pool. It also has wider applicability than the second method; its first-stage problem is not restricted to one for which a network-flow formulation exists but can be based on any MIP model of test assembly.

A critical difference between this method and the big-shadow-test method is that in the latter each of the T tests is assembled from the entire pool exactly to its specifications, whereas in the former they are obtained by splitting one big test selected from the pool. The current method thus offers fewer degrees of freedom when optimizing the T tests than the big-shadow-test method.

6.5   Optimizing BIB Designs

In large-scale educational assessments, such as those conducted by the National Assessment of Educational Progress (NAEP), usually sets of test booklets covering an achievement domain are randomly assigned to students in schools. These booklets have to meet certain specifications. For example, we often want them to have a minimum overlap in items to be able to estimate correlations between scales covered by different booklets.

In the educational assessment literature, a *balanced incomplete-block design* (BIB design) consists of preassembled blocks of items assigned to booklets according to certain principles. (Unfortunately, the use of this term is not entirely in agreement with the experimental-design literature.) These principles can be viewed as constraints on the following design parameters:

1. number of blocks assigned to each booklet;

2. number of booklets to which each block is assigned;

3. number of booklets to which each pair of blocks is assigned.

An example of a BIB design from the 1996 NAEP Grade 8 Mathematics Project with 13 blocks of items, 26 booklets, and each pair of blocks assigned to at least one booklet is given in Table 6.2.

Although it is already difficult to assemble test booklets for a BIB design if a large number of content constraints have to be imposed, an even more challenging task is to optimize such designs (for example, to assemble the booklets such that an optimal match exists between the difficulties of the items and prior knowledge of the ability distributions of the schools in certain strata in the population). Optimization becomes possible if the task is modeled as an MIP problem.

Let $b = 1, ..., B$ denote the booklets that are to be assembled from blocks $j = 1, ..., N$. Because we have constraints on the assignment of pairs of blocks, we need a second index, $k = 1, ..., N$, for the blocks. The decision variables necessary to model the problem are

$$x_{jb} = \begin{cases} 1 & \text{if block } j \text{ is assigned to booklet } b \\ 0 & \text{otherwise,} \end{cases} \quad (6.54)$$

$$z_{jkb} = \begin{cases} 1 & \text{if the pair of blocks } (j, k) \text{ is assigned to booklet } b \\ 0 & \text{otherwise.} \end{cases} \quad (6.55)$$

A BIB design requires the following set of constraints in the model:

$$\sum_{j=1}^{N} x_{jb} \gtreqless \kappa_1, \quad \text{for all } b, \quad (6.56)$$

$$\sum_{b=1}^{B} x_{jb} \gtreqless \kappa_2, \quad \text{for all } j, \quad (6.57)$$

$$\sum_{b=1}^{B} z_{jkb} \gtreqless \kappa_3, \quad \text{for all } j < k, \quad (6.58)$$

Booklets	Blocks												
	1	2	3	4	5	6	7	8	9	10	11	12	13
1				X	X				X				
2				X				X			X		
3		X		X								X	
4	X				X			X					
5				X						X			X
6							X				X	X	
7	X		X						X				
8	X			X			X						
9		X			X					X			
10							X	X		X			
11						X		X					X
12	X									X	X		
13				X	X	X							
14					X							X	X
15			X							X		X	
16			X	X							X		
17		X					X		X				
18			X	X		X							
19			X	X					X				
20	X	X											X
21			X				X						X
22			X			X					X		
23									X		X		X
24							X	X				X	
25	X					X						X	
26						X			X	X			

TABLE 6.2. Feasible BIB design for the 1996 NAEP Grade 8 Mathematics Project.

$$2z_{jkb} \leq x_{jb} + x_{kb}, \quad \text{for all } b \text{ and } j < k, \tag{6.59}$$

$$z_{jkb} \geq x_{jb} + x_{kb} - 1 \quad \text{for all } b \text{ and } j < k, \tag{6.60}$$

$$x_{jb} \in \{0, 1\}, \quad \text{for all } b \text{ and } j, \tag{6.61}$$

$$z_{jkb} \in \{0, 1\}, \quad \text{for all } b \text{ and } j < k. \tag{6.62}$$

The constraints in (6.56) require that the number of blocks per booklet satisfy bounds κ_1, the constraints in (6.57) impose bounds κ_2 on the number of booklets per block, and the constraints in (6.58) impose bounds κ_3 on the number of booklets per pair of blocks. To qualify as a BIB design, at a minimum, (6.58) should contain a lower bound larger than or equal to one on the number of booklets for each pair of blocks. The constraints in (6.59) and (6.60) are necessary to make the assignment consistent; they guarantee that the pair of blocks (j, k) is assigned if and only if the individual blocks j and k are. Observe that these constraints have the same form as the item-overlap constraints in (6.22) and (6.23). The last two constraints in the model define the ranges of the variables.

The objective function for the model has to be formulated using the decision variables x_{jb} and/or z_{jkb}. Also, in a real-life application the model has to be extended with a set of content constraints on the booklets.

The approach is based on the assumption that the items in the pool have been prepackaged in blocks. This practice is often followed to guarantee a balanced composition of the booklets and/or to make them fit a uniform time slot available for administering the booklets. But this step is not necessary. Such constraints can also be met if the booklets are assembled directly from the pool. As a matter of fact, as we will see in the empirical example with a BIB design below, prepackaging items in blocks is a strategy that forces us to give up much of the leeway that otherwise could have been used for optimization.

6.6 Empirical Examples

Several examples of the assembly of multiple tests are given. The first two examples are for a set of three parallel forms of the LSAT. (For empirical examples with a much larger number of tests, see Section 11.5.3.) The item pool and the test specifications were the same as those for the problem of a single version with an absolute target for its information function in Section 5.1.6. In the first example, the three forms were assembled using the standard simultaneous approach in (6.3)–(6.13). The objective function was that based on the minimax principle in (6.14)–(6.17) with $w_t = 1$ for each form. The TIFs of the three forms are shown in the upper panel of Figure 6.2.

In addition, three parallel forms of the LSAT were assembled using the big-shadow-test method in Section 6.3. The method was implemented in two steps. At the first step, one form of the LSAT and a shadow test twice as big were assembled. At the second step, two additional forms of the LSAT were assembled. At each step, we used the same minimax principle in (6.14)–(6.17). The TIFs for this set of forms are shown in the lower panel of Figure 6.2. Both methods produced sets of tests with TIFs that were parallel for all practical purposes. In addition, it hardly appears possible to prefer the results for one method over the other.

The third example consists of a set of two tests assembled for a study with a pretest-posttest design. These two tests were assembled from the same LSAT pool and were required to satisfy the same set of constraints. We assembled these tests using the standard simultaneous approach in (6.3)–

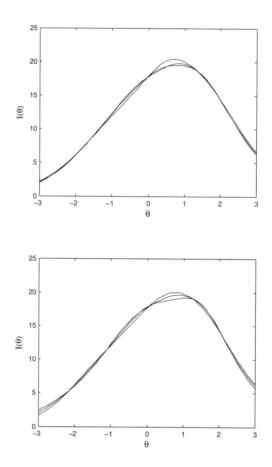

FIGURE 6.2. Information functions of three parallel forms of the LSAT assembled using the method of simultaneous assembly (top) and the big-shadow-test method (bottom).

(6.13). The only difference from the previous examples was that the posttest was required to have a TIF shifted to the right over a distance of 1.2 on the θ scale. The targets for the TIFs were realized using a generalization of the minimax objective in (5.14)–(5.17) to two tests with different targets. (See the description of this generalization at the end of the introduction to Section 6.2.). The TIFs obtained for the two tests are shown in Figure 6.3.

The fourth example consists of a set of seven tests assembled for a three-stage adaptive testing system with one test at the first stage and two tests at the second and third stages. The LSAT consists of three different sections,

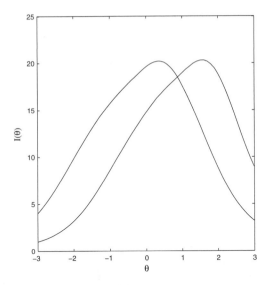

FIGURE 6.3. Information functions of two versions of the LSAT assembled for a pretest-posttest study with a shift in location equal to 1.2.

which were assigned to these stages in an arbitrary order. For the first stage, the test was required to meet 29 content constraints, and for the second and third stages there were 53 and 32 constraints, respectively. The first-stage test was required to meet a uniform relative target at θ_k =-1.2, 0, and 1.2. The assembly of this test was therefore an application of the maximin principle in (5.25)–(5.27) with $\mathcal{R}_k = 1$ for $k = 1, 2, 3$. The sets of three tests for the second and third stages were required to have single peaks at the same selection of θ values; that is, the TIF of the easy test was maximized at $\theta_k = -1.2$, that for the average test at $\theta_k = 0$, and that for the difficult test at $\theta_k = 1.2$. Each set of three tests was assembled simultaneously using a generalization of the same maximin principle with the same relative target values $\mathcal{R}_{kt}$ for each test.

The TIFs obtained for the seven tests are displayed in Figure 6.4. These TIFs thus have the maximum height possible given the sets of content constraints for the sections in the item pool. In addition, each of the TIFs has the shape we would expect for this multistage testing application. The differences in height between the TIFs for the second and third stages follow from the number of content constraints for these stages (53 vs. 32) as well as the number of items in the two sections of the pool available (240 vs. 305).

The last example consists of *post hoc* optimization of the design for the 1996 Grade 8 Mathematics NAEP project. An example of a feasible design

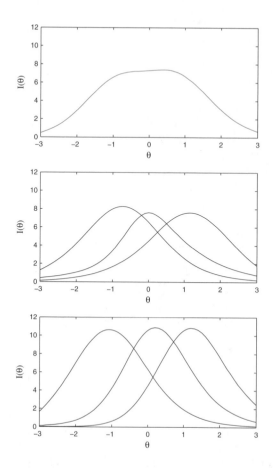

FIGURE 6.4. Information functions for a set of subtests for a multistage testing system (top: stage 1; middle: stage 2; bottom: stage 3).

for this study was already shown in Figure 6.2. The bounds on the constraints in (6.56)–(6.58) used in the project were an equality bound $\kappa_1 = 3$ on the number of blocks per booklet, an upper bound $\kappa_2 = 6$ on the number of booklets per block, and a lower bound $\kappa_3 = 1$ on the number of booklets per pair of blocks. In total, 26 booklets had to be assembled. We assumed that ten booklets had to be assembled to perform best for schools at the 50th percentile of the estimate of the national distribution found in the 1996 project and eight booklets each to perform best at the 25th and 75th percentile. To achieve this objective, we minimized the differences between the expected (relative) item scores at these percentiles and a target value of .50 using the minimax principle.

This example was one of the two reported in this book for which the MIP solver could not find a solution in reasonable time. It can be shown that for the total of 13 blocks and the values for the bounds in (6.56)–(6.58) the constraints could only be satisfied at equality for all bounds. In fact, we thus had a severely constrained problem, with huge numbers of equality constraints, and the reason why we could not find a solution is expected to reside in this nature of the problem. However, a solution was found using the method of simulated annealing in Section 4.5.2; for the implementation chosen for this method, see the references in the literature section at the end of this chapter.

The solution we found is shown in Table 6.3. All expected (relative) item scores for the three populations were in the range of .536–.836, with an average deviation from the target value equal to .217. A better solution would have been possible if the items had been assigned directly to the booklets. We would then have missed all implicit equality constraints on the composition of the 13 blocks and had much more space for optimization.

This might be a good point to remind the reader again that the most important results in the first four examples in this section are not visible in Figures 6.2–6.4. Exactly as required, each of the tests in these figures satisfied all of its content constraints.

6.7 Literature

Sequential approaches to the assembly of sets of parallel tests with a second stage of heuristic corrections were presented in Ackerman (1989), Wang and Ackerman (1998), Luecht (1998), and Luecht and Hirsch (1992), whereas Adema (1990b) explored a sequential approach to the problem of assembling a set of tests for a two-stage testing system.

The first to investigate a simultaneous approach to the problem of assembling a set of parallel tests was Boekkooi-Timminga (1987). A simultaneous approach with test information controlled by constraints was given in Glas (1988); his application was to construct a set of tests with equal accuracy of measurement at a common cutoff score. Sanders and Verschoor (1998) used a simultaneous approach to assemble a set of tests to be item-by-item parallel in their classical item indices. Their method was a generalization of the test-splitting method in Section 5.4.2.

The big-shadow-test method has its origins in Adema (1990a, chapter 5), where it was applied to solve the problem of assembling a set of parallel tests. The method was generalized in van der Linden (1998c) and van der Linden and Adema (1998) to deal with any type of multiple-test assembly. These authors used the name "dummy-test approach" for the method; it

Booklet	Blocks												
	1	2	3	4	5	6	7	8	9	10	11	12	13
1	x									x	x		
2						x		x			x		
3		x				x						x	
4							x		x	x			
5		x				x					x		
6				x		x	x						
7	x						x	x					
8	x					x			x				
9											x	x	x
10					x		x				x		
11			x						x		x		
12			x							x		x	
13	x	x	x										
14	x			x								x	
15						x				x			x
16			x				x						x
17								x	x			x	
18		x		x						x			
19			x		x	x							
20						x		x		x			
21		x				x			x				
22				x					x				x
23	x					x							x
24		x						x					x
25				x	x						x		
26					x	x			x				

TABLE 6.3. Optimal feasible BIB design for the 1996 NAEP Grade 8 Mathematics Project.

has been replaced by "big-shadow-test method" in this chapter to emphasize its analogy with the shadow-test method for item selection in adaptive testing (Section 9.1). The generalization of the method to multiple shadow tests discussed in Section 6.3.1 has not yet been investigated.

A solution to the problem of assembling a set of parallel tests based on the idea of item-pool splitting was investigated in Boekkooi-Timminga (1990a). Network-flow formulations for the assembly of a set of tests with parallel information functions were given in Armstrong, Jones, and Kunce (1998) and Armstrong, Jones, and Wu (1992), whereas Armstrong, Jones, Li, and Wu (1996) compared the results of a network-flow approach with those by the Luecht heuristic. A network-flow formulation for the problem of classically parallel tests was published in Armstrong, Jones, and Wang (1994). Wu (2001) showed how simultaneous and network-flow solutions for the problem of assembly of sets of tests for use in a multistage testing system can be found.

The alternative method based on the idea of splitting one big single test into a set of parallel tests was explored in Adema (1992a).

An excellent introduction to the notion of balanced incomplete-block design in educational assessments is Johnson (1992). A more extensive treatment of the problem of optimizing sets of test booklets for use in educational assessments, with a discussion of alternative objectives, is given in van der Linden (1998c) and van der Linden, Veldkamp, and Carlson (2004). The latter should also be consulted for the implementation of the method of simulated annealing used in the empirical example in Section 6.6.

6.8 Summary

1. If a set of tests has to be assembled, the set typically is required to have one or more attributes at the multiple-test level. Examples of these attributes are the requirements that the tests be parallel, differ systematically in difficulty or information function, cover different collections of content specifications, and show a certain degree of item overlap.

2. If the tests are assembled sequentially, the procedure operates as a greedy heuristic at the level of the set of tests. Hence, the quality of each subsequent test can be expected to decrease quickly. It is possible to improve on a set of sequential solutions using a second-stage heuristic, such as one that swaps items between tests until a more satisfactory uniform result is obtained.

3. A second disadvantage of sequential test assembly is the possible infeasibility of later problems in the sequence. Effective second-stage heuristics for solving this type of infeasibility are not known.

4. Exact solutions to problems with multiple tests are obtained by solving a single model for the simultaneous assembly of the tests. A model for simultaneous assembly can be derived from any model for the assembly of a single test by: (i) replacing the decision variables by doubly indexed variables; (ii) generalizing the objective function over the set of tests; (iii) adding constraints to deal with item overlap; and (iv) choosing appropriate bounds in the constraints for each test. None of the features of the models for single tests met in Chapter 5 need to be sacrificed.

5. It is possible to specify bounds on item overlap in problems with multiple tests. If the bounds are on the number of items common to pairs of tests, the operation entails the necessity of an additional set

of decision variables for each pair and large numbers of additional constraints in the model. Such bounds therefore lead to a strong increase in problem size.

6. If problems with multiple tests become too large, an appropriate backup method is the big-shadow-test method. This method solves the problem as a sequence of smaller simultaneous problems. At each step in the sequence, a smaller set of tests is assembled along with one or more shadow tests representing the specifications of the remaining tests. The only purpose of the shadow tests is to balance the quality of the current and future tests and prevent the infeasibility of tests assembled later in the sequence.

7. Alternative backup methods for the case of assembling a set of parallel tests have been investigated. Each of these is based on the idea of splitting the item pool or a smaller collection of items in it. These methods do not seem to have the same general applicability as the big-shadow-test method, and their generalization to sets of nonparallel tests has not yet been explored.

8. The assembly of sets of test booklets for use in an educational assessment from a set of prepackaged blocks of items can be modeled as an MIP problem with constraints on the number of blocks per booklet, the number of booklets per block, and the number of pairs of booklets per block. Alternatively, the problem can be modeled as a multiple-test-assembly problem with selection of the items directly from the pool.

6.9 Exercises

6.1 Formulate the test-assembly model for the example in Table 6.1.

6.2 In Exercise 5.11, we formulated a model for a test with an item-by-item match between the values for the item-difficulty parameter and the values of a reference test. Formulate a version of this model for the problem of assembling T tests matching the reference test.

6.3 Formulate a test model for the assembly of two tests with different lengths but TIFs that are as close as possible at a set of points θ_k, $k = 1, ..., K$.

6.4 Formulate a model for the problem of assembling three parallel versions of a test of knowledge of psychological theory. Each test should consist of ten multiple-choice items on perception, ten constructed-response items on information processing skills, ten items on language formation, and no items that have been administered earlier more than a three times. In addition, the three tests should have maximum information at a cutoff score $\theta = 1$.

6.5 Suppose we want to assemble three 80-item tests from a pool of 700 items. We want the overlap between each pair of tests to be no larger than five items. Calculate the number of extra variables and constraints needed in the model to satisfy this requirement.

6.6 Formulate a version of the standard model for the big-shadow-test approach in Section 6.3 for the assembly of two regular tests and one shadow test of size $T - 2$. The model should only have the test-level constraints in (6.28)–(6.35).

6.7 Formulate a model for the network-flow approach in Section 6.4 for the assembly of a set of T tests with test-level constraints on categorical attributes $c \in C$. Add a test-level constraint on a quantitative attribute q to the problem. Would it be possible to add constraints on enemy items?

6.8 Formulate the set of constraints for a multiple-test problem for use in an assessment with a balanced incomplete-block design in which: (i) the number of blocks per booklet should not be smaller than 3 or larger than 4; (ii) the number of booklets per block should not be smaller than 5; and (iii) each *triplet* of blocks should be assigned to at least one booklet.

6.9 Formalize the objectives for each of the three stages in the example with the multistage testing problem in Section 6.6.

7
Models for Assembling Tests with Item Sets

Tests with sets of items organized around common stimuli are popular because of the efficiency of their format. By combining more than one item with the same stimulus, we are able to ask questions using more complex stimuli, such as reading passages, descriptions of cases, or problems with data in a set of tables or graphs, without having to sacrifice too many items for the test to meet the time limit. But the presence of such sets in the item pool complicates the process of assembling the test in the following ways:

1. Attributes at two additional levels in the test are possible, namely at the item-set and stimulus levels. Hence, new constraints to deal with these attributes have to be included in the model.

2. More than one set of decision variables is necessary to select both the items and stimuli in the test.

3. Logical constraints have to be added to the model to make the selection of items and stimuli consistent.

Attributes at the item-set level are typically of the same type as those at the test level. For example, they consist of the size of the item set, the distribution of item contents in the set, the average p-value of the set, and its total expected response time. On the other hand, attributes at the stimulus level often resemble those at the item level. They may include such types as content classification, word counts, and the presence of certain stimulus material (e.g., graphics). The presence of item-set and stimulus attributes not only leads to new constraints at these levels but to new constraints at the test level as well, for example, constraints on the total number of sets in the test and the total word count for the stimuli.

The use of special decision variables to deal with item-set problems was already touched on in Section 3.2.3, where certain items were assigned the status of a pivot item and their variables implied the selection of a stimulus as well. In the next section, we will generalize this idea and work with different sets of variables for the selection of items and stimuli.

The necessity of consistent selection of items and stimuli involves the following two logical requirements for each item and stimulus in the pool:

1. An item is selected if and only if its stimuli is.

2. If any of the items in a set is selected, a bounded number of them are to be selected.

Below we will show how to formulate these requirements efficiently; that is, with a minimum increase in the number of variables and constraints in the model.

The purpose of this chapter is not only to show how set-based test-assembly problems can be modeled and solved. How to do this has been known for some time, but until recently the complexity of the problems for a realistic item pool did not always admit a solution close enough to optimality in realistic time. To deal with this complexity, several alternative methods and heuristics were introduced. These alternatives are no longer necessary for the typical problem size in the current testing practice, but they do offer nice insights into the general solution strategies available in case we happen to run into a large problem. For this reason, we discuss a selection of them in Sections 7.2–7.5.

7.1   Simultaneous Selection of Items and Stimuli

In spite of the presence of item sets in the pool, the test-assembly problem still belongs to the domain of constrained combinatorial optimization. The only changes are that: (i) we now have to search the pool for an optimal *combination of items and stimuli,* and (ii) the constraint set becomes more complex. An efficient way to enumerate all possible combinations of items and stimuli in the pool (see Section 3.1) is by using separate sets of decision variables for each of them. In this section, we will demonstrate how these variables can be used to model the objective function and constraints that define an optimal feasible combination.

In practice, item pools sometimes have a mixed nature, and the test may be required to have both discrete items and items in sets. For generality, we present a model for the selection of items and stimuli for the mixed case. The special cases of fully set-based and fully discrete problems follow directly from this model.

We suppose the item pool has $S - 1$ sets with a stimulus. These stimuli are denoted as $s = 1, ..., S - 1$. In addition, the pool has a set of discrete items; we represent this set by a dummy stimulus $s = S$. The items nested under stimulus s are denoted as $i_s = 1, ..., I_s$. This nested type of coding reflects the structure of the item pool; we always know which items are in which set. It is for this reason that we do not need separate variables for the item sets. (But, as will be shown in the next section, an alternative approach with variables only at this level is possible.)

The decision variables are binary variables z_s for the stimuli and binary variables x_{i_s} for the items, which are defined as follows:

$$z_s = \begin{cases} 1 & \text{if stimulus } s \text{ is assigned to the test} \\ 0 & \text{otherwise,} \end{cases} \tag{7.1}$$

$$x_{i_s} = \begin{cases} 1 & \text{if item } i_s \text{ is assigned to the test} \\ 0 & \text{otherwise.} \end{cases} \tag{7.2}$$

Both the stimuli and items can have quantitative and categorical attributes. We use q_s and q_{i_s} as generic symbols for the values of stimulus s and item i_s for a quantitative attribute. A special quantitative item attribute is the value of the IIF for a person with ability level θ, which is denoted as $q_{i_s} = I_{i_s}(\theta)$ for item i_s. Subsets of items and stimuli in the pool that share a common categorical attribute are represented by sets of indices V_c^{item} and V_c^{stim}, respectively. Finally, in addition to the sets of item enemies V_e^{item}, we use V_e^{stim} to denote sets of stimulus enemies.

We present the standard model for a test-assembly problem with item sets and a quantitative objective function as a more general version of the standard problem with discrete items in Section 4.1. For lack of typographical space, we have to leave out the references to the items and stimuli in the descriptive labels we add to the constraints. If a constraint is defined on variables x_{i_s}, it is automatically understood to be on an item attribute or a higher-level attribute defined using item attributes; if it is on variables z_s, it deals with a stimulus attribute or a higher-level version thereof.

The standard model is

$$\text{optimize} \sum_{s=1}^{S} \sum_{i_s=1}^{I_s} q_{i_s} x_{is} \text{ or } \sum_{s=1}^{S-1} q_s z_s \quad \text{(objective)} \tag{7.3}$$

subject to possible constraints at the following levels:

Test Level

$$\sum_{s=1}^{S} \sum_{i_s=1}^{I_s} x_{i_s} \gtrless n, \quad \text{(number of items)} \tag{7.4}$$

$$\sum_{s=1}^{S-1} z_s \gtreqless m, \quad \text{(number of stimuli)} \tag{7.5}$$

$$\sum_{s=1}^{S} \sum_{i_s \in V_c^{\text{item}}} x_{i_s} \gtreqless n_c^{\text{item}}, \quad \text{for all } c, \quad \text{(categorical attributes)} \tag{7.6}$$

$$\sum_{s=1}^{S} \sum_{i_s=1}^{I_s} q_{i_s} x_{i_s} \gtreqless b_q^{\text{item}}, \quad \text{(quantitative attributes)} \tag{7.7}$$

$$\sum_{s \in V_c^{\text{stim}}} z_s \gtreqless n_c^{\text{stim}}, \quad \text{for all } c, \quad \text{(categorical attributes)} \tag{7.8}$$

$$\sum_{s=1}^{S-1} q_s z_s \gtreqless b_q^{\text{stim}}, \quad \text{(quantitative attributes)} \tag{7.9}$$

$$\sum_{i_s \in V_e^{\text{item}}} x_{i_s} \leq 1, \quad \text{for all } e, \quad \text{(enemy items)} \tag{7.10}$$

$$\sum_{s \in V_e^{\text{stim}}} z_s \leq 1, \quad \text{for all } e; \quad \text{(enemy stimuli)} \tag{7.11}$$

Item-Set Level

$$\sum_{i_s=1}^{I_s} x_{i_s} \gtreqless n_s^{\text{set}} z_s, \quad \text{for all } s \leq S-1, \quad \text{(number of items per set)} \tag{7.12}$$

$$\sum_{i_s \in V_c^{\text{item}}} x_{i_s} \gtreqless n_c^{\text{set}} z_s, \quad \text{for all } c \text{ and } s \leq S-1, \quad \text{(categorical attributes)} \tag{7.13}$$

$$\sum_{i_s=1}^{I_s} q_{i_s} x_{i_s} \gtreqless b_q^{\text{set}} z_s, \quad \text{for all } s \leq S-1; \quad \text{(quantitative attributes)} \tag{7.14}$$

Stimulus Level

$$\sum_{s \in V_1^{\text{stim}}} z_s = n_1^{\text{stim}}, \quad \text{(categorical attributes)} \tag{7.15}$$

$$\sum_{s \in V_0^{\text{stim}}} z_s = 0, \quad \text{(categorical attributes)} \tag{7.16}$$

$$q_s z_s \leq b_q^{\text{stim, max}}, \quad \text{for all } s \leq S-1, \quad \text{(quantitative attributes)} \tag{7.17}$$

$$b_q^{\text{stim, min}} z_s \leq q_s, \quad \text{for all } s \leq S-1; \quad \text{(quantitative attributes)} \tag{7.18}$$

Item Level

$$\sum_{i_s \in V_1^{\text{item}}} x_{i_s} = n_1^{\text{item}}, \quad \text{(categorical attribute)} \tag{7.19}$$

$$\sum_{i_s \in V_0^{\text{item}}} x_{i_s} = 0, \quad \text{(categorical attributes)} \tag{7.20}$$

$$q_{i_s} x_{i_s} \leq b_q^{\text{item, max}}, \quad \text{for all } i \text{ and } s, \quad \text{(quantitative attribute)} \tag{7.21}$$

$$b_q^{\text{item, min}} x_{i_s} \leq q_{i_s}, \quad \text{for all } i \text{ and } s; \quad \text{(quantitative attributes)} \tag{7.22}$$

Definition of Variables

$$x_{i_s} \in \{0,1\}, \quad \text{for all } i \text{ and } s, \tag{7.23}$$

$$z_s \in \{0,1\}, \quad \text{for all } i. \tag{7.24}$$

The constraints in this model should be interpreted as follows: Those in (7.4) and (7.5) control the length of the test, n, and the number of stimuli or item sets in it, m. The composition of the test is controlled by the constraints in (7.6)–(7.11). The bounds n_c^{item} and n_c^{stim} in the constraints in (7.6) and (7.8) can be used to obtain the required distribution of the categorical item and stimulus attributes in the test, whereas the constraints in (7.7)–(7.9) require sums of the quantitative items and stimulus attributes to meet the bounds b_q^{item} and b_q^{stim}. The constraints in (7.10) and (7.11) preclude the occurrence of more than one item from the sets of enemies V_e^{item} and more than one stimulus from the sets of enemies V_e^{stim}.

At the item-set level, (7.12) is used to impose bounds n_s^{set} on the number of items per set and (7.13) and (7.14) to impose bounds n_c^{set} and b_q^{set} on the categorical and quantitative attributes of the sets. These three types of constraints are logical; they are the only ones that involve both item and stimulus variables. The role of z_s on the right-hand side of these constraints is to impose the desired bounds only if stimulus s is chosen (that is, if $z_s = 1$); otherwise the right-hand sides are equal to zero and no item from the set is chosen. It is assumed that at least one of the constraints in (7.12)–(7.14) is used for each item set. Otherwise, the variables for the items and stimuli would not not necessarily be consistent.

Also, just as for the earlier constraints with the variables for the pivot items in Section 3.2.3, we can use (7.12)–(7.14) only to impose a combination of a lower and upper bound on the size of the sets or their attributes. If we have to impose a lower bound only, the best strategy is to add a constraint with an inactive upper bound; for example, we could set the upper bound on the number of items per stimulus in (7.12) equal to the size of the set available in the pool (see Exercise 3.6).

Finally, observe that z_s must be present in *each* item-set constraint. If we used these variables only in the constraints on the number of items per set in (7.15), which may seem a natural restriction, the total collection of item-set constraints would become inconsistent and the model would have no solution.

The two sets of constraints at the stimulus level in (7.15)–(7.18) and item level in (7.19)–(7.22) are entirely analogous. We can use (7.15) and (7.16) and (7.19)–(7.20) to include numbers of items and stimuli (bounded by n_1^{item} and n_1^{stim}) with certain special (combinations of) categorical attribute(s) in the sets V_1^{item} and V_1^{stim} in the test or exclude items and stimuli with undesirable attributes in the sets V_0^{item} and V_o^{item}, respectively. The constraints in (7.17) and (7.18) and in (7.21) and (7.22) impose upper and lower bounds on the values of the individual stimuli and items in the tests for the quantitative attributes q_s and q_{i_s}, respectively.

As for the choice of objective, two different types of quantitative functions are offered in (7.3), one in terms of the item variables and one in terms of the stimulus variables. These two types have been given to show that the degree of adaptation of the earlier objective functions in Chapter 3 of this book necessary to deal with the presence of item sets is minor. If the objective function is defined in terms of the item variables, usually the introduction of the double sum in (7.3) suffices, and the formulation of a function of stimulus variables is straightforward.

As a more substantive example of an objective function, a typical choice in the current practice of IRT-based large-scale testing is to assemble a test to a set of absolute target values for its information function. If we want to use the minimax criterion introduced for the case of a test with discrete items only in (5.18)–(5.21), the adaptation necessary to deal with item sets is

$$\text{minimize } y \tag{7.25}$$

subject to

$$\sum_{s=1}^{S} \sum_{i_s=1}^{I_s} I_{i_s}(\theta_k) x_{i_s} \leq T_k + y, \quad \text{for all } k, \tag{7.26}$$

$$\sum_{s=1}^{S} \sum_{i_s=1}^{I_s} I_{i_s}(\theta_k) x_{i_s} \geq T_k - y, \quad \text{for all } k, \tag{7.27}$$

$$y \geq 0. \tag{7.28}$$

7.2   Power-Set Method

An alternative formulation of the problem of set-based test assembly is discussed in this section. It leads to a model with different variables and constraints that is nevertheless equivalent to the method in Section 7.1 in the sense that it has exactly the same optimal solution (provided there is a unique solution). We return to the discussion of the exact differences between the two models at the end of this section.

This alternative formulation is based on a conceptual reorganization of the item pool, in which each item set is replaced by the collection of all possible subsets of it. Because in set theory the collection of all possible subsets of a set is known as its power set, we call this method the *power-set method*. The test-assembly problem can then be reformulated as that of selecting an optimal combination of subsets from the pool that has to meet a set of constraints. The constraint set has to include the requirement that we select no more than one subset for each of the stimuli $s = 1, ..., S - 1$. If the size of the item sets in the test is bounded, which often is the case in practice, we can restrict ourselves to a pool consisting of the set of all *feasible* subsets for every stimulus s; that is, subsets that meet the given bounds on their size. This step permits us to reduce the number of variables, which easily becomes prohibitively large in this approach.

We denote the subsets for stimulus s as $p_s = 1, 2, ..., P_s$. Index p_s is thus the pth element in the power set for stimulus $s = 1, ..., S - 1$. We formulate the model for the mixed case with item sets and discrete items and keep dummy stimulus S to denote the set of discrete items in the pool. The 0-1 variables for the selection of subset p for stimulus s are denoted as z_{p_s}. In addition, we keep the variables x_{iS} for the selection of item iS from the set of discrete items. (Observe the capital S in the last two symbols and when we use them below.)

Because the pool now has subsets instead of sets, attributes formerly at the item-set or stimulus levels need to be redefined at the level of the subsets. The new definitions are as follows:

k_{p_s}: number of items in subset p_s;
q_{p_s}: sum of values for quantitative attribute q of items in subset p_s;
k_{cp_s}: number of items in subset p_s with categorical attribute c;
k_{1p_s}: number of items in subset p_s and attribute set V_1^{item};
v_{0p_s}: indicator variable equal to one if subset p_s contains an item from attribute set V_0^{item} and equal to zero otherwise;
V_c^{stim}: set of subsets p_s with a stimulus with categorical attribute c;
V_e^{item}: set of subsets p_s and items iS with an enemy relation;
V_e^{stim}: set of subsets p_s with stimuli with an enemy relation.

The power-set approach offers the following alternative to the model in (7.3)–(7.24):

$$\text{optimize } \sum_{s=1}^{S-1} \sum_{p=1}^{P} q_{p_s} z_{p_s} + \sum_{iS=1}^{I_S} q_{iS} x_{iS} \text{ or } \sum_{s=1}^{S-1} \sum_{p=1}^{P} r_{p_s} z_{p_s} \quad \text{(objective)}$$
(7.29)

subject to possible constraints at the following levels:

Test Level

$$\sum_{s=1}^{S-1} \sum_{p=1}^{P} k_{p_s} z_{p_s} + \sum_{iS=1}^{I_S} x_{iS} \gtrless n, \quad \text{(number of items)} \quad (7.30)$$

$$\sum_{s=1}^{S-1} \sum_{p=1}^{P} z_{p_s} \gtrless m, \quad \text{(number of stimuli)} \quad (7.31)$$

$$\sum_{s=1}^{S-1} \sum_{p=1}^{P} k_{cp_s} z_{p_s} + \sum_{iS \in V_c^{\text{item}}} x_{iS} \gtrless n_c^{\text{item}}, \quad \text{for all } c, \quad \text{(categorical attributes)}$$
(7.32)

$$\sum_{s=1}^{S-1} \sum_{p=1}^{P} q_{p_s} z_{p_s} + \sum_{iS=1}^{I_S} q_{iS} x_{iS} \gtrless b_q^{\text{item}}, \quad \text{(quantitative attributes)} \quad (7.33)$$

$$\sum_{p_s \in V_c^{\text{stim}}} z_{p_s} \gtreqless n_c^{\text{stim}}, \quad \text{for all } c, \quad \text{(categorical attributes)} \tag{7.34}$$

$$\sum_{s=1}^{S-1} \sum_{p=1}^{P} q_s z_{p_s} \gtreqless b_q^{\text{stim}}, \quad \text{(quantitative attributes)} \tag{7.35}$$

$$\sum_{p_s \in V_e^{\text{item}}} z_{p_s} + \sum_{i_S \in V_e^{\text{item}}} x_{i_S} \leq 1, \quad \text{for all } e, \quad \text{(enemy items)} \tag{7.36}$$

$$\sum_{p_s \in V_e^{\text{stim}}} z_{p_s} \leq 1, \quad \text{for all } e; \quad \text{(enemy stimuli)} \tag{7.37}$$

Item-Set/Stimulus Level

$$\sum_{p=1}^{P} z_{p_s} \leq 1 \quad \text{for all } s \leq S - 1, \quad \text{(at most one set per stimulus)} \tag{7.38}$$

$$\sum_{p=1}^{P} k_{cp_s} z_{p_s} \gtreqless n_c^{\text{set}}, \quad \text{for all } c \text{ and } s \leq S - 1, \quad \text{(categorical attributes)} \tag{7.39}$$

$$\sum_{p=1}^{P} q_{p_s} z_{p_s} \gtreqless b_q^{\text{set}}, \quad \text{for all } s \leq S - 1, \quad \text{(quantitative attributes)} \tag{7.40}$$

$$\sum_{s \in V_1^{\text{stim}}} \sum_{p=1}^{P} z_{p_s} = n_1^{\text{stim}}, \quad \text{(categorical attributes)} \tag{7.41}$$

$$\sum_{s \in V_0^{\text{stim}}} \sum_{p=1}^{P} z_{p_s} = 0, \quad \text{(categorical attributes)} \tag{7.42}$$

$$q_s z_{p_s} \leq b_q^{\text{stim,max}} \quad \text{for all } p \text{ and } s \leq S - 1, \quad \text{(quantitative attributes)} \tag{7.43}$$

$$b_q^{\text{stim,min}} z_{p_s} \leq q_s \quad \text{for all } p \text{ and } s \leq S - 1; \quad \text{(quantitative attributes)} \tag{7.44}$$

Item Level

$$\sum_{s=1}^{S-1} \sum_{p=1}^{P} k_{1p_s} z_{p_s} + \sum_{i_S \in V_1^{\text{item}}}^{I_S} x_{i_S} = n_1^{\text{item}}, \quad \text{(categorical attributes)} \tag{7.45}$$

$$\sum_{s=1}^{S-1} \sum_{p=1}^{P} v_{0p_s} z_{p_s} + \sum_{i_S \in V_0^{\text{item}}}^{I_S} x_{i_S} = 0; \quad \text{(categorical attributes)} \tag{7.46}$$

Definition of Variables

$$z_{p_s} \in \{0,1\}, \quad \text{for all } i, \tag{7.47}$$

$$x_{i_S} \in \{0,1\}, \quad \text{for all } i_S. \tag{7.48}$$

The differences between this model and that in the previous section are:

1. Nearly all expressions are defined in terms of subset variables z_{p_s}; the only other variables are the variables x_{i_S} for the discrete items in the set S.

2. The constraints in (7.38) have been added to the model to guarantee that for each stimulus no more than one subset in the pool is chosen.

3. As all items have been prepackaged in possible item sets with an associated stimulus, the selection of items and stimuli is coordinated implicitly. Hence, the model no longer contains the logical constraints in (7.12)–(7.14).

4. For the same reason, the earlier distinction between constraints at the item-set and stimulus levels disappears. The constraints in (7.38)–(7.40) contain sums over p for each s. However, because (7.38) admits a value $z_{p_s} = 1$ for no more than one value of p, (7.39) and (7.40) are in fact equivalent to the earlier item-set-level constraints.

5. We have left the item-level constraints in (7.21) and (7.22) out of the model and assumed that they were met when formulating the subsets p_s and set of discrete items S.

With a power-set approach, the objective with absolute target values for the TIF in (7.25)–(7.28) requires the definition of a subset information function for each p_s, which is simply the sum of its IIFs. Denoting this function as $I_{p_s}(\theta_k)$, the constraints in (7.26) and (7.27) become

$$\sum_{s=1}^{S-1} I_{p_s}(\theta_k) z_{p_s} + \sum_{i_S=1}^{S} I_{i_S}(\theta_k) x_{i_S} \leq \mathcal{T}_k + y, \quad \text{for all } k, \tag{7.49}$$

$$\sum_{s=1}^{S-1} I_{p_s}(\theta_k) z_{p_s} + \sum_{i_S=1}^{S} I_{i_S}(\theta_k) x_{i_S} \geq \mathcal{T}_k - y, \quad \text{for all } k. \tag{7.50}$$

As already observed, in spite of the different variables and expressions, the current and previous models are entirely equivalent in the sense that if a unique solution exists for a problem, either model will return it. As both the number of variables and the number of constraints in the power-set method are much larger, the simultaneous model in (7.3)–(7.24) is more efficient and should be preferred.

7.3   Edited-Set Method

To implement the power-set approach, the item pool has to be preprocessed; each item set has to be replaced by its power sets or collection of all of its feasible subsets. The item-set attributes also have to be recalculated at the level of all of these subsets. It is possible to go one step further and ask test specialists to inspect the item sets and *edit* each of them in the sense of removing the least desirable items from them. If bounds on the size of the item sets in the test exist, the removal could be continued until each set meets its bounds.

As a result, the model for simultaneous selection of items and stimuli in (7.3)–(7.24) requires fewer item variables. If the sets have been edited to meet the bounds on them, we can also drop the constraints on the set size in (7.12). For the power-set method, we obtain a smaller collection of subsets, and the number of variables is also reduced. Observe, however, that in this approach, even if the sets are edited to meet existing bounds on their size, we still need to formulate the model for the collection of all possible subsets for each edited set; otherwise we would give up the possibility of selecting a smaller number of items from the sets in the pool.

As a matter of fact, it is always favorable to preprocess the item pool and remove items that are undesirable for some reason. The test assembler should be aware, however, of the fact that if too many items with critical features are removed from the pool, it may no longer be possible to find a test that meets all specifications. That is, the editing of the sets should not result in an infeasible problem.

7.4   Pivot-Item Method

The idea of using pivot items in set-based test assembly was already met in Section 3.2.3. Whereas, in the previous method, the least desirable items are removed from the sets, the pivot-item method starts at the other extreme by asking the test specialist to identify the most desirable item in the set. Formally, a *pivot item* is defined as an item that is always selected for the test if and only if its stimulus is selected. In practice, a pivot item is the item in the set that, according to the test specialist, has the best combination of attributes with respect to its stimulus.

For each set only one item needs to have the status of a pivot item. Let i_s^* be the index of the pivot item for stimulus s. Because of the formal definition of a pivot item, it holds for its decision variable $x_{i_s^*}$ that

$$x_{i_s^*} = z_s, \text{ for all } s. \tag{7.51}$$

We can therefore use the variable for a pivot item as a carrier of the attributes of both its stimulus and item set, and we can drop the stimulus variables in the model in (7.3)–(7.24). The only thing necessary to implement a pivot-item approach is to replace the decision variables z_s by $x_{i_s^*}$ throughout the model; no redefinition of attributes or constraints whatsoever is required. The constraints in (7.12)–(7.14) still guarantee that items and stimuli are chosen together as sets.

Test assembly with pivot items leads to a reduction of the number of variables in the recommended model of simultaneous selection of items and stimuli in (7.3)–(7.24). This reduction is not obtained at the price of any loss of flexibility; all previous types of constraints are still possible.

7.5   Two-Stage Method

In this approach, we split the larger problem of selecting items and stimuli into two smaller problems that are solved in two subsequent stages: a first stage of stimulus selection and a second stage in which the items for these stimuli are selected. The model for the first stage has only stimulus variables; the model for the second stage has a small subset of the original item variables.

Unlike all previous approaches, this approach is sequential. Therefore, all of our earlier warnings against sequential procedures (Sections 4.6 and 6.1) apply. The potential danger is unfortunate choices at stage 1 and, consequently, less than optimal results or even infeasibility at stage 2. Using effective heuristics tricks to minimize the occurrences of such choices is therefore essential.

In the next two sections, we describe a few tricks that could be followed in the first stage and formulate models for the two stages. For simplicity, we only address the case of set-based item selection; generalization to the mixed case of set-based and discrete items is straightforward.

7.5.1   Stage 1: Selection of Stimuli

The model for this stage can be best understood as a reduction of the model for simultaneous selection of items and stimuli in Section 7.1. To formulate the model, we need the following new definitions:

k_s: number of items in set s;
k_{cs}: number of items in set s with categorical attribute c;
q_s^{item}: sum of values of the items for quantitative attribute q in set s.

The model has the following standard form

$$\text{optimize} \sum_{s=1}^{S} q_s z_s \quad \text{(objective)} \tag{7.52}$$

subject to possible constraints at the following levels:

Test Level

$$\sum_{s=1}^{S} k_s z_s \geq n, \quad \text{(number of items)} \tag{7.53}$$

$$\sum_{s=1}^{S} z_s = m, \quad \text{(number of stimuli)} \tag{7.54}$$

$$\sum_{s=1}^{S} k_{c_s} z_s \geq n_c^{\text{item}}, \quad \text{for all } c, \quad \text{(categorical item attributes)} \tag{7.55}$$

$$\sum_{s=1}^{S} q_s^{\text{item}} z_s \geq b_q^{\text{item}}, \quad \text{(quantitative item attributes)} \tag{7.56}$$

$$\sum_{s \in V_c^{\text{stim}}} z_s \geq n_c^{\text{stim}}, \quad \text{for all } c, \quad \text{(categorical stimulus attributes)} \tag{7.57}$$

$$\sum_{s=1}^{S} q_s z_s \geq b_q^{\text{stim}}, \quad \text{(quantitative stimulus attributes)} \tag{7.58}$$

$$\sum_{s \in V_e^{\text{stim}}} z_s \leq 1, \quad \text{for all } e; \quad \text{(enemy stimuli)} \tag{7.59}$$

Stimulus Level

$$n_s^{\text{set}} z_s \leq k_s, \quad \text{for all } s, \quad \text{(number of items per set)} \tag{7.60}$$

$$n_c^{\text{set}} z_s \leq k_{cs}, \quad \text{for all } c \text{ and } s, \quad \text{(categorical item attributes)} \tag{7.61}$$

$$b_q^{\text{set}} z_s \leq q_s^{\text{item}}, \quad \text{for all } s, \quad \text{(quantitative item attributes)} \tag{7.62}$$

$$\sum_{s \in V_1^{\text{stim}}} z_s = n_1^{\text{stim}}, \quad \text{(categorical attributes)} \tag{7.63}$$

$$\sum_{s \in V_0^{\text{stim}}} z_s = 0, \quad \text{(categorical attributes)} \tag{7.64}$$

$$q_s z_s \leq b_q^{\text{stim,max}}, \quad \text{for all } s, \quad \text{(quantitative attributes)} \tag{7.65}$$

$$b_q^{\text{stim,min}} z_s \leq q_s, \quad \text{for all } s; \quad \text{(quantitative attributes)} \tag{7.66}$$

Definition of Variables

$$z_s \in \{0, 1\}, \quad \text{for all } i. \tag{7.67}$$

The differences between this model and that for the simultaneous selection of items and stimuli in Section 7.1 are:

1. The model contains stimulus variables only.

2. All item attributes have been aggregated at the stimulus level. For example, instead of using a categorical attribute at the item level, we used the number of items with the attribute in the set, k_{cs}, as an attribute for its stimulus. Similarly, we used the sum of the values for the quantitative attribute of the items in the set, q_s^{item}, as the stimulus attribute.

3. Because of this aggregation, the original constraints at the item-set level in (7.12)–(7.14) now return as constraints at the stimulus level in (7.60)–(7.62). In point 5 below, we explain why we formulated these constraints with a lower bound and ignored possible upper bounds.

4. Some of the constraints in the original problem have been postponed until stage 2. These are the constraints on the enemy items in (7.10) and the entire collection of item-level constraints in (7.19)–(7.22).

5. All constraints at the test level, except those on the number of stimuli in (7.54) and enemy stimuli in (7.59), have been formulated with lower bounds. This measure is to maximize our degrees of freedom in stage 2. If upper bounds had been imposed, we might have constrained away larger sets with items needed later. If no lower bounds had been imposed, we might select sets that are too small and be faced with a shortage of sets in stage 2.

The objective function in this model has been formulated for a quantitative test attribute defined in terms of stimulus variables. If the actual objective is based on item variables, aggregation is necessary and q_s in (7.52) has to be replaced by a sum of quantitative item attributes. Some of the objectives discussed in this book entail one or more constraints with an upper bound on a quantitative attribute. For these, it is recommended to *average* the attribute over the items in the sets instead of summing them. An example of this averaging is given for the constraints with absolute target values in (7.26) and (7.27). These constraints are scaled down entirely to the item level as:

$$S^{-1} \sum_{s=1}^{S} \overline{I}_s(\theta_k) z_s \leq n^{-1} \mathcal{T}_k + y, \quad \text{for all } k, \tag{7.68}$$

$$S^{-1} \sum_{s=1}^{S} \overline{I}_s(\theta_k) z_s \geq n^{-1} \mathcal{T}_k - y, \quad \text{for all } k, \tag{7.69}$$

where $\overline{I}_s(\theta_k)$ is the average value of the IIFs for the items in set s at θ_k, and n is the intended test length. This measure is only necessary for stage 1. When in the next stage the items are selected, we return to the standard item-level formulation of these constraints (Exercise 7.5).

7.5.2   Stage 2: Selection of Items from Sets

In stage 2, the pool is reduced to a collection of m item sets. We denote these sets by the same index s as before, which now runs over $1, ..., m$. The items in set s are still denoted as $i_s = 1, ..., I_s$.

The standard model for stage 2 is

$$\text{optimize} \sum_{s=1}^{m} \sum_{i_s=1}^{I_s} q_{i_s} x_{is} \quad \text{(objective)} \tag{7.70}$$

subject to possible constraints at the following levels:

Test Level

$$\sum_{s=1}^{m} \sum_{i_s=1}^{I_s} x_{i_s} \gtrless n, \quad \text{(number of items)} \tag{7.71}$$

$$\sum_{s=1}^{m} \sum_{i_s \in V_c^{\text{item}}} x_{i_s} \gtrless n_c^{\text{item}}, \quad \text{for all } c, \quad \text{(categorical attributes)} \tag{7.72}$$

$$\sum_{s=1}^{m} \sum_{i_s=1}^{I_s} q_{i_s} x_{i_s} \gtrless b_q^{\text{item}}, \quad \text{(quantitative attributes)} \tag{7.73}$$

$$\sum_{i_s \in V_e^{\text{item}}} x_{i_s} \leq 1, \quad \text{for all } e; \quad \text{(enemy items)} \tag{7.74}$$

Item-Set Level

$$\sum_{i_s=1}^{I_s} x_{i_s} \leq n_s^{\text{set,max}}, \quad \text{for all } s, \quad \text{(number of items per set)} \tag{7.75}$$

$$\sum_{i_s=1}^{I_s} x_{i_s} \geq n_s^{\text{set,min}}, \quad \text{for all } s, \quad \text{(number of items per set)} \tag{7.76}$$

$$\sum_{i_s \in V_c^{\text{item}}} x_{i_s} \gtrless n_c^{\text{set}}, \quad \text{for all } c \text{ and } s, \quad \text{(categorical attributes)} \tag{7.77}$$

$$\sum_{i_s=1}^{I_s} q_{i_s} x_{i_s} \gtrless b_q^{\text{set}}, \quad \text{for all } s; \quad \text{(quantitative attributes)} \tag{7.78}$$

Item Level

$$\sum_{i_s \in V_1^{\text{item}}} x_{i_s} = n_1^{\text{item}}, \quad \text{(categorical attribute)} \tag{7.79}$$

$$\sum_{i_s \in V_0^{\text{item}}} x_{i_s} = 0, \quad \text{(categorical attributes)} \tag{7.80}$$

$$q_{i_s} x_{i_s} \leq b_q^{\text{max}}, \quad \text{for all } i \text{ and } s, \quad \text{(quantitative attribute)} \tag{7.81}$$

$$b_q^{\text{min}} x_{i_s} \leq q_{i_s}, \quad \text{for all } i \text{ and } s; \quad \text{(quantitative attributes)} \tag{7.82}$$

Definition of Variables

$$x_{i_s} \in \{0, 1\}, \quad \text{for all } i \text{ and } s. \tag{7.83}$$

The differences between this model and that for stage 1 are:

1. The model contains item variables only.

2. All stimulus-level constraints and test-level constraints on stimulus attributes have already been realized in stage 1. Consequently, they have been removed from the model.

3. In stage 1, all item-level constraints and constraints with upper bounds were omitted; in the current model, they have been restored.

4. The constraints on the size of the item sets with upper bounds in (7.75) and lower bounds in (7.76) have been presented explicitly. Although the latter were already imposed in (7.60), it is necessary to do so again in stage 2. If these constraints had been left out, the solution might contain fewer sets than required, compensating for the loss of sets by making some of the remaining sets larger than permitted.

7.5.3 *Alternative Version*

The preceding method involves a dramatic reduction of the number of variables in its models relative to the simultaneous model in (7.3)–(7.24). But the reduction in stage 1 is disadvantageous if we are left with a pool at stage 2 that no longer contains a feasible solution. The trick of removing all constraints with upper bounds in stage 1 minimizes the likelihood of this happening, but, like all previous sequential methods, no 100% guarantee of a feasible solution exists.

An alternative trick is to select a larger than necessary number of item sets in stage 1. The only thing required to implement this version of the two-stage method is an increase of the right-hand-side coefficient of (7.54) to a number larger than the m stimuli actually needed. As all other constraints are based on lower bounds, they need not be adapted. In stage 2, we select the final stimuli and items simultaneously using the model in Section 7.1, which is then defined over a smaller portion of the pool.

7.6   Empirical Example

To investigate the differences in performance among all of these methods, they were used to assemble the two sections of the LSAT with an item-set structure. These sections are labeled here as SA and SB. The composition

	Item Pool			Test		
Section	# Items	Stimuli	Set Size	# Items	Stimuli	Set Size
SA	208	24	5–11	22–24	4	5–7
SB	240	24	8–12	26–28	4	5–8

TABLE 7.1. Number of items and stimuli in the pool and needed in the test.

of the item pool used in this study and the required numbers of items and stimuli for the two sections are given in Table 7.1.

The only method excluded from this example was the power-set method (Section 7.2), the reason being the large number of subsets possible for each item set in the LSAT pool and, hence, the large number of variables this using this method would entail. For example, the item pool for section SB contained between 8 and 12 items for each set, whereas only 5–8 items per set had to be selected for the section. If we restrict ourselves to feasible subsets, the number of variables required for only one set in the pool would have been equal to

$$\binom{12}{5} + \binom{12}{6} + \binom{12}{7} + \binom{12}{8} = 3{,}003. \tag{7.84}$$

To account for all 24 item sets in the pool, the number of variables would have to be as large as 72,072.

For the methods with pivot items and edited sets, test specialists from the Law School Admission Council were asked to select the pivot items and edit the sets. As for the size of the edited sets, the specialists were free to stop removing items from them as long as the result met the bounds on their size in the test specifications (see Table 7.1). The alternative version of the two-stage method in Section 7.5.3 was implemented with twice as many item sets selected in stage 1 as actually required for the test.

For both sections, we specified an absolute target for their information functions. These targets are depicted in Figure 7.1, along with the information functions for the two pools scaled down to the required size of the test from the two sections. The figures show general agreement between the distribution of information in the pool and the distribution required for the two tests. For each method, five target values were specified at $\theta_k = -1.8$, $-0.9, 0, 0.9$, and 1.8. The targets for the two tests were approximated using the maximin criterion in (7.25)–(7.28). The total number of variables and constraints for the methods in this example are given in Table 7.2.

For each method, a feasible solution was found, except for the alternative version of the two-stage method, for which the collection of sets selected in stage 1 did not offer a feasible solution in stage 2. Inspection of the results showed that feasibility could be obtained by relaxing one of the item-set constraints in the stage 1 model; the only change needed was the replacement of an "=2" constraint by a less stringent "≤ 3" constraint.

The TIFs found for the two sections assembled are given in Figures 7.2 and 7.3. Both figures have separate panels for the results by the simulta-

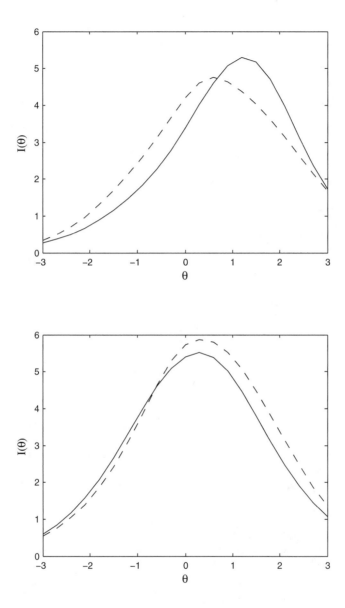

FIGURE 7.1. Pool information functions (dashed lines) and targets for section information functions (bold line) for sections SA (top) and SB (bottom). The pool information functions have been scaled down to the required section length.

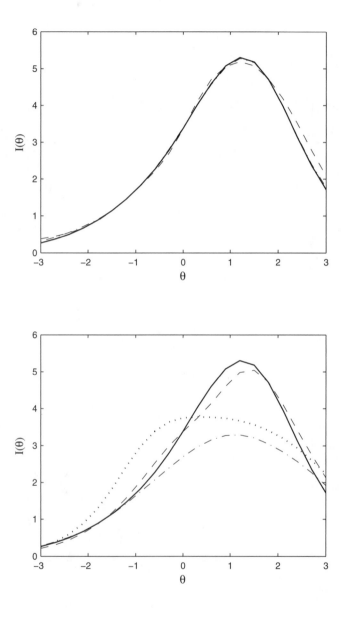

FIGURE 7.2. Information functions for section SA. Top: simultaneous method (dash-dotted line) and pivot-item method (dashed line). Bottom: edited-set method (dashed line), two-stage method (dash-dotted line), and alternative two-stage method (dotted line). The bold line is the target for the information functions.

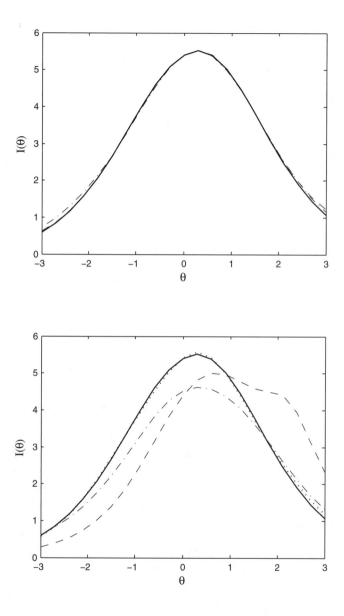

FIGURE 7.3. Information functions for section SB. Top: simultaneous method (dash-dotted line) and pivot-item method (dashed line). Bottom: edited-set method (dashed line), two-stage method (dash-dotted line), and alternative two-stage method (dotted line). The bold line is the target for the information functions.

Method	Variables	Constraints
Simultaneous Method		
Section SA	233	91
Section SB	265	109
Pivot-Item Method		
Section SA	209	91
Section SB	241	109
Edited-Set Method 3		
Section SA	25	41
Section SB	25	60
Two-Stage Method (Stage 1)		
Section SA	25	29
Section SB	25	37
Two-Stage Method (Stage 2)		
Section SA	33*	36
Section SB	37*	58
Alternative Two-Stage Method (Stage 1)		
Section SA	25	29
Section SB	25	37
Alternative Two-Stage Method (Stage 2)		
Section SA	74*	57
Section SB	88*	75

TABLE 7.2. Number of variables and constraints for each method. (Starred numbers are dependent on the output of stage 1.)

neous method and the pivot-item method (upper panel) and the edited-set method and the two-stage methods (lower panel). This division reflects our expectations: We expected the TIFs for the simultaneous method to match their targets nearly perfectly, comparable with the results for the earlier case of a single test for the LSAT without item sets presented in the lower two panels of Figure 5.2. For the pivot-item method, we expected a slightly less satisfactory fit; this method also involves simultaneous selection but with the additional constraints that four items from the set of pivot items in the pool be chosen (see the column with the number of stimuli in Table 7.1). Because this number of additional constraints was low, its impact was expected to be minor. Both expectations were confirmed by the results in Figures 7.2 and 7.3.

The edited-set method and the two versions of the two-stage method are heuristic methods. In addition, they entail extra constraints, which reduced the effective size of the item pool considerably. (See the column with the number of variables in Table 7.2.) We therefore expected the results to be much less favorable. These expectations were also confirmed. But, as the lower panels of Figures 7.2 and 7.3 show, there were important differences between the results for these methods. The best results were obtained for the edited-set method. The performances of the two versions of the two-stage method varied wildly: Both versions produced a poor TIF for section SA (Figure 7.3) but better TIFs for section SB, with the TIF for the alternative version of the two-stage method suddenly approaching perfection. The erratic pattern for this alternative version is typical of most heuristic methods of test assembly; it is generally impossible to predict with certainty how close their solutions will be to optimality.

7.7   Literature

There does not exist much literature on the problem of set-based test assembly. The same methods as in this chapter are discussed in van der Linden (2000b). The method with power sets was suggested in Swanson and Stocking (1993). Luecht and Hirsch (1992) incorporated the same idea in the Luecht heuristic. The method with pivot items was introduced in van der Linden (1992).

7.8   Summary

1. The problem of set-based test assembly involves a search for the best combination of items and stimuli in the pool that meets all constraints. To identify all possible combinations, we use separate decision variables for the items and the stimuli.

2. The problem also involves the necessity of new types of constraints to deal with test specifications that address the stimulus and item-set attributes in the test. As a result, the set of constraints is usually much larger than for a pool of discrete items.

3. Exact solutions for set-based test-assembly problems can be found using a model for the simultaneous selection of items and stimuli, with logical constraints to coordinate their selection.

4. The power-set method is an alternative method of simultaneous selection, which consists of the following steps: (i) forming all possible candidate sets from the item sets in the pool, (ii) aggregating the item attributes at the level of these sets, and (iii) formulating a model based entirely on the variables for the selection of these sets. This method does not need any constraints to coordinate the selection of items and stimuli, but it does require constraints to prevent the selection of more than one candidate set per stimulus.

5. Pivot items are items selected if and only if their stimulus is selected. The status of pivot item is assigned by test specialists evaluating

their attributes. If each set in the pool has a pivot item, we can use them as carriers of the properties of their stimuli and no longer need stimulus variables in the model. The use of pivot items thus leads to a reduction of variables but no loss of flexibility in formulating constraints.

6. In the method with edited items, we ask the test specialist to remove the least desirable items from the sets. This method leads both to a dramatic reduction of the number of item variables in the model for simultaneous selection and the number of set variables in the power-set method. This reduction may result in a less satisfactory result, however.

7. An obvious heuristic is to split set-based test assembly problems into two smaller problems that are solved in two different stages—a first stage in which the stimuli are selected, and a second stage in which items are assigned to the selected stimuli. This heuristic is sequential and may suffer from less than optimal results or even infeasibility in the second stage due to unfortunate selection in the first stage. Both outcomes occurred in the empirical example in Section 7.6 of this chapter.

7.9   Exercises

7.1 Reformulate the constraints in Exercises 3.2(c)–(f) and 3.4(c).

7.2 Use 0-1 variables for the selection of items and/or stimuli to formulate the following constraints:

   (a) The test should have no item sets with more than two items with a data display.

   (b) All stimuli with a newspaper clip should be in the test.

   (c) The average value for the difficulty parameter of the items per set should not be smaller than 1.5.

   (d) The total number of items on optics in the sets for stimuli 5–9 should not be larger than 2.

   (e) Stimulus 7 should be in the test if and only if stimulus 8 is in the test.

   (f) Stimuli 22 and item 8 for stimulus 27 should not be in the same test.

7.3 Use 0-1 variables for the selection of items and/or stimuli to formulate the following objectives:

(a) The total word count for the stimuli should be as close as possible to 750.

(b) Minimize the difference between the average readability of the items in the set and the readability of its stimulus.

(c) Minimize the total previous exposure of the stimuli in the test.

(d) Maximize the number of items with sets that are not required to have more than five items.

(e) Minimize the difference between the total number of items in sets and the number of discrete items in the test.

7.4 Use both 0-1 variables for the selection of the items and/or stimuli and, when necessary, auxiliary 0-1 variables ζ to formulate the following conditional constraints:

(a) The overlap between the items in the sets for stimuli 8 and 14 should not be larger than 3.

(b) The number of sets for which the number of items with a constructed response format exceeds the number of items with a multiple-choice format should not be smaller than 10.

(c) If a stimulus has more than one item with a majority or minority orientation, the number of items with a majority and minority orientation should be equal to one another.

7.5 Why should the quantitative attribute in (7.68) and (7.69) be averaged instead of summed? Why should we sum and not average in stage 2 of this method?

8
Models for Assembling Tests Measuring Multiple Abilities

At first sight, the problem of assembling a test from a pool calibrated under a multidimensional model may seem to involve a straightforward generalization of the objective functions for the unidimensional problems in Chapters 5–7. For example, if the model is the two-dimensional logistic model in (1.17), it may seem as if all we have to do is specify target values for the "test-information function" over a grid of points $(\theta_{1k}, \theta_{2l})$, $k = 1, ..., K$ and $l = 1, ..., L$, and define an objective function with respect to these values.

This impression is incorrect for the following two reasons. First, different cases of multidimensional test assembly exist, each going back to a different evaluation of the multidimensional ability structure in the pool. To choose an appropriate multidimensional model for test assembly, we first have to determine which case applies. Second, if the response model is multidimensional, Fisher's information measure in (1.19) and 1.20) does not remain the simple function of θ for a unidimensional model but becomes an *information matrix*. It is not immediately clear how to specify a target for this matrix, let alone how to assemble a test to meet it.

In the following sections, we first discuss five different cases of multidimensional test assembly from which we have to choose one before we assemble a test. The next section analyzes Fisher's information matrix for a multidimensional model and shows how to derive a set of linear objectives for the minimization of the variance functions of the ability estimators from it. In subsequent sections, we present the basic models for assembling a multidimensional test for an absolute and a relative target for these variance functions, and we show how to apply these models to the five different cases.

We also discuss generalizations of other types of objectives to multidimensional test assembly, including the objectives of matching observed-score distributions and matching a test item by item to a reference test. The chapter is concluded with an empirical example.

8.1 Different Cases of Multidimensional Testing

The fact that an item pool is sensitive to more than one ability is not always intentional but sometimes happens by accident; for example, because the test is taken by students who have been exposed to curricula with a different emphasis on different types of knowledge or skills. It can also happen out of necessity. This case arises when the ability of interest can only be measured by items with a format sensitive to another ability; for example, when an essentially nonverbal ability has to be tested by items with a verbal component.

Another reason why we have to distinguish between different cases of multidimensional test assembly is an ability structure for the test we may have in mind. For example, we may require the test to have sections for which different abilities are dominant. In a slight abuse of this term, which has a more precise definition in factor analysis, we will refer to the structure of a test with one dominant ability per section as a *simple structure.*

The cases discussed in the next sections therefore differ with respect to:

1. whether the abilities are intentional or a "nuisance";

2. whether or not the test should have a simple structure for its abilities.

For convenience, in this chapter, we assume that the two-dimensional response model in (1.17) has been fitted to the pool. The generalization to more than two abilities does not involve any new complications. Also, the differences between the models in this chapter mainly reside in their objective functions. As in the preceding chapters, we will therefore skip a discussion of the constraints needed to deal with the content specifications of the test. Any of the constraints met in a test-assembly models elsewhere in this book can be inserted into a model for a multidimensional problem.

8.1.1 Both Abilities Intentional

In this case, the item pool has been designed to measure two abilities. The test is scored with a separate estimate of each ability for each person. This case has hardly been used in real-life testing. But with the current advances in the statistical treatment of multidimensional response models, it is expected to become operational soon. One of the main advantages of this case over that of two separate tests measuring a single ability is an increase in the accuracy of scoring. This increase can be realized by using information on the correlation between θ_1 and θ_2 in the pool when estimating the values of these two parameters.

As will be shown below, the case of two intentional abilities can be solved using an approach based on the two-dimensional grid of points $(\theta_{1k}, \theta_{2l})$ proposed in the introduction to this chapter. The only difference is that we now have to derive an appropriate objective function over the grid from the information matrix for the two-dimensional response model.

8.1.2   One Nuisance Ability

As already noted, an item pool designed to measure a single ability sometimes appears to be sensitive to another ability. This other ability is then a nuisance in the sense that we would have preferred a pool that is not sensitive to it.

Ignoring the nuisance ability by trying to fit a unidimensional model to the pool does not work. The nuisance ability would then bias the scores and give the impression that some of the items in the test "function differentially" (i.e., show different response functions for subpopulations with different distributions for the nuisance ability). The only possible way to get rid of a nuisance ability is by acknowledging its presence, fitting a multidimensional model with a parameter for it, and ignoring the estimates of this parameter.

If an item pool measures a nuisance ability, tests from it should be assembled to optimize the accuracy of the estimator of the intentional ability. Contrary to expectations, we should not try to minimize the accuracy of the estimator for the nuisance ability simultaneously or to put a lower bound on it. We simply ignore this estimator, and the same should be done for its accuracy. Any attempt to also optimize or constrain a test with respect to the estimator of a nuisance ability is likely to result in a lower accuracy of the estimator of the intentional ability (Exercise 8.1).

8.1.3   Composite Ability

Sometimes an item pool measures more than one intentional ability but the test has to be scored by a single number. This happens, for example, because the tradition of a single score existed before the item pool evolved to multidimensionality or because the test is used for decision-making (e.g., selection) and the decision makers find multiple scores difficult to handle.

An attractive solution to this problem is to define a convex combination of the intentional ability parameters (that is, a combination

$$\lambda\theta_1 + (1 - \lambda)\theta_2, \quad 0 \le \lambda \le 1, \tag{8.1}$$

with weights λ and $1 - \lambda$) and score the test using an estimate of this combination. This solution forces us to be explicit about our weights for the two abilities instead of using implicit weights implied by some arbitrary score or by calibrating the items under a unidimensional model that does not fit the responses.

If the linear combination in (8.1) is chosen as the new parameter of interest, the test should be assembled to optimize its estimator. How this can be done will be shown below.

8.1.4 Simple Structure of Multidimensional Abilities

This case arises if all abilities are intentional and the test is required to consist of different sections with a different dominant ability. This structure is desirable if the test is released after it has been administered and the test takers are encouraged to inspect its items for an interpretation of their scores (see Section 1.2.7 on item mapping). They can then use a different section for each score. Observe that, although the scores can be interpreted best using different sections, they are still calculated from the responses to the entire test.

This case is one in which all abilities are intentional at the level of the test, but at the level of the individual sections one ability should be treated as intentional and the others as a nuisance. Assembling a set of different sections for a test with this structure is actually an instance of the problem of multiple-test assembly dealt with in Chapter 6. The only difference is the adjustment needed to deal with the multidimensionality of the pool.

8.1.5 Simple Structure of Unidimensional Abilities

If an item pool does not fit a unidimensional model, it can still consist of subpools that do fit such a model. If so, the notion of a test with a simple ability structure boils down to one of a test with sections with items selected from different subpools. A test with this structure has the same attractive possibility of score interpretation as the preceding case, but the scores are now calculated from the responses to individual sections.

This case also implies a multiple-test-assembly problem. However, because each section is assembled from a different pool, the sections do not have to compete for the best items in a pool. Therefore, simultaneous assembly is not necessary, and the sections can be assembled sequentially from their pools (see Section 6.1). Because this type of assembly is straightforward, we will not return to it in this chapter.

8.2 Variance Functions

For a dichotomous model with two ability parameters, such as the two-dimensional logistic model in (1.17), Fisher's information for a test of n

items is the 2×2 matrix

$$I(\theta_1, \theta_2) = \begin{bmatrix} \sum\limits_{i=1}^{n} a_{1i}^2 p_i q_i & \sum\limits_{i=1}^{n} a_{1i}a_{2i} p_i q_i \\ \sum\limits_{i=1}^{n} a_{1i}a_{2i} p_i q_i & \sum\limits_{i=1}^{n} a_{2i}^2 p_i q_i \end{bmatrix}, \tag{8.2}$$

where $p_i = p_i(\theta_1, \theta_2)$ is the probability of a correct response and $q_i = 1 - p_i$ the probability of an incorrect response. For the unidimensional case, the relation in (1.18) showed that the information measure is asymptotically equal to the inverse of the variance of the ability estimator. Analogously, for the multidimensional case, it can be shown that, asymptotically, the information matrix and the covariance matrix of the two ability estimators are one another's inverse.

Inverting (8.2) yields

$$\mathrm{Var}(\widehat{\theta}_1, \widehat{\theta}_2 \mid \theta_1, \theta_2) = \begin{bmatrix} \dfrac{\sum\limits_{i=1}^{n} a_{2i}^2 p_i q_i}{|I(\theta_1,\theta_2)|} & -\dfrac{\sum\limits_{i=1}^{n} a_{1i}a_{2i} p_i q_i}{|I(\theta_1,\theta_2)|} \\ -\dfrac{\sum\limits_{i=1}^{n} a_{1i}a_{2i} p_i q_i}{|I(\theta_1,\theta_2)|} & \dfrac{\sum\limits_{i=1}^{n} a_{1i}^2 p_i q_i}{|I(\theta_1,\theta_2)|} \end{bmatrix}, \tag{8.3}$$

where

$$|I(\theta_1,\theta_2)| = \left(\sum_{i=1}^{n} a_{1i}^2 p_i q_i\right)\left(\sum_{i=1}^{n} a_{2i}^2 p_i q_i\right) - \left(\sum_{i=1}^{n} a_{1i}a_{2i} p_i q_i\right)^2 \tag{8.4}$$

is the determinant of the information matrix in (8.2), which is assumed to be nonzero because otherwise (8.3) is not determined. (For example, this assumption excludes the case where $a_{1i} = a_{2i}$ for all items.)

The diagonal elements of (8.3) are the variances of $\widehat{\theta}_1$ and $\widehat{\theta}_2$ given (θ_1, θ_2). Observe that these variances depend not only on the ability parameter for their own estimator but also on the other parameter. The off-diagonal elements of (8.3) are the covariances of $\widehat{\theta}_1$ and $\widehat{\theta}_2$ given (θ_1, θ_2).

The two variances can be written more explicitly as

$$\mathrm{Var}(\widehat{\theta}_1 \mid \theta_1, \theta_2) = \frac{\sum\limits_{i=1}^{n} a_{2i}^2 p_i q_i}{\left(\sum\limits_{i=1}^{n} a_{1i}^2 p_i q_i\right)\left(\sum\limits_{i=1}^{n} a_{2i}^2 p_i q_i\right) - \left(\sum\limits_{i=1}^{n} a_{1i}a_{2i} p_i q_i\right)^2} \tag{8.5}$$

and

$$\mathrm{Var}(\widehat{\theta}_2 \mid \theta_1, \theta_2) = \frac{\sum\limits_{i=1}^{n} a_{1i}^2 p_i q_i}{\left(\sum\limits_{i=1}^{n} a_{1i}^2 p_i q_i\right)\left(\sum\limits_{i=1}^{n} a_{2i}^2 p_i q_i\right) - \left(\sum\limits_{i=1}^{n} a_{1i}a_{2i} p_i q_i\right)^2}. \tag{8.6}$$

We will treat these two variances as a function of (θ_1, θ_2) and use the name *variance function* for them. It is customary to assume that the test is long enough for these functions to approximate the actual conditional variances of the two ability estimators closely enough for practical application.

Graphical examples of the two variance functions in (8.5) and (8.6) for a small fictitious test are given in Figure 8.1. The values for a_{1i} in this example were approximately twice as large as those for a_{2i}; hence the lower surface for $\widehat{\theta}_1$. Both surfaces also have a "valley" that is typical of the two-dimensional response model in (1.17). The variances of $\widehat{\theta}_1$ and $\widehat{\theta}_1$ are relatively high if θ_1 and θ_2 are both small or large; that is, if the sum $a_{1i}\theta_1 + a_{2i}\theta_2$ in (1.17) is much smaller or larger than b_i for all items. In this case, the response probabilities approach 0 or 1, and the test is not informative. If the sum $a_{1i}\theta_1 + a_{2i}\theta_2$ approximates b_i for the items, the response probabilities go to .50 and the test becomes informative.

8.3   Linearization of the Problem

The two variance functions in (8.5) and (8.6) can be written as a function of 0-1 decision variables for the selection of the items. Division of the expressions in (8.5) and (8.6) by their numerator yields

$$\text{Var}(\widehat{\theta}_1 \mid \theta_1, \theta_2) = \left[\sum_{i=1}^{n} a_{1i}^2 p_i q_i x_i - \frac{\left(\sum_{i=1}^{n} a_{1i}a_{2i}p_i q_i x_i \right)^2}{\sum_{i=1}^{n} a_{2i}^2 p_i q_i x_i} \right]^{-1} , \qquad (8.7)$$

$$\text{Var}(\widehat{\theta}_2 \mid \theta_1, \theta_2) = \left[\sum_{i=1}^{n} a_{21i}^2 p_i q_i x_i - \frac{\left(\sum_{i=1}^{n} a_{1i}a_{2i}p_i q_i x_i \right)^2}{\sum_{i=1}^{n} a_{1i}^2 p_i q_i x_i} \right]^{-1} . \qquad (8.8)$$

The functions are not linear in the variables; it is therefore impossible to introduce them directly as objective functions in one of the approaches to multiobjective test assembly used earlier in this book. In the following sections, we show two different ways of transforming a multidimensional test-assembly problem with objectives based on variance functions into a linear model.

8.3.1   Linear Decomposition

Although the variance functions in (8.7) and (8.8) are not linear in their decision variables, they consist of components that do have a linear form.

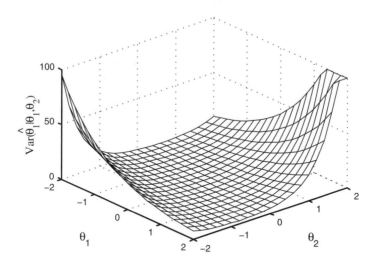

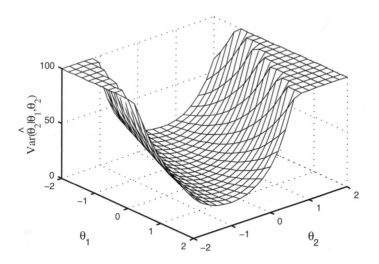

FIGURE 8.1. Examples of the variances function of $\widehat{\theta}_1$ (top) and $\widehat{\theta}_2$ (bottom) for a two-dimensional test, with considerably larger values for a_{1i} than for a_{2i}.

In fact, the functions remind us of the earlier problem of maximizing coefficient α in Section 5.2.1. Maximization of α also led to a function that was nonlinear but consisted of two linear components. In the model in (5.34)–(5.37) that we proposed for this case, one component was used as our objective function and the other as a constraint. A comparable approach is followed here.

If we want to minimize the value of the variance function of $\widehat{\theta}_1$ for a fixed pair of values (θ_1, θ_2), (8.7) shows that the items should be selected such that

$$\sum_{i=1}^{n} a_{1i}^2 p_i q_i x_i \text{ is maximal,} \tag{8.9}$$

$$\sum_{i=1}^{n} a_{2i}^2 p_i q_i x_i \text{ is maximal,} \tag{8.10}$$

and

$$\sum_{i=1}^{n} a_{1i} a_{2i} p_i q_i x_i \text{ is minimal.} \tag{8.11}$$

These objectives cannot be optimized simultaneously for a given pool of items. Particularly if our primary objective is to select a combination of items with a maximum value for (8.9), we are immediately faced with a trade-off between (8.10) and (8.11). Because the latter contains the products of the parameters a_{1i} and a_{2i}, a low value for (8.11) is only possible if the items have low values for a_{2i}; that is, when (8.10) also takes a low value. Since (8.7) contains the square of (8.11), if our interest is in the variance function for the estimator of θ_1, the best choice is to sacrifice the objective in (8.10) and choose items with low values for a_{2i}. Of course, the values of the difficulty parameter b_i cannot be ignored, but their role is minor. They have an impact only through the products $p_i q_i$ in (8.9)–(8.11), which typically show much less variation than the two discrimination parameters.

Observe that these three objectives (8.9)–(8.11) are symmetric in θ_1 and θ_2. If our primary interest is in minimizing the variance function for the estimator of θ_2, we have to select items with high values for a_{2i} and low values for a_{1i}.

This analysis suggests a test-assembly model in which we choose the minimization of

$$\sum_{i=1}^{n} a_{1i} a_{2i} p_i q_i x_i$$

as our objective and impose constraints on

$$\sum_{i=1}^{n} a_{1i}^2 p_i q_i x_i$$

and

$$\sum_{i=1}^{n} a_{2i}^2 p_i q_i x_i$$

with bounds that reflect our relative interest in the two variance functions.

8.3.2 Linear Approximation

Another approach is to minimize a linear approximation to a weighted sum of the variance functions. Let w_1 and w_2 be our weights for the accuracy of the estimators $\widehat{\theta}_1$ and $\widehat{\theta}_2$, respectively. The function that has to be approximated is

$$w_1 \text{Var}(\widehat{\theta}_1 \mid \theta_1, \theta_2) + w_2 \text{Var}(\widehat{\theta}_2 \mid \theta_1, \theta_2). \tag{8.12}$$

A standard approximation is that based on the first two terms of the Taylor expansion of (8.12) about the point $(\theta_{1k}, \theta_{2l})$. This approximation can be shown to result in

$$d_{1kl} \sum_{i=1}^{n} a_{1i}^2 p_{ikl} q_{ikl} + d_{2kl} \sum_{i=1}^{n} a_{2i}^2 p_{ikl} q_{ikl} + d_{3kl} \sum_{i=1}^{n} a_{1i} a_{2i} p_{ikl} q_{ikl}, \tag{8.13}$$

where $p_{ikl} = p_i(\theta_{1k}, \theta_{2l})$ and d_{1kl}, d_{2kl}, and d_{3kl} are constants calculated from the weights w_1 and w_2 and the partial derivatives of $p_i(\theta_1, \theta_2)$ at $(\theta_1, \theta_2) = (\theta_{1k}, \theta_{2l})$. This expression is linear in the items and can be used directly in an integer programming model for test assembly.

The criterion in (8.12) can be viewed as a weighted version of the A-criterion (see Section 4.7 and the discussion in Section 8.4.1 below). An attractive feature of the expression in (8.13) is that it is the result of a Taylor approximation to the criterion of D-optimality, too; the only adaptation necessary is a change in the values of coefficients d_{1kl}, d_{2kl}, and d_{3kl}. However, empirical research suggests that the approximation is not always satisfactory, and it is not yet known under which conditions we could rely on it. Besides, we are not in favor of approaches to multiobjective test assembly based on weighted combinations of objectives, especially if strong trade-offs between them exist. This is the case for the objectives in (8.9)–(8.11) because these expressions are controlled by common parameters a_{1i} and a_{2i}. The remainder of this chapter is therefore based on the linear decomposition approach in the preceding section.

8.4 Main Models

If we want to optimize each of the objectives in (8.9)–(8.11) over the grid points $(\theta_{1k}, \theta_{2l})$, with $k = 1, ..., K$ and $l = 1, ..., L$, the total number of objectives is equal to $3KL$. This number is much larger than in the problem of assembling a unidimensional test with K target values for its information function. It thus becomes critical to have explicit control over all objectives. For this reason, we prefer a model of the minimax type that minimizes the maximum of the expression in (8.11) over the grid points $(\theta_{1k}, \theta_{2l})$.

We will present two models, one for the case of relative targets for the two variance functions and one for the case of absolute targets.

8.4.1 Model for Relative Targets

The following model can be used:

$$\text{minimize } y \tag{8.14}$$

subject to

$$\sum_{i=1}^{I} a_{1i} a_{2i} p_{ikl} q_{ikl} x_i \leq y, \quad \text{for all } k \text{ and } l, \tag{8.15}$$

$$\sum_{i=1}^{I} a_{1i}^2 p_{ikl} q_{ikl} x_i \geq w_{1kl} \kappa, \quad \text{for all } k \text{ and } l, \tag{8.16}$$

$$\sum_{i=1}^{I} a_{2i}^2 p_{ikl} q_{ikl} x_i \geq w_{2kl} \kappa, \quad \text{for all } k \text{ and } l, \tag{8.17}$$

$$\sum_{i=1}^{n} x_i = n, \tag{8.18}$$

$$x_i \in \{0, 1\}, \quad \text{for all } i, \tag{8.19}$$

$$y \geq 0, \tag{8.20}$$

with $p_{ikl} = p_i(\theta_{1k}, \theta_{2l})$ and $q_{ikl} = 1 - p_{ikl}$.

The constraints in (8.15) require the expression in (8.11) to take values at the points $(\theta_{1k}, \theta_{2l})$ not larger than a common bound, y. This bound is minimized in (8.14). The constraints in (8.16) and (8.17) impose lower bounds on the expressions in (8.9) and (8.10), where κ is a fixed common factor in the bounds, and w_{1kl} and w_{2kl} are relative weights that control the shapes of the two variance functions over the points $(\theta_{1k}, \theta_{2l})$, $k = 1, ..., K$ and $l = 1, ..., L$, respectively. The values for the factor and weights are selected by the test assembler.

Choice of Bounds

As discussed in Section 8.3.1, minimization of the expression in (8.15) has a downward effect on the two expressions in (8.16) and (8.17). Because both expressions are constrained by lower bounds, we can expect the solution to be at or closely above these bounds. By manipulating the size of the weights w_{1kl} and w_{2kl} and the common factor κ, we have explicit control of all three left-hand-side expressions in (8.15) and (8.16).

As for the choice of weights, the following two principles hold:

1. The differences *between* the two sets of weights $\{w_{1kl}\}$ and $\{w_{2kl}\}$, with $k = 1, ..., K$ and $l = 1,...,L$, determine the relative heights of the two variance functions for $\widehat{\theta}_1$ and $\widehat{\theta}_2$.

2. The differences *within* these two sets of weights determine the relative shapes of the separate variance functions over the ability space.

The values for the weights w_{1kl} and w_{2kl} thus have no absolute meaning. The only thing that counts is their ratio. (Compare this with the discussion of the specification of relative targets for a TIF in Section 5.1.1.)

As for κ, the idea is to solve the model for a sequence of trial values for this factor and pick the solution with the pair of variance functions that best approaches our ideal. An obvious strategy for choosing trial values is to begin with a low value and continue with a series of increments until one of the lower bounds in (8.16) and (8.17) becomes too large and no feasible solution is left. If the range of possible values for κ is unknown, it is efficient to begin with a set of large increments. During a second stage, we can then zoom in, searching the neighborhood of the best solution for improvements. An empirical example of this strategy for a two-dimensional test-assembly problem with relative targets for its variance functions will be given in Section 8.6.

Criterion of Optimality

In Section 4.7 on the optimal design approach to test assembly, we discussed the criteria of D- and A-optimalities. The expressions for these criteria in (4.30) and (4.31) used in the optimal design literature were simple because they were for the independent estimators of a set of unidimensional ability parameters. However, if we have a model with multiple ability parameters, their estimators are dependent. This fact is demonstrated by the nonzero covariances in (8.3). The dependence complicates the criterion of D-optimality, which now involves minimization of the determinant of the covariance matrix in (8.3). But the criterion of A-optimality remains a simple sum of the variances of the estimators in (8.5) and (8.6).

The model in (8.14)–(8.20) along with the strategy of trial values for κ can be viewed as an application of a weighted version of the criterion of A-optimality. The weights are introduced to define the status of the abilities that the test measures; that is, to indicate which abilities are intentional and a nuisance.

Interestingly, the same model can also be used for an application of the criterion of D-optimality. The only change needed is manipulation of the bounds in (8.16) and (8.17) until we find a solution with the best values for the determinant of the information matrix in (8.3) over the grid of $(\theta_{1kl}, \theta_{2kl})$. We are not entirely in favor of this approach because it forces us to give up our explicit weights for the relative accuracy of the test with respect to the individual abilities it measures.

8.4.2 Model for Absolute Targets

If a new test has to be parallel to a reference test, the variance functions of both tests should be identical. From the values of the item parameters for the reference test, we can calculate its values for the left-hand expressions in (8.15)–(8.17). Let κ_{0kl}, κ_{1kl}, and κ_{2kl} denote these values. They can be used as absolute targets in a version of the previous model with (8.14)–(8.17) replaced by

$$\text{minimize } y \tag{8.21}$$

subject to

$$\sum_{i=1}^{I} a_{1i} a_{2i} p_{ikl} q_{ikl} x_i \leq \kappa_{0kl} + y, \quad \text{for all } k \text{ and } l, \tag{8.22}$$

$$\sum_{i=1}^{I} a_{1i} a_{2i} p_{ikl} q_{ikl} x_i \geq \kappa_{0kl} - y, \quad \text{for all } k \text{ and } l, \tag{8.23}$$

$$\sum_{i=1}^{I} a_{1i}^2 p_{ikl} q_{ikl} x_i \leq \kappa_{1kl} + y, \quad \text{for all } k \text{ and } l, \tag{8.24}$$

$$\sum_{i=1}^{I} a_{1i}^2 p_{ikl} q_{ikl} x_i \geq \kappa_{1kl} - y, \quad \text{for all } k \text{ and } l, \tag{8.25}$$

$$\sum_{i=1}^{I} a_{2i}^2 p_{ikl} q_{ikl} x_i \leq \kappa_{2kl} + y, \quad \text{for all } k \text{ and } l, \tag{8.26}$$

$$\sum_{i=1}^{I} a_{2i}^2 p_{ikl} q_{ikl} x_i \geq \kappa_{2kl} - y, \quad \text{for all } k \text{ and } l. \tag{8.27}$$

8.4.3 Applications to Different Cases

Because the weights w_{1kl} and w_{2kl} in (8.14)–(8.20) offer us explicit control over the relative size of the accuracy of the estimators $\widehat{\theta}_1$ and $\widehat{\theta}_2$, putting appropriate constraints on them is key to the applications of the model to the different cases of multidimensional test assembly discussed in Section 8.1. How these weights should be constrained in these cases is discussed in this section.

We will not discuss these cases of multidimensional test assembly for the model with absolute targets in (8.21)–(8.27). The only purpose of this model is to assemble a test to match a reference test, regardless of its ability structure.

Both Abilities Intentional

The case where both abilities were intentional suggests an application in which the weights w_{1kl} and w_{2kl} for the two variance functions are pointwise equal over the grid $(\theta_{1k}, \theta_{2l})$. This case thus amounts to a choice of bounds in (8.16) and (8.17) subject to the restrictions

$$w_{1kl} = w_{2kl}, \quad \text{for all } k \text{ and } l. \tag{8.28}$$

Otherwise, the values for w_{1kl} and w_{2kl} can be chosen to produce the common shape for the variance functions we have in mind; for instance, weights that produce lower variance functions where the majority of the persons are expected, or lower functions at lower values of $(\theta_{1k}, \theta_{2l})$ because the test is used for diagnosing test takers with poor performances.

One Nuisance Ability

If the pool is sensitive to a nuisance ability, we should ignore this ability and introduce a target only for the intentional ability. If θ_2 is the nuisance ability, all we have to do is to set

$$w_{2kl} = 0, \quad \text{for all } k \text{ and } l, \tag{8.29}$$

that is, guarantee that the constraints for the estimator of this ability in (8.17) cannot become active. If positive values for w_{2kl} were selected, these constraints could become active, and the result for the variance function for $\widehat{\theta}_1$ would be less favorable. (See the discussion of ignoring variance functions for nuisance abilities in Section 8.1.2.)

Composite Ability

The model in (8.14)–(8.20) was developed for separate variance functions for the two ability estimators and not for a single variance function for a composite ability. As a simple estimator of the linear composite in (8.1), a plug-in estimator can be chosen; that is, the same linear combination of the individual estimators, $\lambda\widehat{\theta}_1 + (1-\lambda)\widehat{\theta}_2$. The variance of $\lambda\widehat{\theta}_1 + (1-\lambda)\widehat{\theta}_2$ given (θ_1, θ_2) is equal to

$$\lambda^2 \mathrm{Var}(\widehat{\theta}_1 \mid \theta_1, \theta_2) \quad + \quad (1-\lambda)^2 \mathrm{Var}(\widehat{\theta}_2 \mid \theta_1, \theta_2)$$
$$+ \quad \lambda(1-\lambda)\mathrm{Cov}(\widehat{\theta}_1, \widehat{\theta}_2 \mid \theta_1, \theta_2). \tag{8.30}$$

The first two terms in this expression are the variance functions in (8.5) and (8.6); the last term is the covariance function defined by the off-diagonal elements in (8.3).

This variance function is based on the same three expressions as in (8.9)–(8.11). Formulating a test-assembly model with this function is certainly possible. But it is easier to apply a transformation to the discrimination parameters in the response model that rotates the ability space to a space that has the composite ability $\lambda\theta_1 + (1 - \lambda)\theta_2$ as one of its dimensions. The case then becomes one with one dimension representing an intentional ability and the other a nuisance ability, and the model in (8.14)–(8.20) with the constraint on the weights in (8.29) can be used (Exercise 8.3).

Simple Multidimensional Structure of Abilities

We assume that the sections have been coded such that θ_1 is the intentional ability for section 1 and θ_2 for section 2. In addition, we use the index $t = 1, 2$ to denote the two sections of the test and use 0-1 variables x_{it} for the selection of item i for section t.

The version of the model in (8.14)–(8.20) needed for the case of a simple structure for the test is

$$\text{minimize } y \tag{8.31}$$

subject to

$$\sum_{i=1}^{I} a_{1i} a_{2i} p_{ikl} q_{ikl} x_{it} \leq y, \quad \text{for all } k, l, \text{ and } t, \tag{8.32}$$

$$\sum_{i=1}^{I} a_{1i}^2 p_{ikl} q_{ikl} x_{it} \geq w_{1tkl} \kappa, \quad \text{for all } k, l, \text{ and } t, \tag{8.33}$$

$$\sum_{i=1}^{I} a_{2i}^2 p_{ikl} q_{ikl} x_{it} \geq w_{2tkl} \kappa, \quad \text{for all } k, l, \text{ and } t, \tag{8.34}$$

$$\sum_{i=1}^{I} x_{it} = n_t, \quad \text{for all } t, \tag{8.35}$$

$$x_{it} \in \{0, 1\}, \quad \text{for all } i \text{ and } t, \tag{8.36}$$

$$y \geq 0, \tag{8.37}$$

with the following constraints on the selection of the weights in (8.33) and (8.34):

$$w_{1tkl} = 0 \text{ and } w_{2tkl} = 1 \text{ if } t = 2, \quad \text{for all } k \text{ and } l, \tag{8.38}$$

$$w_{1tkl} = 1 \text{ and } w_{2tkl} = 0 \text{ if } t = 1, \quad \text{for all } k \text{ and } l. \tag{8.39}$$

The differences between this model and the original one in (8.14)–(8.20) are:

1. The variables in the model have been indexed by the sections in the test.

2. The same has been done for the weights in the lower bounds in (8.33) and (8.34).

3. Extra constraints have been added in (8.35) to control the length of the sections.

Because of the extra index for the weights, we are able to formulate the restrictions in (8.38) and (8.39). These restrictions help us to ignore the estimators of the nuisance abilities at the level of the individual sections in the test.

8.5   Alternative Objectives for Multidimensional Test Assembly

In Chapter 5, in addition to models for the assembly of a unidimensional test for a target for its information function, we also presented models for classical test assembly (Section 5.2), matching an observed-score distribution for the test (Section 5.3), and item matching (Section 5.4). It does not make sense to generalize classical test assembly to the multidimensional case, but the generalization of the two other types of models to this case is straightforward.

8.5.1   Matching Observed-Score Distributions

The model for matching an observed-score distribution in (5.50)–(5.55) followed from a necessary and sufficient condition for two tests to have the same observed-score distribution. This condition, which was given in (5.47), was on the probabilities of a correct answer for the two tests. The condition is neutral as to the question of where these probabilities come from; they can be calculated from any type of response model, provided the two tests are calibrated on the same scale.

If the reference test is calibrated under a two-dimensional response model, the set of target values in (5.48) can be calculated as

$$T_{rkl} = \sum_{j=1}^{n} p_{ikl}^{r}, \quad r = 1, ..., R, \tag{8.40}$$

for $k = 1, ..., K$ and $l = 1, ..., L$, where p_{ikl}^{r} is the rth power of the response probability $p_i(\theta_{1k}, \theta_{2l})$ in (1.17) and R is the largest value of r adopted in the test-assembly model.

To assemble a test from a two-dimensional pool to match an observed-score distribution on a reference test (Section 5.3), we can use the same model as in (5.50)–(5.55) but have to replace the constraints in (5.51) and (5.52) by

$$\sum_{i=1}^{I} p_{ikl}^{r} x_i \leq T_{rkl} + w_r y, \quad \text{for all } k, l, \text{ and } r \leq R, \tag{8.41}$$

$$\sum_{i=1}^{I} p_{ikl}^r x_i \geq \mathcal{T}_{rkl} + w_r y, \quad \text{for all } k, l, \text{ and } r \leq R. \tag{8.42}$$

8.5.2 Item Matching

Generalization of the models for item matching discussed in Section 5.4 is also straightforward. In fact, if the items are matched on the item parameters in a multidimensional response model, the only thing we have to do is define the measure for the distance between two items in (5.57) on these parameters. Thus, if we want to assemble a test to be item-by-item parallel to a reference test or to split a test into two parallel halves, we should define this metric as

$$\delta_{ij} = [w_1(a_{1i} - a_{2j}) + w_2(a_{2i} - a_{2j}) + w_3(b_i - b_j)]^{-1/2} \tag{8.43}$$

for items i and j and select the appropriate model from Section 5.4.

8.5.3 Other Generalizations of Unidimensional Problems

Generalizing the models for multiple-test assembly (Chapter 6) and pools with item sets (Chapter 7) to the multidimensional case does not yield any new complications. An example of a model for the assembly of multiple multidimensional tests was already given in (8.31)–(8.37). If a multidimensional pool has item sets, we should use the same types of variables for item and stimulus selection and the same logical constraints to keep their values consistent as in the standard model in (7.3)–(7.24).

8.6 Empirical Example

The model for multidimensional test assembly in (8.14)–(8.20) was applied to a mathematics item pool for the ACT Assessment Program. The pool consisted of 176 items for which the two-dimensional logistic response model in (1.17) yielded a satisfactory fit. A 50-item test was assembled.

The two abilities were identified as an algebra ability and a geometry ability. The items in the pool were classified with respect to three algebra and three geometry areas, as well as three different levels of skill (basic skill, application, analysis). The model for the assembly of the test therefore had to be extended by nine constraints to deal with the existing specifications with respect to these classifications.

Both abilities were deemed to be equally important, and we settled on relative targets for the two variance functions with a flat shape over the ability space. It follows from (8.28) that these targets can be implemented by choosing

$$w_{1kl} = w_{2kl} = 1, \quad \text{for all } k \text{ and } l, \tag{8.44}$$

κ	μ	σ
.0	1.59	.92
.1	1.59	.92
.2	1.59	.92
.3	1.59	.92
.4	1.56	.83
.5	1.34	.51
.6	1.31	.38
.7	1.28	.37
.8	1.17	.32
.9	1.07	.28
1.0	1.06	.27
1.1	1.12	.29
1.2	1.20	.34
1.3	1.85	.48
1.4	*	*

TABLE 8.1. Mean and standard deviation of values of two variance functions. (Note: * denotes an infeasible solution)

for the weights in the lower bounds in (8.16) and (8.17). This choice effectively sets these lower bounds equal to κ. This common bound was imposed at the points $(\theta_{1k}, \theta_{2l})$ in the grid defined by all possible combinations of $\theta_{1k}, \theta_{2l} = -2.0, -1.8, ..., 1.8, 2.0$.

We ran the model for a series of values for κ with increments of .1 until the model became infeasible. This happened for $\kappa = 1.4$.

Since in each run of the model we obtained values for the two variance functions at a large set of grid points, we only report their mean (μ) and standard deviation (σ) in Table 8.1. A lower mean implies a lower height of the variance functions, whereas a lower standard deviation implies a flatter shape. The best results were obtained for $\kappa = 1.0$ with $\mu = 1.06$ and $\sigma = .27$.

Plots of the two variance functions for the test assembled for $\kappa = 1.0$ are given in Figure 8.2. The variance function for $\widehat{\theta}_2$ appeared to be flatter, while that for $\widehat{\theta}_1$ showed a slight upward curve for the higher θ_1 values over the entire range of θ_2 values. This increase in variance is the result of a combination of a relative scarcity of items in the pool with good discriminating power along θ_1 in this area in combination with an unfavorable ratio of the test length to the pool size.

It is instructive to diagnose the pattern in the solutions for the range of values for κ in Table 8.1. From $\kappa = 0$ through $\kappa = .3$, the constraints in (8.16) and (8.17) are not yet active at any of the points $(\theta_{1k}, \theta_{2l})$, and the solution remains the same. They then improve until $\kappa = 1.0$, for which

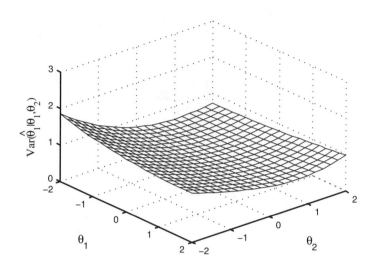

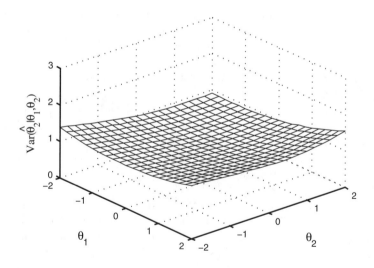

FIGURE 8.2. Variance functions of $\widehat{\theta}_1$ (top) and $\widehat{\theta}_2$ (bottom) for a two-dimensional test assembled to flat targets.

the best solution is obtained. After $\kappa = 1.0$, the constraints become more and more severe, and the solution deteriorates. When $\kappa = 1.4$, the model becomes overconstrained and no solution is left. The pattern in these solutions corresponds exactly with our motivation of the model in (8.14)–(8.20) in Section 8.4.1.

8.7   Literature

References to the multidimensional logistic response model used as an example in this chapter were given in the literature section of Chapter 1.

Not much literature on multidimensional test assembly is available. The different cases of multidimensional testing in Section 8.1, the linear decomposition of the weighted sum of the variance function in Section 8.3.1, and the ideas underlying the models in Section 8.4 have been introduced in van der Linden (1996). An empirical study of multidimensional test assembly from the point of view of multiobjective decision-making is given in Veldkamp (1999). The linear approximation to a weighted combination of variance functions in Section 8.3.2 was proposed in Veldkamp (2002); this reference should also be consulted for an empirical comparison between the results of multidimensional test assembly based on this approximation, a greedy heuristic, and a random method. More details on the model for multidimensional test assembly with a target for its observed-score distribution can be found in van der Linden and Luecht (1998).

The more challenging part of multidimensional test assembly is the establishment of statistical criteria for accurate estimation of the ability parameters. Once a criterion has been derived and linearized, formulation of a test-assembly model for it becomes relatively straightforward. Readers with an interest in the statistical treatment of ability estimation in multidimensional adaptive test assembly should consult Luecht (1996), Segall (1996, 2000), van der Linden (1999b), and Veldkamp and van der Linden (2002).

8.8   Summary

1. If tests are assembled from a pool with items sensitive to more than one ability, we have to distinguish between the cases in which (i) the abilities are intentional or a "nuisance" and (ii) the test is or is not required to have a simple ability structure. If all abilities are intentional but the test has to be scored by a single number, the best strategy is to score the test with respect to an explicit linear composite of the abilities.

2. For a response model with more than one ability parameter, Fisher's information measure is a matrix. The matrix is (asymptotically) equal to the inverse of the covariance matrix of the estimators of the ability parameters.

3. A useful objective for multidimensional test assembly is minimization of the (weighted) variance functions of the ability estimators, which are the diagonal elements of the (asymptotic) covariance matrix taken as a function of the value of the ability parameters.

4. This objective is a weighted version of the criterion of A-optimality in the optimal design literature discussed in Section 4.7. It is also possible to minimize the determinant of the covariance matrix—an objective known as the criterion of D-optimality in the literature. But we then lose our explicit weights for the relative accuracy of the test with respect to the individual abilities it measures.

5. To use this objective in an integer programming approach to test assembly, it has to be linearized. One possible strategy is linear decomposition; that is, choosing one of the linear components of the variance functions as the objective function and imposing appropriate constraints on the other components. Another strategy is linear approximation based on a Taylor expansion of a weighted sum of the variance functions.

6. The first strategy offers explicit control of the relative importance of the variance functions. The conditions under which the linear approximations in the second strategy are satisfactory are not yet known.

7. If one of the abilities measured by the test is a nuisance, the constraints for its variance function in the multidimensional test-assembly model should be made inactive. If our interest is in a linear composite of the abilities, it is convenient to rotate the ability space such that one dimension coincides with the composite and the other dimensions can be treated as nuisances. If the test is required to have a simple ability structure, a multidimensional version of a model for multiple-test assembly can be used.

8. Generalization of the unidimensional models for matching observed-score distributions, matching a test item by item to a reference test, and splitting a test into parallel halves in the earlier chapters to the case of multidimensional test assembly is straightforward. The same holds for the assembly of multiple tests and tests from multidimensional pools with item sets.

8.9 Exercises

8.1 Suppose one of the two abilities measured by a two-dimensional item pool is a nuisance. Use the objectives in (8.9)–(8.11) to explain why it may be disadvantageous to have a constraint or objective in the model with respect to this ability.

8.2 Suppose the model in (8.14)–(8.20) is formulated over a grid of points $(\theta_{1k}, \theta_{2l})$ consisting of all possible combinations of the values $(-2, -1, 0, 1, 2)$. Propose a set of weights $\{w_{1kl}, w_{2kl}\}$ for the case where: (i) the variance function for $\widehat{\theta}_1$ should have a flat surface, (ii) the variance function for $\widehat{\theta}_2$ should have a "valley" for $(\theta_{1k}, \theta_{2l}) = ((-2, 2), (-1, 1), (0, 0), (1, -1), (2, -2)$, and (iii) the surface for $\widehat{\theta}_1$ and the valley for $\widehat{\theta}_2$ should be at the same height.

8.3 Derive the transformation that rotates the ability space of the two-dimensional response model in (1.17) to a space with $\lambda\theta_1 + (1-\lambda)\theta_2$ as its first dimension. Why does this transformation not involve difficulty parameter b_i? Calculate the transformation for the special case in which θ_1 and θ_2 are weighted equally.

9
Models for Adaptive Test Assembly

In adaptive test assembly, items are selected from the pool in a sequential fashion. The response to a new item is used to update the test taker's ability estimate, and the next item is then selected to have maximum accuracy at the updated estimate. Adaptive tests are highly efficient. Extensive computer simulations have shown that to yield equally accurate ability estimates, adaptive tests require only 40–50% of the items needed for a fixed test.

Large-scale adaptive testing became possible in the 1990s when the computer revolution led to PCs that were powerful enough to perform real-time ability estimation and item selection at the testing site. Until then, adaptive testing had been restricted to an occasional experimental program run on a mainframe computer or to the use of approximate, computationally less intensive procedures for ability estimation and item selection.

One approximate procedure was multistage testing in which adaptation took place only at the level of a few alternative subtests, with estimation of θ replaced by simple number-correct scoring of the subtests. Also, to avoid the use of computers, experiments with paper-and-pencil adaptive testing at the level of the individual items were conducted using a testing format known as flexilevel testing. In this format, the test taker answered the items by scratching an alternative on the answer sheet, whereupon a reference to the next item on the test form became visible. The form was organized such that the difficulty of the items went up after a correct response and down after an incorrect response. The absolute size of the adjustments followed a predetermined sequence of numbers. This item-selection procedure, more generally known in statistics as a Robbins-Monro procedure, was also tried in the early computerized versions of adaptive testing.

At first, research on adaptive testing was primarily statistical and addressed such topics as the relative efficiency of adaptive tests versus fixed tests, alternative criteria for item selection, simplifying methods for updating ability estimates, the stabilization of ability estimators as a function of test length, and the impact of the choice of the initial item. But the introduction of large-scale adaptive testing in the 1990s marked the beginning of a whole new era of adaptive-testing research.

For one thing, it became clear that it was not enough for adaptive tests to be statistically efficient. In addition, they had to meet the same content specifications as their paper-and-pencil predecessors, which created a dilemma because when items are selected adaptively, each test taker gets a different set of items from the pool. Next, the issue of how to deal with adaptive tests from pools with set-based items quickly became manifest. An even more urgent new problem was item security. By its very nature, an adaptive-testing algorithm tends to capitalize on a small set of high-quality items in the pool; if the item pool is used for some time, those items become vulnerable to security breaches. An equally serious, though less generally understood, problem is that of differential speededness in adaptive testing. Since test takers get different sets of items, some may end up with a set that is very time-intensive, whereas others have ample time to answer their items. Finally, as the practice of releasing the items after the test became no longer affordable for adaptive testing, the question of how to use item content to report test scores in an informative fashion announced itself quickly.

The parallels between these early developments in adaptive test assembly and those after Birnbaum introduced his approach to fixed test assembly in 1968 are conspicuous. As was already pointed out in Section 1.2.8, Birnbaum's approach focused exclusively on the statistical aspects of testing, too. To become realistic, it had to be adjusted to problems with elaborate sets of content specifications and more complicated types of item pools. Moreover, the initial heuristic techniques for item selection developed to implement Birnbaum's method had to be replaced by flexible algorithms with optimal results. Basically, the same challenges were met again when the first large-scale adaptive-testing programs were launched in the 1990s.

In this chapter, we will show how the optimal test-assembly approach in the previous chapters can also be used to solve the problems in adaptive testing above. We will first model adaptive test assembly from a pool of discrete items as an instance of 0-1 programming. The result will be a modification of the standard test-assembly model for a single fixed test presented in Section 4.1. Although the model changes only a little, a major difference with fixed-form test assembly is that an updated version of the model has to be solved for the selection of each subsequent item in the test. We will then discuss a few alternative objective functions for adaptive testing and extend our standard model with the different sets of constraints necessary to solve the various new problems discussed above. Some of these constraints are direct generalizations of the ones we used to extend the model for a fixed test in Section 4.1 to those for the special problems in Chapters 5–8, whereas others require a bit more ingenuity.

Because both our basic model for adaptive test assembly and all additional constraints remain linear in the decision variables, the branch-and-bound searches discussed in Section 4.2 can also be used to run an adaptive-testing program. As a matter of fact, thanks to a special feature of adaptive item selection, much faster implementations of these searches than for fixed test assembly are possible, which enables us to execute them in real time.

9.1   Shadow-Test Approach

In Section 2.3, we classified the objective used in adaptive testing as a quantitative objective at the item level. The objective was modeled in Section 3.3.1 as

$$\text{maximize} \sum_{i \in R} I_i(\widehat{\theta}) x_i \quad \text{(maximum information)} \tag{9.1}$$

subject to

$$\sum_{i \in R} x_i = 1, \quad \text{(selection of one item)} \tag{9.2}$$

$$x_i \in \{0, 1\}, \quad \text{for all } i, \quad \text{(range of variables)} \tag{9.3}$$

where R denotes the items in the pool that the person has not yet taken and $\widehat{\theta}$ is his or her current ability estimate.

The representation is not yet realistic for the following reasons:

1. For a complete test, a set of these problems has to be solved, one for each of its items.

2. For each of the problems in this set, we have to update the estimate $\widehat{\theta}$ in the objective function.

3. The problems in the set are dependent in the sense that once an item has been administered, it cannot be chosen again in a later problem.

Thus, the model in (9.1)–(9.3) needs to be reformulated. We will do this first for adaptive testing with a random test length and then for the case of a fixed test length.

9.1.1   Random Test Length

In early research on adaptive testing, the ideal of a stopping rule based on a common level of accuracy of the final ability estimator θ for all test takers was advocated. This ideal can easily be realized by estimating the accuracy of $\widehat{\theta}$ online, monitoring the estimates, and stopping when a predetermined threshold is passed.

This case of a random test length can be modeled as follows. Let $g = 1, 2, \ldots$ denote the items in the adaptive test. We use $\widehat{\theta}^{(g-1)}$ to represent the update of the ability estimate after the first $g - 1$ items; this update is thus used to select the gth item. Furthermore, we use R_g to denote the set of items in the pool that is still available for administration when the gth item for the adaptive test is selected.

The previous model for the selection of the kth item can then be reformulated as:

$$\text{maximize} \sum_{i \in R_g} I_i(\widehat{\theta}^{(g-1)}) x_i \quad \text{(maximum information)} \tag{9.4}$$

subject to

$$\sum_{i \in R_g} x_i = 1, \quad \text{(selection of one item)} \tag{9.5}$$

$$x_i \in \{0, 1\}, \quad \text{for all } i. \quad \text{(range of variables)} \tag{9.6}$$

This model depicts adaptive test assembly as a process in which after each new response the ability estimate $\widehat{\theta}^{(g-1)}$ and the set of items R_g are updated and the model is run again to select the next item. The only difference with the preceding model is that (9.1) and (9.2) are now formulated explicitly as a *dynamic* objective function and constraint.

9.1.2   Fixed Test Length

The ideal of a common level of accuracy for the ability estimator was soon abandoned in favor of adaptive testing with the same fixed number of items for all persons who take the test. Typically, this length is chosen to guarantee a desirable minimum level of accuracy over the ability range for which the test is used. The choice of a fixed test length was necessary to deal with the requirement that each test taker get a test assembled for a common set of content specifications. A more mundane reason was that adaptive-testing sessions cannot be planned efficiently if the time spent on the test is not known in advance. In this chapter, we further focus on the case of adaptive test assembly with a fixed test length.

To select an adaptive test of fixed length, we could simply run the model in (9.4)–(9.6) and stop after a fixed number of items has been administered. But a much more useful model arises if we adopt an explicit constraint on the test length in the model. If we do so, we also must have a constraint that sets the variables of the items already administered equal to one.

The result is the following set of models for $g = 1, ..., n$:

$$\text{maximize} \sum_{i=1}^{I} I_i(\widehat{\theta}^{(g-1)}) x_i \quad \text{(maximum information)} \tag{9.7}$$

subject to

$$\sum_{i=1}^{I} x_i = n, \quad \text{(test length)} \tag{9.8}$$

$$\sum_{i \in \overline{R}_g} x_i = g - 1, \quad \text{(previous items)} \tag{9.9}$$

$$x_i \in \{0, 1\}, \quad \text{for all } i, \quad \text{(range of variables)} \tag{9.10}$$

where $\overline{R}_g$ is the set of items not in R_g; that is, the items already administered. Observe that (9.9) is a single constraint that sets each of the $g - 1$ variables in $\overline{R}_g$ equal to one; this type of constraint was already introduced in (3.28).

Instead of selecting one item, this model selects an entire test of n items with maximum information at $\widehat{\theta}^{(g-1)}$. The item that is administered as the gth item in the adaptive test is the one among the $n - g$ free items with the maximum value of $I_i(\widehat{\theta}^{(g-1)})$. Thus, the original objective of an item with maximum information at the ability estimate is now realized through a two-stage optimization procedure in which:

1. a test of length n with maximum information at $\widehat{\theta}^{(g-1)}$ is assembled;

2. the free item in this test with maximum information at $\widehat{\theta}^{(g-1)}$ is selected.

Although at first sight the model in (9.7)–(9.10) may look somewhat overdone, it has an attractive feature: Its constraint set can be extended with whatever other content constraint we find useful. Because the same set of constraints is imposed on each of the n tests assembled for the test takers, the adaptive test automatically satisfies each of its constraints. We document this feature as an explicit principle:

Any type of constraint available to give a fixed test a certain feature can be inserted in the basic model in (9.7)–(9.10) to give an adaptive test the same feature.

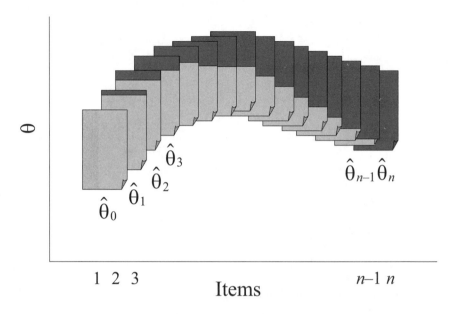

FIGURE 9.1. Graphical representation of the shadow-test approach to adaptive test assembly.

9.1.3   Definition of Shadow Tests

Tests calculated by the model in (9.7)–(9.10) are known as *shadow tests* in adaptive testing. Their name reminds us of the big-shadow-test method for multiple-test assembly in Section 6.3. In this method, shadow tests were assembled to keep a sequence of test-assembly problems feasible with respect to their constraints. The same principle is implemented at the item level by (9.7)–(9.10). Items in a shadow test that are not selected for administration are returned to the pool; they are made available again when the shadow test is reassembled at the next update of $\hat{\theta}$. Their only purpose is to keep the adaptive test feasible with respect to its constraints when an individual item is selected.

A graphical representation of the shadow-test approach (STA) to adaptive testing is given in Figure 9.1. The horizontal axis represents the sequence of items in the adaptive test and the vertical axis the ability measured by the item pool. The vertical position of the shadow tests corresponds with the current ability estimate; the higher the test, the larger the estimate. Also, a higher position indicates that the preceding response was correct and a lower position that it was incorrect. The smaller differences between the vertical positions of the shadow tests toward the end of the test reflect the stabilization of the ability estimates. The darker portions of the shadow test represent the items already administered and the lighter portions the parts that are reassembled at the new ability estimate. The last test is the actual adaptive test that has been administered; it automatically meets the common set of content constraints imposed on each of the individual shadow tests.

9.1.4 Standard Model for a Shadow Test

For a pool of discrete items, the standard model for a shadow test follows directly from the model for a fixed test introduced in Section 4.1. For the selection of item $g = 1, ..., n$, the model is

$$\text{maximize} \sum_{i=1}^{I} I_i(\hat{\theta}^{(g-1)})x_i \quad \text{(objective)} \tag{9.11}$$

subject to possible constraints at the following levels:

Test Level

$$\sum_{i=1}^{I} x_i = n, \quad \text{(test length)} \tag{9.12}$$

$$\sum_{i \in V_c} x_i \gtrless n_c, \quad \text{for all } c, \quad \text{(categorical attributes)} \tag{9.13}$$

$$\sum_{i=1}^{I} q_i x_i \gtrless b_q; \quad \text{(quantitative attributes)} \tag{9.14}$$

Subtest Level

$$\sum_{i \in \overline{R}_g} x_i = g - 1; \quad \text{(previous items)} \tag{9.15}$$

Item Level

$$\sum_{i \in V_1} x_i = n_1, \quad \text{(categorical attributes)} \tag{9.16}$$

$$\sum_{i \in V_0} x_i = 0, \quad \text{(categorical attributes)} \tag{9.17}$$

$$q_i x_i \leq b_q^{\max}, \quad \text{for all } i, \quad \text{(quantitative attributes)} \tag{9.18}$$

$$b_q^{\min} x_i \leq q_i, \quad \text{for all } i, \quad \text{(quantitative attributes)} \tag{9.19}$$

$$\sum_{i \in V_e} x_i \leq 1, \quad \text{for all } e; \quad \text{(enemies)} \tag{9.20}$$

Definition of Variables

$$x_i \in \{0,1\}, \quad \text{for all } i. \quad \text{(range of variables)} \tag{9.21}$$

Observe that, except for the objective function in (9.11) and the extra constraint in (9.15), the model is identical to that for a single fixed test with discrete items. This fact illustrates our earlier observation that an adaptive test can be given any feature possible for a fixed test.

The only dynamic quantities in the model are the objective function and constraint in (9.11) and (9.15). The updates of the objective function make the selection of the items adaptive with respect to the interim ability estimates and, in doing so, give the test its favorable statistical features for the estimation of θ. The updates of the constraint force the new items in the shadow test to have attributes that complement the attributes of the items already administered with respect to the other constraints in (9.9)–(9.20) (Exercise 9.1).

9.1.5 Calculating Shadow Tests

Shadow tests in adaptive testing have to be calculated in real time. It is therefore important to use a fast implementation of the branch-and-bound search discussed in Section 4.2. Fortunately, such implementations are possible because of a special feature of the set of n models for the shadow tests in (9.11)–(9.21).

The differences between the models for two subsequent shadow tests reside in the updates of (9.11) and (9.15). Generally, the collection of feasible tests in a test-assembly problem is determined only by the constraints in the model. The changes in the objective function in (9.11) thus do not have any impact on this set. On the other hand, the update of the constraint in (9.15) does have an impact. But since the update consists only of the fixing of one more decision variable, and all other constraints in (9.11)–(9.21) remain the same, the collection of feasible tests for the next problem is always a subset of the collection for the preceding problem. More importantly, since the variable is fixed at the value found in the solution of the preceding solution, this solution remains feasible for the next problem. Finally, because the value of the objective function changes gradually between subsequent shadow tests, new shadow tests tend to be found in the neighborhood of their predecessor in the feasible collection.

This argument shows that the preceding shadow test is a good initial solution in a branch-and-bound algorithm for the calculation of a shadow test. In all our applications, this choice has dramatically sped up the search for shadow tests. For problems with constraint sets and item pools comparable to those in the empirical examples in the next section, the current integer solver in *CPLEX* (Section 4.2.5) finds the shadow tests in a split second.

When selecting the first item in the adaptive test, no previous shadow test is available. However, an initial solution can easily be calculated before the adaptive testing program is operational. All we have to do is choose a typical value for θ in the objective function in (9.11) and calculate a solution. Because the content constraints remain identical for all test takers, the same initial solution can be used for each of them.

As an aside, we observe that the same argument shows that the presence of the constraints on the previous items in (9.15) can never be a reason for a shadow test to become infeasible. If an initial shadow test can be assembled, all later problems are feasible. Because the shadow tests for all test takers are subject to a common set of content constraints, it follows that if the item pool has at least one feasible test, the STA will never run into feasibility problems.

9.1.6 Empirical Example

Computer simulations of a 50-item adaptive version of the *Law School Admission Test* (LSAT) were conducted. The item pool was the same pool of 753 items used in the previous examples for the LSAT. The full set of specifications for the test was used, including the specifications needed to deal with the item-set structure of two of the three sections in the test. (The topic of how to model adaptive tests with item sets will be addressed in Section 9.3.) The only difference with the earlier paper-and-pencil version of the LSAT was a proportional reduction of the bounds in the constraints to account for the reduction of the test length to 50 items. The number of variables and constraints needed to model the three sections were: 232 variables and 179 constraints for Section SA, 264 variables and 218 constraints for Section SB, and 305 variables and 30 constraints for Section SC.

The order of the sections in the adaptive test was (i) SC, (ii) SA, and (iii) SB. This order allowed the ability estimator in the objective function to stabilize somewhat before the more severely constrained sections were introduced. The test administrations were replicated for 100 test takers at $\theta = -2.0, -1.5, ..., 2.0$. The first item in the test was selected at a common value $\hat{\theta} = 0$ for all test takers. The updates of the ability estimates were calculated using the expected a posteriori (EAP) estimator with a uniform prior distribution.

The study was repeated a second time without any of the content constraints on the items. The differences between the results for these two studies enable us to evaluate the efficiency of the STA in the presence of large numbers of constraints on the test.

Because the test takers were simulated, we knew their true ability levels and were able to estimate the bias and mean-squared error (MSE) in their ability estimates. Figure 9.2 shows the estimated bias as a function of the true values in the simulation study after 10, 20, 30, and 40 items were administered. The differences between the functions for adaptive testing

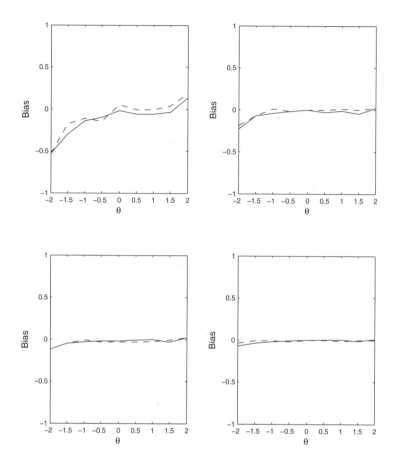

FIGURE 9.2. Bias functions for $n = 10$ and 20 (top) and $n = 30$ and 40 (bottom) for adaptive testing with (solid line) and without (dashed line) content constraints.

with and without the constraints were already small after $n = 10$ items but, for all practical purposes, disappeared with the increase in test length. Essentially the same results were observed for the MSE functions in Figure 9.3.

The main conclusion from this study is that the presence of large sets of content constraints on the tests did not have any noticeable impact on the quality of the ability estimation, and the STA appeared to be an efficient way to impose these constraints.

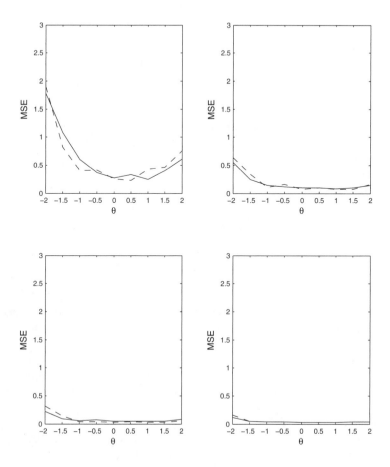

FIGURE 9.3. MSE functions for $n = 10$ and 20 (top) and $n = 30$ and 40 (bottom) for adaptive testing with (solid line) and without (dashed line) content constraints.

9.1.7 Discussion

There exists a fundamental dilemma between sequential and simultaneous item selection in adaptive testing: To realize the objective of maximum information, items have to be selected sequentially with an update of the ability estimate in the objective function after each item. But to realize the constraints on the test, they have to be selected simultaneously. If they were selected sequentially, we could easily run into the problems illustrated in Table 4.1: After a few items, it would become impossible to select a new item without violating a constraint and/or making a suboptimal choice. The STA solves the dilemma by treating adaptive test assembly as a *sequence of n simultaneous optimization problems*. The importance of this principle was already explained in Section 6.3 when we introduced the big-shadow-test method for the assembly of multiple tests.

Another way to view the STA is as a *projection* method. At each ability update, the STA projects the remaining part of the adaptive test for the test taker and picks the best item from this projection.

It is instructive to compare this interpretation of the STA with an application of the Swanson-Stocking heuristic in adaptive testing (Section 4.4.3) known as the weighted-deviations method (WDM) for adaptive testing. The WDM selects the items using the criterion of a weighted sum of projections of the deviations of the contributions of the items from the bounds in the constraints of the model. Suppose $g-1$ items have been administered. The weighted sum was formulated in (4.20) as

$$\sum_{h=1}^{H} w_h \left| \pi_{i_g h} - b_h \right|,\qquad(9.22)$$

where $h = 1, ..., H$ denote the constraints on the test, b_h their bounds, and $\pi_{i_g h}$ the prediction of the contribution of item i to constraint h when selected as the gth item in the test. The prediction is calculated according to (4.19) as

$$\pi_{i_g h} = \sum_{j=1}^{g-1} a_{i_j h} + a_{i_g h} + (n - g)\frac{\sum\limits_{i \in R_g \setminus \{i_g\}} a_{ih}}{(I - g)}.\qquad(9.23)$$

The first term in this prediction is the sum of the attribute values $a_{i_g h}$ in constraint h for the first $g - 1$ items in the test, the second term is the attribute value of candidate item i, and the last term equals $n - g$ times the average attribute value calculated over all remaining items in the pool.

The last term of (9.23) is the actual projection of the remaining part of the adaptive test for each constraint h by the WDM. But it is unlikely that the pool contains a feasible subset of $n - g$ items with average values for H attributes equal to these projections. Therefore, the WDM is vulnerable to constraint violation. The STA uses the *best feasible subset* of $n - g$ items in the pool at the ability estimate as a projection and does not suffer from this problem.

9.2   Alternative Objective Functions

The standard model for a shadow test in (9.11)–(9.21) offers a menu of options from which a choice has to be made to accommodate our applications. Several of these options will be discussed later in this chapter. We first discuss a few alternative choices for the objective function in (9.11). The discussion will be rather concise; for a more elaborate treatment of these objectives, we refer to the literature on the statistical aspects of adaptive testing at the end of this chapter.

9.2.1 Kullback-Leibler Information

The objective function in (9.11) is based on Fisher's information measure in (1.18). A useful alternative measure for adaptive testing is *Kullback-Leibler information*. For item i, this information is defined as

$$K_i(\widehat{\theta}, \theta) = \mathcal{E}\left[\ln \frac{p_i(\widehat{\theta})^{U_i}[1 - p_i(\widehat{\theta})]^{1-U_i}}{p_i(\theta)^{U_i}[1 - p_i(\theta)]^{1-U_i}}\right], \tag{9.24}$$

where $p_i(.)$ is the response function for the 3PL model in (1.16), U_i is the random response on item i for a test taker with true ability θ, and $\widehat{\theta}$ is the estimate of θ. The expectation is taken with respect to the distribution of U_i at $\widehat{\theta}$.

Since θ is unknown, it should be integrated out of (9.24), preferably over its posterior distribution. Let $f(\theta \mid u_{i_1}, ..., u_{i_{g-1}})$ denote the density of the posterior distribution of θ after the responses $(u_{i_1}, ..., u_{i_{g-1}})$ to the first $g-1$ items. The ith item is selected such that

$$K_i(\widehat{\theta}) = \int K_i(\widehat{\theta}, \theta) f(\theta \mid u_{i_1}, ..., u_{i_{g-1}}) d\theta \tag{9.25}$$

is maximal.

This criterion can easily be adopted in the model for the shadow test. The only thing we have to do is replace the objective function in (9.11) by

$$\text{maximize} \sum_{i=1}^{I} K_i(\widehat{\theta}^{(g-1)}) x_i. \tag{9.26}$$

The gth item in the adaptive test is then the one in the shadow test with a maximum value for (9.25).

An attractive feature of Kullback-Leibler item selection is its robustness to the uncertainty on $\widehat{\theta}$ in the beginning of the test. Another attractive feature is that the criterion for item selection in (9.25) generalizes easily to multidimensional response models. We will show this generalization in an application of the STA to multidimensional adaptive testing in Section 9.7.

9.2.2 Bayesian Item-Selection Criteria

Although the use of information measures dominates, item selection in adaptive testing is a natural area for the application of Bayesian criteria.

One obvious criterion is to select the items that minimize the expected posterior variance of θ.

Suppose we evaluate the candidacy of item i in the pool for administration as the gth item in the test. If item i is selected, the posterior variance of θ can be expected to be

$$\mathcal{E}[\text{Var}(\theta \mid u_{i_1}, ..., u_{i_{g-1}}, U_i)], \tag{9.27}$$

where the expectation is taken with respect to the posterior predictive distribution of U_i given the responses $(u_{i_1}, ..., u_{i_{g-1}})$. This expected value is a useful criterion for item selection; it tells us what reduction of posterior variance of θ to expect if item i is administered.

A shadow-test approach with this criterion has the objective function

$$\text{minimize} \sum_{i=1}^{I} \mathcal{E}\left[\text{Var}(\theta \mid u_{i_1}, ..., u_{i_{g-1}}, U_i)\right] x_i. \tag{9.28}$$

This function results in the selection of a test with the $n - g$ items with the largest reductions of the expected posterior variance of θ possible given all constraints on the test. The item that is administered is the one with the smallest value for (9.27).

Other Bayesian criteria are possible, all of which share the fact that they are defined for the posterior distribution of θ given the preceding item responses. In fact, if the Kullback-Leibler measure is integrated over the posterior distribution, as we suggested for (9.25), it can also be considered as a Bayesian criterion for item selection.

9.3   Adaptive Testing with Item Sets

If the item pool contains set-based items, the model for the shadow test in (9.11)–(9.21) should be adjusted to the model for the simultaneous selection of items and stimuli in (7.3)–(7.24). Obviously, we retain the objective function in (9.11) as well as the constraint on the previous items in (9.15). The only addition necessary is a constraint on the previous stimuli in the test comparable to (9.15).

Let $l = 1, ..., m$ represent the stimuli in the adaptive test, and suppose that the test taker has already seen the first $l - 1$ stimuli. We use R_l to denote the set of stimuli in the pool available for selection as the lth stimulus in the test. Thus, $\overline{R}_l$ is the set of $l-1$ stimuli already administered. Analogously to (9.15), the following constraint has to be added to the model:

$$\sum_{s \in \overline{R}_l} z_s = l - 1. \tag{9.29}$$

This constraint must be updated every time a new stimulus is administered.

Typically, if a new stimulus becomes active, we want to continue administering items for it until the bounds on the number of items in (7.12) are satisfied. This practice is supported by the updates of (9.29). Once the first item for a stimulus is selected, (9.29) sets the decision variable for the stimulus equal to one. Consequently, the bounds on the number of items in (7.12) become active and remain so during the rest of the test. We are therefore able to administer the best items from the set until no free item in it is left. Then, an item for a new stimulus is selected and the process is repeated (Exercise 9.2).

Two of the three sections of the LSAT in the example in Section 9.1.6 were set-based. The model for the shadow tests for these two sections in the example was exactly as described here.

9.4   Controlling Item Exposure

It is necessary to control the exposure rates of the items in adaptive testing. The objective of maximum information in (9.11) involves a preference for the small subset of items in the pool with information functions that dominate the IIFs of all other items in the pool over an interval of θ. Without control, these items would be frequently seen by test takers and easily passed on to a person who takes the test later.

The preference for the subset of most informative items is mitigated somewhat by the content constraints imposed on the test. To satisfy the constraints, it becomes necessary to select items with less than optimal information at the ability estimate. But then if the item pool has relatively few items with the combinations of attributes required by the constraints, these items easily become overexposed.

In this section, we discuss three different methods of item-exposure control for the STA. Two of these methods are based on the idea of adding one or more constraints to the model for the shadow test with a direct impact on the item-exposure rates; they differ only in the type of constraint that is imposed. The other method is an implementation of the well-known Sympson-Hetter method for the STA. Furthermore, in Chapter 11 we will discuss a few approaches to item-pool design for adaptive testing that prevent tendencies to overexpose items by building special constraints into the design of the item pool.

9.4.1   Alpha Stratification

Although the selection of items with maximum information at the test taker's ability estimate $\widehat{\theta}$ makes intuitive sense, it is not necessarily a strategy that is always good. In the beginning of the test, when the errors in $\widehat{\theta}$ are relatively large, the item with the highest peak for its information function at $\widehat{\theta}$ is not necessarily the one with the highest peak at the *true* θ value of the test taker. For example, it is easy to find two points on the ability scale in Figure 1.4, one for a test taker's true ability and the other for an estimate of it, where the best item at the latter is not the best at the former. Furthermore, if we select the items with the highest peaks for their information functions early in the test, we cannot use them later when the estimates $\widehat{\theta}$ are close to the true θ.

In alpha-stratified adaptive testing, we select less informative items first and postpone the selection of the more informative items until the end of the test. This strategy is implemented by stratifying the pool on the values of item-discrimination parameter a and restricting the selection of the items to the consecutive strata in the pool. That it is effective to stratify the pool on the values of a for the items instead of their more complicated information functions follows from the analysis of the impact of a on the IIF at the end of Section 1.2.4.

The option of alpha stratification is discussed here not because of its potentially beneficial impact on ability estimation but because of its tendency toward more uniform item usage. It prevents the adaptive-testing algorithm from capitalizing on a small subset of items with high values for a and enforces a more uniform distribution of the items in the test on this parameter.

Alpha stratification can be implemented simply by introducing a new constraint into the model for the shadow tests. Suppose the item pool has been stratified into strata Q_p, with $p = 1, ..., P$. The question of how to stratify a pool is postponed until Section 11.5.1. We assume that fixed numbers of items n_p are selected from the strata. The constraint to be imposed on the shadow tests is

$$\sum_{i \in Q_p} x_i = n_p. \tag{9.30}$$

The set Q_p in this constraint is updated after $n_1, ..., n_P$ items in the test; (9.30) is thus another example of a dynamic constraint on an adaptive test. Because fixed numbers of items are selected from each stratum, the constraint on the total length of the adaptive test in (9.12) is redundant and can be removed from the model.

If the strata in the pool are chosen to be narrow, the only remaining parameter with an impact on the information functions of the items is the difficulty parameter b_i. (The guessing parameter has hardly any impact on item selection in adaptive testing.) It has therefore been suggested to simplify item selection for alpha-stratified adaptive testing and select the items from the strata with their values for b closest to $\widehat{\theta}^{(g-1)}$. This suggestion implies an objective with a goal value for the shadow test (see Section 3.3.3).

Minimax implementation of this objective leads to the replacement of (9.11) by

$$\text{minimize } y \tag{9.31}$$

subject to

$$\left(b_i - \widehat{\theta}^{(g-1)}\right) x_i \leq y, \quad \text{for } i \in Q_p, \tag{9.32}$$

$$\left(b_i - \widehat{\theta}^{(g-1)}\right) x_i \geq -y, \quad \text{for } i \in Q_p. \tag{9.33}$$

Empirical Example

The 50-item adaptive version of the LSAT in Section 9.1.6 was used to evaluate the impact of the alpha-stratification constraint in (9.30) on the exposure rates of the items. The item pool was divided into $P = 5$ strata each with 20% of the items. The maximum values of a for the successive strata were: .559, .700, .813, .959, and 1.686. From each stratum, $n_p = 10$ items were selected for the test.

The model for the shadow test had all earlier content constraints for the LSAT, but the item-set structure for two of its sections was ignored. We simulated test administrations both with and without alpha stratification. For the case with alpha stratification, we also used the objective function in (9.31)–(9.33). The two cases were repeated with all content constraints removed from the model, which enabled us to evaluate the impact of alpha stratification on the exposure rates above and beyond the impact of the content constraints.

The distributions of the exposure rates of the 753 items in the pool for the four cases are displayed in Figure 9.4. For adaptive testing both with and without content constraints, the exposures rates with the alpha-stratification constraint were much closer to uniformity than without the constraint. The presence of the content constraints in the model did not have any discernible impact on these distributions. Although alpha stratification did have a favorable impact on the exposure rates, the results still show high rates for a few items in the pool.

We conclude that the introduction of the alpha-stratification constraint in the model appears to be an effective method for obtaining a more uniform distribution of the item-exposure rates. To reduce the rates for the last few items, stricter control is necessary, however. Stricter control is obtained if we increase the number of strata, P. But the problem would then likely become overconstrained, and the statistical quality of the ability estimates might deteriorate seriously.

More importantly, in practice, we always want to control the *conditional* exposure rates of the items at a series of well-chosen θ values because control of the marginal rates only does not preclude the possibility of high rates

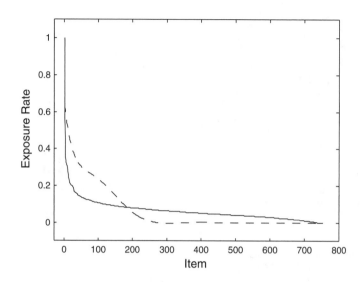

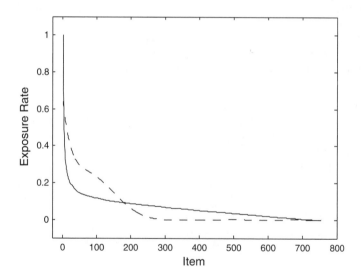

FIGURE 9.4. Item-exposure rates for adaptive testing without (dashed line) and with (solid line) alpha stratification for the cases without (top) and with (bottom) content constraints on the test. The items are ordered by exposure rate.

for test takers with ability levels close to each other. Without conditional control, it would still be easy for such test takers to share items.

Alpha stratification by itself does not control the conditional exposure rates of all items. We are therefore more in favor of combining a smaller number of strata with additional probabilistic control of the conditional item-exposure rates. The following sections describe two such probabilistic methods that can be used with the STA.

9.4.2 Sympson-Hetter Method

The Sympson-Hetter method reduces the exposure rates of the more popular items by introducing a probability experiment in the adaptive-testing algorithm that is conducted after each item has been selected. The experiment is to decide if the item is actually administered or if it is rejected in favor of the item with the next-highest information at $\widehat{\theta}$.

For the case of conditional item-exposure control, the Sympson-Hetter experiment can be modeled as follows. Let S_i be the event of item i being selected and A_i the event of item i being administered. The conditional probabilities of these events given θ are denoted as $P(S_i \mid \theta)$ and $P(A_i \mid \theta)$, respectively. The probabilities $P(A_i \mid \theta)$ are the expected conditional exposure rates of the items. An item cannot be administered without being selected. Thus, $P(S_i \mid A_i, \theta) = 1$. It therefore holds that

$$P(A_i \mid \theta) = P(A_i \mid S_i, \theta)P(S_i \mid \theta). \tag{9.34}$$

For a given item pool and set of constraints on the tests, the probabilities $P(S_i \mid \theta)$ are fixed for all items. The conditional probabilities $P(A_i \mid S_i, \theta)$ serve as control parameters for the experiment. By manipulating these probabilities for items with $P(S_i \mid \theta) > 0$, their expected exposure rates can be increased or decreased. To find the optimal values for these parameters at a set of θ values, we iteratively adjust them in a series of simulations of adaptive test administrations prior to the operational use of the test until they are below an upper limit, $r^{\max}$. The limit is set by the program administrator (Exercise 9.4).

If the test is operational, the Sympson-Hetter experiment is usually implemented as follows: Instead of selecting the most informative item at $\widehat{\theta}$, an ordered list with a number of the most informative items is identified. The control probabilities $P(A_i \mid S_i, \widehat{\theta})$ for the items are those at the θ values closest to $\widehat{\theta}$. The probabilities are renormed (i.e., their sum for the list is set equal to one), and one item is sampled from this list that conducts the multinomial experiment defined by the control probabilities. All items on the list more informative than the item sampled are removed from the pool, and all items less informative items than the sample are returned to the pool.

A longer list of items for the Sympson-Hetter experiment implies lower exposure rates for the more popular items in the pool. But if the list becomes too long, we lose too many good items during the test, and pay a price in the form of less accurate ability estimation. In practice, we compromise between these two tendencies. For the STA, a natural candidate for the list is the set of free items in the shadow test; they are the most informative items given all content constraints in the model. However, for a shorter adaptive test, this set may become too small toward the end of the test.

9.4.3 Multiple-Shadow-Test Approach

An effective way to get a larger set of free items is to use a *multiple-shadow-test approach* (MSTA). In this approach, at each step, a set of parallel shadow tests is selected, and the experiment is conducted over the list of the most informative items assembled from the free items in these tests. At first sight, it may seem cumbersome to implement an MSTA, but the only thing required to do so is to adjust the model for the single shadow test in (9.11)–(9.21) to that for simultaneous selection of multiple tests.

As an example, we formulate the core of a model for an adaptive test with set-based items and omit possible content constraints:

$$\text{maximize } y \quad \text{(objective)} \tag{9.35}$$

subject to

$$\sum_{i=1}^{S} \sum_{i=1}^{I_s} I_{i_s}(\hat{\theta}^{(g-1)}) x_{i_s t} \geq y, \quad \text{for all } t, \quad \text{(test information)} \tag{9.36}$$

$$\sum_{t=1}^{T} x_{i_s t} \leq 1, \quad \text{for all } i_s \in R_g, \quad \text{(item overlap)} \tag{9.37}$$

$$\sum_{t=1}^{T} z_{st} \leq 1, \quad \text{for all } s \in R_l, \quad \text{(stimulus overlap)} \tag{9.38}$$

$$\sum_{i_s \in \overline{R}_g} x_{i_s t} = g - 1, \quad \text{for all } t, \quad \text{(previous items)} \tag{9.39}$$

$$\sum_{s \in \overline{R}_l} z_{st} = l - 1, \quad \text{for all } t, \quad \text{(previous stimuli)} \tag{9.40}$$

$$\sum_{i_s=1}^{I_s} x_{i_s t} \geq n_s^{\text{set}} z_s, \quad \text{for all } s \text{ and } t, \quad \text{(number of items per set)} \tag{9.41}$$

$$x_{i_s t} \in \{0, 1\}, \quad \text{for all } i, s \text{ and } t, \quad \text{(range of variables)} \tag{9.42}$$

$$z_{st} \in \{0, 1\}, \quad \text{for all } s \text{ and } t. \quad \text{(range of variables)} \tag{9.43}$$

Observe that the decision variables z_{st} and $x_{i_s t}$ are now for the assignment of stimulus s and the items in its set $i_s = 1_s, ..., I_s$ to shadow test t, respectively. Of course, for the MSTA to be effective, we do not want the free items and stimuli in the shadow tests to overlap; hence the constraints in (9.37) and (9.38). The constraints in (9.39) and (9.40) guarantee the presence of the previous items and stimuli in each of the shadow tests. The constraints in (9.41) do not only control the size of the item sets but also coordinate the values of the variables z_{st} and $x_{i_s t}$. If the set sizes are not constrained, alternatively the constraint in (7.13) or (7.14) should be used to play this role (see the discussion in Section 7.1).

Empirical Example

We introduced Sympson-Hetter exposure control in the 50-item adaptive version of the LSAT in Section 9.1.6 using the MSTA. The number of parallel shadow tests was equal to $T = 2$. At each step, the Sympson-Hetter experiment was conducted over all free items in the two shadow tests.

To set the values of the control parameters in (9.34), we conducted an iterative series of simulated administrations of the LSAT for test takers with abilities equal to $\theta = -2.0, -1.5, ..., 2.0$. For each θ value, the limit for the exposure rates was $r^{\max} = .25$. To get stable estimates of the exposure rates, 1,000 administrations were simulated for each θ value. The values for the control parameters were adjusted according to the standard procedure for the Sympson-Hetter method. (See the literature at the end of this chapter.) Even though we ran a series of 21 simulations for each θ value, we were unable to produce a set of values for the control parameters with all exposure rates below the limit. The best results were obtained in the 15th iteration; the values found in this iteration were used in the main study.

In the main study, CAT administrations both without and with Sympson-Hetter exposure control were simulated. For the case without control, we used the STA with a single shadow test, whereas for the case with control, we used the MSTA.

Figure 9.5 shows the distributions of the conditional exposure rates for the item pool at $\theta = -2.0, -1.5, ..., 2.0$ for the two cases. Without exposure control, the conditional exposure rates were much too high for a considerable number of items. The introduction of control reduced the rates to below .25 for nearly all of the items. The only exceptions were sets of 5–10 items for each of the θ values with exposure rate slightly above .25. The maximum rate of .29 among these items occurred only once. These exceptions were due to the fact that no entirely satisfactory set of values for the control parameters could be found, a result not uncommon for the Sympson-Hetter method.

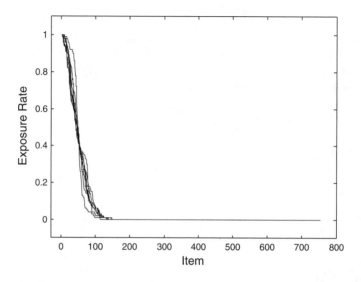

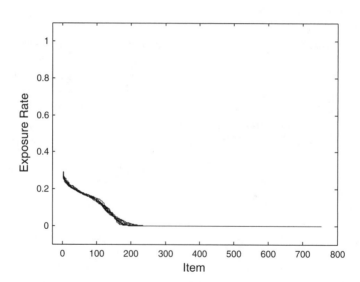

FIGURE 9.5. Conditional item-exposure rates at $\theta = -2.0, -1.5, \ldots, 2.0$ for adaptive testing without (top) and with (bottom) Sympson-Hetter exposure control. The items are ordered by exposure rate.

9.4.4   Method with Ineligibility Constraints

Finding appropriate values for the control parameters in the Sympson-Hetter method is quite time-consuming. In the preceding example, 189 computer simulations were required to identify the set of values with acceptable exposure rates (21 simulations at nine θ values each). Also, every time the item pool is updated and/or the adaptive-testing algorithm changed, the control parameters have to be adjusted anew.

An alternative approach is based on the idea of eligibility decisions for the items in the pool. These decisions are based on probability experiments, too. But unlike the Sympson-Hetter method, the experiments are conducted only once for each test taker—before the test begins. If item i is decided to be ineligible for the test taker, the following *ineligibility constraint* is added to the model for the shadow tests:

$$x_i = 0. \tag{9.44}$$

If an item is decided to be eligible, no constraint is added.

Obviously, the lower the probability of eligibility for an item, the lower its exposure rate. But if an item is eligible, it is not necessarily selected for administration. It is therefore not immediately clear what values the eligibility probabilities should have to constrain the exposure rates to a given range. Appropriate goal values for these probabilities can, however, be derived in the following way.

In addition to the event A_i introduced for (9.34), we define event E_i as item i being eligible for a test taker. For an unfavorable combination of item pool and content constraints, adding a large number of ineligibility constraints could make the shadow-test model infeasible. We therefore define F as the event of the shadow test remaining feasible after all eligibility constraints have been added to the model. The event of the model becoming infeasible is denoted as $\overline{F}$. If infeasibility happens, the model for the shadow test is solved with all ineligibility constraints removed. We discuss the likelihood of $\overline{F}$ and its consequences for the exposure rates of the items below.

An item can be administered only if it is eligible or the ineligibility constraints are removed from the model because it is infeasible. Thus, $P(E_i \cup \overline{F} \mid A_i, \theta) = 1$, and, analogous to (9.34),

$$P(A_i \mid \theta) = P(A_i \mid E_i \cup \overline{F}, \theta) P(E_i \cup \overline{F} \mid \theta). \tag{9.45}$$

It follows that the requirement that all expected exposure rates $P(A_i \mid \theta)$ be below a limit $r^{\max}$ is met if

$$P(E_i \cup \overline{F} \mid \theta) P(A_i \mid E_i \cup \overline{F}, \theta) \leq r^{\max} \tag{9.46}$$

for all i. This inequality does not impose any direct constraint on the probabilities of item eligibility, $P(E_i \mid \theta)$. But using probability calculus,

(9.46) can be shown to lead to the bound on these probabilities

$$P(E_i \mid \theta) \leq 1 - \frac{1}{P(F \mid \theta)} + \frac{r^{\max} P(E_i \cup \overline{F} \mid \theta)}{P(A_i \mid \theta) P(F \mid \theta)}, \qquad (9.47)$$

with $P(A_i \mid \theta) > 0$ and $P(F \mid \theta) > 0$. (For a derivation, see Exercise 9.5.)

Suppose e persons have taken the tests, and we want the items with a tendency to overexpose to meet the upper bound $r^{\max}$. The ineligibility constraints for test taker $e + 1$ are then drawn with probabilities

$$P^{(e+1)}(E_i \mid \theta) = 1 - \frac{1}{P^{(e)}(F \mid \theta)} + \frac{r^{\max} P^{(e)}(E_i \cup \overline{F} \mid \theta)}{P^{(e)}(A_i \mid \theta) P^{(e)}(F \mid \theta)}, \qquad (9.48)$$

with $P^{(e)}(F \mid \theta) > 0$ and $P^{(e)}(A_i \mid \theta) > 0$. The superscripts in these probabilities denote their status with respect to the succession of the test takers. Observe that all probabilities on the right-hand-side bound are for the preceding test taker e, while the eligibility probability on the left-hand side is for the new test taker $e + 1$. Also, the inequality in (9.47) has been replaced by an equality.

The right-hand side of (9.48) can be easily estimated for an operational adaptive testing program using counts of the events A_i, F, and E_i. We recommend recording the counts conditional on the final ability estimates for the test takers, $\widehat{\theta}_n$. Since conditional exposure rates are robust with respect to small changes in θ, the impact of the remaining estimation error in $\widehat{\theta}_n$ can be disregarded.

The bounds on the probabilities in (9.48) are *self-adaptive*. As soon as $P^{(e)}(A_i \mid \theta)$ becomes larger than $r^{\max}$ for a test taker in the program, probability $P^{(e+1)}(E_i \mid \theta)$ goes down, whereas if $P^{(e)}(A_i \mid \theta)$ becomes smaller than $r^{\max}$, it goes up again. (For a derivation, see Exercise 9.6.) This feature of self-adaptation permits us to apply this type of exposure control in an operational testing program without any previous adjustment of control parameters. The exposure rates of the items automatically adapt to optimal levels. The same holds if we have to change the item pool during operational testing; for instance, to remove some items with security breaches.

The only precaution that has to be taken is setting $P^{(e+1)}(E_i \mid \theta) = 1$ until a shadow test is found and the item has been administered once at the ability level. This measure is necessary to satisfy the conditions of $P^{(e)}(F \mid \theta) > 0$ and $P^{(e)}(A_i \mid \theta) > 0$ for (9.48).

For a well-designed item pool, the ineligibility constraints will hardly ever lead to infeasibility. If it does, the adaptive nature of (9.48) automatically corrects for the extra exposure of the items in the test due to the removal of the constraints.

Empirical Example

The empirical example with the adaptive version of the LSAT in the preceding section was repeated with the Sympson-Hetter exposure-control method replaced by the method with random ineligibility constraints discussed in this section. All other aspects of the earlier study remained the same, except that we were a bit more ambitious and set the limit on the conditional exposure rates at $r^{\max} = .2$. We simulated 3,000 administrations for test takers at $\theta = -2.0, -1.5, ..., 2.0$ each.

The distributions of the conditional exposure rates for the cases without and with exposure control are shown in Figure 9.6. For the case with control, the exposure rates were effectively reduced to below .20. Due to the remaining estimation error in the right-hand-side probabilities of (9.48), a few items exceeded the limit by .01–.02, however.

We also recorded the number of times the model for the shadow test was feasible in this study. No cases of infeasibility were observed.

9.5 Controlling the Speededness of the Test

Test items differ as to the amount of time they require. An obvious factor with an impact on the time an item requires is its difficulty, but other factors, such as the amount of reading or encoding of symbolic information that is required, also play a role.

If the test is fixed, each test taker gets the same set of items. Consequently, the test is equally speeded for each of them. But if the test is adaptive, each test taker gets a different set, and the test easily becomes *differentially speeded*. Some of the test takers may then be able to complete their test early, whereas others run out of time. If this happens, the test can lose much of its validity.

One solution to the problem of differential speededness would be to choose the time limit for the test takers as a function of the time intensity of the items he or she gets. This strategy is technically possible as soon as we have good estimates of the time required by the items but is bound to run into practical problems, such as the impossibility of planning adaptive testing sessions efficiently.

Another solution would be to keep a common time limit for all test takers but to stop the test as a function of the time intensity of the items administered. This strategy leads to a different test length for different test takers and therefore has the disadvantage of less accurate ability estimates for some of them. It also becomes difficult for the test to satisfy a common set of content specifications for all test takers.

A better solution therefore is to *constrain* the test to become equally speeded for all test takers. This approach requires good estimates of the time intensity of the items. But if they have been pretested by seeding

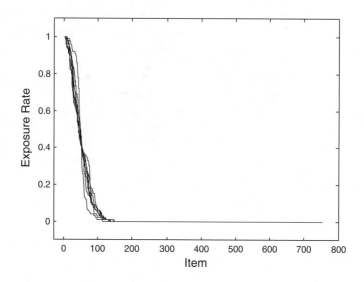

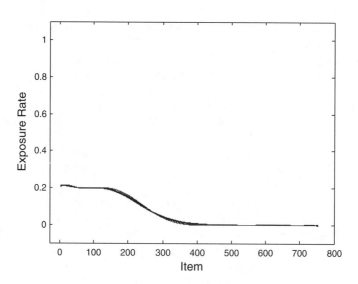

FIGURE 9.6. Conditional item-exposure rates at $\theta = -2.0, -1.5, \ldots, 2.0$ for adaptive testing without (top) and with (bottom) probabilistic ineligibility constraints. The items are ordered by exposure rate.

them into regular adaptive-test administrations, their response times have been automatically recorded, and estimates of the time parameters of the items can easily be obtained as part of regular item calibration. We discuss a lognormal model for the response times on test items that had excellent fit to a data set used in the empirical study later in this section and then show what constraints can be used to make a test equally speeded.

9.5.1   Response-Time Model

The response-time model is for the distribution of random variable T_i for the response time of a person operating at speed τ on item i. In addition to the person parameter, the model has two item parameters, one for the time intensity of item i, β_i, and the other for its discriminating power, α_i.

The model has the density function

$$f(t_i; \tau, \alpha_i, \beta_i) = \frac{\alpha_i}{t_i \sqrt{2\pi}} \exp\left\{ -\frac{1}{2} [\alpha_i(\ln t_i - (\beta_i - \tau))]^2 \right\}, \qquad (9.49)$$

which is known as the lognormal density because it is identical to the density of a normal distribution for the logarithm of the response time. This model is not yet identified; we therefore propose the following constraint on the speed parameters for the persons $j = 1, ..., N$ in the data set:

$$\sum_{j=1}^{N} \tau_j = 0. \qquad (9.50)$$

The speed parameter τ and time-intensity parameter β_i are both on a scale from $-\infty$ to ∞, while the discrimination parameter takes values from 0 to ∞. Observe that the distribution of $\ln T_i$ has expected value $\beta_i - \tau$. Thus, the more time the item requires or the slower the person operates, the larger the expected logtime for the test taker on the item. The difference between t_i and the expected value $\beta_i - \tau$ is modified by the discrimination parameter α_i. The larger this parameter, the smaller the variance of the distribution, and the better the item discriminates between the response-time distributions of persons operating at a speed just above and below β_i.

Just as for the parameters in the IRT model, the estimates of the values of item parameters β_i and α_i are treated as their true values during the operational use of the item pool. For details on this estimation procedure, see the literature at the end of this chapter.

We discuss two different types of control, one based on the features of the items only and another that also corrects for the individual speed of the test takers. Which type of control is appropriate depends on what the test was designed to measure. Following up on our discussion of the different cases of multidimensional testing in Section 8.1, the following two different cases are distinguished:

1. Both speed and ability are intentional factors measured by the test. In this case, it would be better to score the test with separate estimates of θ and τ, but this is not yet current practice. Instead, typically a single score is supposed to reflect a combination of ability and speed. In this hybrid type of testing, the test has a time limit that is supposed to put the test takers under certain pressure. The limit has to be equally effective for all test takers. But since the test is adaptive, each test taker gets a different selection of items, and we have to control the selection of the items for their time intensity.

2. Ability is intentional but speed is a nuisance factor. In this case, the test is in fact a power test, and the scores can be interpreted as an estimate of θ only. The test may have a time limit for practical reasons, but we do not want the limit to be effective, let alone put a different amount of pressure on different test takers. In this case, item selection has to be controlled both for the test taker's speed and the time intensity of the items to prevent the test taker from running out of time.

9.5.2 Ability and Speed as Intentional Factors

If the calibration sample is large and can be viewed as a random sample from the population of test takers, the identifiability constraint in (9.50) sets the average speed of the population of test takers equal to zero. As a consequence, the time-intensity parameter β_i becomes the expected logtime on item i for an average test taker in the population.

If the total time available for the test, t_{tot}, is well-chosen for the majority of the test takers, item selection can be controlled for differences in time intensity between the items by including the following constraint in the model for the shadow test:

$$\sum_{i=1}^{I} \exp(\beta_i) x_i \leq t_{\text{tot}}, \tag{9.51}$$

where the exponential transformation is needed because β_i is on the logtime scale.

We assume that (9.15) is present in the model for the shadow test so that the left-hand sum of this constraint automatically contains the values of β_i for the items already administered.

The constraint in (9.51) makes item selection equally speeded for all test takers at the level of the total test. If stricter control is required, in the sense of more homogeneous speededness throughout the test, we can also impose the constraint at the level of subsequent blocks of items in the test.

The constraint in (9.51) ignores the differences in the dispersion of the total time on the test between different test takers. For an adaptive test of regular length, this is not much of a problem. Because the total time is the *sum* of the response times on the items, the standard deviation of the total time quickly decreases with increasing length of the test (Exercise 9.8).

9.5.3   Speed as a Nuisance Factor

If speed is a nuisance factor according to the definition of the test, we should estimate the test takers' speed during the test and use these estimates as well to create unspeeded tests for all test takers.

Suppose the response times on the first $g - 1$ items have already been recorded, and we are to select the gth item in the test. The maximum-likelihood estimate of the test taker's speed parameter τ after $g - 1$ items can be shown to be equal to

$$\widehat{\tau}^{(g-1)} = \sum_{i \in \overline{R}_g} (\beta_i - \ln t_i)/(g - 1). \tag{9.52}$$

The estimate is used in the following constraint on the test:

$$\sum_{i=1}^{I} \exp(\beta_i - \widehat{\tau}^{(g-1)})x_i \leq t_{\text{tot}}. \tag{9.53}$$

This constraint thus controls the expected total time of the test takers on the test, no matter how fast they work.

A more sophisticated version of (9.53) is possible if we update our estimates of τ in a Bayesian fashion (i.e., as the posterior distribution of τ given the response times on the previous items, $t_{i_1}, ..., t_{i_{g-1}}$). The posterior distribution of τ can be used to predict the time distribution for each of the remaining items in the pool for the test taker, which are known to also be lognormal for the model in (9.49). (For a derivation, see the literature section at the end of this chapter.) Let $f(t_i \mid t_{i_1}, ..., t_{i_{g-1}})$ denote the density of the predicted response-time distribution for item i in the remaining set of items in the pool, R_g. It is easy to calculate the πth percentiles of these distributions, which we denote as $t_i^{\pi_g}$. The following constraint on the shadow tests should be used:

$$\sum_{i \in \overline{R}_g} t_i + \sum_{i \in R_g} t_i^{\pi_g} x_i \leq t_{\text{tot}}. \tag{9.54}$$

This constraint restricts the sum of the actual response times on the first $g-1$ items and π_gth percentiles of the predicted response-time distributions on the $n - g$ free items in the shadow test by the total amount of time available for the test. It makes sense to specify a sequence of percentiles for the successive items that increases toward the end of the test. Such a sequence makes the predictions more conservative when less time is left.

Just as discussed for the constraint in (9.51) on the item parameters only, (9.53) and (9.54) can also be imposed at the level of subsequent blocks of items to realize a more homogeneous level of unspeededness throughout the test.

In principle, for this second type of control, if test takers understand the procedure, they may try manipulating the choice of items; for example, by working more slowly initially than they need to and speeding up later in the test, when the algorithm selects items that require less time. If the item parameters in the IRT model do not correlate with the parameters in the response-time model, such strategies have no impact on the ability estimates. If these parameters do correlate, they can only have an impact on the accuracy of the estimates of θ because of less than optimal item selection. But if θ is estimated statistically correctly, such strategies cannot introduce any bias in the estimates that would be advantageous to the test taker.

Empirical Example

A simulation study was conducted in which the Bayesian constraint in (9.54) was used to control the speededness of the test. We used the adaptive version of the Arithmetic Reasoning Test from the Armed Services Vocational Aptitude Battery (ASVAB). The item pool was a previous pool of 186 items for this test calibrated using the 3PL model in (1.16). The test has a length of 15 items and is administered without any content constraints. An initial analysis of the actual response times in the data set showed that the time limit of 39 minutes (2,340 seconds) for the test was rather generous and the test thus could be viewed as a power test. This impression justifies the use of (9.54) to avoid differences in speededness between test takers due to the adaptive nature of the test.

The response-time model we used was the lognormal model with a different parameterization, which involved the constraint $\alpha_i = \alpha$ on the discrimination parameter for all items in the pool. The model showed a satisfactory fit to the response times of a sample of $N = 38,357$ test takers.

The items were selected to have maximum information at the interim estimates of $\dot{\theta}$. The first item was selected to be optimal at $\widehat{\theta}^{(0)} = 0$. Interim estimates during the test were obtained using expected a posteriori (EAP) estimation with a uniform prior distribution for the first estimate. The percentile chosen for the posterior predicted response-time distributions in (9.54) was the 50th percentile for the selection of the first item, but we moved linearly to the 95th percentile for the selection of the last two items in the test. The prior distribution of τ was a normal distribution with mean and variance equated to the mean and variance of the distribution of τ estimated from the sample of persons in the data set. After each item, the test taker's response time was used to update this prior distribution in a Bayesian fashion.

We simulated test takers with abilities $\theta = -2.0, 1.5, ..., 2.0$ and speed $\tau = -.6, -.3, 0, .3,$ and $.6$. This range of values for the speed parameter covered the estimated values for the sample of test takers for the version of the response-time model used in this study.

We first simulated test administrations without the response-time constraint. The average times used by the test takers at the different ability and speed levels are reported in the first panel of Figure 9.7. The major impression from the results is that the majority of the test takers have ample time to complete the test, which therefore can be viewed as a power test. Of course, the slower test takers used more time, but this finding does not necessarily point to differential speededness of the test but only to individual differences between test takers. However, the fact that a minority of the test takers ran out of time does reveal that the test was differentially speeded.

We then repeated the study with the response-time constraint in (9.54) added to the shadow-test model. The results are given in the second panel of Figure 9.7. This time, all test takers were able to meet the limit of 2,340 seconds. Also, the amount of time they used was distributed much more uniformly over τ. These results were obtained in spite of the fact that the test takers operated at exactly the same levels of speed as in the first study!

To stretch the limit, we also repeated the study with a time limit equal to $t_{\text{tot}} = 34$ minutes (2,040 seconds) and then $t_{\text{tot}} = 29$ minutes (1,740 seconds). The third and fourth panels in Figure 9.7 show the time used by the test takers for these limits. Again, the response-time constraint appeared to be effective. In spite of the decrease in time available, the test takers had no difficulty completing the test in time, and the distributions of the times they needed to complete the test were more uniform still.

It may be surprising to note that the test takers who ran out of time in the unconstrained version of the test were those with a low value for τ but a *high* value for θ. (See the upper left panel of Figure 9.7.) This result can be explained by the correlation of .65 between the item-difficulty parameter b_i and the time-intensity parameter β_i we found for the data set. As a result of this correlation, adaptive selection of the items for the more able test takers led not only to items that were more difficult toward the end of the test but also to items that were more time-intensive. Consequently, the slower test takers among them ran out of time.

9.6 Reporting Scores on a Reference Test

To enhance the interpretation of test scores, testing agencies usually give the test taker a sample of the test items. In a program with a group-based fixed test administered only once, the test itself can be released for this purpose, but this practice is not possible for adaptive tests. The

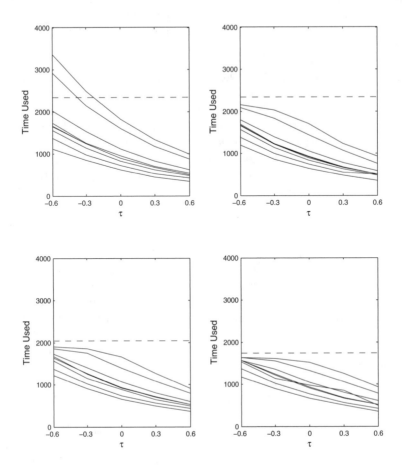

FIGURE 9.7. Average time used by examinees of different levels of ability θ and speed τ for the cases without the time constraint (top left) and with the time constraint and a time limit of 2,340 seconds (top right), 2,040 seconds (bottom left), and 1,740 seconds (bottom right). All curves are ordered by θ, with $\theta = 2.0$ for the highest curves and $\theta = -2.0$ for the lowest curves. The dashed lines indicate the time limits.

testing agency would then have to replenish the item pool too frequently—an activity that not only would entail prohibitively large costs but could also be expected to lead to a quick deterioration of the quality of the pool.

A standard solution for an adaptive-testing program is to give the test takers a paper-and-pencil test with items representative of the pool as a reference test. If the test takers' ability estimates, $\widehat{\theta}$, have been equated to the number-correct scores on the reference test, X, the reference test can be used to evaluate their performances on the adaptive test.

Typical equating methods used to transform $\widehat{\theta}$ to a number-correct score on the reference test are traditional equipercentile equating or true-score equating using the test characteristic function $\tau(\theta)$ in (1.22) for the reference test. If equipercentile equating is used, both the adaptive test and the reference test have to be administered to random samples from the population of test takers, and estimates of the population distributions of $\widehat{\theta}$ and X need to be used to find the score transformation. This equating study is not necessary if the test characteristic function of the reference test, $\tau(\theta)$, is used. This function follows directly from the response functions of the items in the reference test, and substitution of the final estimate $\widehat{\theta}$ on the adaptive test into $\tau(\theta)$ gives an estimate of the test taker's true number-correct score on the reference test.

Both score transformations can be shown to be seriously biased in the presence of measurement error on the reference test and adaptive test. The reason for this bias is the use of a common transformation for all test takers, which has to compromise between their different error distributions along the scales of the two tests. An alternative is to use a local transformation at the position of the test taker on this scale. The discussion of such techniques is beyond the scope of this book. But an alternative that does fit the subject of this book can be derived from the constraints for matching observed-score distributions in Section 5.3.

When applied to adaptive testing, we impose the condition on the sums of powers of the response probabilities in (5.47) on the shadow tests. Let $j = 1, ..., n$ denote the items in the reference test. Suppose we are to assemble the shadow test for the selection of the gth item in the adaptive test. Analogous to (5.48), the target values are now the known constants

$$\mathcal{T}_{r(g-1)} = \sum_{j=1}^{n} p_j^r(\widehat{\theta}^{(g-1)}), \quad \text{for } r \leq R, \tag{9.55}$$

where R is the condition in (5.47) with the highest order used. These target values have to be met by the shadow test; that is, by

$$\sum_{i=1}^{I} p_i^r(\widehat{\theta}^{(g-1)})x_i, \quad \text{for } r \leq R. \tag{9.56}$$

These target values are enforced by imposing the following constraints on the shadow tests:

$$\sum_{i=1}^{I} p_i^r(\widehat{\theta}^{(g-1)})x_i \leq \mathcal{T}_{r(g-1)} + \delta, \quad \text{for all } r \leq R, \tag{9.57}$$

$$\sum_{i=1}^{I} p_i^r(\widehat{\theta}^{(g-1)})x_i \geq \mathcal{T}_{r(g-1)} - \delta, \quad \text{for all } r \leq R, \tag{9.58}$$

where δ is a small tolerance needed to avoid infeasibility due to an equality constraint in the model; see the discussion of (3.50) in Section 3.2.4.

A critical difference with the constraints for the case of a fixed test in Section 5.3 is that (9.57) and (9.58) control the conditions in (5.47) only at the current estimate $\widehat{\theta}_{g-1}$, while in (5.51) and (5.52) they are controlled at a fixed series of values θ_k, $k = 1, ..., K$. In the example for a fixed test in Section 5.3.4, we saw that the best results were obtained for the cases with control at two or three θ values. We therefore recommend adding constraints at the values $\widehat{\theta}_{g-1} + \varepsilon$ and $\widehat{\theta}_{g-1} - \varepsilon$, where ε is a constant chosen by the test administrator. The target values for the reference test at these points, $\mathcal{T}_{r(g-1)}^{+\varepsilon}$ and $\mathcal{T}_{r(g-1)}^{-\varepsilon}$, are calculated analogously to (9.55).

These target values are enforced by the following additional constraints:

$$\sum_{i=1}^{I} p_i^r(\widehat{\theta}^{(g-1)} + \varepsilon)x_i \leq \mathcal{T}_{r(g-1)}^{+\varepsilon} + \delta, \quad \text{for all } r \leq R, \tag{9.59}$$

$$\sum_{i=1}^{I} p_i^r(\widehat{\theta}^{(g-1)} + \varepsilon)x_i \geq \mathcal{T}_{r(g-1)}^{+\varepsilon} - \delta, \quad \text{for all } r \leq R, \tag{9.60}$$

$$\sum_{i=1}^{I} p_i^r(\widehat{\theta}^{(g-1)} - \varepsilon)x_i \leq \mathcal{T}_{r(g-1)}^{-\varepsilon} + \delta, \quad \text{for all } r \leq R, \tag{9.61}$$

$$\sum_{i=1}^{I} p_i^r(\widehat{\theta}^{(g-1)} - \varepsilon)x_i \geq \mathcal{T}_{r(g-1)}^{-\varepsilon} - \delta, \quad \text{for all } r \leq R. \tag{9.62}$$

Unlike the fixed set of constraints in (5.51) and (5.52), the current set is dynamic. It imposes the conditions in (5.47) at a window about $\widehat{\theta}^{(g-1)}$ of size 2ε, which stabilizes if $\widehat{\theta}^{(g-1)}$ does.

We do not yet expect this application to automatically work as well as the one for the fixed test in Section 5.3. One reason is that the best combination of choices of values for δ and ε still has to be determined. Another is that an unfortunate initialization of $\widehat{\theta}^{(0)}$ may lead to an initial series of wild estimates with response functions of the selected items that are hard to compensate for later in the test, when $\widehat{\theta}$ is close to the test taker's true θ. In fact, it may well be that control at a fixed series of well-chosen θ values works equally well or even better than (9.57)–(9.62) for an adaptive test. Both points require further research.

This research is worth the effort because automatic equating of an adaptive test to a reference test entails two major advantages. First, the equating is local; that is, conditional on the final ability estimate of the test taker. As indicated in Section 5.3.3, this type of equating is strong and satisfies the important requirement of equitability: It yields equated scores with the same error distribution as the test taker would have had on the reference test. Second, by imposing the conditions in (5.47) on an adaptive test, the test automatically produces the same *observed number-correct scores* as the reference test. No additional score transformation is needed. The test taker can interpret his or her number-correct score on the adaptive test directly as the number of items he or she would have had correct on the reference test. More amazingly, because the adaptive test is equated to the *same* reference test for all test takers, their scores are also equated mutually: Different test takers can directly compare their numbers of items correct even though they received a different selection of items from the pool.

Empirical Example

The set of constraints in (9.57)–(9.62) was used in a simulation study with adaptive-test administrations from the same item pool for the LSAT used in the examples in the preceding sections. We first assembled a fixed test from the pool and then randomly took a set of nested reference tests from it, with test lengths of $n = 10$, 20, 30, and 40 items; that is, the reference test of 10 items was nested in the test of 20 items, and so on.

No constraints were imposed on the adaptive test. The tolerance parameter δ was set at .5. This choice is equivalent to a half score point on the number-correct scale. During a tryout of this study, we discovered a few cases of infeasibility later in the adaptive test due to first estimates $\widehat{\theta}$ that were far off. If this happened, the algorithm increased the value of δ by .2. The parameter ε was always kept at .5. The target values in the constraints in (9.59)–(9.62) were thus calculated at $\widehat{\theta}^{(g-1)} - .5$, $\widehat{\theta}^{(g-1)}$, and $\widehat{\theta}^{(g-1)} + .5$. Three different replications of the study were conducted, in which the constraints in (9.57)–(9.62) were imposed for (i) $r = 1$, (ii) $r = 1$ and 2, and (iii) $r = 1$, 2, and 3.

We used a Bayesian initialization of $\widehat{\theta}$, where $\widehat{\theta}^{(0)}$ was calculated using regression on a background variable that was assumed to correlate .60 with θ. The prior distribution was also provided by the correlation with the background variable. Subsequent estimates of θ were expected a posteriori (EAP) estimates. (For details on this procedure, see the literature section at the end of this chapter.)

Adaptive test administrations were simulated for 30,000 test takers randomly sampled from a standard normal distribution for θ. For each simulated test taker, we recorded the number-correct score after $n = 10$, 20, 30, and 40 items. The distributions of these scores for the 30,000 test takers are shown in Figures 9.8–9.10. The observed-score distributions on the reference tests were calculated using the Lord-Wingersky algorithm with a standard normal distribution for θ. (For this algorithm, see the literature section at the end of this chapter.)

The results for the set of constraints with $r = 1$, 2 and $r = 1$, 2, 3 were quite close. Also, they were generally better than those for $r = 1$ only. For the lengths of 30 and 40 items, the number-correct score distributions on the adaptive test matched those on the reference test reasonably well.

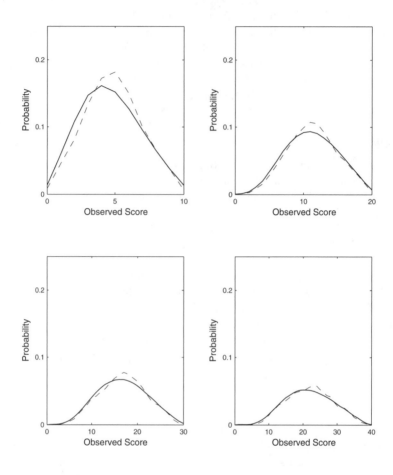

FIGURE 9.8. Observed-score distributions on an adaptive test (dashed lines) and a reference test (solid line) for $n = 10$ and 20 (top) and $n = 30$ and 40 (bottom) $(r = 1)$.

For the shorter test lengths, there was still a mismatch. The question of whether the results for the test lengths of 30 and 40 items, which are typical lengths for real-world adaptive tests, are good enough for score-reporting purposes is subject to further research. This research should involve other choices of δ and ε as well as the alternative of permanent control at a fixed series of values θ_k, $k = 1, ..., K$. Also, the bias and accuracy of this equating method should be evaluated against the alternatives based on the test characteristic function and traditional equipercentile equating.

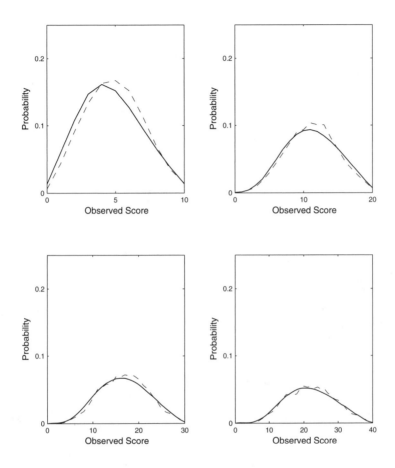

FIGURE 9.9. Observed-score distributions on an adaptive test (dashed lines) and a reference test (solid line) for $n = 10$ and 20 (top) and $n = 30$ and 40 (bottom) $(r = 1, 2)$.

In this study, we also checked the impact of the constraints on the statistical quality of the final ability estimator for the test. There was no discernible loss of accuracy over the main portion of the θ scale. At the extremes of the scale, there was some loss, equivalent to only a few test items. This loss could thus easily be compensated for by making the test slightly longer.

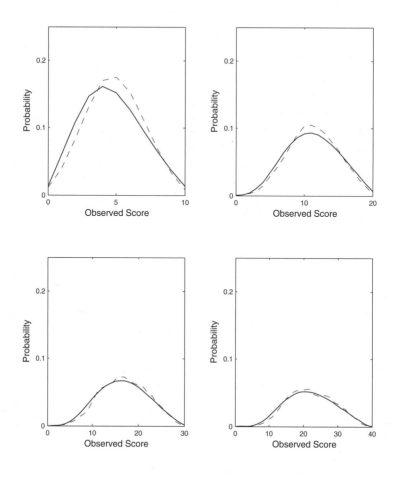

FIGURE 9.10. Observed-score distributions on an adaptive test (dashed lines) and a reference test (solid line) for $n = 10$ and 20 (top) and $n = 30$ and 40 (bottom) ($r = 1, 2, 3$).

9.7   Multidimensional Adaptive Test Assembly

9.7.1   Minimizing Error Variances

If the item pool is multidimensional, the model for the shadow tests can be derived from the standard model for the assembly of a fixed multidimensional test in (8.14)–(8.20). In Section 8.4.3, we showed how to specialize this model to different cases of multidimensional test assembly by imposing certain restrictions on the sets of weights in the key constraints in (8.16) and (8.17). These cases included multidimensional testing in which all abilities measured by the items are intentional, cases where only some of them are intentional and the others are a nuisance, and cases of testing with an interest in a linear combination of the abilities.

The modification of the model in (8.14)–(8.20) that is required for a multidimensional model for shadow tests in adaptive testing is straightforward. As before, we formulate the model for the selection of the gth item in the adaptive test. The updates of the estimates of the two ability parameters after the first $g - 1$ items are denoted as $\widehat{\theta}_1^{(g-1)}$ and $\widehat{\theta}_2^{(g-1)}$. For brevity, we denote the probabilities of correct and incorrect responses under the two-dimensional model in (1.17) at these estimates as

$$p_i^{(g-1)} = p_i(\widehat{\theta}_1^{(g-1)}, \widehat{\theta}_2^{(g-1)}), \tag{9.63}$$

$$q_i^{(g-1)} = 1 - p_i(\widehat{\theta}_1^{(g-1)}, \widehat{\theta}_2^{(g-1)}).$$

The core of the shadow-test version of the model in (8.14)–(8.20) is

$$\text{minimize } y \tag{9.64}$$

subject to

$$\sum_{i=1}^{I} a_{1i} a_{2i} p_i^{(g-1)} q_i^{(g-1)} x_i \leq y, \tag{9.65}$$

$$\sum_{i=1}^{I} a_{1i}^2 p_i^{(g-1)} q_i^{(g-1)} x_i \geq w_1 \kappa, \tag{9.66}$$

$$\sum_{i=1}^{I} a_{2i}^2 p_i^{(g-1)} q_i^{(g-1)} x_i \geq w_2 \kappa, \tag{9.67}$$

$$\sum_{i=1}^{n} x_i = n, \tag{9.68}$$

$$\sum_{i \in \overline{R}_g} x_i = g - 1, \tag{9.69}$$

$$x_i \in \{0, 1\}, \quad \text{for all } i, \tag{9.70}$$

$$y \geq 0. \tag{9.71}$$

If the item pool contains set-based items, the constraint in (9.29) has to be added to this model.

Observe that we no longer control two variance functions over an entire grid of points in the ability space, that is, at points $(\theta_{1kl}, \theta_{2kl})$, with $k = 1, ..., K$ and $l = 1, ..., L$, as we did for the assembly of a fixed test in Chapter

8, but only control the variances of the ability estimators at $(\theta_1, \theta_2) = (\widehat{\theta}_1^{(g-1)}, \widehat{\theta}_2^{(g-1)})$. For this reason, the original sets of weights in (8.16) and (8.17) specialize to the two relative weights w_1 and w_2 in (9.66) and (9.67).

If both θ_1 and θ_2 are intentional, the weights should be chosen to reflect the relative importance of minimization of the variance of $\widehat{\theta}_1$ relative to the variance of $\widehat{\theta}_2$. If both objectives are equally important, we should choose

$$w_1 = w_2 = 1, \tag{9.72}$$

which means that the weights can be removed from (9.66) and (9.67).

If θ_2 is a nuisance ability, we should choose

$$w_1 = 1, \tag{9.73}$$

$$w_2 = 0. \tag{9.74}$$

This choice puts all weight on the constraint in (9.66) and makes (9.67) redundant.

The criterion for picking the best item from the free items in the shadow test follows directly from the definition of the variances of estimators $\widehat{\theta}_1$ and $\widehat{\theta}_2$ in (8.5) and (8.6). To evaluate the candidacy of item i, we calculate projections for these variances after administration of item i at the current estimate $(\theta_1, \theta_2) = (\widehat{\theta}_1^{(g-1)}, \widehat{\theta}_2^{(g-1)})$. We propose using the following projections derived from (8.5) and (8.6):

$$\mathrm{Var}(\widehat{\theta}_1^{(g-1+i)} \mid \widehat{\theta}_1^{(g-1)}, \widehat{\theta}_2^{(g-1)}) = \frac{A_2}{A_1 A_2 - A_{12}}, \tag{9.75}$$

$$\mathrm{Var}(\widehat{\theta}_2^{(g-1+i)} \mid \widehat{\theta}_1^{(g-1)}, \widehat{\theta}_2^{(g-1)}) = \frac{A_1}{A_1 A_2 - A_{12}}, \tag{9.76}$$

with

$$A_1 = \sum_{j \in \overline{R}_g \cup \{i\}} a_{1j}^2 p_j^{(g-1)} q_j^{(g-1)}, \tag{9.77}$$

$$A_2 = \sum_{j \in \overline{R}_g \cup \{i\}} a_{2j}^2 p_j^{(g-1)} q_j^{(g-1)}, \tag{9.78}$$

$$A_{12} = \sum_{j \in \overline{R}_g \cup \{i\}} a_{1j} a_{2j} p_j^{(g-1)} q_j^{(g-1)}, \tag{9.79}$$

where $\overline{R}_g$ still denotes the set of $g - 1$ items already administered.

The item with the minimal value for

$$w_1 \mathrm{Var}(\widehat{\theta}_1^{(g-1+i)} \mid \widehat{\theta}_1^{(g-1)}, \widehat{\theta}_2^{(g-1)}) + w_2 \mathrm{Var}(\widehat{\theta}_2^{(g-1+i)} \mid \widehat{\theta}_1^{(g-1)}, \widehat{\theta}_2^{(g-1)}) \tag{9.80}$$

is the best item for administration. The values of the weights w_1 and w_2 in this sum are subject to the same restrictions as in (9.72) or (9.73) and (9.74).

The expression (9.80) represents a weighted version of the criterion of
A-optimality discussed in Section 8.4.1 for the case of a fixed test. Alternatively, we could use the criterion of D-optimality and evaluate projections
of the determinant of the covariance matrix in (8.3) for each of the free
items in the shadow test (Exercise 9.10).

9.7.2 Computational Aspects

Although the criterion for the second-stage selection of the item in (9.80)
can easily be calculated in real time for the set of free items in the shadow
test, the computation time required to calculate the shadow tests is an as
yet unexplored aspect of multidimensional adaptive testing. As discussed
in Section 8.4.1, the model in (9.63)–(9.71) should be solved for a sequence
of increments of κ, and the best solution according to (9.80) should be
picked. The empirical example with a fixed test in Section 8.6 illustrated
this approach. With adaptive test assembly, the computations have to be
performed in real time.

It is possible to optimize these computations along the same lines as in
Section 9.1.5. If we start the constraints in (9.66) and (9.67) with a large
value for κ and relax by small decreases of κ, the preceding solution is
always in the feasible space of the next problem and is an attractive initial
solution for the next shadow test. However, except for the case of adaptive
testing for a linear combination of abilities (see the literature at the end
of this chapter), we do not yet have much experience with this type of
multidimensional adaptive-test assembly, and our computational ideas still
have to be tried out empirically.

9.7.3 Maximizing Kullback-Leibler Information

An alternative approach to multidimensional adaptive testing is to choose
an objective function for the shadow-test model based on the multivariate
version of the posterior expected Kullback-Leibler information in (9.26). As
already observed in Section 9.2.1, the generalization of the Kullback-Leibler
measure to more than one dimension only involves the replacement of the
unidimensional response model in (9.24) by the two-dimensional model in
(1.17). Likewise, in (9.25) we have to integrate the multidimensional version
of this measure over the joint posterior distribution of (θ_1, θ_1) given the
previous responses $(u_{i_1}, ..., u_{i_{g-1}})$.

To maximize Kullback-Leibler information in multidimensional adaptive
testing, the objective function in the standard model for the shadow test
in (9.11)–(9.21) has to be replaced by

$$\text{maximize} \sum_{i=1}^{I} K_i(\widehat{\theta}_1^{(g-1)}, \widehat{\theta}_2^{(g-1)}) x_i. \tag{9.81}$$

The only price we pay for using this objective function is that the different cases of multidimensional test assembly introduced in Section 8.4.3 can no longer be addressed with explicit weights for the ability dimensions, as we were able to do for (9.66), (9.67), and (9.80). But alternative ways to address these cases do exist.

We discuss the following three cases:

1. If θ_1 and θ_2 are both intentional abilities, the free item in the shadow test with the largest contribution to (9.81) should be selected. This criterion leads to the selection of items that are most informative in the sense of giving the best discrimination between the current estimates $(\widehat{\theta}_1^{(g-1)}, \widehat{\theta}_2^{(g-1)})$ and the points in the two-dimensional ability space at which the posterior distribution is concentrated.

2. If θ_1 is intentional but θ_2 is a nuisance ability, we recommend the following change for the objective function in (9.81): (i) Substitute the current estimate $\widehat{\theta}_2^{(g-1)}$ for θ_2 in the denominator of the Kullback-Leibler information in (9.24) and (ii) perform the integration in (9.25) over the marginal posterior distribution of θ_1 given $(u_{i_1}, ..., u_{i_{g-1}})$. As a result of this change, the items in the shadow test become most informative with respect to the variation in the two-dimensional ability space in the direction along the θ_1 axis, while the variation along the θ_2 axis is ignored.

3. If one is interested in a linear combination $\lambda\theta_1 + (1-\lambda)\theta_2$, with $0 < \lambda < 1$, following our earlier suggestion in Section 8.4.3, we recommend rotating the ability space such that this combination coincides with the first dimension in the new space. The case then becomes identical to the preceding case.

9.7.4 Empirical Examples

We simulated administrations of a 50-item adaptive test for the three different cases of multidimensionality in the preceding section using the same pool of 176 mathematics items for the ACT Assessment Program as in the empirical example with a fixed multidimensional test in Section 8.6. For each case, the items were selected using the modification of the Kullback-Leibler information criterion in (9.81) above. Otherwise, the model for the shadow test was entirely identical to the model for the fixed test in the example in Section 8.6. The test was started with $(\widehat{\theta}_1^{(0)}, \widehat{\theta}_2^{(0)}) = (0,0)$ for each simulated test taker. The ability estimates were updated using joint EAP estimation.

The case where we are interested in a linear combination of abilities had equal weights $\lambda = .5$. That is, we used $\xi_1 = .5\theta_1 + .5\theta_2$ as the intentional ability and $\xi_2 = -.5\theta_1 + .5\theta_2$ as the nuisance ability. The case was implemented using the transformations $a_1^* = a_1 + a_2$ and $a_2^* = a_2 - a_1$ for the two discrimination parameters. (See Exercise 8.3 for details.)

The test administrations were simulated at the 441 different combinations of $\theta_1, \theta_2 = -2.0, -1.8, ..., 2.0$. At each combination, we calculated the average variances in (8.5) and (8.6) for the final estimates $\widehat{\theta}_1$ and $\widehat{\theta}_s$ across the replications. The number of replications at each different combination was equal to 25. The plots with average variances were smoothed using a standard procedure in *Matlab*.

The results for the case where θ_1 and θ_2 are both intentional are given in Figure 9.11. As expected, the two plots show surfaces at about the same height. The fact that the test was adaptive led to an improvement of the surfaces relative to those for the fixed test where θ_1 and θ_2 are intentional in Figure 8.2. The fact that the improvement was modest is due to the unfavorable size of the item pool in relation to the test length.

Figure 9.12 shows the estimates of the two variance functions for the case where θ_1 is the only intentional ability. Since the item selection no longer had to compromise between the variances of the estimators of two intentional ability parameters, the surface for $\widehat{\theta}_1$ was more favorable than in Figure 9.11, while, as expected, the surface for $\widehat{\theta}_2$ was less favorable.

An excellent variance function was obtained for the linear combination of interest, ξ_1, in the third case. As Figure 9.13 shows, the surface was not only low but also nearly uniform over the entire space of combinations of values of ξ_1 and ξ_2 studied. Apparently, the items in this pool were written and selected with this kind of combination of abilities in mind. Of course, the large improvement in the variance of the estimator of ξ_1 in Figure 9.13 relative to that of θ_1 in Figure 9.12 was obtained at the price of a much deteriorated variance for the combination ξ. But the latter did not interest us.

9.8   Final Comments

So far, we have only discussed adaptive test assembly with adaptation at the level of individual items. Alternative options are testlet-based adaptive testing, multistage adaptive testing, and adaptive linear on-the-fly testing. These alternatives have a decreasing level of adaptation: In testlet-based adaptive testing, the ability estimate is updated after testlets of 3–5 items, in multistage adaptive testing after longer subtests, and in linear on-the-fly testing the possibility of adaptation arises only if the individual tests given to test takers are assembled to be optimal at an *a priori* estimate of their ability derived from background information; for instance, an earlier test score.

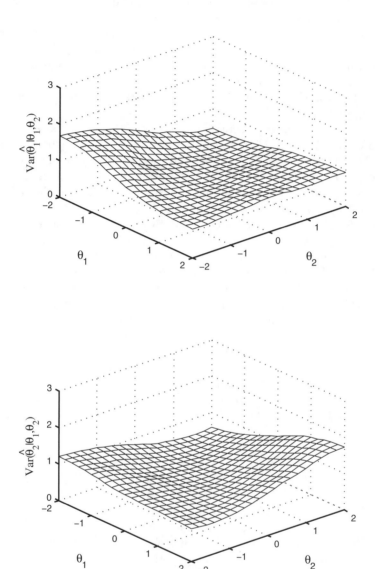

FIGURE 9.11. Estimated variance functions for $\widehat{\theta}_1$ (top) and $\widehat{\theta}_2$ (bottom) for a two-dimensional test with both θ_1 and θ_2 intentional abilities.

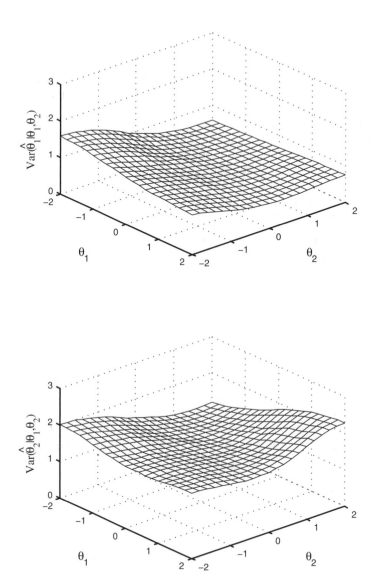

FIGURE 9.12. Estimated variance functions for $\widehat{\theta}_1$ (top) and $\widehat{\theta}_2$ (bottom) for a two-dimensional test with θ_1 an intentional ability and θ_2 a nuisance ability.

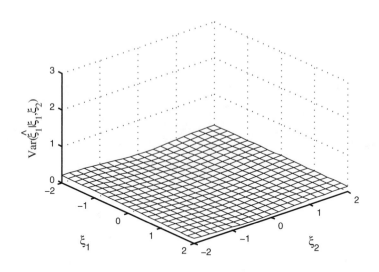

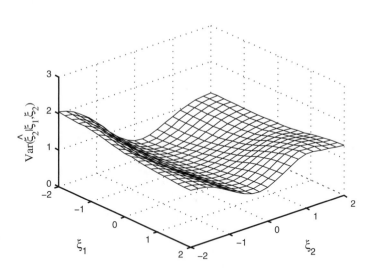

FIGURE 9.13. Estimated variance functions for $\widehat{\xi}_1$ (top) and $\widehat{\xi}_2$ (bottom) for a two-dimensional test with $\xi_1 = .5\theta_1 + .5\theta_2$ an intentional ability and $\xi_2 = -\theta_1 + .5\theta_2$ a nuisance ability.

The two main reasons for accepting a lower level of adaptation that have been put forward are: (i) the wish to have content specialists review intact units in the test before they become operational, and (ii) the opportunity for test takers to go back and review their response to an earlier item. The former is certainly a valid reason. If one wants the content specialist to review units in the test because the results of automated test assembly cannot be trusted (for example, because the items have not yet been coded completely), adaptation is only possible at the level of these intact units.

But the latter is not valid; in adaptive testing, it is always possible to have test takers review earlier items. An obvious strategy is to give them permission to go back to any of the last m items they have taken and change their response if they find it necessary to do so. The only consequence is the necessity to recalculate the current ability estimate from the likelihood for the response vector with the corrected responses. The test is then continued with the new estimate.

In fact, this type of item review is much more efficient than the review offered in testlet-based or multistage adaptive testing, where updating the ability estimate is always postponed until a fixed number of items have been answered. Typically, test takers change their responses only for an occasional item. In this case, the revision of the ability estimate can be expected to lead to a minor change, particularly after the first ten items or so.

An instructive way to view testlet-based, multistage, and adaptive linear on-the-fly testing is as severely restricted versions of the STA. The graphical representation of the method in Figure 9.1 shows that the STA is the case of adaptive testing with the largest number of stages (n) as well as the largest choice of alternative test units (all items in the set of feasible tests in the pool) available at each stage. The other forms of adaptive testing are obtained by restricting the number of stages and/or the number of units available after an update. The restriction is maximal for adaptive linear on-the-fly testing, which is in fact equivalent to an STA with only one shadow test. Obviously, the price for these restrictions is lower precision of the test scores.

9.9   Literature

Pioneering work on adaptive test assembly was reported in Lord (1970; 1971; 1980, chapter 10) and in numerous research reports by David J. Weiss of the University of Minnesota (see Weiss, 1982). More recent treatments of adaptive testing have been given in van der Linden and Glas (2000) and Wainer (2000), while Parshall, Spray, Kalohn, and Davey (2002) should be consulted for the more practical aspects of adaptive testing.

The shadow-test approach (STA) was introduced in van der Linden and Reese (1998) and further extended in van der Linden (2000a). The weighted-deviations method (WDM) was published in Stocking and Swanson (1993). For an extensive comparison between the STA and the WDM, see van der Linden (2005d); a case study with these two approaches is reported in Robin, van der Linden, Eignor, Steffen and Stocking (2004).

The idea of using use Kullback-Leibler information as an objective in adaptive test assembly was formulated in Chang and Ying (1996). Alternative Bayesian criteria for item selection in adaptive testing were proposed in van der Linden (1998d) and van der Linden and Pashley (2000).

Chang and Ying (1999) were the first to suggest the use of alpha stratification in adaptive test assembly. The implementation of alpha stratification using a shadow test with (9.30)–(9.33) was investigated in van der Linden and Chang (2003). The Sympson-Hetter method of item-exposure control for adaptive testing was presented in Sympson and Hetter (1985); a case study with an application of this method to the adaptive version of the Armed Services Vocational Aptitude Battery (ASVAB) can be found in Hetter and Sympson (1997). Stocking and Lewis (1998) suggest using a conditional version of the Sympson-Hetter method, whereas formal properties of the Sympson-Hetter method and some alternative adjustment schemes for its control parameters are presented in van der Linden (2003). For details of the multiple-shadow-test approach (MSTA), the reader should consult Veldkamp and van der Linden (submitted). The method of item-exposure control based on random ineligibility constraints was introduced in van der Linden and Veldkamp (2004); a derivation of the bounds on the ineligibility probabilities in (9.47) as well as a proof of their property of self adaptation can be found in this reference. For the conditional version of this method, see van der Linden and Veldkamp (submitted). A review of all current methods of item-exposure control will be offered in Segall (in preparation).

The version of the lognormal model for response times was formulated in van der Linden (2005a); this reference should also be consulted for statistical methods for calibrating an item pool and testing the fit of this model against response-time data. The Bayesian constraint on the predicted response times for the test taker in (9.54) was introduced in van der Linden, Scrams, and Schnipke (1999). For other uses of response times to improve adaptive testing, see van der Linden (in preparation).

The idea of equating number-correct scores on an adaptive test to those on a reference test using an adaptive version of the constraints for matching observed-score distributions was developed in van der Linden (2001a). Details of the procedure for the Bayesian initialization of the ability estimator used in the empirical example in Section 9.6 are given in van der Linden (1999a).

Multidimensional adaptive testing with the criterion of minimum error variance for a linear combination of abilities in (9.79) was examined in van der Linden (1999b), whereas a more systematic treatment of multidimensional adaptive testing with the posterior expected Kullback-Leibler criterion is given in Veldkamp and van der Linden (2002). For a case study of multidimensional adaptive testing with the STA, see Li (2002). A Bayesian version of the criterion of D-optimality for use in adaptive test assembly was studied in Luecht (1996) and Segall (1996, 2000).

9.10 Summary

1. In adaptive test assembly, items for the test are selected sequentially; each subsequent item is selected to be most informative at an update of the test taker's ability estimate calculated after the preceding response.

2. Adaptive tests have to be assembled to three different sets of constraints: (i) content constraints representing the test specifications, (ii) dynamic constraints necessary to implement the process of adaptation, and (iii) extra constraints to deal with such new problems in adaptive-testing programs as the necessity to constrain the exposure rates of the items, make the test equally speeded for each test taker, and equate the scores to a reference test released for score interpretation.

3. In a shadow-test approach (STA), the constraints are imposed on shadow tests assembled prior to the selection of a new item. Shadow tests are fixed tests that (i) have maximum information at the current ability estimate, (ii) meet all constraints, and (iii) contain all items already taken by the person. The item that is actually administered is the most informative free item in the shadow test. Because each shadow test meets all constraints, the adaptive test always does also.

4. The models used to assemble shadow tests are the same integer programming models as for fixed tests. The only modifications necessary are: (i) the addition of the second and third sets of constraints mentioned in the first point of this summary and (ii) the replacement of an objective function that controls the TIF at a series of fixed values θ_k, $k = 1, ..., K$, by a function that maximizes to the value of the TIF only at the current estimate $\widehat{\theta}_{g-1}$.

5. The STA can be viewed as a projection method for adaptive item selection. At each next ability estimate, it predicts the optimal feasible remaining part of the test and picks the best item from it for administration.

6. The STA can also be viewed as a solution to the dilemma invoked by the combination of sequential item selection and the fact that the constraints can only be satisfied if all items are selected simultaneously. The STA resolves this dilemma by treating adaptive test assembly as a sequence of n simultaneous optimization problems.

7. Adaptive test assembly can be conducted with objectives other than maximizing Fisher's information; for example, objectives based on Kullback-Leibler information and/or Bayesian objectives based on the posterior distribution of θ updated during the test.

8. If the pool contains set-based items, the model for the shadow tests can be derived from the standard model for the simultaneous selection of items and stimuli in Chapter 7. The model then has to be extended with a constraint that sets the variables of the stimuli already chosen equal to one.

9. An effective way to reduce the item-exposure rates of the more popular items in the pool is through alpha stratification; that is, restricting the selection of the items to subsequent strata in the pool with increasing values for the item-discrimination parameter. Alpha stratification can be implemented by adopting a special constraint in the shadow-test model.

10. An alternative way to reduce the exposure rates for the more popular items is through probabilistic control using the Sympson-Hetter method. The method can be implemented effectively using a multiple-shadow-test approach (MSTA) with the Sympson-Hetter experiment conducted over a list of items composed from the free items in parallel shadow tests. The model for the MSTA can be derived from the standard model for the simultaneous selection of multiple tests in Chapter 6.

11. A more efficient form of probabilistic exposure control is through random ineligibility constraints on the items in the pool. The constraints can be drawn with probabilities that are self-adaptive (that is, they automatically maintain the item-exposure rates at optimal levels and do not require any previous adjustment of control parameters).

12. Adaptive tests tend to be differentially speeded in the sense that some test takers get selections of items that require more time than others. If the items have been calibrated under a response-time model, the test can be made equally speeded by including a special constraint in the model for the shadow tests.

13. If the speed at which the test takers operate is an intentional part of the ability measured by the item pool, the constraint should be

based on the item parameters in the response-time model only. But if it is a nuisance factor, the constraint should be based both on the item and person parameters in the model.

14. Number-correct scores on adaptive tests can be automatically equated to scores on a reference test released for score interpretation by including an adaptive version of the constraints for matching the observed-score distribution in Section 5.3 in the model for the shadow tests. These constraints also allow for a direct comparison of the number-correct scores of different persons taking the adaptive test.

15. If the item pool is multidimensional, the model for the shadow tests can be derived from the standard model for the assembly of a fixed multidimensional test in Chapter 8. The item that is actually administered is the item with a minimal value for a weighted projection of the variances of the ability estimators. The weights offer direct control of the relative importances of these variances in the different cases of multidimensional testing discussed in Chapter 8.

16. Alternatively, the model for the shadow tests can be given an objective function based on a multidimensional generalization of (posterior) expected Kullback-Leibler information. This option allows us to deal with different cases of multidimensional testing, too, but without explicit weights for the individual ability estimators.

17. Testlet-based adaptive testing, multistage testing, and adaptive linear on-the-fly testing are restricted versions of the STA, with smaller numbers of stages at which the ability estimate is updated and smaller numbers of test units to choose from after the updates. The price paid for these restrictions is lower precision of the test score.

9.11   Exercises

9.1 Formulate a version of the standard model for a shadow test in (9.11)–(9.21) for the case of an adaptive test with random test length in Section 9.1.1.

9.2 In Section 9.3, the next stimulus in an adaptive test is identified by the most informative free item in the shadow test. An alternative criterion would be to select the free stimulus in the shadow test with the largest average information for its items. Which criterion is best?

9.3 Show that the sum of the exposure rates of the items in the pool in adaptive testing is always equal to the test length, n. What is the effect on the other items in the pool of lowering the exposure rate of an item with a tendency toward overexposure to less than $r^{\max}$?

For an adaptive test of 15 items, would it be possible to design an exposure-control method that forces the exposure rates of all items in a pool of 350 to be between .05 and .10?

9.4 Let $t = 1, 2, \ldots$ be the iteration steps in a sequence of adaptive-testing simulations conducted to adjust the control parameters $P(A_i \mid S_i, \theta)$ in the Sympson-Hetter method. After each step, we have new estimates of the probabilities of selecting the items, $P^{(t)}(S_i \mid \theta)$. The Sympson-Hetter method uses the following adjustment rule for the control parameters:

$$
P^{(t+1)}(A_i \mid S_i, \theta) = \begin{cases} 1 & \text{if } P^{(t)}(S_i \mid \theta) \leq r^{\max}, \\ r^{\max}/P^{(t)}(S_i \mid \theta) & \text{if } P^{(t)}(S_i \mid \theta) > r^{\max}. \end{cases}
$$

Motivate the adjustment of the control parameters for $P^{(t)}(S_i \mid \theta) > r^{\max}$. Does it make sense to set the control parameters equal to 1 if $P^{(t)}(S_i \mid \theta) \leq r^{\max}$? Formulate a few alternatives for this part of the adjustment rule.

9.5 Show that the upper bound for $P(E_i \mid \theta)$ in (9.47) follows from (9.46) along with the assumption that $P(E_i \cap F \mid \theta) = P(E_i \mid \theta)P(F \mid \theta)$. How reasonable is this independence assumption?

9.6 For a well-designed adaptive test, the probability of a feasible test for test taker e can be expected to be equal to $P^{(e)}(F \mid \theta) = 1$. Use this condition to show the property of self-adaptation for the updates of the probabilities of item eligibility in (9.47).

9.7 Motivate the choice of the constraint on the time intensities of the items in the shadow test in (9.50) using the identifiability constraint in (9.49) and the fact that t_{tot} has been chosen to be large enough for the population of test takers.

9.8 Suppose the response times of the test takers have a common standard deviation of 30 seconds for all items in the pool. What would be your estimate of the standard deviation of the total time for a test taker on a test of 25 items?

9.9 In the empirical example in Section 9.5.3, we began the test with the 50th percentile of the posterior predicted response-time distributions in the constraint in (9.53). Why is this choice reasonable? Why does it make sense to move to the 95th percentile for the selection of the last two items in the test.

9.10 Suppose both abilities measured by the items in a two-dimensional pool are intentional. In addition, suppose it holds that if the weights w_1 and w_2 for an adaptive test are set as in (9.71), the STA meets the criterion of D-optimality (i.e., it minimizes the determinant of the covariance matrix in (8.4)). Formulate the criterion for item selection that has to replace (9.80) if the items from the shadow test are selected to be D-optimal?

10
Designing Item Pools for Programs with Fixed Tests

As has become clear in the previous chapters, our interest in this book is not in the design of an individual test but of a *program of tests*. This choice is in line with the modern practice of testing, with its emphasis on item banking, multiple testing occasions, the possible reuse of items, and the assembly of tests to different specifications from the same item pool (see Section 1.2.1). If we were interested only in the design of a single test administration, it would be more efficient to write the items directly for the test, review them, and pretest a trial version of the test. In fact, we would then return to the classical practice of standardized testing (see Section 1.1.1).

Consequently, the models for item-pool design in this chapter are also at the level of an entire testing program. But, of course, no item pool can support a testing program forever, and we have to limit our planning horizon. We do so by assuming explicit parameters for the number of parallel forms of each test to be administered in the program.

The models in this chapter are for different types of testing programs. The simplest program is one that administers parallel forms of a single test. A more complicated type of program is one with parallel forms of multiple tests, where, not surprisingly, a further complication arises if one or more of the tests consists of item sets.

A solution to a design model is a blueprint for the item pool that tells us what items to write. The blueprint is optimal in that it minimizes a cost function; the nature of this function is explained in this chapter.

It is possible to use the design models in this chapter in a one-shot approach in which no test forms are assembled until the item pool is complete.

But a more dynamic application, in which the item pool is still developed while test forms are already assembled, seems more realistic. We will therefore introduce dynamic versions of the models, which enable us to adapt our blueprint permanently to the actual practice of item writing and test assembly.

Before introducing the models, we have to make our notion of an item pool, which in the general testing parlance seems to encompass virtually any collection of items, somewhat more precise. A basic distinction is between a master pool and an operational pool. We define a *master pool* as an inventory of test items maintained by the testing organization and an *operational pool* as a pool of items from which the test forms are actually assembled. Typically, a master pool is much less structured than an operational pool. Its items may be in various stages of development, while the items in an operational item pool have passed all preparatory stages and the pool is ready for test assembly.

The design models in this chapter are for calculating an optimal blueprint for an operational item pool. The blueprint has all the information required to instruct the item authors. The items can be written directly for the operational pool. But, as an interim step, they can also be collected in the master pool first. The development of the operational pool then involves the additional step of assembling the operational pool to the blueprint. This step is common for programs with adaptive testing but less so for programs with fixed tests, where the distinction between a master pool and an operational pool typically is only conceptual.

All design models in this chapter are integer programming models. Consequently, it is easy to solve them; basically, all we have to do is use an IP solver to calculate a solution. Nevertheless, the best way to view these models is not as test-assembly models with fully relaxed integer variables but as a generalization of the optimal design approach discussed in Section 4.7 that includes the full set of item attributes as well as all constraints required to represent the test specifications in the program. It is recommended to reread Section 4.7 at this point, particularly the list of critical differences between optimal test design and optimal test assembly at the end of it.

10.1   Definition of Design Space

A key notion in this chapter is that of a design space for the item pool. A *design space* $\mathcal{D}$ is defined as the Cartesian product of all item attributes figuring in the specifications of the tests in the program. These attributes can be of any of the types distinguished in Chapter 2, though several of the logical attributes that may occur in test specifications do not play any role in item-pool-design problems (see below).

The design space is often high-dimensional and large. On the other hand, it makes no sense to consider all possible values for the quantitative attributes. We therefore assume that each quantitative attribute is represented by a smaller set of values for it. This assumption basically reduces $\mathcal{D}$ to a multivariate table, with each cell representing a combination of attribute values.

We will refer to these combinations as the *design points* $d = 1, ..., D$ for the item pool. The order of the individual attributes in d, as well as the order in which the combinations are represented in $\mathcal{D}$, is not important; we assume that they have been fixed in a known way. The only thing that matters is that each design point d represents a possible combination of attribute values

$$(\text{attribute } 1, \text{attribute } 2, ...) \tag{10.1}$$

for a potential item in the pool. Unlike the optimal design approach in Section 4.7, the current points thus represent a potentially wide range of attributes, running from classifications of item content, format, and cognitive level to such attributes as statistical item parameters, word counts, and expected response times for the items.

If the values are chosen well, the reduction of a quantitative attribute to a smaller set of discrete values is not dramatic. Typically, the results are robust with respect to minor variations in the values of the quantitative attributes. A case in point are the values for the item parameters in the 3PL model in (1.16). The reduction of these parameters to a smaller set of values reminds us of a similar decision made in Chapter 5, where we decided to consider target values for TIFs only at a few discrete values θ_k, $k = 1, ..., K$.

We will use (a_d, b_d, c_d) to denote the values of the item parameters at point d. At each point, the combination of values for the three parameters fixes the item-information function in (1.21). We will use $I_d(\theta)$ to denote the function at point d. Typically, in test assembly, we constrain large sums of these functions, and the sums are reasonably robust with respect to small deviations in the parameter values for some of the items.

It is important to note that each possible test from the item pool can be represented by an array of integers

$$(x_1, ..., x_D), \tag{10.2}$$

which tells us how many items in the test have the combination of attributes at point $d = 1, ..., D$. The integers x_d are *not* restricted to 0-1 values; a test can have more than one item with the same attributes. In a design model for an item pool, these integers do not represent an existing test. Instead, they are *decision variables* that allow us to calculate how many items in the pool are required at each point d to assemble all tests in a program.

It makes sense to optimize the design of an item pool for a program with respect to the costs involved in the production of the items. To this end, we introduce a cost function, φ_d. This function, which will be further explored in Section 10.4, represents the costs of writing an item with the combinations of attributes at $d = 1, ..., D$.

We first apply our ideas to the problem of designing an item pool for a program with parallel forms of a single test and then generalize the model to the case of a program with parallel forms of multiple tests.

10.2   Programs with Parallel Forms of a Single Test

As already alluded to, the model will be formulated using the decision variables

$$x_d = \text{number of items at point } d \in \mathcal{D}. \tag{10.3}$$

Suppose the pool has to support a planning period with N parallel forms of the test. The number of items at design point d needed in the pool is then

$$N_d = N x_d. \tag{10.4}$$

These numbers enable us to define a design or a *blueprint for the item pool* as the array

$$(N_1, ..., N_D). \tag{10.5}$$

This array can also be viewed as a collection of *item blueprints*; for each design point, we know exactly what combination of attributes its items should have. The expression (10.5) can therefore be used to instruct the item authors or as input to item-generation software.

To represent the constraints on the categorical attributes of the test, we use the earlier sets V_c as our generic notation for a partition of $\mathcal{D}$ in which each set of points represents a different category of an attribute c. That is, if $d \in V_c$, the attribute at d belongs to category c. Likewise, we use q_d as the generic symbol for the value of a quantitative attribute q at design point d. We have already defined $I_d(\theta)$ as the IIF associated with the item-parameter values at point d. For a program with N parallel forms, it is unlikely that the forms have to be assembled to a relative target. We therefore assume that their information function has to meet absolute target values $\mathcal{T}_k$ at θ_k, $k = 1, ..., K$.

10.2.1   Standard Design Model

Following is our standard model for calculating an optimal blueprint for a program with parallel forms of a single test:

$$\text{minimize } \sum_{d=1}^{D} \varphi_d x_d \quad \text{(minimal costs)} \tag{10.6}$$

subject to possible constraints at the following levels:

Test Level

$$\sum_{d=1}^{D} I_d(\theta_k) x_d \gtreqless \mathcal{T}_k, \quad \text{for all } k, \quad \text{(test information)} \qquad (10.7)$$

$$\sum_{d=1}^{D} x_d \gtreqless n, \quad \text{(test length)} \qquad (10.8)$$

$$\sum_{d \in V_c} x_d \gtreqless n_c, \quad \text{for all } c, \quad \text{(categorical attributes)} \qquad (10.9)$$

$$\sum_{d=1}^{D} q_d x_d \gtreqless b_q; \quad \text{(quantitative attributes)} \qquad (10.10)$$

Item Level

$$\sum_{d \in V_1} x_d = n_1, \quad \text{(special combinations of attributes)} \qquad (10.11)$$

$$\sum_{d \in V_0} x_d = 0; \quad \text{(special combinations of attributes)} \qquad (10.12)$$

Definition of Variables

$$x_d \in \{0, 1, ...\}, \quad \text{for all } d. \quad \text{(range of variables)} \qquad (10.13)$$

The objective in (10.6) is minimization of the total cost of item production, which is to be realized subject to the constraints in (10.7)–(10.13). The constraints represent the specifications of the test forms in the program. The constraints in (10.7) guarantee a TIF that meets the target values $\mathcal{T}_k$ at θ_k, $k = 1, ..., K$, whereas the constraints in (10.8) control the test length. The constraints in (10.9) and (10.10) represent the usual options of categorical and quantitative constraints at the test level. To be able to include items with certain desirable combinations of attributes in the test or exclude undesirable combinations, the constraints in (10.11) and (10.12) are available. The decision variables x_d are defined to take (nonnegative) integer values in (10.13).

It is instructive to reflect on the precise differences between (10.6)–(10.13) and the model for the assembly of a single test in (4.1)–(4.10), from which it is obviously derived. The differences are as follows:

1. The variables are not for the combinatorial problem of selecting a combination of items from an existing pool but represent the number of items with the different combinations of attribute values needed in the pool to assemble the test. Hence, they are no longer restricted to 0-1 values but are fully integer.

2. Just as in (4.1), the objective function in (10.6) is still formulated for a test-level quantity, but the quantity is now the value of the cost function for a single test form in the program.

3. All test specifications are dealt with as constraints. Although most of the models for IRT-based test assembly in Chapter 5 had an objective function formulated for the TIF, the change is not critical. For example, if the test forms will be assembled using (5.9)–(5.12), the TIF approximates the target values $\mathcal{T}_k$ from above. Likewise, (10.7) can be used to include the TIF in a small band just above a target function.

4. The design model does not have an equivalent to the constraints on enemy items in (4.9) simply because we do not have any items yet. Constraints on enemy items are only required when review of an actual item pool leads to the detection of a few sets of items that appear to exclude each other. If certain combinations of item attributes are expected to increase the likelihood of enemy items in the pool, we can restrict the number of items with these combinations by using

$$\sum_{d \in V_e} x_d \leq 1, \quad \text{for all } e, \tag{10.14}$$

where the sets V_e are the sets with such combinations of attributes. These sets may consist of single points d.

5. The model also misses the quantitative item-level constraints in (4.7) and (4.8). If a range of values for a quantitative attribute has to be excluded, a direct way of dealing with these requirements is to avoid the range in our choice of design points $d = 1, ..., D$.

6. Just as in (4.5) and (4.6), the remaining item-level constraints in (10.11) and (10.12) can be used to include or avoid items with certain combinations of categorical attributes. But in fact they have become more general; they now also allow us to include or avoid items at design points d with combinations of categorical attributes with certain quantitative attribute values.

10.3   Programs with Parallel Forms of Multiple Tests

A more interesting case arises if the item pool has to serve a collection of tests $t = 1, ..., T$ during the planning period. These tests are different in that they have to satisfy different sets of bounds for the constraints; for example, a different test length or content distribution, or different sets of target values for their TIFs. But since the specifications of each test are still formulated using the same set of attributes, the same design space holds for the entire set of tests.

In principle, this design problem could be solved using the preceding model for each separate test and adding the values of the decision variables for the solutions. This approach would not lead to any of the usual problems involved in the sequential assembly of multiple tests discussed in Section 6.1; in the current application, the solutions would no longer have to "compete for the best items in the pool," and there is thus no danger of a deteriorating value of the objective function or of later problems becoming infeasible.

But unless the size of the problem is too large, a simultaneous approach is to be preferred: First, it is always more convenient to get a solution as the result of a single run of a model. This point holds particularly if the model is used in a series of updates in the dynamic implementation of a design model to be discussed in Section 10.7 below. Second, a simultaneous model enables us to deal with the possible overlap required between test forms.

For the case where the number of variables in the model becomes too large, we present a (somewhat less general) alternative simultaneous model below.

10.3.1   Simultaneous Model

The following set of variables is needed to formulate the model:

$$x_{dt} = \text{number of items at point } d \in \mathcal{D} \text{ for test } t. \tag{10.15}$$

Suppose N_t parallel forms are to be assembled for test t during the planning period. The total number of items needed in the pool at design point d is then

$$N_d = \sum_{t=1}^{T} N_t x_{dt}. \tag{10.16}$$

The blueprint for the item pool is now the array of the numbers in (10.16) for $d = 1, ..., D$.

Following is our standard model for calculating an optimal blueprint for a program with parallel forms of multiple tests:

$$\text{minimize} \sum_{t=1}^{T} \sum_{d=1}^{D} \varphi_d x_{dt} \quad \text{(minimal costs)} \tag{10.17}$$

subject to possible constraints at the following levels:

Test Level

$$\sum_{d=1}^{D} I_d(\theta_k) x_{dt} \gtreqless \mathcal{T}_{kt}, \quad \text{for all } k \text{ and } t, \quad \text{(test information)} \tag{10.18}$$

$$\sum_{d=1}^{D} x_{dt} \gtreqless n_t, \quad \text{for all } t, \quad \text{(test length)} \tag{10.19}$$

$$\sum_{d \in V_c} x_{dt} \gtreqless n_{ct}, \quad \text{for all } c \text{ and } t, \quad \text{(categorical attributes)} \tag{10.20}$$

$$\sum_{d=1}^{D} q_d x_{dt} \gtreqless b_{qt}, \quad \text{for all } t; \quad \text{(quantitative attributes)} \tag{10.21}$$

Item Level

$$\sum_{d \in V_1} x_{dt} = n_{1t}, \quad \text{for all } t, \quad \text{(special combinations of attributes)} \tag{10.22}$$

$$\sum_{d \in V_0} x_{dt} = 0, \quad \text{for all } t; \quad \text{(special combinations of attributes)} \tag{10.23}$$

Definition of Variables

$$x_{dt} \in \{0, 1, ...\}, \quad \text{for all } d \text{ and } t. \quad \text{(range of variables)} \tag{10.24}$$

Analogous to the model for a program with a single test, (10.17)–(10.24) is a direct generalization of the model for the simultaneous assembly of multiple tests in (6.3)–(6.13). It does not, however, have any equivalent to the item-overlap constraints in (6.4). The reason is the same as for the absence of the enemy constraints in the preceding model; the only thing a design model has to guarantee is an item pool with the right number of items with the various combinations of attributes for the tests to be assembled in the program. The model in (10.17)–(10.24) does so for a program with no item overlap between its test forms.

10.3.2   Item Overlap

If the program admits reuse of items in test forms, the design model has to be adjusted. For notational convenience, we restrict our treatment to the model for a program with constraints on the common numbers in two tests, t and t'.

Analogous to the case of the simultaneous assembly of a pair of tests in (6.19), we need to add the following variables to the model:

$$z_{dtt'} = \text{number of items at point } d \in \mathcal{D} \text{ for tests } t \text{ and } t', \tag{10.25}$$

for all d. The version of the model in (10.17)–(10.24) that admits a number of common items in tests t and t' between bounds $n_{tt'}^{\max}$ and $n_{tt'}^{\min}$ is

$$\text{minimize} \sum_{d=1}^{D} \varphi_d(x_{dt} + x_{dt'} + z_{dtt'}) \tag{10.26}$$

subject to possible constraints at the following levels:

Test Level

$$\sum_{d=1}^{D} I_d(\theta_k)(x_{dt} + z_{dtt'}) \gtreqqless \mathcal{T}_{kt}, \quad \text{for all } k, \quad \text{(TIF of } t) \tag{10.27}$$

$$\sum_{d=1}^{D} I_d(\theta_k)(x_{dt'} + z_{dtt'}) \gtreqqless \mathcal{T}_{kt'}, \quad \text{for all } k, \quad \text{(TIF of } t') \tag{10.28}$$

$$\sum_{d=1}^{D} (x_{dt} + z_{dtt'}) \gtreqqless n_t, \quad \text{(length of } t) \tag{10.29}$$

$$\sum_{d=1}^{D} (x_{dt'} + z_{dtt'}) \gtreqqless n_{t'}, \quad \text{(length of } t') \tag{10.30}$$

$$\sum_{d} z_{dtt'} \leq n_{tt'}^{\max}, \quad \text{(overlap)} \tag{10.31}$$

$$\sum_{d} z_{dtt'} \geq n_{tt'}^{\min}, \quad \text{(overlap)} \tag{10.32}$$

$$\sum_{d \in V_c} (x_{dt} + z_{dtt'}) \gtreqqless n_{ct}, \quad \text{for all } c, \quad \text{(categorical attributes of } t) \tag{10.33}$$

$$\sum_{d \in V_c} (x_{dt'} + z_{dtt'}) \gtreqqless n_{ct'}, \quad \text{for all } c, \quad \text{(categorical attributes of } t') \tag{10.34}$$

$$\sum_{d=1}^{D} q_d(x_{dt} + z_{dtt'}) \gtreqqless b_{qt}, \quad \text{(quantitative attributes of } t) \tag{10.35}$$

$$\sum_{d=1}^{D} q_d(x_{dt'} + z_{dtt'}) \gtreqqless b_{qt'}; \quad \text{(quantitative attributes of } t') \tag{10.36}$$

Item Level

$$\sum_{d \in V_1} (x_{dt} + z_{dtt'}) = n_{1t}, \quad \text{(special combinations of attributes of } t) \tag{10.37}$$

$$\sum_{d \in V_0} (x_{dt} + z_{dtt'}) = 0, \quad \text{(special combinations of attributes of } t) \tag{10.38}$$

$$\sum_{d \in V_1} (x_{dt'} + z_{dtt'}) = n_{1t'}, \quad \text{(special combinations of attributes of } t') \tag{10.39}$$

$$\sum_{d \in V_0} (x_{dt'} + z_{dtt'}) = 0; \quad \text{(special combinations of attributes of } t') \tag{10.40}$$

Definition of Variables

$$z_{dtt'} \in \{0, 1, ...\}, \quad \text{for all } d, \quad \text{(range of variables)} \qquad (10.41)$$

$$x_{dt}, x_{dt'} \in \{0, 1, ...\}, \quad \text{for all } d. \quad \text{(range of variables)} \qquad (10.42)$$

The following differences exist between the model in (10.26)–(10.42) and the preceding model for a program without overlap:

1. The decision variables x_{dt} for test t have been replaced by $x_{dt} + z_{dtt'}$. The same has been done for test t'. These substitutions redefine the variables x_{dt} and $x_{dt'}$ as the number of *unique items* for tests t and t' at design point d, whereas $z_{dtt'}$ is the number of *common items* at d in tests t and t'.

2. In the objective function, the costs for the common items have been included only once.

3. The new constraints in (10.31) and (10.32) control the size of the overlap between the two tests t and t'.

Observe that the model does not need any constraints analogous to (6.22) and (6.23) to keep the values of the variables x_{dt}, $x_{dt'}$, and $z_{dtt'}$ consistent. The reason is the same as for the absence of certain constraints in the preceding models: Design models do not assign any actual items to tests; the only thing they have to guarantee is that the right number of items for each design point be available in the item pool. The increase of the number of constraints in the design model for a program with item overlap is thus much smaller than the one entailed by the model for the actual assembly of the test forms in (6.20)–(6.24).

If it is necessary to restrict the overlap between tests only to items with certain attribute combinations, the following constraint should be added to the model:

$$\sum_{d \in V_0} z_{dtt'} = 0, \qquad (10.43)$$

where V_0 now is the set of points $d \in \mathcal{D}$ for which no overlap is permitted.

Of course, the numbers N_d for the blueprint in (10.16) have to be adjusted for the overlap between the variables x_{dt} and $x_{dt'}$. For a set of T tests, these numbers are now equal to

$$N_d = \sum_{\{t,t'\}} x_{dt} + x_{dt'} + z_{dtt'}, \qquad (10.44)$$

where $\{t, t'\}$ denotes the set of all possible pairs of the T tests. Each of the terms in (10.44) is the sum of the number of unique items for t and t' plus the number of common items in the pair.

10.3.3 Model with Aggregated Bounds

If the design space for the model in (10.17)–(10.24), and hence its number of variables, becomes large, a simultaneous solution is still possible using a version of the model similar to (10.6)–(10.13) but with aggregated bounds. We first present the model and then explain its features.

$$\text{minimize} \ \sum_{d=1}^{D} \varphi_d x_d \quad \text{(minimal costs)} \tag{10.45}$$

subject to possible constraints at the following levels:

Test Level

$$\sum_{d=1}^{D} I_d(\theta_k) x_d \gtreqless \sum_{t=1}^{T} \mathcal{T}_k, \quad \text{for all } k, \quad \text{(test information)} \tag{10.46}$$

$$\sum_{d=1}^{D} x_d \gtreqless \sum_{t=1}^{T} n_t, \quad \text{(test length)} \tag{10.47}$$

$$\sum_{d \in V_c} x_d \gtreqless \sum_{t=1}^{T} n_{ct}, \quad \text{for all } c, \quad \text{(categorical attributes)} \tag{10.48}$$

$$\sum_{d=1}^{D} q_d x_d \gtreqless \sum_{t=1}^{T} b_q; \quad \text{(quantitative attributes)} \tag{10.49}$$

Item Level

$$\sum_{d \in V_1} x_d = \sum_{t=1}^{T} n_{1t}, \quad \text{(special combinations of attributes)} \tag{10.50}$$

$$\sum_{d \in V_0} x_d = ; \quad \text{(special combinations of attributes)} \tag{10.51}$$

Definition of Variables

$$x_d \in \{0, 1, ...\}, \quad \text{for all } d. \quad \text{(range of variables)} \tag{10.52}$$

The bounds in this model are equal to the sums of the original bounds over all tests $t = 1, ..., T$ in (10.17)–(10.24). This type of model works best if it has categorical constraints only; a solution to it can always be split into sets of different numbers of items required for each category in the individual tests. But this additivity does not necessarily hold if quantitative constraints are present. For example, the fact that the sum of the item-information functions meets the sum of target values in (10.46) does not necessarily imply the existence of subsets of items that meet the values for the individual tests. We do not expect this to be much of a problem for larger programs, with the exception of the case in which the TIFs of the tests are to be constrained at different points θ_k (Exercise 10.4).

10.3.4   Discussion

So far, the design models have been rather straightforward modifications of some of the earlier models for test assembly in this book. As a matter of fact, the modifications invariably led to models simpler than their originals. This feature is the result of the fact that we were able to leave out certain constraints because they

1. did not apply to design problems, such as the (logical) constraints on enemy items and item overlap, or

2. could be met more directly by our definition of the design space.

If the pool has to be designed for a program with item sets, we will introduce a comparable modification for the model for set-based test assembly in (7.3)–(7.24), but this time the result appears to be somewhat more complicated. Before discussing this case, we first address an issue touched upon only briefly so far, namely the idea of using a cost function to optimize the blueprint of an item pool.

10.4   Cost Function

The cost function φ_d represents our estimates of the production costs of an item for the design points $d \in \mathcal{D}$. Item production usually involves several steps, such as (i) the actual writing of the item, (ii) one or more reviews, (iii) pretesting, (iv) the amount of fixing necessary, and (v) the final decision to accept or reject the item. Usually, the costs of some of these steps—for example, the cost of reviewing and pretesting—are approximately equal for all items. Since we use the cost function in an optimization problem, all constant components can be removed from it without changing the solution. Basically, it suffices if the function covers only the costs of (i) writing an item and (ii) the risk of having to fix or reject it.

Ideally, we have direct estimates of all relevant costs. These may be available as the result of earlier research on the testing program or as currently budgeted costs. If the program is new, we may be able to start with rough initial estimates and update them when we gather more experience with the item-production process. A formal framework for doing so will be presented in Section 10.7.

If no direct cost estimates are available, it makes sense to look for proxies of item-writing costs. Again, since we use this function in an optimization problem only, proxies of monotonic functions of the costs work equally well. Examples of such proxies are: (i) the average time needed to write an item for the various attribute combinations, (ii) the frequencies with which items for these combinations have been written in the past, and (iii) the number of times such items have been rejected as the result of review and/or pretesting.

Also, it is seldom necessary to have cost estimates based on the entire combination of attributes that defines $\mathcal{D}$. Often, a few known attributes dominate the costs. For example, it is a well-known experience that it is more difficult to write items with a multiple-choice format than with a constructed-response format or items with more alternatives if this is a relevant attribute. In such cases, our estimate of φ_d can be chosen to vary mainly with these attributes. Conversely, we sometimes have attributes known to show hardly any variation at all. An example is guessing parameters c in the 3PL model in (1.16) when the number of response alternatives of the items is fixed. Such attributes should be removed from the definition of $\mathcal{D}$; they lead to a simplification of the cost function.

In the empirical examples in Sections 10.6 and 10.7.3, we used a simple proxy for the cost function derived from a previous item pool for the same testing program. It was based on the assumption that items with attribute combinations written more frequently in the previous history of the program apparently were easier to write, showed less risk of being rejected, and were thus obtained at lower cost.

Even if this assumption leads to an incorrect estimate of the actual costs, it makes sense to optimize the design of an item pool capitalizing on the patterns of frequencies of attribute combinations in a representative item pool reflected in this type of cost function. The choice enables us to automatically account for the empirical correlations between the attributes in $\mathcal{D}$; that is, the design model guarantees an item pool that supports the required set of test forms but avoids combinations less likely to be written due to tendencies for specific attributes to correlate (for example, item content and difficulty). The benefits become even stronger if we add the item authors involved in the program as a categorical attribute to the design space (see Section 10.7.2).

The main point put forward in this section is that we often have access to more sources of information on the costs of item production for a testing program than we may realize. It is always advantageous to improve the design of the item pool using as much information from these sources as possible.

10.4.1 Smoothing Cost Functions

If we have inaccurate estimates of φ_d for some points of $\mathcal{D}$, or no estimates at all, we may be able to improve our cost function by using a smoothing technique. Of course, smoothing only makes sense for the quantitative attributes in the design space. In the examples in Sections 10.6 and 10.7.2, we used a simple technique known as *k-nearest-neighbor regression*. In this technique, the smoothed cost estimate at design point d is calculated as the average of the estimates of the costs in a neighborhood of d. Let φ_d^*

denote the smoothed cost at d, and suppose we work with a neighborhood of size k. It then holds that

$$\varphi_d^* = k^{-1} \sum_{d' \in N_k(d)} \varphi_{d'}, \qquad (10.53)$$

where the neighborhood of d, $N_k(d)$, is defined as the set of the k points in $\mathcal{D}$ closest to d.

The size of the neighborhood determines the degree of smoothing. Usually, a neighborhood that includes the first one or two neighbors in each direction suffices. For the cost function used in the example in Section 10.6, smoothing was effective in the areas of the design space with only an occasional point with lack of data but became less effective for areas with sparser data. This point suggests that it might be worthwhile to look into the application of an adaptive smoothing technique, with the size of the neighborhood defined as a function of the data.

If we have direct estimates of all major cost components but estimates of the full costs for a subset of the points only, we could also use a model-based technique. For example, we could fit parametric regression models to the data and generalize the result for the best-fitting model to the entire space. With this approach, smoothness is imposed directly by the model.

10.5   Item Sets

If the program has set-based tests, the design model can be derived from the model for the simultaneous selection of items and stimuli in (7.3)–(7.24). This time the adjustment reaches a bit farther since the model now has to be formulated for two design spaces simultaneously: one for the items and one for the stimuli. We will formulate the model for the case of a program with parallel forms of multiple tests.

10.5.1   Simultaneous Model

Analogous to design space $\mathcal{D}$ for the items, we now need a space $\mathcal{E}$ with points $e = 1, ..., E$, for the stimuli. This space is defined as the Cartesian product of all stimulus attributes in the test specifications. Typically, the number of stimulus attributes is much smaller than the number of item attributes; the same therefore holds for the size of $\mathcal{E}$. Also, it is rare to have statistical parameters for stimuli. But if they do occur, the choice of design points $e = 1, ..., E$ should be representative of their range of empirical values.

A model for the design of a set-based item pool has separate variables for the numbers of stimuli and items, each indexed by its own design points.

The variables are

$$z_{et} = \text{number of stimuli at point } e \in \mathcal{E} \text{ for test } t \qquad (10.54)$$

and

$$x_{d_e t} = \text{number of items at point } d \in \mathcal{D} \text{ for stimulus } e \text{ and test } t. \quad (10.55)$$

The model will have special constraints to relate the two sets of variables to one another.

If N_t parallel forms of test t are to be assembled during the planning period, the numbers of stimuli and items needed at points e and d are

$$N_e = \sum_{t=1}^{T} N_t z_{et} \qquad (10.56)$$

and

$$N_{d_e} = \sum_{t=1}^{T} N_t x_{d_e t}. \qquad (10.57)$$

Hence, the blueprint in (10.5) is now replaced by the following two arrays:

$$(N_1, ..., N_E) \qquad (10.58)$$

and

$$\begin{pmatrix} N_{1_1} & \cdots & N_{1_E} \\ \cdots & \cdots & \cdots \\ N_{D_1} & \cdots & N_{D_E} \end{pmatrix}. \qquad (10.59)$$

In addition, we need separate functions to represent the costs of producing an item and a stimulus. We use the function φ_e for the costs of a stimulus with the attributes at design point $e \in \mathcal{E}$, and the function φ_{d_e} for the cost of an item at design point $d \in \mathcal{D}$ for a stimulus at $e \in \mathcal{E}$. Observe that these definitions allow for an interaction between the two spaces on the costs of item writing. If no interaction exists, the functions φ_{d_e} simplify to

$$\varphi_{d_e} = \varphi_d \quad \text{for all } e, \qquad (10.60)$$

and the same simplification holds for the decision variables for the items (see below).

To denote categorical attributes for the items and stimuli, we use sets V_c^{item} and V_c^{stim}, whereas the quantitative attributes for the items and stimuli are denoted as q_{d_e} and q_e, respectively. The rest of our other notation is analogous to the model for assembling tests with item sets in (7.3)–(7.24).

The standard model for a program with item sets is

$$\text{minimize} \sum_{t=1}^{T} \left(\sum_{e=1}^{E} \sum_{d=1}^{D} \varphi_{d_e} x_{d_e t} + \sum_{e=1}^{E} \varphi_e z_{et} \right) \quad \text{(minimal costs)} \quad (10.61)$$

subject to possible constraints at the following levels:

Test Level

$$\sum_{e=1}^{E} \sum_{d=1}^{D} I_d(\theta_k) x_{d_e t} \gtreqless T_{kt}, \quad \text{for all } k \text{ and } t, \quad \text{(test information)} \quad (10.62)$$

$$\sum_{e=1}^{E} \sum_{d=1}^{D} x_{d_e t} \gtreqless n_t, \quad \text{for all } t, \quad \text{(test length)} \quad (10.63)$$

$$\sum_{e=1}^{E} z_{et} \gtreqless m_t, \quad \text{for all } t, \quad \text{(number of stimuli)} \quad (10.64)$$

$$\sum_{e=1}^{E} \sum_{d \in V_c^{\text{item}}} x_{d_e t} \gtreqless n_{ct}^{\text{item}}, \quad \text{for all } c \text{ and } t, \quad \text{(categorical attributes)}$$
$$(10.65)$$

$$\sum_{e=1}^{E} \sum_{d=1}^{D} q_d x_{d_e t} \gtreqless b_{qt}^{\text{item}}, \quad \text{for all } t, \quad \text{(quantitative attributes)} \quad (10.66)$$

$$\sum_{e \in V_c^{\text{stim}}} z_{et} \gtreqless n_{ct}^{\text{stim}}, \quad \text{for all } c \text{ and } t, \quad \text{(categorical attributes)} \quad (10.67)$$

$$\sum_{e=1}^{E} q_e z_{et} \gtreqless b_{qt}^{\text{stim}}, \quad \text{for all } t; \quad \text{(quantitative attributes)} \quad (10.68)$$

Item-Set Level

$$\sum_{d=1}^{D} x_{d_e t} \gtreqless n_t^{\text{set}} z_{et}, \quad \text{for all } e \text{ and } t, \quad \text{(number of items per set)} \quad (10.69)$$

$$\sum_{d \in V_c^{\text{item}}} x_{d_e t} \gtreqless n_{ct}^{\text{set}} z_{et}, \quad \text{for all } c, e, \text{ and } t, \quad \text{(categorical attributes)}$$
$$(10.70)$$

$$\sum_{d=1}^{D} q_{d_e} x_{d_e t} \gtreqless b_{qt}^{\text{set}} z_{et}, \quad \text{for all } e \text{ and } t; \quad \text{(quantitative attributes)}$$
$$(10.71)$$

Stimulus Level

$$\sum_{e \in V_1^{\text{stim}}} z_{et} = n_{1t}^{\text{stim}}, \quad \text{for all } t, \quad \text{(special combinations of attributes)}$$
$$(10.72)$$

$$\sum_{e \in V_0^{\text{stim}}} z_{et} = 0, \quad \text{for all } t; \quad \text{(special combinations of attributes)}$$
$$(10.73)$$

Item Level

$$\sum_{d \in V_1^{\text{item}}} x_{d_e t} = n_{1t}^{\text{item}}, \quad \text{for all } t, \quad \text{(special combinations of attributes)}$$
$$(10.74)$$

$$\sum_{d \in V_0^{\text{stim}}} x_{d_e t} = 0, \quad \text{for all } t; \quad \text{(special combinations of attributes)}$$
$$(10.75)$$

Definition of Variables

$$x_{d_e t} \in \{0, 1, ...\}, \quad \text{for all } d, e, \text{ and } t, \quad \text{(range of variables)} \qquad (10.76)$$

$$z_{et} \in \{0, 1, ...\}, \quad \text{for all } e \text{ and } t. \quad \text{(range of variables)} \qquad (10.77)$$

The objective function in (10.61) does not weigh the costs for the items and stimuli differently; both are assumed to be on the same scale.

The constraints at the item-set level in (10.69)–(10.71) have the same structure as those in the test-assembly model in (7.12)–(7.14) in spite of the fact that the current variables are no longer restricted to 0-1 values. They operate as follows: If $z_{et} = 0$ in (10.69), no stimulus is assigned to point e, and neither are any items to the combination of any $d \in D$ with e. If $z_{et} = 1, 2, ...$, the constraints in (10.69) guarantee the assignment of multiples of n_t^{set} items to the combinations of $d \in D$ with e. Comparable control on the item-set attributes is exerted by the constraints in (10.70) and (10.71). As already noted in Section 7.1, some of these constraints, with upper bounds on the item-set attributes, should always be included in the model. If the test specifications do not imply upper bounds, dummy constraints should be used (Exercise 3.6).

Finally, no quantitative constraints are formulated at the stimulus level. If certain ranges of quantitative attributes for stimuli have to be avoided, it is much more efficient to exclude them in our choice of design points $e \in \mathcal{E}$.

10.5.2 Three-Stage Approach

The model in (10.61)–(10.77) is for the calculation of a joint blueprint for the items and stimuli, with immediate assignment of the number of items to the stimuli for which they have to be written. If the problem is too large, and the item-writing costs show no interaction (that is, if (10.60) holds), we can also design the pool using a method consisting of the following three stages:

1. calculating an optimal blueprint for the stimuli using a model analogous to the one in (10.17)–(10.24) defined on $\mathcal{E}$;.

2. calculating an optimal blueprint for the items using the model for a program with multiple tests in (10.17)–(10.24);

3. assigning the items to the sets for the stimuli using a network-flow model with the points $d \in \mathcal{D}$ as supply nodes and the individual stimuli needed at $e \in \mathcal{E}$ as demand nodes (Exercise 10.7).

It may seem unusual to split a problem for a single pool into three separate stages, but, again, the solution we seek is for a design problem, and all it should enable us to do is calculate an optimal combination of the item and stimulus blueprints in (10.58) and (10.59). Of course, once this combination has been calculated, the items and stimuli for the individual sets have to be produced in a coordinated fashion.

10.6   Calculating Solutions

All design models discussed so far were IP models that can be solved using a commercial solver (Section 4.2.5). If correct implementation decisions are made, we expect no special problems. For example, in problems with item sets, it is efficient to have the solver branch on the stimulus variables before the item variables (see Section 4.2.2).

If the problem still appears to be too large, we may feel inclined to resort to the approximation algorithm in Section 4.2.4, but another, simpler alternative is definitely more attractive. The alternative is to drop the integer constraints on the variables and solve the relaxed model using one of the standard implementations of the simplex algorithm.

The solution will then contain some variables with fractional values, but these can be rounded upward. The only effect of this rounding is a few extra items, but the pool will still support the assembly of the tests planned for it. Besides, it is always sensible to plan some spare items. The general problems discussed for the application of this rounding heuristic to problems with 0-1 variables (see Section A1.5) can be ignored when they are applied to item-pool-design problems.

Nevertheless, it is always recommended to reduce the size of the problem as much as possible. One possible reduction has already been mentioned: If an attribute shows hardly any empirical variation, it should be removed from the definition of the design space. Besides, if the test consists of sections with independent sets of specifications, it is simpler to calculate separate blueprints for the parts of the item pool that have to support the individual sections. (See the empirical example below.) As a final example, we refer to a possible choice between the simultaneous model for a program with multiple tests and the model with aggregated bounds in (10.45)–(10.52). Our recommendation is to use the latter when (i) the simultaneous problem becomes too large, (ii) no overlap constraints between tests are required, and (iii) a relaxed solution with rounding is not acceptable for some reason.

Infeasibility is not expected to be a problem in item-pool design, the reason being that, unlike test assembly, where an item pool may run into an occasional supply problem because of bad planning, all models are formulated over a design space with unlimited capacity. If equality constraints on quantitative attributes are avoided, and the usual care is taken with respect to the consistency of the constraints (Section 3.2.4), the model always has a feasible solution.

Section	# Attributes	# Design Points	# Constraints
SA			
Items	5	1,920	70
Stimuli	4	8	1
SB			
Items	6	6,144	97
Stimuli	4	31	6
SC			
Items	5	11,520	65

TABLE 10.1. Summaries of the design spaces for the three different sections of the pool.

Empirical Example

An item pool was designed for a fictitious program with three different versions of the LSAT: one version with the regular target for the TIF and two versions with the targets shifted .6 to the left and .6 to the right. Each version had to satisfy the full set of content specifications for the test.

As indicated in earlier examples, the LSAT contains three sections, one section with discrete items and two sections that are set-based. We calculated the parts of the blueprint for each of these three sections in the pool separately. For the section with discrete items, we used the design model for programs with multiple tests in (10.17)–(10.24). For the sections with item sets, we used the three-stage approach in Section 10.5.2. An application of the simultaneous model for a program with item sets in (10.61)–(10.77) will be discussed in a second example for the LSAT in Section 10.7.3.

Summaries of the design spaces for the three different sections of the pool are given in Table 10.1. Although the items were assumed to fit the 3PL model in (1.16), we ignored the guessing parameter c in the definition of the design space because all items in a section had the same number of alternatives and this parameter has a negligible impact on the optimal design of an item pool. Item information functions $I_d(\theta)$ were calculated using the average value of c for a previous pool of 5,316 items for the LSAT. Our definition of the item space was based on eight equally spaced values for discrimination parameter a and ten values for difficulty parameter b; both sets of values covered the actual range of values for these parameters in the same previous item pool.

Our cost function was also derived from this previous item pool. We first classified the items and stimuli according to the design points. (The quantitative attributes were classified using the shortest distance as criterion.) Let η_d denote the number of items in our classification at point d of the item space. The cost function we used was based on the proxy

$$\varphi_d = f\left(\frac{1}{\eta_d + \delta}\right), \tag{10.78}$$

with $f(.)$ a monotonically increasing function and δ an arbitrary constant close to zero that is needed to avoid infinite costs at points with $\eta_d = 0$. In fact, because (10.78) yields the same result for any choice of $f(.)$, we simply used $\varphi_d = (\eta_d + \delta)^{-1}$. Although the item pool had a total of 5,316 items, the number was still small relative to the size of our design spaces (see Table 10.1). We therefore smoothed the function using the method of k-nearest-neighbor regression outlined in Section 10.4.1. The method was applied over the quantitative coordinates of d only. That is, for each point d, we calculated the average value of $(\eta_d + \delta)^{-1}$ over the neighborhood defined by the quantitative coordinates of d and assigned the average value as the smoothed value φ_d^* to d. The size of the neighborhood varied with the sparseness of points with $\eta_d = 0$ in the space.

The three models appeared to have a unimodular structure (for a definition of this structure, see the more technical literature at the end of Appendix 1), which guarantees a solution that is fully integer for the relaxed version of the model. Since the solutions are just arrays of numbers of the form displayed in (10.58) and (10.59), it is no use showing them here.

10.7   Dynamic Versions of Design Models

Although the presentation of the design models in the preceding sections seems to suggest a one-shot approach to item-pool development, testing organizations seldom have the time and resources to wait until the pool is complete before beginning test assembly. In this section, we therefore present a dynamic version of the design models that can be used to guide the item-writing process while tests are assembled.

In fact, a more dynamic form of item-pool design helps us to address an issue we have not yet discussed: Although it is relatively easy to write items with the prespecified categorical attributes and with such quantitative attributes as reading time and word counts, it becomes more difficult to realize item blueprints that include the classical item parameters and IRT parameters reviewed in Chapter 1. Only recently have we begun to learn more about what makes an item difficult. But writing items with a prespecified combination of values for a difficulty and discrimination parameter is still beyond our reach. As we will see below, a dynamic use of the design models earlier in this chapter helps us to manage the item-writing process and to adapt it to the actual developments in the item pool.

10.7.1   Dynamic Models

We use the case of a program with multiple tests as an example. If the item pool is developed on a continuous basis, the process can be based on a series of updates of the blueprint for the item pool, each consisting of the following steps:

1. establishing the number of parallel forms of each test to be assembled in the next planning period;

2. updating the model in (10.17)–(10.24) to account for the current composition of the item pool;

3. updating the cost function in the model using the cumulative experiences with item writing;

4. running the model to determine the number of new items that have to be written for each design point $d \in \mathcal{D}$ in the next planning period.

The updates in steps 2–4 can be based on an aggregated version of the model in (10.17)–(10.24) that accounts for the numbers of items with the different attribute combinations already present in the pool. Let p be the planning period for which the new update is needed. The composition of the item pool at the end of period $p - 1$ can be represented by the array

$$(\eta_1^{(p-1)}, ..., \eta_D^{(p-1)}). \tag{10.79}$$

We want to know the number of new items at each point d that have to be written for p. Hence, we replace the decision variables in (10.15) by

$$x_{dt}^{(p)} = \text{number of items at point } d \in \mathcal{D} \text{ for test } t \text{ in period } p. \tag{10.80}$$

In addition, let $N_t^{(p)}$ be the number of forms for test t planned for period p. The supplement of the item pool required for the assembly of these test forms is thus

$$(N_1^{(p)}, ..., N_D^{(p)}), \tag{10.81}$$

with

$$N_d^{(p)} = \sum_{t=1}^{T} N_t^{(p)} x_{dt}^{(p)}. \tag{10.82}$$

The experiences with item writing during the preceding $p - 1$ periods can be used to update the cost function. For example, if the function in (10.78) is chosen, we can use the new data in (10.79) for an update of the function. Let $\varphi_d^{(p)}$ denote the update for period p.

The model for the supplement of the current item pool for period p is

$$\text{minimize } \sum_{t=1}^{T} \sum_{d=1}^{D} \varphi_d^{(p)} x_{dt}^{(p)} \quad \text{(minimal costs)} \tag{10.83}$$

subject to possible constraints at the following levels:

Test Level

$$\sum_{d=1}^{D} I_d(\theta_k) \left(\eta_d^{(p-1)} + \sum_{t=1}^{T} N_t^{(p)} x_{dt} \right) \gtreqless \sum_{t=1}^{T} N_t^{(p)} \mathcal{T}_{kt}, \quad \text{for all } k, \tag{10.84}$$

$$\sum_{d=1}^{D} \left(\eta_d^{(p-1)} + \sum_{t=1}^{T} N_t^{(p)} x_{dt} \right) \gtreqless \sum_{t=1}^{T} N_t^{(p)} n_t, \tag{10.85}$$

$$\sum_{d \in V_c} \left(\eta_d^{(p-1)} + \sum_{t=1}^{T} N_t^{(p)} x_{dt} \right) \gtreqless \sum_{t=1}^{T} N_t^{(p)} n_{ct}, \quad \text{for all } c, \tag{10.86}$$

$$\sum_{d=1}^{D} q_d \left(\eta_d^{(p-1)} + \sum_{t=1}^{T} N_t^{(p)} x_{dt} \right) \gtreqless \sum_{t=1}^{T} N_t^{(p)} b_q; \tag{10.87}$$

Item Level

$$\sum_{d \in V_1} \left(\eta_d^{(p-1)} + \sum_{t=1}^{T} N_t^{(p)} x_{dt} \right) = \sum_{t=1}^{T} N_t^{(p)} n_{1t}, \tag{10.88}$$

$$\sum_{d \in V_0} \left(\eta_d^{(p-1)} + \sum_{t=1}^{T} N_t^{(p)} x_{dt} \right) = 0; \tag{10.89}$$

Definition of Variables

$$x_{dt} \in \{0, 1, ...\}, \quad \text{for all } d \text{ and } t. \tag{10.90}$$

The aggregated bounds in this model remind us of the model in (10.45)–(10.52), but this time all sums are weighted by the number of planned test forms, $N_t^{(p)}$. The decision variables are also summed over the tests using the same weights. The presence of $\eta_d^{(p-1)}$ in each of the constraints corrects the number of items needed at point d for the number of items already available in the pool. Observe that the objective function in (10.83) is not corrected for these numbers; it does not make sense to minimize the cost of items that have already been written.

As in (10.45)–(10.52), the use of the aggregated bounds in the constraints does not lead to automatic satisfaction of the quantitative constraints at the level of the individual test forms to be assembled from the new pool. But, again, for larger programs we do not expect this to be much of a problem.

10.7.2 Item Author as Attribute

If the program has a fixed group of item authors, an attractive management tool becomes possible: We can add the item authors as an explicit (categorical) attribute to the design space for the item pool. As each design point is then associated with a specific item author, the solution to the model in (10.83)–(10.90) automatically assigns item blueprints to optimal authors. Of course, this option becomes more advantageous the larger the interaction between the item authors and the other item attributes on the costs; that is, if it appears to be easier for some item authors to produce an item with a given combination of attributes than for others.

For a new program, we may not immediately be able to specify cost functions for individual item authors. But we could start with a function based on their preferences, and move to more empirical estimates if information relevant to the actual costs is accumulated in the program. Each period, the item-writing assignments then become better adjusted to the actual skills of the item authors.

Usually, item authors have restricted capacities. These restrictions can be introduced as constraints in the design model. Let $w = 1, ..., W$ denote the set of item authors and V_w the subset of a point in $\mathcal{D}$ with item author w as attribute. If each item author has a maximum capacity of n_w items, the set of constraints required for period p is

$$\sum_{d \in V_w} \sum_{t=1}^{T} N_t^{(p)} x_{dt}^{(p)} \leq n_w, \quad \text{for all } w. \tag{10.91}$$

To date, we do not have much practical experience with dynamic use of item-pool design models. If more experience is gathered, we expect new tools and ideas for tuning item-pool development to item-writing skills to become available. The only point we want to advocate right now is that in a more dynamic environment item-pool management can only be successful if we permanently have a clear picture of what kinds of items are needed to supplement the item pool. Updates of the blueprints based on the model in (10.83)–(10.90) provide us with useful pictures.

In the next section, we discuss a few results from a simulation study conducted to follow the developments in the costs of item writing for different scenarios based on the model in (10.83)–(10.90).

10.7.3 Empirical Example

The fictitious testing programs simulated in this study consisted of two parallel forms of three different tests for one of the sections of the LSAT. The three tests differed only in the location of their TIF, but all other specifications were identical. The total number of test forms to be assembled during each simulated planning period was thus equal to six. The operational item pools used for this program consisted of 350 items, whereas each test form had 50 items. Ideally, the pools thus had just enough items to assemble one spare form for each program.

We used a previous pool of 2,436 items for this study. The items were collected from different sources but all were written for the LSAT. The dis-

Scenario	Initial Pool	Management	Item Writing
1	+	+	+
2	+	+	−
3	+	−	+
4	+	−	−
5	−	+	+
6	−	+	−
7	−	−	+
8	−	−	−

TABLE 10.2. Summary of features of eight different scenarios in simulation study.

tribution of the items in this pool was used to estimate the cost function in (10.78). The function was smoothed with respect to the item difficulty and discrimination parameter using the method of k-nearest-neighbor regression outlined in Section 10.4.1. As in the other examples in this chapter, the guessing parameter was ignored.

Eight different scenarios of item-pool development were simulated, each based on a different combination of the following three factors:

1. Initial operational item pool optimal or less than optimal. The optimal pool was assembled using a blueprint calculated according to the simultaneous model in (10.17)–(10.24). For the condition with a less than optimal pool, we assembled five test forms and sampled the remaining 100 items randomly from the old item pool.

2. Item-pool management optimal or less than optimal. Optimal item-pool management was simulated using the dynamic version of the design model in (10.83)–(10.90). Less than optimal management consisted of sampling the blueprints for the new items randomly from the old pool.

3. Item writing optimal or less than optimal. In both cases, the quantitative attributes of the items were perturbed randomly. For the case of less than optimal item writing, the perturbations were larger. For example, for the b parameter, the absolute error was uniform in the interval between .20 and .30, whereas for the case of optimal item writing it was between .15 and .20.

To make the eight scenarios, which are summarized in Table 10.2, more realistic, each of them had a mild form of item attrition (outdated items, detected flaws, etc.). The attrition was simulated to have a level of 5%; that is, in each scenario, after each planning period, a random sample of 5% of the items from the pool was deleted. The items were replaced using the item-writing style simulated for the scenario.

The eight different scenarios were evaluated using the following two criteria:

| | Initial Pool: Optimal | | | | | | | |
| | Scenario 1 | | Scenario 2 | | Scenario 3 | | Scenario 4 | |
Period	Forms	Costs	Forms	Costs	Forms	Costs	Forms	Costs
1	6.0	.17	6.0	.17	6.0	.17	6.0	.17
2	6.0	.17	6.0	.50	4.6	.47	3.8	1.63
3	6.0	.17	6.0	.38	3.3	.47	2.0	1.73
4	6.0	.17	6.0	.50	2.2	.47	1.1	1.45
5	6.0	.17	6.0	.37	2.2	.49	1.0	1.56
6	6.0	.17	6.0	.42	1.6	.51	0.4	2.13

| | Initial Pool: Less than Optimal | | | | | | | |
| | Scenario 5 | | Scenario 6 | | Scenario 7 | | Scenario 8 | |
Period	Forms	Costs	Forms	Costs	Forms	Costs	Forms	Costs
1	5.0	.48	5.0	.48	5.0	.48	5.0	.48
2	3.3	.17	3.0	.39	3.4	.48	2.6	1.71
3	4.4	.19	4.0	.65	2.6	.47	1.8	1.09
4	5.2	.18	4.2	.66	2.0	.51	1.2	1.36
5	5.4	.18	4.4	.41	1.1	.45	1.0	1.26
6	6.0	.17	3.0	.53	1.1	.50	0.2	1.53

TABLE 10.3. Number of feasible test forms and average cost per item during six planning periods for eight different scenarios of item-pool development.

1. average number of feasible forms that could be assembled from the pool during the planning periods;

2. average cost per item written during the planning periods.

Each scenario was replicated five times. The average results across replications are shown in Table 10.3. As expected, the first scenario yielded the best results. For each of the six periods, all six forms in the program could be assembled. In addition, the first scenario had the lowest costs of item writing, and the costs did not change over time. A comparison between scenarios 2 and 3 shows that it was better to have optimal management with less than optimal item writing than the other way around, particularly as to the number of forms that could be assembled. In scenario 4, both management and item writing were less than optimal. The results show a strong interaction effect: The number of feasible test forms as well as the cost per item deteriorated much faster than could have been expected on the basis of the results for scenarios 2 and 3.

As the results for scenario 5 show, the combination of optimal management and item writing was able to undo most of the negative effects of the less than optimal initial item pool on the item-writing costs, but it was much harder to assemble the required number of test forms. Optimal management (scenario 6) and optimal item writing only (scenario 7) produced approximately the same number of test forms as for scenario 5 but at a higher cost level. In scenario 8, both management and item writing were less than optimal, and the program deteriorated much faster over time.

10.8 Assembling an Operational Item Pool

If an operational pool has to be assembled from a master pool, two different cases may apply:

1. If the master pool contains all items listed in the blueprint for the operational pool, we can simply pick the items from it. The selection does not involve any kind of optimization.

2. If the statistical item parameters play a more dominant role, we typically have the less than ideal case of having more than enough items with the required combinations of attributes for each design point d, except for the values for the item parameters, which are somewhat off-target.

The second case involves an optimization problem. For each point d, we have to select N_d items from the master pool with values for the item parameters closest to the design point that has the required combination of all other attributes. The problem can easily be solved manually or by a simple sorting algorithm. However, we present an optimization model for this problem, mainly because we will need a generalization of it for the more complicated case of assembling a system of rotating item pools for adaptive testing addressed in Section 11.5.5. The model will be formulated for the item parameters in the 3PL model. As before, the guessing parameter is ignored. But, if necessary, it can easily be included in the objective function. The same holds for other quantitative attributes that may be troublesome.

Let V_d be the set of items in the master pool that have the required combination of attributes at d, except for the values for discrimination parameter a and difficulty parameter b. These sets need to be considered only at the points d with $N_d > 0$. Points with $N_d = 0$ play no role; items at these points are not required for the operational pool. The set of points $d \in \mathcal{D}$ with $N_d > 0$ is denoted as W.

We use (a_i, b_i) for the values of item $i \in V_d$ for the two parameters, and (a_d, b_d) for the values required at their design point $d \in W$. The following measure is for the distance between the actual values of item i and the values at its point d

$$\delta_{id} = \sqrt{(b_i - b_d)^2 + w^2(a_i - a_d)^2}, \tag{10.92}$$

where weight w should be used to compensate for the scale differences between the two parameters. The measure is an instance of (5.57), which was used for the problem of matching a test to a reference test in Section 5.4.1. An obvious choice of weight is

$$w = (b^{\max} - b^{\min})/(a^{\max} - a^{\min}), \qquad (10.93)$$

with the superscripts denoting the maximum and minimum values of the parameters in the master pool.

Let x_{id} be the 0-1 variable for the assignment of item $i \in V_d$ to point d. If an item is assigned to point d, it is assumed to be assigned to the operational pool as well.

The model is as follows:

$$\text{minimize} \sum_{d \in W} \sum_{i \in V_d} \delta_{id} x_{id} \qquad (10.94)$$

subject to

$$\sum_{i \in V_d} x_{id} = N_d, \quad \text{for all } d \in W, \quad \text{(content constraints)} \qquad (10.95)$$

$$x_{id} \in \{0, 1\}, \quad \text{for all } i \in V_d \text{ and } d \in W. \quad \text{(range of variables)} \qquad (10.96)$$

The solution to the model assigns the best items to each point d subject to the optimal blueprint defined by the numbers N_d in (10.95).

10.9   Final Comment

This chapter did not cover all possible optimization problems that can be met in the practice of item-pool design and development. For example, for a testing program, it may be important to maintain a constant quality of its operational pools over time. If the pools are assembled sequentially, the usual evil associated with sequential assembly can be expected to strike again: Earlier item pools are then likely to contain better items.

Solutions to this problem are possible, for instance, by assembling a set of parallel pools, keeping one pool and returning all but one of these pools to the master pool. This measure guarantees that the future item pool always contains a subset of items with the same quality as the current operational pool. An optimization model for the problem of simultaneous assembly of multiple pools is formulated in Section 11.5.5. If the problem becomes too large, we could use a generalized version of the big-shadow-test method in Section 6.3 and assemble one new operational pool and a *shadow pool* that is the aggregate of a set of future pools. The items in the shadow pool are then returned to the master pool.

Another example of a problem we have not yet discussed is the design of item pools for programs with tests of a special format. Although we will discuss the problem of item-pool design for programs with adaptive tests in the next chapter, programs with testlet-based or multistage adaptive testing are not addressed in this book. The same holds for programs with a random sampling of fixed tests for the individual test takers ("linear on-the-fly testing").

Research on these and other topics is being done, and hopefully the results will reach the testing literature before too long.

10.10   Literature

If the composition of an item pool is unbalanced, the quality of the tests is low and we may even run the risk of an infeasible problem. In this sense, the composition of the item pool is "our most important constraint on test-assembly problems." It is therefore amazing that the problem of item-pool design has received so little attention in the psychometric literature. Fortunately, the situation changed somewhat when large-scale adaptive testing programs were introduced and testing organizations became aware of the impact of the item pool on the exposure rates of the items.

The first to introduce integer programming in item-pool design was Boekkooi-Timminga (1991). Her model was for the improvement of an existing pool calibrated under the Rasch model; its objective was maximization of the TIFs of the tests to be assembled from it.

This chapter approaches the problem of item-pool design as an optimization problem over a design space for the item pool. It borrowed this perspective from optimal design theory in statistics (Section 4.7). For an introduction to optimal design in statistics and applications to test design, we refer to the literature section at the end of Chapter 4. The basic ideas were introduced in van der Linden, Veldkamp, and Reese (2000). This reference should also be consulted for details of the empirical example in Section 10.6. Dynamic versions of item-pool design models were suggested in the same paper; they were developed further in Ariel, van der Linden, and Veldkamp (in press). The example in Section 10.7.3 was also taken from Ariel, van der Linden, and Veldkamp (in press). A review of several other aspects of item-pool design for programs with fixed tests is offered in Veldkamp, van der Linden, and Ariel (2003). For the k-nearest-neighbor regression method proposed as a smoother for the cost functions in this chapter, see, for example, Hastie, Tibshirani and Friedman (2001, chapters 2 and 13).

10.11   Summary

1. The problem of item-pool design should be addressed at the level of a program of tests. The two basic programs addressed in this chapter are programs with parallel forms of single tests and programs with parallel forms of multiple tests.

2. Design models are formulated over a design space $\mathcal{D}$ defined as the Cartesian product of all item attributes figuring in the specifications of the tests in the program. Quantitative attributes are represented by a set of discrete values. Points in $\mathcal{D}$ are referred to as design points.

3. Design models have decision variables defined as the number of items with the combinations of attributes at the design points required in the pool. The models have constraints that represent the specifications of the tests in the program and minimize an objective function representing the costs of writing the items.

4. Design models are integer programming models that can be solved using a regular IP optimizer. An optimal blueprint for the item pool is calculated from the solution to a design model. The blueprint defines the combinations of attributes of the items to be written for the pool.

5. The notion of optimal item-pool design was motivated by the theory of optimal design for parameter estimation in statistics. The differences between the design models in this chapter and those for parameter estimation problems in statistics are: (i) an extension of the design space to include all nonstatistical attributes of the problem, (ii) the presence of a large collection of constraints representing the test specifications, and (iii) the replacement of an objective function for the accuracy of the estimator by a cost function.

6. Design models for programs with single and multiple tests resemble the earlier models for test assembly in this book, except for the following differences: (i) the decision variables are no longer restricted to 0-1 values but are fully integer, (ii) all test specifications, including those for the TIF, are dealt with as constraints, (iii) logical constraints on enemy items and item overlap between tests are not required, and (iv) quantitative constraints at the item level are not required.

7. Cost functions for item writing can be based on direct estimates of the costs of the items. But they can also be based on such proxies as (i) the amount of time required to write items to their blueprints, (ii) the risk of having to fix or reject an item, or (iii) the number of items in a previous item pool of the program with the attributes associated with the design points.

8. Since the cost functions are used in an optimization problem, monotone functions of (proxies to) actual costs work equally well. We can therefore eliminate all constant components in our estimates and focus on costs varying with the more dominant item attributes.

9. For larger design spaces, it is recommended to improve the cost estimates by using a smoothing technique or fitting a model to the estimates.

10. If the program has set-based items, the design model should be formulated over the joint design spaces for the items and stimuli. The optimal blueprint for the item pool shows which items to write for which stimuli.

11. It is possible to design an item pool in a more continuous fashion, with items being written while tests are already being assembled. We then use a dynamic version of the design model that allows us to calculate an optimal update of the blueprint for each subsequent planning period.

12. If the program has a fixed group of item authors, it is attractive to add them as categorical attributes to the design space. The model then automatically assigns item blueprints to optimal item authors. If the authors have restricted capacity, the restrictions can be included as constraints in the design model.

13. If an operational pool is to be assembled from a master pool, the assembly can be done using a simple optimization model. The model assigns the items in the master pool to the points in the design space that minimize the deviations of the actual values for the statistical item parameters from the values at their design points, subject to the condition that the blueprint is realized with respect to all other attributes that describe these points.

10.12 Exercises

10.1 Define the design space for the test specifications in Exercise 3.8. How many design points does this space have. What could be done to reduce the size of the space?

10.2 Formulate the design model for a program with five parallel forms of the tests in Exercise 3.8, with the test length constrained to be equal to $n = 30$ instead of being minimized, assuming we have estimates of the cost function for the items.

10.3 Reformulate the model in Exercise 10.2 for an extension of the program with eight parallel forms of a test with the same content specifications but the bounds on the TIF imposed at $\theta = 0$ and $\theta = 2$.

10.4 Formulate the version of the model in Exercise 10.3 with aggregated bounds in Section 10.3.3.

10.5 Formulate the version of the model in Exercise 10.3 for the case where the two types of tests should have an overlap between four and eight items.

10.6 A testing program consists of six parallel forms of a set-based physics test on the following four topics: static electricity, magnetism, current electricity, and light. The test should have two sets on each topic. The number of items per set should be 4–6, while the total number of items should equal 40. For each item set, the number of items measuring the use of a physical law should not be smaller than the number measuring knowledge of a concept or a principle. At most, 18 items should require computational activity. No more than four of the stimuli should contain a description of an experiment. Formulate the model for the optimal blueprint of the item pool, assuming we have estimates of the cost functions for the stimuli and items.

10.7 Formulate the models for the three-stage approach in Section 10.5.2 for the design problem in Exercise 10.6.

11

Designing Item Pools for Programs with Adaptive Tests

A blueprint of an item pool for an adaptive testing program is the same type of array $(N_1, ..., N_D)$ over the design space for the program as in the preceding chapter. But the numbers can no longer be calculated from the solution $(x_1, ..., x_D)$ to a single design model. The reason is, of course, that in adaptive testing each individual test taker gets a different selection of items adapted to his or her response vector. Consequently, there exists no single item pool that is optimal for the response vectors of all test takers. We therefore use a Monte Carlo method and *simulate* adaptive test administrations for ability levels randomly sampled from the population of test takers. The design space serves as the item pool in this simulation. The optimal blueprint for the program is estimated using counts of the number of times each point in the design space is visited during the simulations.

The simulations are conducted using the shadow-test approach (STA) to adaptive testing. The STA comes in handy because the model for the shadow tests enables us to impose the full set of specifications for the adaptive test on the selection of the items. Besides, its objective function can be used to optimize the design with respect to a cost function. In fact, the model for the shadow test in the simulations now becomes our design model for the item pool.

One of the key features of the shadow-test model in this application is that it is fully dynamic; each time an item is administered, all constraints in the model are updated. In spite of these updates, the model is less complicated than the standard model for the assembly of shadow tests in Chapter 9. For the same reason as for the design models in Chapter 10, we can suspend most of the logical constraints implied by the test specifications. The same also holds for the item-ineligibility constraints introduced in Chapter 9 to control the exposure rates of the items. These constraints are replaced by a simple adjustment of the results from the simulations.

Operational item pools in adaptive testing programs are typically assembled from a master pool. The basic model for assembling an operational pool to a blueprint was already presented in Section 10.8. The model does not change if the pool is used for adaptive testing; we therefore do not need to discuss it again. Instead, attention will be paid to a few new problems that may emerge when preparing an item pool for adaptive testing. For example, we will discuss how to optimally stratify an item pool for use in adaptive testing with alpha stratification (Section 9.4.1). In addition, we will present an intuitively attractive principle for assembling an item pool from a master pool that can be used as an alternative to the basic item-pool-assembly model in Section 10.8 if no blueprint for the pool is available. Finally, we will show how to assemble a system of item pools for rotating among testing sites to minimize the risk of item compromise.

11.1   Programs with a Single Adaptive Test

The basic idea is thus to simulate adaptive test administrations for test takers $j = 1, ..., J$ with ability levels randomly sampled from the population for which the pool is designed. The items in these administrations have the combinations of attributes at the points in the design space $\mathcal{D}$ defined by the specifications of the adaptive test (Section 10.1).

Relative to regular adaptive testing, two modifications are required: First, analogous to a program with fixed tests, we have to reformulate the model for the assembly of a shadow test in (9.11)–(9.21) as an IP model over the design space. Second, we have to formulate a rule for selecting items from the shadow test for administration to the simulated test takers.

11.1.1   Design Model for Shadow Tests

We use decision variables x_d to represent the number of items selected at the design points $d = 1, ..., D$. More precisely, these variables are defined as

$$x_d = \text{number of } \textit{free} \text{ items at design point } d \text{ in the shadow test.} \quad (11.1)$$

In the model, these variables are combined with counters for the number of items at each of the points $d \in \mathcal{D}$ already administered to the test taker. Specifically, we use $\eta_d^{(j,g-1)}$ to denote the number of items with the combination of attributes at d already administered to test taker j during the first $g - 1$ items in the test.

Just as for design models for programs with fixed tests, we control the TIF using constraints with lower bounds representing values of a target function $\mathcal{T}(\theta)$. But each time, only one bound is active. As before, we use $\widehat{\theta}_j^{(g-1)}$ to denote the ability estimate of test taker j after $g-1$ items in the adaptive test. The bound on the TIF active in the shadow test for the gth item is the value of the target function $\mathcal{T}(\theta)$ at $\theta = \widehat{\theta}_j^{(g-1)}$. The bound is denoted as $\mathcal{T}_j^{(g-1)}$.

The design model for the shadow test for the selection of the gth item is the following adjusted version of the standard model for the assembly of shadow tests in (9.11)–(9.21):

$$\text{minimize} \sum_{d=1}^{D} \varphi_d x_d \quad \text{(objective)} \tag{11.2}$$

subject to possible constraints at the following levels:

Test Level

$$\sum_{d=1}^{D} I_d(\widehat{\theta}_j^{(g-1)})(\eta_d^{(j,g-1)} + x_d) \geq \mathcal{T}_j^{(g-1)}, \quad \text{(test information)} \tag{11.3}$$

$$\sum_{D=1}^{D} (\eta_d^{(j,g-1)} + x_d) = n, \quad \text{(test length)} \tag{11.4}$$

$$\sum_{d \in V_c} (\eta_d^{(j,g-1)} + x_d) \gtreqless n_c, \quad \text{for all } c, \quad \text{(categorical attributes)} \tag{11.5}$$

$$\sum_{D=1}^{D} q_d(\eta_d^{(j,g-1)} + x_d) \gtreqless b_q; \quad \text{(quantitative attributes)} \tag{11.6}$$

Item Level

$$\sum_{d \in V_1} (\eta_d^{(j,g-1)} + x_d) = n_1, \quad \text{(special combinations of attributes)} \tag{11.7}$$

$$\sum_{d \in V_0} (\eta_d^{(j,g-1)} + x_d) = 0; \quad \text{(special combinations of attributes)} \tag{11.8}$$

Definition of Variables

$$x_d \in \{0, 1, ...\}, \quad \text{for all } d. \quad \text{(range of variables)} \tag{11.9}$$

The points $d \in D$ for which the shadow test has a value $x_d \geq 1$ are the *active design points* during the selection of item g. The item selected for administration has the combination of attributes at the active point with the minimum value for the cost function φ_d.

At first sight, it might seem more attractive to select an item at the design point with maximum information at $\widehat{\theta}_j^{(g-1)}$. However, since the bounds in (11.3) are imposed on each shadow test, the adaptive test automatically realizes values for the TIFs close to the target function $\mathcal{T}(\theta)$ for the population of test takers. More importantly, since the objective is to find the item pool with minimum cost, the same objective should be used when selecting items for administration.

If an item with attributes at point d is administered, its counter $\eta_d^{(j,g-1)}$ is updated. As a result of these updates, after J simulated test takers, we are able to calculate the array of counts

$$(\eta_1, ..., \eta_D) \tag{11.10}$$

with

$$\eta_d = \sum_{j=1}^{J} \eta_d^{(j,n)}, \tag{11.11}$$

where $\eta_d^{(j,n)}$ is the last update of $\eta_d^{(j,g-1)}$ for test taker j.

It is instructive to compare the design model in (11.2)–(11.9) with the earlier design model for a program with a single fixed test in (10.6)–(10.13), as well as with the standard model for the assembly of a shadow test in (9.11)–(9.21):

1. Most of the model in (11.2)–(11.9) follows from (10.6)–(10.13) upon substitution of the expression $\eta_d^{(j,g-1)} + x_d$ for the variables x_d in the constraints. The set of counters $\eta_d^{(j,g-1)}$, $d \in \mathcal{D}$, represents the items in the shadow test that have already been administered. The set of decision variables x_d represents the number of free items in the shadow test.

2. Analogous to (10.83), the substitution does not take place for the objective function in (11.2). It only makes sense to minimize the costs of items not yet administered; the costs of items that have already been administered are fixed.

3. Because of the presence of the counters in the model, the constraint on the previous $g - 1$ items in the model for the assembly of shadow tests in (9.15) can be omitted.

4. For the same reason as for the design models for fixed tests in Chapter 10, both the constraints on enemy items and the item-level constraints on quantitative attributes have been omitted.

5. In the shadow-test model in (9.11)–(9.21), the ability estimate $\widehat{\theta}^{(g-1)}$ and the constraint on the previous items in (9.15) are the only expressions updated after each new item. In the current model, the counts $\eta_d^{(j,g-1)}$ and target value $\mathcal{T}_j^{(g-1)}$ are also updated. As a consequence, each constraint in the model is dynamic.

The substitution of $\eta_d^{(j,g-1)} + x_d$ for x_d parallels the one in the model for the update of an item-pool blueprint in (10.83)–(10.90), which was introduced to correct this model for the attributes of the items already in the pool at the beginning of a new planning period.

In practical applications, the design model in (11.2)–(11.9) may have to be extended with a few of the special features of adaptive testing discussed in Chapter 9, such as alpha stratification or control of speededness. Each new constraint entailed by these extensions has to be subjected to the same substitution. Not surprisingly, the only extension that is more complicated is adaptive testing with item sets. In Section 11.3, we will show how to optimize a blueprint for a pool with set-based items.

11.1.2   Blueprint without Item-Exposure Control

In the adaptive-testing jargon, the counts in (11.10) are the number of times an item at $d \in \mathcal{D}$ was "exposed" to a random test taker. The simulations thus yield estimates of the (marginal) exposure rates of the items at the points $d \in \mathcal{D}$ that are equal to η_d/J.

If the adaptive test has no item-exposure control, the blueprint for the item pool follows directly from these exposure rates. For any point with a positive rate, the item pool should have an item. In view of the generalizations below, we formulate the conclusion slightly more formally and define the blueprint for the item pool as the array

$$(N_1, ..., N_D) \tag{11.12}$$

with

$$N_d = \text{int}\left(\frac{\eta_d}{J}\right), \tag{11.13}$$

where the int(.) function returns the first integer value not smaller than its argument.

It generally holds that the average exposure rate for an item pool in adaptive testing is equal to n/I, where n is the length of the adaptive test and I the size of the item pool (Exercise 9.3). An estimate of this average can be calculated directly from (11.10) as

$$\frac{\sum_{d=1}^{D} \eta_d}{JD}. \tag{11.14}$$

Ignoring the rounding operation, the size of the item pool corresponding with the exposure rates η_d/J in (11.13) is thus equal to

$$I^* = \frac{nJD}{\sum_{d=1}^{D} \eta_d}. \tag{11.15}$$

If for some reason a larger item pool, with a size minimally equal to $I^{\min} > I^*$, is required, the numbers in (11.13) should therefore be replaced by

$$N_d = \text{int}\left(\frac{\eta_d I^{\min}}{J I^*}\right). \tag{11.16}$$

11.1.3 Blueprint with Marginal Item-Exposure Control

For the case of item-exposure control, one might have expected special constraints in the model for the shadow tests, especially the item-ineligibility constraints in (9.43). The reason we did not include them is the same as for the omission of the constraints on enemy items and item overlap: there are no actual items yet, and there is thus nothing to control. Rather, we design the item pool such that the necessity of item-exposure control for the actual adaptive test (that is, the expected number of ineligibility constraints on its shadow tests) is minimized.

This goal can be realized using the following simple adjustment. Let $r^{\max}$ still denote the upper bound on the marginal item-exposure rates. The blueprint can then be calculated from the estimates η_d/J from the simulated test administrations as

$$(N_1, ..., N_D) \tag{11.17}$$

with

$$N_d = \text{int}\left(\frac{\eta_d}{J r^{\max}}\right), \tag{11.18}$$

The division by $r^{\max}$ in the argument guarantees that the share of the total exposure for each of the N_d items at d is not larger than $r^{\max}$. If the item pool is required to have a predetermined minimum size, a correction similar to that in (11.16) should be applied to (11.18) (Exercise 11.1).

11.1.4 Blueprint with Conditional Item-Exposure Control

If conditional exposure rates of the test have to be controlled, the counts should be recorded for a partitioning of the θ scale into a collection of small intervals. If the intervals are indexed by $k = 1, ..., K$, their counts can be denoted as $\eta_d^{(k)}$. Likewise, the number of test takers sampled from interval k can be denoted as $J^{(k)}$.

Since all conditional exposure rates have to be controlled simultaneously, we propose to calculate the blueprint for the item pool such that the maximum conditional exposure rate over the K intervals satisfies $r^{\max}$. The blueprint is then given by

$$N_d = \text{int}\left(\max_k\left\{\frac{\eta_d^{(k)}}{J^{(k)} r^{\max}}\right\}\right). \tag{11.19}$$

The price paid for this slightly conservative approach is an item pool that is somewhat larger than actually required for most of the test takers. To realize a prespecified minimum size for the item pool, a correction similar to (11.16) should be applied (Exercise 11.1).

11.1.5   Empirical Example

A Monte Carlo study based on the model in Section 11.1.1 was conducted to design an item pool for an adaptive version of the quantitative portion of the Graduate Management Admission Test (GMAT). The specifications of the test involved eight different attributes: five content attributes and the three item parameters for the response model in (1.16). We chose representative sets of nine values for the discrimination parameter and 14 values for the difficulty parameter and ignored the guessing parameter. The total number of design points was equal to 12,096. The IIFs at the design points were calculated using the values for the difficulty and discrimination parameters associated with the design points along with the average value for the guessing parameter in a previous pool of 397 items. The total number of constraints in the model for the shadow tests was equal to 30.

The cost function was the one in (10.78) estimated from the same previous pool. No attempt was made to smooth this function, which was thus rather coarse. Because we had no target for the information function of the GMAT, the constraint in (11.3) was replaced by the following weighted combination of test information at the ability estimates and the cost function:

$$\text{maximize } w_1 \sum_{d=1}^{D} I_d(\widehat{\theta}_j^{(g-1)}) x_d + w_2 \sum_{d=1}^{D} \varphi_d x_d, \tag{11.20}$$

with a negative value for w_2.

The administrations were simulated for θ values sampled from $N(1,1)$, which seemed a reasonable guess for the GMAT population. Consequently, the initial ability estimate was set equal to $\widehat{\theta}^{(0)} = 1$ for each simulated test taker. The estimates were updated using the expected a posteriori (EAP) estimator with a noninformative prior distribution.

The key result from the simulated test administrations was the estimate of the exposure rates, η_d/J, that enables us to calculate an optimal blueprint for any upper limit on the item-exposure rates for the GMAT using (11.18) or (11.19). Because the result was an array of 12,096 numbers, it is not shown here.

11.2 Programs with Multiple Adaptive Tests

Two different programs with multiple adaptive tests are discussed: (i) a program in which tests with different specifications are administered from the same item pool, and (ii) a program in which tests with the same specifications are administered from different item pools.

11.2.1 Different Tests from the Same Item Pool

In the first type of program, the test specifications are different in the sense that they require different bounds for some of the constraints on the shadow tests. This definition includes the case of different subsets of constraints for different tests, which can be realized by selecting values for some of the bounds that make their constraint inactive. By changing the bounds, the tests may thus have different lengths, different targets for their information functions, different content distributions, and so on.

To the author's knowledge, programs with different adaptive tests from the same item pool do not yet exist. But they are technically possible and offer several advantages over programs in which the same set of tests is administered from different pools.

An attractive area of application for such programs is multidimensional adaptive testing. In Section 9.7, several cases of multidimensional adaptive testing with different combinations of intentional and nuisance abilities were discussed (see also Section 8.1). Tests for different combinations can be administered from the same multidimensional item pool. If the model for adaptive testing with minimum error variance in (9.63)–(9.70) is used, the only operation involved in the transition from one test to another is a change of the weights in the constraints that define the different cases of multidimensionality. Comparable operations are possible for the model with maximization of the Kullback-Leibler information in Section 9.7.3.

Applications for which such programs are welcome are testing for admission and placement with different success criteria, such as testing for admission to different educational programs or for placement in different jobs in an organization. Current testing for these purposes consists mainly of batteries of unidimensional tests with different weighting of their scores for different criteria. However, instead of *post hoc* weighing of scores, both the validity and efficiency of the test can be improved by designing pools with items that reflect the multidimensional complexities of the criteria and imposing the weights directly on the selection of the items using the test-assembly model in (9.63)–(9.70).

Relative to a program with a single test, designing an item pool for a program with multiple adaptive tests hardly involves any extra work. The only thing that has to be done is to repeat the simulated administrations for each test, with an appropriate change of the constraints in the model for the shadow tests. The ability levels of the test takers in the simulations have to be sampled from the different populations to which the tests are to be administered, with sample sizes proportional to the size of the populations. The blueprint for the item pool is calculated by aggregating the counts in (11.11) over the different tests.

11.2.2 Same Test from Different Item Pools

An example of the second type of program is adaptive testing with rotating item pools. In this application, which has been proposed to discourage test takers from trying to share items, different versions of the item pool are rotated among the testing sites. Because the tests, and hence the item pools, should be parallel, the design of a system of rotating pools does not involve anything new. For each of these pools, the same blueprint applies. In Section 11.5.5, we will discuss the problem of how to assemble such systems of pools simultaneously.

11.3 Item Sets

Just as for the problem of designing a set-based item pool for a program with fixed tests addressed in Section 10.5, we use separate design spaces $\mathcal{D}$ for the items and $\mathcal{E}$ for the stimuli. The blueprints for the numbers of items and stimuli have the same format as the arrays in (10.58) and (10.59).

11.3.1 Design Model

Following (10.54) and (10.55), the decision variables for the items and stimuli are denoted as z_e and x_{d_e}, whereas we use φ_e and φ_{d_e} to denote the cost functions. As before, $g = 1, ..., n$ and $l = 1, ..., m$ denote the items and stimuli in the adaptive test, respectively. For notational convenience, we suppose the item set for stimulus $l - 1$ has been completed and that item g is the first item selected for the lth stimulus.

A key difference with the problem of an item pool of discrete items is that when selecting a new stimulus in the simulated test administrations we also have to account for the stimuli already administered. Therefore, we introduce counters for the number of stimuli at $e \in \mathcal{E}$ administered to the test taker. Specifically, in addition to $\eta_d^{(j,g-1)}$, we use $\mu_e^{(j,l-1)}$ to denote the number of stimuli at point e administered to test taker j during the first $l - 1$ stimuli in the test.

The model for the shadow test for the selection of the gth item is as follows:

$$\text{minimize} \sum_{e=1}^{E} \sum_{d=1}^{D} \varphi_{d_e} x_{d_e} + \sum_{e=1}^{E} \varphi_e z_e \qquad (11.21)$$

subject to possible constraints at the following levels:

Test Level

$$\sum_{e=1}^{E}\sum_{d=1}^{D} I_{d_e}(\hat{\theta}_j^{(g-1)}) \left(\eta_{d_e}^{(j,g-1)} + x_{d_e} \right) \geq \mathcal{T}_j^{(g-1)}, \tag{11.22}$$

$$\sum_{e=1}^{E}\sum_{d=1}^{D} \left(\eta_{d_e}^{(j,g-1)} + x_{d_e} \right) = n, \tag{11.23}$$

$$\sum_{e=1}^{E} \left(\mu_e^{(j,l-1)} + z_e \right) = m, \tag{11.24}$$

$$\sum_{e=1}^{E} \sum_{d\in V_c^{\text{item}}} \left(\eta_{d_e}^{(j,g-1)} + x_{d_e} \right) \gtrless n_c^{\text{item}}, \quad \text{for all } c, \tag{11.25}$$

$$\sum_{e=1}^{E}\sum_{d=1}^{D} q_d \left(\eta_{d_e}^{(j,g-1)} + x_{d_e} \right) \gtrless b_q^{\text{item}}, \tag{11.26}$$

$$\sum_{e\in V_c^{\text{stim}}} \left(\mu_e^{(j,l-1)} + z_e \right) \gtrless n_c^{\text{stim}}, \quad \text{for all } c, \tag{11.27}$$

$$\sum_{e=1}^{E} q_e \left(\mu_e^{(j,l-1)} + z_e \right) \gtrless b_q^{\text{stim}}; \tag{11.28}$$

Item-Set Level

$$\sum_{d=1}^{D} \left(\eta_{d_e}^{(j,g-1)} + x_{d_e} \right) \gtrless n^{\text{set}} \left(\mu_e^{(j,l-1)} + z_e \right), \quad \text{for all } e, \tag{11.29}$$

$$\sum_{d=1}^{D} \left(\eta_{d_e}^{(j,g-1)} + x_{d_e} \right) \gtrless n_c^{\text{set}} \left(\mu_e^{(j,l-1)} + z_e \right), \quad \text{for all } e, \tag{11.30}$$

$$\sum_{d=1}^{D} \left(\eta_{d_e}^{(j,g-1)} + x_{d_e} \right) \gtrless b_q^{\text{set}} \left(\mu_e^{(j,l-1)} + z_e \right), \quad \text{for all } e; \tag{11.31}$$

Stimulus Level

$$\sum_{e\in V_1^{\text{stim}}} \left(\mu_e^{(j,l-1)} + z_e \right) = n_1^{\text{stim}}, \tag{11.32}$$

$$\sum_{e\in V_0^{\text{stim}}} \left(\mu_e^{(j,l-1)} + z_e \right) = 0; \tag{11.33}$$

Item Level

$$\sum_{d\in V_1^{\text{item}}} \left(\eta_{d_e}^{(j,g-1)} + x_{d_e} \right) = n_1^{\text{item}}, \tag{11.34}$$

$$\sum_{d\in V_0^{\text{stim}}} \left(\eta_{d_e}^{(j,g-1)} + x_{d_e} \right) = 0; \tag{11.35}$$

Definition of Variables

$$x_{d_e} \in \{0, 1, ...\}, \quad \text{for all } d \text{ and } e, \tag{11.36}$$

$$z_e \in \{0, 1, ...\}, \quad \text{for all } e. \tag{11.37}$$

The descriptive labels for the constraints are omitted because of lack of space; however, they parallel those in (10.61)–(10.77). Observe that, except for the objective function, we have not only substituted $\eta_{d_e}^{(j,g-1)} + x_{d_e}$ for x_{d_e} but also $\mu_e^{(j,l-1)} + z_e$ for z_e. Together, counters $\eta_d^{(j,g-1)}$ and $\mu_e^{(j,l-1)}$ represent the part of the shadow test that has already been administered. As a result, the earlier constraints on the previous items and stimuli in (9.15) and (9.29) could be omitted. Also, recall that the item-level constraints in (11.29)–(11.31) should always have an upper bound (Section 7.1).

The points $e \in \mathcal{E}$ for which the shadow test has a value $z_e > 0$ are the *active design points* during the selection of a stimulus. Let $e^{(l)}$ be the point at which the current stimulus, l, was chosen. We now need rules for selecting the items as well as the stimuli. We propose the following rules:

1. The items are selected at the active points $d_{e^{(l)}}$ in $\mathcal{D}$ associated with the current stimulus point $e^{(l)}$. The criterion for selecting an item is a minimum value for the cost function for the items, $\varphi_{d_{e^{(l)}}}$. Item selection from this subset of points is continued until the shadow test has no free items for the current stimulus. (That is, a new solution has a value for $z_{e^{(l)}}$ one lower than the current value.) We then select a new stimulus.

2. The new stimulus is chosen to be the stimulus at the active point e with the lowest costs for an item set associated with it. The cost of the item set is calculated as

$$\varphi_e + \frac{\displaystyle\sum_{d=1}^{D} \varphi_{d_e} x_{d_e}}{\displaystyle\sum_{d=1}^{D} x_{d_e}}, \tag{11.38}$$

where x_{d_e} has the value for the current shadow test. The criterion is equal to the cost of the stimulus plus the average costs of the items associated with it.

The condition to select items for stimulus point $e^{(l)}$ until the shadow test has a solution with a lower value for its decision variable $z_{e^{(l)}}$ guarantees that the items are treated at the level of an entire set. If a set has been administered, the competition between the stimulus points opens up again, and the test is allowed to move to another point (or stay at the same point if this appears to be more advantageous).

The item-set level constraints in (11.29)–(11.31) guarantee that the active points in $\mathcal{D}$ and $\mathcal{E}$ are always consistent. The updates of $\widehat{\theta}^{(g-1)}$ in the constraint on the test-information function in (11.22) introduce a tendency for other points in $\mathcal{D}$ and $\mathcal{E}$ to become active after a new item and/or stimulus is selected.

11.3.2 Calculating the Blueprint

For brevity, the calculations are presented for a program with control of the marginal exposure rates only. The generalization to conditional rates is straightforward (Exercise 11.2).

In addition to (11.10) and (11.11), we now also have the counts of the number of stimuli at the points $e \in \mathcal{E}$,

$$\mu_e = \sum_{e-1}^{E} \mu_e^{(j,m)}, \tag{11.39}$$

where $\mu_e^{(j,m)}$ is the last update of $\mu_e^{(j,l-1)}$ for test taker j. Since the exposure rate of an item can never exceed the rate of its stimulus, it makes sense to apply the rounding in (11.13) to the counts for the stimuli and then calculate the blueprint for the items.

If the upper limit on the exposure rates is $r^{\max}$, the blueprint for the stimuli can be written as

$$(N_1, ..., N_E), \tag{11.40}$$

with

$$N_e = \text{int}\left(\frac{\mu_e}{Jr^{\max}}\right). \tag{11.41}$$

Due to the upward rounding in (11.41), we get extra stimuli in the pool. As a result, we also need a few extra items to complete the sets for these stimuli. Let

$$\varepsilon_e = \text{int}\left(\frac{\mu_e}{Jr^{\max}}\right) - \frac{\mu_e}{Jr^{\max}} \tag{11.42}$$

be the effect of the rounding. It is proposed to calculate the blueprint for the items as

$$\begin{pmatrix} N_{1_1} & \cdots & N_{1_E} \\ \cdots & \cdots & \cdots \\ N_{D_1} & \cdots & N_{D_E} \end{pmatrix}, \tag{11.43}$$

with

$$N_{d_e} = \text{int}\left(\frac{(1+\varepsilon_e)\eta_{d_e}}{Jr^{\max}}\right). \tag{11.44}$$

If a minimum size for the item pool has been set in advance, a correction similar to (11.16) should be applied.

11.4   Calculating Shadow Tests

The only difference with the regular case of adaptive test assembly discussed in Section 9.1.5 is that the shadow tests are calculated over a design space much larger than the actual pool. Hence, they take much more time.

On the other hand, the goal is not to simulate real-time CAT administrations. Besides, the entire process of item-pool development is rather time-intensive, and a day or so spent on simulations to optimize the design of the pool should be a worthwhile investment.

In principle, the only points in the design space that we need to address in the model are those that become active during the simulations. Since the computing time depends directly on the number of points, the time can be lowered by looking for methods to reduce the design space. A key factor in this reduction is the cost structure of the problem; points with prohibitively large costs are unlikely ever to become active and could be removed from the model. Methods for identifying such points in advance have not yet been researched in detail.

11.5   Some Remaining Topics

In adaptive testing, it is common practice to assemble the operational item pool from a master pool. The model for this problem was already presented in Section 10.8. In this section, we address a few remaining topics of item-pool development for adaptive testing, namely (i) optimizing item-pool stratification, (ii) item-pool assembly without a blueprint for the pool, and (iii) the assembly of a system of rotating item pools for adaptive testing.

11.5.1   Stratifying an Item Pool

To introduce alpha stratification in adaptive testing, the item pool has to be stratified on the item-discrimination parameter, a. During the test, a fixed number of items are selected from each subsequent stratum.

Alpha stratification can be implemented by inserting the constraints in (9.30) into the model for the shadow test. The definition of these constraints was based on two different arrays, one that defines the strata in the pool,

$$(Q_1, ..Q_P), \qquad (11.45)$$

and another that defines the number of items to be administered from the strata,

$$(n_1, ..., n_P). \qquad (11.46)$$

In this section, we address the question of how to stratify an operational item pool for which the stratification $(Q_1, ..Q_P)$ has already been determined. The more important question of how to *design* a new item pool for alpha-stratified adaptive testing appears to be too complicated. We then have to optimize simultaneously (i) a blueprint $(N_1, ..., N_D)$ with respect to a cost function over $\mathcal{D}$ and (ii) a stratification $(Q_1, ..Q_P)$ for the blueprint with respect to a statistical criterion. The only possible approach seems to be a trial-and-error method in which we try to find the best values for $(N_1, ..., N_D)$ given trial values for $(Q_1, ..Q_P)$, or conversely.

Since adaptive testing with alpha stratifications has been studied mainly for the objective function in (9.31)–(9.33), we discuss a model for the joint stratification of a given item pool on item parameters a and b. Stratification on both parameters allows us to choose from items with a wide range of values for the difficulty parameter within every stratum Q_p visited during the test.

The idea is to replace the original space by a new two-dimensional attribute space $\mathcal{D}$ defined by item-difficulty parameter b and discrimination parameter a only. The points in this space form a grid with coordinates for b that are representative of the range of values b_i in the item pool and the coordinates for a in $(Q_1, ..., Q_d)$. (Of course, we are free to choose new coordinates for a if that results in a better solution.)

As in the model in Section 10.8, we assign the items $i = 1, ..., I$ in the pool to the attribute points $d \in \mathcal{D}$ such that the sum of the distances between the items and the points is minimized. If we choose the same distance measure as in (10.92), the model is

$$\text{minimize} \sum_{i=1}^{I} \sum_{d=1}^{D} \delta_{id} x_{id} \tag{11.47}$$

subject to

$$\sum_{d=1}^{D} x_{id} = 1, \quad \text{for all } i, \quad \text{(supply)} \tag{11.48}$$

$$\sum_{i=1}^{I} x_{id} = n_d, \quad \text{for all } d, \quad \text{(demand)} \tag{11.49}$$

$$x_{id} \leq 1, \quad \text{for all } i \text{ and } d, \quad \text{(range of variables)} \tag{11.50}$$

where n_d is the prespecified number of items needed at point d.

Because of the equality constraints in (11.48) and (11.49), the model has the form of a (semiassignment) network-flow problem. (A full assignment problem arises if $n_d = 1$ for all d.) As discussed in Section A1.4, we therefore relaxed the integer constraints on the values of x_{id} in (11.50). The result is a fast solution that is always fully integer.

11.5.2   Empirical Example

The model for optimal stratification in (11.47)–(11.50) was applied to a pool of 360 items for an adaptive version of the quantitative test of the

# Items	Stratum 1 90	Stratum 2 90	Stratum 3 90	Stratum 4 90
Parameter a				
Mean	.53	.75	.93	1.26
SD	.11	.10	.13	.21
Range	.26–.73	.54–.99	.63–1.23	.98–2.00
Parameter b				
Mean	−.10	−0.03	.13	.54
SD	1.18	1.03	.92	.60
Range	−2.89–2.02	−2.89–1.79	−2.47–1.76	−.92–1.21

TABLE 11.1. Results for the GRE item pool for an application of the stratification model in (10.126)–(10.129).

Graduate Record Examination (GRE). The pool was calibrated using the 3PL model in (1.16).

We chose an attribute space of 20 points defined by the four values .55, .74, .95, and 1.28 for parameter a and the five values −2.0, −1.0, 0, 1.0, and 2.0 for parameter b. Both sets of values were representative of the actual range of the values of the items in the pool for the two parameters. (The parameter values for b were scaled to have a mean of zero.) To each of the 20 points $d \in \mathcal{D}$ we assigned $n_d = 18$ items. The items were assigned using the distance measure in (10.92) with the weights in (10.93) calculated for the actual ranges of parameter values in the item pool.

The results from the stratification are summarized in Table 11.1. The means, standard deviations, and ranges for parameter a show the desired differences between the four strata. There is some overlap between the ranges, which is the result of our attempt to get uniform distributions for the values of parameter b within each stratum. It appeared somewhat difficult to realize both goals simultaneously; particularly the range of b for the highest stratum deviates from the other strata. This deviation is the result of substantial correlation between the two item parameters in the pool (.44). The deviation was thus the price paid for the fact that an arbitrary item pool was taken instead of one specially optimized for adaptive testing with alpha stratification.

11.5.3 Assembling an Item Pool as a Set of Fixed Test Forms

At face value, an item pool may seem to serve an adaptive testing program best if the distribution of points at which the items in the pool have maximum information follows the distribution of θ for the population of test takers. We would then have sufficient items everywhere along the θ scale. Also, as the two distributions have identical shapes, the item pool would have the same built-in type of exposure control pursued in the calculation of the item-pool blueprint in (11.17)–(11.19). This point of view is not correct, however; it overlooks the fact that the test has to meet a set of content specifications as well. For each estimate of θ during the test, we need not be able to find an informative item close to it but an informative shadow test that meets each of the content specifications.

A practical advantage of this method over the standard model for item-pool assembly in Section 10.8 is that no blueprint for the item pool is required. It can be used directly to assemble an operational item pool from any master pool (though we get better results if the items have been written to an optimal blueprint for the operational pool).

Suppose the operational item pool is assembled as a set of fixed test forms with the following two features:

1. Each form meets all constraints to be imposed on the test.

2. The distribution of the points at which the forms have maximum information reflects the ability distribution of the population of test takers.

For a pool of this type, the STA would always be able to find a shadow test close to the current estimate of θ. And since the distribution of the locations of the peaks of the TIFs reflects the ability distribution of the test takers, we would always have more shadow tests available in areas where we have more test takers and thus introduce a trend to more uniform item exposure as well. (Of course, shadow tests always contain the items that were optimal at the different θ values visited earlier by the test taker, but this feature of adaptive test assembly cannot be avoided.)

A set of fixed test forms with these two features can easily be assembled using one of the regular models for the assembly of multiple tests in Chapter 6. In the empirical example below, we used the model for simultaneous assembly in (6.3)–(6.13) in combination with a relative target value for the TIF of each individual test. The target values were imposed using the following version of the maximin principle in (5.25)–(5.27) for multiple-test problems:

$$\text{maximize } y \tag{11.51}$$

subject to

$$\sum_{i=1}^{I} I_i(\theta_t)x_{it} \geq y, \quad \text{for all } t, \tag{11.52}$$

$$y \geq 0, \tag{11.53}$$

where the values θ_t are the single values at which the information in test $t = 1, ..., T$ is maximized. Also, observe that (11.52) is (5.26) with $R_k = 1$.

The distribution of the θ_t values should be chosen to follow the ability distribution of the population of test takers. Let $g(\theta)$ denote a density that describes this population. A straightforward method for choosing a set of values $(\theta_1, ..., \theta_T)$ reflecting $g(\theta)$ as closely as possible consists of the following steps:

1. Choose the size of the item pool T times as large as the size of the test length.

2. Partition the θ scale into T intervals, where each interval has an equal portion of the probability mass in $g(\theta)$ (ignoring the extremes of the tails).

3. Choose points θ_t, $t = 1, ..., T$, to represent these T intervals; for example, the points with equal mass in the interval on each side. The distribution of these points reflects the shape of $g(\theta)$ (Exercise 11.3).

11.5.4 Empirical Example

We used a pool of 5,316 items for the LSAT as the master pool from which we assembled an operational pool for the 50-item adaptive version of the test. The pool had to consist of $T = 10$ test forms, each meeting the full set of content constraints for the LSAT. As in some of our earlier examples, we ignored the item-set structure of two of the sections in the test. The population of test takers was assumed to have an $N(0,1)$ distribution. The values θ_t were determined using the method in the preceding section. The total number of variables in the model was equal to 53,161 (5,316 variables for each of the ten forms plus minimax variable y). For the computational aspects of this extremely large example, see our report in Section 4.2.4.

The item pool was evaluated against a second pool in which the distribution of the total information in the pool reflected the population distribution $g(\theta)$. This second pool represents the naive view of item-pool design referred to at the beginning of the preceding section.

To make the second pool otherwise as comparable as possible, it was assembled as a set of ten parallel forms, each satisfying the same set of specifications for the test and with a shape reflecting the standard normal distribution of θ. The only change in the model needed to assemble the second set of test forms was the replacement of (11.52) by

$$\sum_{i=1}^{I} I_i(\theta_k)x_{it} \geq g(\theta_k)y, \quad \text{for all } k \text{ and } t, \tag{11.54}$$

where $g(.)$ is the standard normal density function. Observe that the left-hand side represents the information functions of the test forms and that the right-hand side imposes the population distribution as a common target on each of them.

The information functions of the sets of fixed test forms in the two pools are shown in Figure 11.1. As a consequence of the application of the maximin principle with equal relative target values $R_t = 1$ in (11.51)–(11.53), the information functions for the pool assembled according to the method proposed in this section had peaks of about the same height. In addition, the location of the peaks was denser closer to $\theta = 0$ due to the distribution of points θ_t at which the target values were imposed. The second pool consisted of a set of test forms with information functions that were parallel, each with a shape that, except for its height, reflected the standard normal distribution.

The two pools were evaluated against one another by comparing the results of 1,000 adaptive test administrations simulated at each of the values $\theta = -2.0, -1.5, ..., 2.0$. The shadow-test model for the two series of simulations was the same regular model for the adaptive version of the LSAT. We simulated versions both with and without additional item-exposure control using the method with the ineligibility constraints in Section 9.4.4 with $r_{\max} = .25$.

The bias and MSE functions calculated from the ability estimates for each of the four different conditions are given in Figure 11.2. Both panels show a function for the pool assembled by the method proposed in this section which much better results for the high and low ability values than for the pool with the parallel test forms. This result is entirely due to the fact that the proposed method effectively breaks down the correlations between the item attributes and the item-parameters existing in the master pool and, in doing so, creates a sufficient supply of items close to each point on the θ scale.

Although we used a known true ability distribution $g(\theta)$ in this study to assemble the item pools, in practice this distribution is not known. In an additional study, we assessed the effects of replacing $g(\theta)$ by the distribution of ability estimates $\widehat{\theta}$ for a large sample of test takers from $g(\theta)$. For all practical purposes, the results for the two distributions were identical. The conclusions from this study therefore seem to apply to item-pool assembly with an empirical estimate of the distribution of ability estimates as well.

11.5.5 Assembling a System of Rotating Item Pools

To offer test takers comparable tests in an adaptive testing program with rotating item pools, the pools should be parallel. Let $h = 1, ..., H$ denote the item pools in the system. To achieve parallelness, the H pools should be assembled to the same blueprint. Thus, the problem is a generalization of the problem of assembling a single pool to a blueprint discussed in Section 10.8. A topic of this section is how to solve this more general problem.

As for the case of a single pool, we only have to consider the attribute points $d \in \mathcal{D}$ in the blueprint with $N_d > 0$, and we denote the set of these points as W. Also, we expect the master pool to contain the minimum number of items required with the attribute combinations at the points $d \in W$, except for a (hopefully slight) mismatch for their values for the item-difficulty and discrimination parameters. Specifically, we expect the master pool to have at least HN_d of such items at the points $d \in W$.

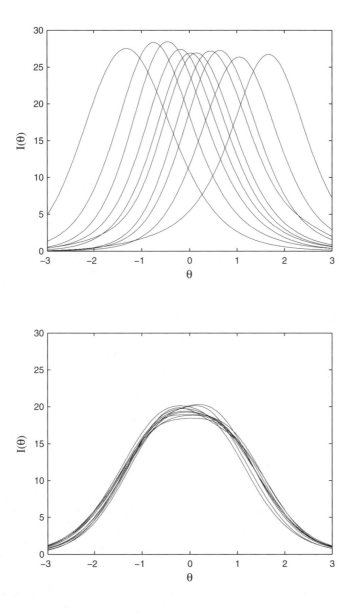

FIGURE 11.1. Ten test forms in the item pool with information functions with maximizers reflecting the standard normal density (top) and ten parallel forms with information functions each reflecting the standard normal density (bottom).

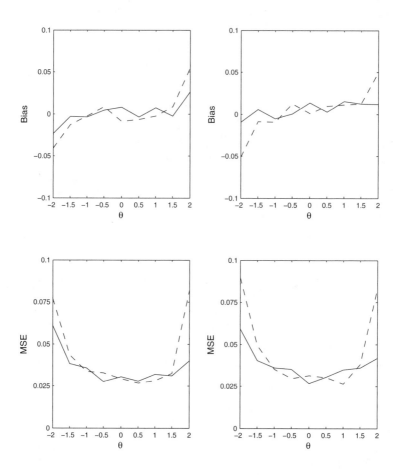

FIGURE 11.2. Bias functions (top) and MSE functions (bottom) for adaptive testing without (left) and with item-exposure control (right). The solid lines are for the item pool assembled according to the proposed method; the dashed lines are for the item pool with parallel forms.

Picking sets of exactly HN_d items from the master pool with the smallest values for the distance measure δ_{id} in (10.92) is a simple task that can be done manually or by a sorting algorithm. Since the pools have to be parallel, each of these sets has to be split into H subsets of N_d items with values (a_i, b_i) for the item parameters that match each other as closely as possible. The H operational pools can then be created by assigning one of the H subsets at the points $d \in W$ to each pool.

Obviously, the problem resembles the two-stage test-splitting problem treated in Section 5.4.2. The only differences are:

1. We now split a collection of test items into item pools instead of a test into subtests.

2. In the second stage of the process, we assign sets of N_d items to the pools instead of individual items to subtests.

The problem can be solved using an adjusted version of the models in the two-stage solution process for the test-splitting problem in Section 5.4.2. For notational convenience, we discuss the models for the case of $H = 2$ item pools.

First-Stage Model

Let $i = 1, ..., 2N_d$ denote the $2N_d$ best items in the set preselected for point $d \in W$. Because each of these sets has to be split into N_d pairs of items, we use a second index $j = 1, ..., 2N_d$. Analogous to (5.56), decision variables x_{ijd} are defined as:

$$x_{ijd} = \begin{cases} 1 & \text{if items } i \text{ and } j \text{ at } d \text{ are assigned to a pair} \\ 0 & \text{otherwise.} \end{cases} \quad (11.55)$$

The pairs of items are found for all sets at $d \in W$ simultaneously using a slight extension of the model in (5.79)–(5.81), which was a more parsimonious alternative to the one in (5.67)–(5.71):

$$\text{minimize} \sum_{d \in W} \sum_{i=1}^{2N_d-1} \sum_{j=i+1}^{2N_d} \delta_{ij} x_{ijd} \quad (11.56)$$

subject to

$$\sum_{i=1}^{j-1} x_{ij} + \sum_{i=j+1}^{2N_d} x_{ji} = 1, \quad \text{for all } j \text{ and } d \in W, \quad (11.57)$$

$$x_{ijd} \in \{0, 1\}, \quad \text{for all } i < j \text{ and } d \in W. \quad (11.58)$$

Observe that the model is separable. If the problem is too large to be solved in a reasonable time, it can be divided into a series of separate problems for subsets of points in W with a joint solution equal to the solution for the full model.

Second-Stage Model

The result from the first stage is a set of I pairs of items, where I is the common size of the two item pools to be assembled. The pairs are denoted as $p = 1, ..., I$, while we use $i_p = 1, 2$ to denote the items in pair p. The set of pairs of items at point $d \in W$ is denoted as V_d.

The problem is to assign the items in every pair p to the item pools $h = 1, 2$ such that each pool satisfies the blueprint $(N_1, ..., N_D)$ and they are as parallel as possible with respect to the item parameters. Rather than matching the pools on the values (a_i, b_i), our proposal is to match them directly on their information functions, which are the quantities actually used when assembling tests from the pools. Analogously to (5.72), decision variables $x_{i_p h}$ are used for the assignment of item i in pair p to pool h.

The version of the second-stage model in (5.73)–(5.78) we need is

$$\text{minimize } y \tag{11.59}$$

subject to

$$\sum_{i=1}^{2} \sum_{p=1}^{I} I_{i_p}(\theta_k)(x_{i_p 1} - x_{i_p 2}) \leq y, \quad \text{for all } k, \tag{11.60}$$

$$\sum_{i=1}^{2} \sum_{p=1}^{I} I_{i_p}(\theta_k)(x_{i_p 1} - x_{i_p 2}) \geq -y, \quad \text{for all } k, \tag{11.61}$$

$$\sum_{p \in V_d} \sum_{i=1}^{2} x_{i_p h} = N_d, \quad \text{for all } d \in W \text{ and } h, \tag{11.62}$$

$$\sum_{h=1}^{2} x_{i_p h} = 1, \quad \text{for all } i \text{ and } p, \tag{11.63}$$

$$x_{i_p h} \in \{0, 1\}, \quad \text{for all } i, p, \text{ and } h. \tag{11.64}$$

It is useful to compare this model with that for the assembly of a single test in (10.94)–(10.96). Although they have different objective functions, the differences between their constraints are more important. The set of constraints in (11.62) is a generalization of (10.95); the constraints now guarantee realization of the same blueprint $(N_1, ..., N_D)$ for each individual pool. The model in (10.94)–(10.96) also misses the constraints in (11.63). These constraints are necessary only in the case of multiple pools; they require that each item be assigned to one pool and thus prevent overlap between pools.

Models for the Case without a Blueprint

If no blueprint for the item pools is available, the optimal numbers $(N_1, ..., N_D)$ are unknown. This lack of knowledge has two different consequences for the problem of assembling a set of parallel item pools:

1. The subset of design points W with $N_d \geq 1$ cannot be identified.

2. The optimal size of the item pool I, which is equal to the sum of the numbers N_d, is unknown.

These consequences suggest an approach in which a preselected portion of the master pool is split into the necessary number of operational pools, requiring the pools to be matched as closely as possible on the combinations of item attributes we select as relevant.

For the version of the problem with $H = 2$ item pools, the proposed method consists of the following steps:

1. Select a set of design points in $\mathcal{D}$ with the combinations of attributes on which the item pools should match.

2. Select the items in the pool with the combinations of categorical attributes at these design points. (If necessary, go back and forth between the current step and the preceding step.)

3. Split the sets of items at these points into pairs with values for the item parameters that match each other as closely as possible.

4. Assign the items in the pairs to different item pools, if necessary with constraints on possible remaining quantitative attributes to match the composition of the pools with respect to these constraints as well.

Let V_d denote the set of items in the master pool with the combination of categorical attributes at the points $d \in \mathcal{D}$ selected in step 1 above. The model in (11.56)–(11.58) can then be used to split each of the sets V_d into the pairs of items referred to in step 3 above. (If some of these sets have an odd number of items, we ignore the item with the worst set of distances δ_{ij} to all other items in V_d.)

In the second stage of the procedure, we use the model in (11.59)–(11.64) to assign the items to the two pools. The only change in the model is the replacement of (11.62) by

$$\sum_{i=1}^{2} x_{i_p h} = 1, \quad \text{for all } p \text{ and } h. \tag{11.65}$$

This change is necessary because we do not have a blueprint with the optimal number of items N_d. Instead, we require that one item from each pair p be assigned to each item pool. How many items with the combinations of attributes at d the two pools will have depends entirely on the composition of the master pool.

If quantitative attributes other than the item parameters are relevant, we can add constraints to the model in (11.59)–(11.64) to force the pools to be parallel with respect to them as well. Specifically, we can force the sum of the values of these attributes to be between the same (tight) bounds for each pool using constraints of the type

$$\sum_{p=1}^{P} \sum_{i=1}^{2} q_{i_p} x_{i_p h} \gtrless b_q, \quad \text{for all } h. \tag{11.66}$$

Another disadvantage of assembling a system of rotating item pools without a blueprint is that they miss the tendency for equal exposure rates for adaptive tests from the pools built into (11.17)–(11.19). It is possible to compensate for this by assigning items expected to be less popular to more than one pool. Because the pools are used randomly, the exposure rates of items assigned to more pools tend to increase.

If this option is used, in the first stage of the procedure, the sets V_d may have to be split into subsets of different sizes. For example, if some of the items are assigned to two pools, the size of the subsets to which they are assigned decreases by one.

For the general case of H pools, we have to replace the no-overlap constraint in (11.63) by

$$\sum_{h=1}^{H} x_{i_p h} \leq n_o^{\max}, \quad \text{for some } i \text{ and } p, \tag{11.67}$$

and

$$\sum_{h=1}^{H} x_{i_p h} \geq n_o^{\min}, \quad \text{for some } i \text{ and } p, \tag{11.68}$$

where $1 < n_o^{\min} \leq n_o^{\max} \leq H$ are the maximum and minimum number of tests these items are allowed to share.

11.5.6   Empirical Example

Two systems of rotating pools were assembled from a master pool consisting of 2,131 items for the section of the LSAT that consists of discrete items only. One system was assumed to have four pools without any item overlap; the other system was assumed to have six pools with item overlap. The amount of overlap was based on the values of the discrimination parameter for the items, the idea being that items with lower values tend to be less popular in adaptive testing. The range of values in the pool was divided into seven equally wide intervals; the items in the highest interval were assigned to one pool only, those in the second highest interval to two pools, and so on.

We addressed the case of no blueprint for the pool and used the second approach above. The section of the test used in this example had items with nine different combinations of categorical attributes for which the set of content specifications implied 20 different constraints. All items in the master pool were classified with respect to these combinations. In the first stage of the assembly process, the collections of items for each of these combinations were split into the maximum number of subsets of size four for the system without item overlap. For the system with item overlap, the size of the subsets was adapted according to the required overlap. The split was made using the version of the first-stage model in (11.56)–(11.58), with the distance measure δ_{ij} in (10.92) for $w = 1$, ignoring the guessing parameter c.

For the second stage, we used the model in (11.59)–(11.64) with the replacement of (11.62) by (11.65) for the system without item overlap and (11.67) and (11.68) for the system with overlap. The model was also extended with a set of constraints of the type in (11.66) to match the pools as closely as possible on one remaining quantitative attribute (word count).

We evaluated the two systems in a study with 1,000 simulated administrations of the adaptive test at each of the values $\theta = -2.0, -1.5, ..., 2.0$ using the STA. To obtain a baseline, we also ran these simulations with the systems of rotating pools replaced by the master pool of 2,131 items. All simulations were thus conducted with approximately the same number of items, but the active pool for the simulated test taker in the system of rotating item pools was much smaller than the master pool.

Figure 11.3 shows the exposure rates of the items for the system with four nonoverlapping and six overlapping pools relative to the master pool. From these plots, it is clear that the method of rotating item pools reduces the exposure rates effectively. Figure 11.4 shows the estimated bias and MSE functions. For each of the three pools, bias appeared to be negligible for all practical purposes. For adaptive testing from the master pool, the MSE was smaller at the lower part of the θ scale than for the two cases with rotating item pools, particularly for the system with overlapping pools. The reason was that in adaptive testing from the master pool we have permanent access to the best items in the pool, whereas for the two other cases only a portion of it was active at a time. The fact that the system with overlapping pools performed worse than the one without overlap was due to the use of the discrimination parameter as the criterion for the size of the overlap; items with lower values for it were assigned to more pools. The differences were more clearly manifest at the lower part of the scale because of the relative scarceness of items in the LSAT pool for this part of the scale.

The conclusion from this study is that using a system of rotating pools appears to be an effective measure to reduce the exposure rates of the more popular items, but the price that has to be paid is an increase in the MSE of the ability estimates that is somewhat higher than expected .

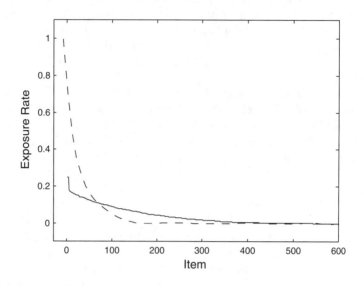

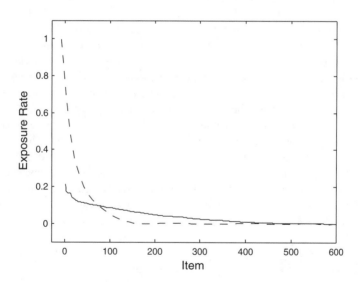

FIGURE 11.3. Item-exposure rates for adaptive testing using a system of rotating item pools (solid lines) with four nonoverlapping pools (top) and six overlapping pools (bottom). The dashed lines are for adaptive testing from the master pool. The items are ordered by their exposure rates; items not shown had zero exposure.

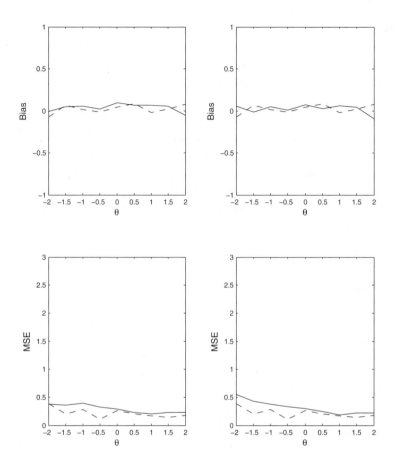

FIGURE 11.4. Bias functions (top) and MSE functions (bottom) for adaptive testing using a system of rotating item pools (solid lines) with four nonoverlapping pools (left) and six overlapping pools (right). The dashed lines are for adaptive testing from the master pool.

11.6   Literature

General discussions of the problem of item-pool design for programs with adaptive tests, with an emphasis on their security, are given in Way (1998), Way, Steffen, and Anderson (1998), and Way, Swanson, Steffen, and Stocking (2001).

The Monte Carlo approach to item-pool design for a program with adaptive testing was introduced in Veldkamp and van der Linden (2000);

an update of the theory and a few new empirical examples are given in Veldkamp and van der Linden (in preparation).

For a derivation of the relation between test length, item pool size, and the sum of exposure rates used in (11.14), see van der Linden (2003, Appendix).

Chang and van der Linden (2003) presented the model for optimal stratification of an item pool for alpha-stratified adaptive testing. The idea of assembling an item pool as a set of fixed test forms was introduced in van der Linden, Ariel, and Veldkamp (2005). Stocking and Swanson (1998) used their weighted-deviations method (WDM; Section 4.4.3) to solve the problem of assembling a system of rotating item pools. The fact that this problem shares much of its structure with the test-splitting problem in Chapter 5 was discussed in Ariel, Veldkamp, and van der Linden (2004). This reference also presents several heuristics for solving this problem, and should also be consulted for more details of the empirical example in Section 11.5.6.

11.7 Summary

1. Design models for programs with adaptive tests are formulated for their shadow tests. The optimal blueprint is calculated using a Monte Carlo study with test administrations at ability levels randomly sampled from the population of test takers. The items administered have the combinations of attributes at the points in the design space.

2. The design model has counters for the number of items administered at each design point. The blueprint for the item pool is calculated from the counts, adjusting them to create uniform (marginal or conditional) exposure of the items.

3. Programs with multiple adaptive tests from a single item pool are technically feasible. They are expected to be particularly efficient for multidimensional item pools used in such applications as testing for admission and placement with multiple criteria because they replace *post hoc* weighting of scores on different tests by a score on a multidimensional test directly assembled to measure the desired combination of intentional abilities.

4. If the program has set-based adaptive tests, the Monte Carlo study is conducted over two design spaces simultaneously, one for the items and the other for the stimuli. The model then has counters both for the items and stimuli administered at the points in the two spaces.

5. Operational pools for adaptive testing are typically assembled from a master pool. The model for assembling an item pool for a program

with adaptive tests is identical to the model for a program with fixed tests in Section 10.8.

6. Item pools for adaptive testing with alpha stratification can be stratified optimally using a semiassignment network-flow model.

7. If no blueprint is available, item pools for adaptive testing can be assembled as a set of fixed test forms that satisfy the specifications of the test and have a distribution of the maximizers of their information functions reflecting the ability distribution of the population of test takers. Such pools always have a shadow test that is optimal at a point close to the current ability estimate of the test takers during the test.

8. The problem of assembling a system of rotating parallel item pools from a master pool resembles the test-splitting problem addressed in Chapter 5. The problem can be solved by assigning items with an optimal match between their item-parameter values to the pools subject to the requirement that each pool realize the same blueprint with respect to all other attributes.

9. A similar approach can be followed if the pools have to be assembled without a blueprint for them. But we are then uncertain as to the set of design points that should be used and the optimal size of the item pool. In addition, the exposure rates of the items have to be controlled by constraints on the number of pools to which each item is assigned.

11.8   Exercises

11.1 Derive an equation for the optimal number of items in the blueprint in (11.18) for the case of marginal exposure control, where the item pool is required to have a minimum size of $I^{\min}$. Do the same for the case of conditional exposure control in (11.18).

11.2 Formulate an equation for the optimal number of items in the blueprint for a set-based item pool in (11.41) and (11.44) for the case of conditional exposure control.

11.3 Suppose we stratify an item pool on discrimination parameter a only but want to impose constraints on the values of the b parameter to get an acceptable item-difficulty distribution per stratum. Formulate a model for this type of stratification. Evaluate the model against the one in (11.47)–(11.50).

11.4 Calculate the values θ_t at which the TIFs for a pool of nine test forms should be optimized to reflect a standard normal distribution using the method proposed in Section 11.5.3. Assume that the last 5% of the mass in each tail can be ignored.

11.5 The problem of assembling a system of rotating item pools can be redefined as a problem of assigning the items in the master pool directly to the subpools. Formulate a model of this type. Evaluate the model against the two-stage procedure in Section 11.5.5.

12
Epilogue

We began the preface to this book with the observation that during the first century of its existence test theory has developed into a mature discipline with powerful models and statistical tools. On the other hand, the development has not shown much spin-off in the form of a technology that helps us "to engineer tests rigorously to our specifications." This book was motivated by the wish to fill this void. At the end of it, it may be appropriate to review the principles that have guided us in our efforts to do so. We consider three principles as crucial.

> Principle 1: *Any specification that a test has to satisfy can be realized by imposing one or more constraints on its composition.*

The chapters in this book contain numerous illustrations of this principle. For some specifications the answer to the question of what constraint to choose was straightforward. Examples are the length of the test, its content distribution, the fact that its information function should deviate from a target function by no more than a prespecified tolerance, and the exclusion of items that are too difficult. Other illustrations of Principle 1 may have been more surprising, such as the level of speededness of a test, a pre-existing observed-score scale that the test should have, an item-by-item match between two tests, a maximum exposure rate for an item pool for adaptive testing, item overlap between tests, the status of an ability as an intentional or a nuisance parameter in a multidimensional test-assembly problem, and the inclusion of items in a set for the same stimulus.

A major effort in this book was directed at establishing menus with constraints for all possible features consumers and developers may want a test to have. Also, we classified the constraints by their level and type and discussed the formal characteristics of constraints for each possible combination of level and type. Finally, we extended the principle to adaptive test assembly, which appeared to be possible through the introduction of the notion of a shadow test.

A test specification can also be formulated as an objective for an optimization problem. But, as we explained in Section 2.3, constraints are actually more useful than objectives. They give us maximum control of attributes, and we know exactly what test we get in advance. Objectives should be reserved for attributes with values for which we are less certain, such as estimates of statistical attributes. In fact, for several of the models in this book, we chose an objective function of a more technical nature that did not contain any test attribute at all. The foremost example of this choice was the objective function used to implement the maximin/minimax principle, which was just an auxiliary variable.

Throughout this book, we have been keen on formulating specifications as *linear* constraints. One reason for this preference was emphasized on many occasions in the earlier chapters: As long as a test-design problem remains linear, there is not much reason to be concerned about the algorithmic aspect of finding a solution. The algorithms reviewed in Chapter 4 always worked for the real-world-size problems used as examples in this book. (This observation should not be taken as an invitation to carelessness, however; see our comment on the skillful test assembler at the end of Section 3.1.) But a second, equally important reason to formulate specifications as linear constraints is that linear constraints can always be formulated independently. That is, we can focus on just one attribute at a time, model the specifications in which it occurs as linear constraints, and insert the constraints into the model. As long as we make no consistency errors (Section 3.2.4), there is no need to be concerned about possible interactions of a new constraint with earlier or later constraints. This basic property of linear programming makes test design most convenient. It enables us to mold our tests simply by adding and removing constraints from the optimization model.

We followed different approaches to formulating specifications as linear constraints. First, often we were able to use the fact that higher-level attributes in the test were additive in item attributes. A straightforward example was the time spent on a test (sum of the response times on its items). Second, occasionally we were able to exploit the possibilities offered by the use of different sets of decision variables; for example, the use of different 0-1 variables for items and stimuli to model the inclusion of items in sets with common stimuli. Third, we also used real-valued auxiliary variables to formulate constraints linearly, primarily in the application of the minimax approach to IRT-based test assembly with an absolute target for the TIF. In this type of test assembly, our actual objective was to minimize the (two-sided) area between the TIF and its target. But we were able to approximate this nonlinear objective by a linear formulation that involved minimization of a common bound at a set of selected θ values. (This approximation also capitalized on the fact that TIFs are smooth mathematical functions!) Fourth, some problems that were nonlinear in their actual objectives could be reformulated using the technique of linear decomposition; that is, decomposing the actual objective into a combination of a linear objective and linear constraints. This approach was used in our examples of classical and multidimensional test assembly. Fifth, sometimes we were able to use a linear statistical approximation to a nonlinear actual objective. An example of this approach was the use of a set of linear constraints on powers of response probabilities in observed-score pre-equating of a test to a reference test. (In fact, the same principle was followed in test assembly with information functions; we use information functions in IRT-based test assembly only because they are convenient asymptotic approximations to the sampling variance of ability estimates.) Lastly, to constrain the exposure rates of items in adaptive testing, we used probabilistic constraints. The constraints that were actually imposed were simple linear item-ineligibility constraints, whereas the more complicated nonlinear aspects of the problem were captured by the probabilities with which they were imposed.

Principle 2: *Constraints should be imposed as early in the test-development process as possible.*

To appreciate the second principle, it is important to understand that constraints are not only imposed when selecting items from a pool. They can also occur as *implicit* constraints that are imposed, for instance, when coding the items in the pool in a special way, adding or excluding certain types of items from the pool, forcing the item-selection process to go through different stages, choosing a testing format, or adjusting a test after it has been assembled.

The history of test design can be viewed as a (sometimes slow) process of adhering to the notion that prevention is better than cure, which motivates the second principle. For example, in large-scale testing programs, it is now common practice to pretest items before they are used operationally. This choice allows us to constrain items with unfortunate statistical attributes or otherwise undesirable behavior out of the test. It is difficult to imagine that the idea of pretesting initially met with considerable resistance, primarily because of concern about item security. The testing industry reacted to these concerns by developing ingenious pretesting designs, after which the resistance disappeared.

It is even harder to remember the times when an *independent* review of new test items was not yet standard practice. In fact, independent review is still lacking in most testing in schools. The quality of teacher-made tests would improve greatly if they were not administered immediately but given to a few colleagues for review first.

These two examples do not exhaust the possibilities for early constraints to prevent later problems. Item pools are frequently treated just as an inventory of items for a content domain, which develops over time. A result of this view may be a large collection of items that are never used or a shortage of items with combinations of attributes that are badly needed. On the other hand, the method of item-pool design proposed in this book was motivated entirely by the principle of early constraint imposition above. In spite of its new terminology and modeling, it is nothing but the idea to impose the test specifications in a program directly on the blueprint for its item pool. By imposing them this early, we increase the likelihood that the specifications can be met if the tests are actually assembled.

In fact, we went back even one step further and suggested imposing the constraints where they can be expected to be most effective—on the authors that have to write the items! In fact, a blueprint for an item pool is just a collection of blueprints for its items. Instead of inviting authors to write items for a content domain and giving them a list of dos and don'ts, it is much more effective to ask them to write their items precisely to the combinations of attributes listed in their blueprints. Our proposal to add item authors for a program as an explicit attribute to the design space and manage the item-pool development process with respect to their capacity (Section 10.7.2) was motivated by the same principle of early constraint imposition.

More subtle applications of the second principle can be met in some of the other topics addressed in this book. For example, our plea to assemble multiple test forms simultaneously rather than sequentially goes back to the same principle. Sequential test assembly always needs to be followed by a second corrective stage to realize a satisfactory solution. Constructive heuristics for test assembly (Section 4.6) suffer from the same problem.

Another application of the second principle is item-exposure control in adaptive testing using the item-ineligibility method (Section 9.4). In the Sympson-Hetter method of exposure control, tendencies toward overexposure are corrected after an item is selected for a test taker, whereas in the item-ineligibility method, constraints on the item-exposure rates are imposed before a test taker begins. Because it corrects only afterward, the Sympson-Hetter method may be removing more items from the pool than are actually required.

One area where the idea of early control has not had much impact on the testing industry is observed-score equating of a fixed or adaptive test to a reference test. The current routine is to ignore the observed-score metric when the test is assembled and then correct by adjusting the test scores afterward. In Sections 5.3 and 9.6, we identified the constraints that can be included in the optimization model to assemble tests with the same observed-score metric as a reference test. Using them prevents an expensive *post hoc* equating study. It also prevents the loss of optimality of the test assembled by the optimization model due to a later change of scoring metric.

As indicated in Section 11.2.1, a comparable case may hold with respect to the predictive validity of a test battery in testing for admission or placement. The current practice is to design unidimensional tests and then use a weighted combination of scores to maximize the validity with respect to a criterion. Alternatively, it may be worth looking into the possibilities of designing a pool with more complex multidimensional items and imposing the weights through the model in (8.14)–(8.20) or (9.63)–(9.70) used to assemble tests from it. Empirical research is needed to determine how much efficiency can be gained if a test battery scored for a combination of abilities is replaced by a test optimally designed to measure the combination.

> Principle 3: *Constraints that do not serve any desired feature of the test should be avoided.*

This principle is the counterpart of Principle 1. It seems straightforward but is not always followed. In particular, it is easily violated by implicit constraints.

Examples of implicit constraints due to forcing an item-selection process to go through different stages are found in the alternative back-up methods for multiple-test assembly discussed in Section 6.4. One method was based on the idea of first splitting a pool into a subpool for each test and then assembling a single test from each subpool. This method involved the rather stringent set of ineligibility constraints in (6.53) on the individual tests. In another method, first a big test was assembled, and this was then split into individual tests. This method should be viewed as one that imposes the composition of the big test as a set of constraints on the assembly of the individual tests. Similar forms of overconstraining occur in the heuristics for the assembly of tests with item sets in Chapter 7, especially in the two-stage methods in Section 7.5.

Another example of implicit constraints are those involved in the choice of the adaptive testing formats discussed in Section 9.8. If the choice is between a fully adaptive, a multistage adaptive, and an adaptive linear on-the-fly format, it is important to be aware of the extra constraints implied by each of these formats relative to the content specifications of the test. As indicated in Section 9.8, both a multistage and a linear on-the-fly format imply a large set of logical constraints to keep their subtests or linear tests together. For the same item pool, the price of a larger number of active constraints is loss of information. It is therefore important to identify the feature that these extra constraints makes possible—in the case of the multistage and linear on-the-fly formats, the possibility of reviewing intact test units before they are used operationally (see Section 9.8) and deciding if it is worth the loss.

Another example of implicit constraints is adaptive testing from rotating item pools (Section 11.5.5). If the system has H pools of equal size, the procedure is equivalent to adaptive testing from a pool with all items but ineligibility constraints on $(H-1)/Hx100\%$ of them. Viewing the use of rotating item pools from this perspective opens up an entire range of alternatives to adaptive testing with rotating item pools—for instance, testing from a large pool with random ineligibility constraints on a smaller portion of the pool. Or constraints only for the part of the pool that has already been exposed. An important problem is then to determine what level of constraining is actually necessary to realize the desired level of security of the items.

In sum, when designing a testing program, we should identify the constraints that represent our test specifications and impose them as early in the developmental process as possible. Also, we should be aware of constraints imposed implicitly during the test-development process, or by our choice of testing format, that do not entail a necessary feature of the test.

Appendix 1
Basic Concepts in Linear Programming

A1.1   Mathematical Programming

Mathematical programming belongs to a field of problem solving that emerged in such areas as operations research, decision analysis, economics, and management science. The problems it addresses typically belong to the daily operations of a business or organization, deal with decisions that have consequences for their costs or profits, and are approached from a managerial point of view; hence, its links with the areas above. Examples of these problems include optimization of a manufacturer's product mix, scheduling production, job assignment, transportation decisions, factory location, inventory control, maintenance, and economic planning.

The reason that mathematical programming approaches can be applied to test-design problems is their formal analogy with some of these examples. For instance, there is not much difference between the formal structure of problems in job assignment and test selection, nor between problems in inventory control and item-pool design.

The problems addressed in mathematical programming are mostly too complicated to be solved intuitively, and more formal approaches involving mathematical modeling and the use of computer algorithms are required. Mathematical programming techniques are frequently implemented in software systems that help users model their problems, calculate solutions under varieties of conditions, and show them how to interpret results. The software used to calculate a solution is often referred to as a *solver* or *optimizer*.

More generally, in mathematical programming, one seeks to optimize an objective for the solution of a decision problem that can be modeled as a function of a set of variables that describe all possible outcomes. These variables are related to each other through one or more constraints on their values.

The general form of a mathematical programming problem is

$$\text{optimize } z = f(x_1, ..., x_n) \tag{A1.1}$$

subject to

$$g_1(x_1, ..., x_n) \underset{>}{\overset{\leq}{=}} b_1,$$

$$...$$

$$g_m(x_1, ..., x_n) \underset{>}{\overset{\leq}{=}} b_m, \tag{A1.2}$$

where $(x_1, ..., x_n)$ are the variables that characterize the problem, $z = f(x_1, ..., x_n)$ is the objective function that is optimized, and $g_j(x_1, ..., x_n)$, $j = 1, ..., m$, are m constraints on the variables with bounds b_j. The constraint set includes constraints that follow from the substantive structure of the problem but also constraints on the range of values the variables can take.

A specific problem is obtained from (A1.1) and (A1.2) by making choices for the variables $(x_1, ..., x_n)$, the functions $f(x_1, ..., x_n)$ and $g_j(x_1, ..., x_n)$, and the bounds b_j. If such choices are made, the general structure of the problem in (A1.1) and (A1.2) specializes. Or, in other words, the problem has been "programmed"; hence the name mathematical programming. Because these choices have to be realistic for the empirical structure of the problem, we also refer to the result as a model.

A1.1.1   Linear Programming

If all functions $f(x_1, ..., x_n)$ and $g_j(x_1, ..., x_n)$ are linear, the problem is known as a *linear programming* (LP) problem. Its standard or canonical form is

$$\text{maximize } z = c_1 x_1 + ... + c_n x_n \tag{A1.3}$$

subject to

$$a_{11} x_1 + ... + a_{1n} x_{1n} \leq b_1,$$

$$...$$

$$a_{m1} x_1 + ... + a_{mn} x_{mn} \leq b_m,$$

$$x_i \geq 0, \quad i = 1, ..., n. \tag{A1.4}$$

Note that in (A1.3) and (A1.4) all variables are nonnegative, the constraints are less-than-or-equal-to inequalities, and the objective function is maximized. This form can always be realized using the fact that:

1. A minimization problem can be converted into a maximization problem by taking the negatives of the coefficients c_i in the objective function.

2. The sense of an inequality can be changed by taking the negatives of coefficients a_{ji} and bound b_j.

3. An equality can be formulated as a combination of two inequalities with the same bound, with a subsequent change of the sense of the larger-than inequality using the preceding operation.

4. Variables that take positive and negative values can be transformed to nonnegative variables by adding a sufficiently large number to their values.

If a problem needs to be reformulated into the form in (A1.3) and (A1.4), its solution can always be transformed back to a solution for the original formulation by performing the inverse operations. In this appendix, we assume that LP problems are always in their standard format. This assumption was ignored everywhere else in this book because we wanted to remain as close as possible to the original formulation of the problems.

Observe that any linear program is completely defined by a vector $\mathbf{c} = (c_i)$ with coefficients for the objective function, a matrix $\mathbf{A} = (a_{ji})$ for the left-hand-side coefficients in the constraints, and a vector of $\mathbf{b} = (b_j)$ for the bounds, with $i = 1, ..., n$ and $j = 1, ..., m$. If we refer to the structure of an LP problem, we refer to the values of these vectors and matrix.

A1.1.2 Nonlinear Programming

If the objective function $f(x_1, ..., x_n)$ is quadratic but all constraints are linear, the problem is known as a *quadratic programming* problem. Techniques for solving quadratic programming problems are available, but frequently it is more advantageous to approximate the original problem by a linear formulation. Examples of linear decomposition and approximation of problems with quadratic objectives are given in Section 5.2.1 (classical test assembly) and 8.3 (multidimensional test assembly).

Different forms of nonlinear programming arise if both the objective function and the constraints are quadratic or take another nonlinear form. Such problems hardly exist in test assembly. If they occur, again the best strategy is to avoid algorithmic complications and approximate them by a linear formulation of the problem.

A1.1.3 Other Forms of Mathematical Programming

If decisions are made under conditions of uncertainty but we have hypotheses on the form of the probability distributions of the conditions, the decision problem becomes one of *stochastic programming*. Problems of stochastic programming have one or more random coefficients, and typically the objective is to optimize an expected value defined over these coefficients.

Another common form of mathematical programming arises if time is an important characteristic of the problem and the outcomes of later decisions depend on outcomes of earlier decisions. Problems of this type belong to the domain of *dynamic programming*.

Sequential and adaptive test assemblies (Section 1.3.1) have both features and can be classified as problems of *stochastic dynamic programming*. Sequential test assembly is not addressed in this book, but we deal with the problem of adaptive testing in Chapter 9. Treatment of adaptive testing as an instance of stochastic dynamic programming is not realistic, however. The probability structure involved in the selection of each possible next item as a function of all possible responses to all possible previous combinations of items quickly becomes unmanageable if the length of adaptive tests increases to realistic values. Instead, we treat adaptive testing as a series of deterministic mixed-integer problems (though the notion of a *stochastic constraint* is introduced to deal with the problem of item-exposure control in adaptive testing in Section 9.4.3).

A1.1.4   Constraints on Variables

If all variables in (A1.3) and (A1.4) are real, the problem is known as an LP problem. If all variables are integer, as was the case for the problems of item-pool design in Chapter 10, the problem is known as an *integer programming* (IP) problem. A special case of IP arises if all variables are 0-1. The problem is then known as a 0-1 IP or *binary programming problem*. Some of the test-assembly problems in this book are pure 0-1 integer or binary programming problems, while others have both integer and real variables. The latter are known as *mixed-integer programming* (MIP) problems. Most of the test-design problems in this book are of this type.

In this book, we also refer to test-assembly problems as problems of combinatorial optimization. Generally, in a combinatorial optimization problem, the task is to identify an optimal combination of elements from a finite set subject to one or more constraints. An optimization problem of this type thus differs fundamentally from that of finding an optimum of a function defined over a real-valued domain in calculus. Because 0-1 variables can be used as indicator variables for the choice of elements from a set, the test-assembly problems we are interested in can appropriately be modeled as 0-1 IP problems.

It is key to note that if the variables in an LP problem are replaced by integer variables, the new problem is more severely constrained; hence the standard practice of formulating the range of these variables as integer constraints at the end of the constraint set of a problem. Conversely, if integer constraints are removed, the new problem becomes less severely constrained, or *relaxed*.

Although the set of feasible solutions for a problem generally becomes smaller if its variables are subjected to integer constraints, it becomes more difficult to find a solution to the problem. This fact, which goes against our intuition, is discussed in Section A1.5 below.

A1.2   Graphical Example

We give a graphical representation of an example of a common LP problem with two variables. This representation helps us to discuss and motivate several basic concepts in linear programming.

A1.2.1   Problem

The problem is that of a small manufacturer who has to decide on the mix of products it should produce. Suppose the choice is between products 1 and 2. Either product is made from materials A, B, and C. To produce one unit of product 1, we need two units of A, one unit of B, and one unit of C, whereas for one unit of product 2 we need one unit of A, one unit of B, and two units of C. Due to inventory restrictions, the company cannot use more than 31, 24, and 20 units of A, B, and C during its planning period. The profit made on the production of one unit of products 1 and 2 is \$25 and \$20, respectively.

Our first step is to identify the variables that help us calculate the best solution to this problem. Clearly, the objective of the company is to maximize its profit, and profit is a function of the number of units of products 1 and 2 that are produced. Let x_1 and x_2 be the variables that represent the number of units of these products. Profit is then $25x_1 + 20x_2$. The only constraints in this problem are those due to the inventory restrictions on the materials A, B, and C. If x_1 and x_2 units of each product are produced, we need $2x_1 + x_2$ units of A, $x_1 + x_2$ units of B, and $x_1 + 2x_2$ units of C.

The LP model we have to solve for the optimal values of x_1 and x_2 is therefore

$$\text{maximize } 25x_1 + 20x_2 \quad \text{(profit)} \tag{A1.5}$$

subject to

$$2x_1 + x_2 \leq 31, \quad \text{(inventory restriction for } A) \tag{A1.6}$$

$$x_1 + x_2 \leq 24, \quad \text{(inventory restriction for } B) \tag{A1.7}$$

$$x_1 + 2x_2 \leq 20, \quad \text{(inventory restriction for } C) \tag{A1.8}$$

$$x_1, x_2 \geq 0. \quad \text{(range of variables)} \tag{A1.9}$$

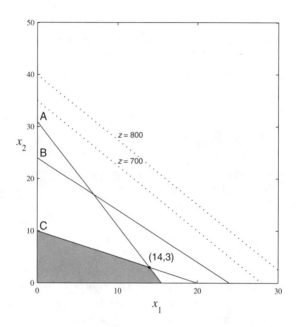

FIGURE A1.1. Graph of the product-mix problem in (A1.5)–(A1.9).

A1.2.2 Graphical Representation

A graph with the problem is given in Figure A1.1. The space of possible solutions for the unconstrained version of the problem consists of all points in the first quadrant. The constraints reduce this space to the subspace of *feasible solutions*. Each of the constraints is met by the half-planes below the lines $x_2 = -2x_1 + 31$ (inventory restriction for A), $x_2 = -x_1 + 24$ (inventory restriction for B), and $x_2 = -.5x_1 + 10$ (inventory restriction for C), respectively. The set of feasible solutions is therefore the intersection of these half-planes, represented by the shaded area in the figure.

For every value z of the *objective function*, we obtain a line $z = 25x_1 + 20x_2$. Two possible lines, for $z = 700$ and 800, are given in the graph. Observe that these lines are parallel and that the line for the larger value of z is higher. Maximization of the objective function means finding the line with the largest possible value for z that intersects the feasible space. Obviously, the largest value is obtained when the line coincides with vertex $(14, 3)$, where the lines $x_2 = -2x_1 + 31$ for A and $x_2 = -.5x_1 + 10$ for B intersect. This point thus represents the *optimal feasible solution*. Its coordinates are the optimal values of x_1 and x_2; they tell us how many units of each product have to be produced to get the maximum profit of $z = 25 \times 14 + 20 \times 3 = 410$.

Although Figure A1.1 is only for a two-variable LP problem with real values, it allows us to illustrate graphically some of the notions in the MIP test-assembly problems with large numbers of variables discussed in this book. In Section 2.4.2, the issue of the number of constraints possible for a test-assembly problem was discussed. The graph illustrates that this number is free as long as the problem remains feasible. A problem remains feasible as long as a new constraint added to it leaves the feasible space intact or "cuts off only a small piece of it."

Possible effects on the feasible space of a new constraint added to the problem in (A1.5)–(A1.9) are illustrated in Figure A1.2. The feasible space in the lower-left portion of this figure is the same as in Figure A1.1. Constraint D is an example of a constraint that would be *redundant* if it were added to the current problem; its presence would not imply any further reduction of the feasible space. Constraint E would entail a reduction of the feasible space but would not make it empty. Its addition would thus keep the problem feasible. But constraint F is an example of one that would make it infeasible. It is met by the points that lie in the half-plane away from the origin, and the intersection of this half-plane with the original feasible space is empty. Constraint F is thus inconsistent with any of the constraints in our original problem. The notion of *inconsistent* constraints is discussed in Section 3.2.4.

Another notion that can be illustrated using Figure A1.1, is that of an *active* constraint introduced in Section 4.1.1. In Figure A1.1, constraints A and C are the only constraints active in the solution: If the problem had been relaxed by leaving out all other constraints, the solution would still have been the same. Whether an constraint is active depends not only on its coefficients but also on those in the objective function; a change in the latter could make other constraints active.

In Section 4.1.1, it was recommended to check the objective function of a test-assembly problem against its constraints before calculating a solution. This check helps us to interpret the solution found and may lead to a more parsimonious formulation of the problem. The idea can be illustrated using Figure A1.1. Because the problem involves maximization, the solution is found in the upper-right corner of the feasible space. Constraints with lower bounds tend to cut off only a portion of the feasible space near its lower-left corner. They are generally inactive and can be left out. But, as discussed in Section 4.1.1, these conclusions involve only tendencies, and we should always be careful. For example, if for some reason the manufacturer in the problem in (A1.5)–(A1.9) had to produce a minimum of five units for product 2, the constraint

$$x_1 \geq 5 \tag{A1.10}$$

would have replaced constraint A as an active constraint in the solution of the problem and we could not have left (A1.10) out.

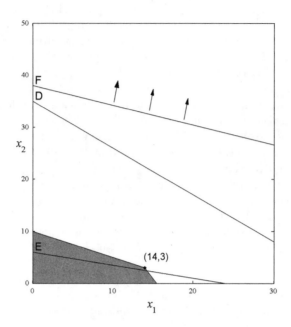

FIGURE A1.2. Example of an LP problem with a redundant constraint (D) and inconsistent constraints $(F$ versus the other constraints).

A1.2.3   Number of Solutions

The shape of the feasible space in Figure A1.1 is the result of a set of linear constraints cutting off the portions of the first quadrant that do not belong to their half-planes. It therefore has straight edges and vertices that point outward. A space of this shape is known as *convex*. A formal definition of a convex space is based on the property that the line connecting any two of its points is always included in it. It is easy to verify visually that this feature holds for the feasible space in Figure A1.1.

Convex spaces can be both *bounded* and *unbounded*. An example of an unbounded feasible space for a two-variable problem with two constraints is given in Figure A1.3. (Note that the formal definition of a convex space still holds for this example but that the more intuitive feature of outward-pointing vertices does not.) If a feasible space is unbounded in the direction in which the objective function is maximized, the solution is unbounded, too. In Figure A1.3, value z of the objective function can be made arbitrarily large without leaving the feasible space.

If the feasible space is bounded, the solution to the problem has to be along the border of the feasible space. The solution is unique if it is at a vertex. But we have infinitely many solutions, each consisting of a different combination of values for the decision variables but with the same value

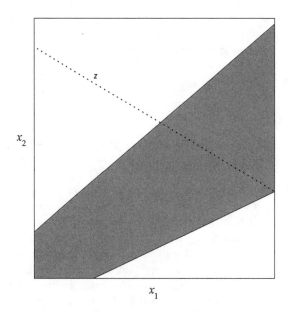

FIGURE A1.3. Example of an LP problem with an unbounded solution.

for the objective function, if the objective function coincides with an edge of the feasible space.

In summary, for each LP problem, the solution set:

1. is empty (problem is infeasible);

2. has one solution (vertex of the feasible space);

3. has infinitely many solutions (all solution points on an edge connecting two vertices); or

4. is unbounded.

This result generalizes to LP problems with more than two variables but does not generally hold for problems with integer variables, for which we can have a finite solution set with more than one solution.

A1.3   Simplex Method

The question of how to find the numerical value of a solution to an LP problem has not yet been addressed. For a standard LP problem, the simplex method is available. The *simplex method* is an iterative method; it begins with an initial solution that is improved on at each next step. We only give a geometric interpretation of the simplex method and refer to the references at the end of this appendix for an algebraic treatment.

The steps taken in the simplex method are:

1. Choose one of the vertices of the feasible space as the initial solution.

2. Move to a new vertex that has a higher value for the objective function.

3. Repeat the previous step until no further improvements are possible. The last vertex visited represents a solution to the problem.

To execute the method, several implementation choices have to be made. For step 1, it is sometimes possible to choose the origin as the point of departure (where all variables are equal to zero), but an advanced start with an initial solution closer to optimality is always attractive. In step 2, the simplex method finds the next vertex in step 2 by embedding the LP problem in a problem with a larger number of variables and replacing the inequality constraints by equalities. A vertex in the original problem corresponds with a combination of values for a subset of the variables in this larger problem. A new vertex is obtained by replacing variables in the current subset. Important implementation decisions on which variables to remove and add are made. Arithmetically, a simplex process proceeds as a series of operations on the coefficients and bounds in the LP problem arranged in a convenient array known as the *simplex tableau*. For an introduction to these operations, see the literature at the end of this appendix.

Although the simplex method has exponential worst-case running time, there are polynomial time algorithms that typically solve problems with large numbers of variables and constraints in a small amount of time. The method has been refined and adapted to problems with special structures and is no longer the only method available to solve LP problems. But it has remained popular, and a version of it known as the *revised simplex method* is the industry standard for LP applications in many fields.

A1.4   Network-Flow Problems

Network-flow, or *transportation*, *problems* are LP problems with a special structure of values for their coefficients and bounds. They have all of the properties of regular LP problems, but their special structure leads to a major simplification of the simplex method. Another attractive feature is that, for a widely used subclass of network-flow problems, the simplex method automatically produces an integer-valued solution. Early examples of network-flow problems dealt with actual transportation problems.

The name "network-flow problem" was introduced later to emphasize the applicability of its models to a larger class of problems.

Suppose we have a transportation problem involving the shipment of a certain commodity from $i = 1, ..., m$ points with a supply of S_i units to $j = 1, ..., n$ different points with a demand of D_j units. The costs of shipping one unit from point i to point j are φ_{ij}. The problem is to find a solution for the variables x_{ij} representing the number of units shipped from i to j. The LP formulation of the problem is

$$\text{minimize} \sum_{i=1}^{m} \sum_{j=1}^{n} \varphi_{ij} x_{ij} \quad \text{(transportation costs)} \tag{A1.11}$$

subject to

$$\sum_{j=1}^{n} x_{ij} \leq S_i, \quad \text{for all } i, \quad \text{(supply)} \tag{A1.12}$$

$$\sum_{i=1}^{m} x_{ij} \geq D_j, \quad \text{for all } j, \quad \text{(demand)} \tag{A1.13}$$

$$x_{ij} \in \{0, 1, ...\}, \quad \text{for all } i \text{ and } j, \quad \text{(range of variables)} \tag{A1.14}$$

with all of their coefficients φ_{ij} and bounds S_i and D_j nonnegative. For the case of $m = 4$ supply points to $n = 3$ demand points, the network is shown in Figure A1.4.

A special case of a network-flow problem is the *assignment problem*, which (1) has equality constraints instead of inequality constraints and (2) the value one for all bounds S_i and D_j. An example of an assignment problem is a scheduling problem in which workers have to be assigned to jobs; for example, minimizing the total time of completion. An example of an assignment problem in test assembly is the item-matching problem discussed in Chapter 5.

In more detail, the two advantages associated with network-flow problems are:

1. The simplex method becomes computationally less intensive: It is easier to choose an initial feasible solution and the only operations on the simplex tableau needed to find the next feasible solution are addition and subtraction.

2. If the bounds S_i and D_j are integer, the set of solutions always contains one with integer values for all values x_{ij}. The simplex method finds this solution.

These two advantages are retained if the problem is allowed to have *transshipment points*; that is, points with both a positive input and a positive output that are located between the pure supply and demand points in the network in Figure A1.4. Several types of test-assembly problems can be approximated by a network-flow formulation (see Section 4.3). Solutions to these problems are found without the computational complexities involved in solving the integer problems discussed in the next section.

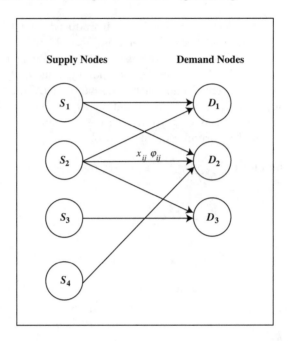

FIGURE A1.4. Example of a network-flow problem with $V = 4$ supply nodes and $W = 3$ demand nodes.

A1.5   Solving Integer Problems

If a problem has integer constraints on its variables, its space of feasible solutions becomes discrete. An example of the feasible space for a small two-variable problem with integer variables is given in Figure A1.5. Observe that this space does not have the convex shape with straight edges and vertices that the problem in Figure A1.1 had. In Section A1.3, the simplex method was intuitively described as an iterative method that walks from vertex to vertex of the feasible space until an optimum is found. This method does not work for a space of discrete points, where we can only walk from single point to single point.

At first sight, a solution to an integer problem seems possible by ignoring the discreteness of the feasible space, using the simplex method for the relaxed version of the problem, and rounding the solution to integer values. The following small example shows why this *rounding heuristic* sometimes is dangerous:

$$\text{maximize } 35x_1 + 30x_2 \tag{A1.15}$$

subject to

$$21x_1 + 14x_2 \le 60, \tag{A1.16}$$

$$x_1, x_2 = 0, 1, \dots . \tag{A1.17}$$

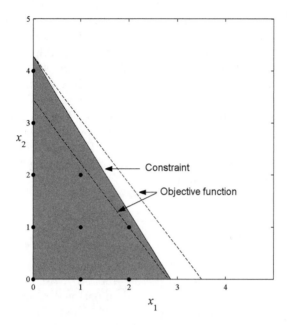

FIGURE A1.5. Example of an IP problem for which the rounding heuristic yields a solution with values for the decision variables entirely different from those for the exact solution.

The feasible space for this problem is represented by the bold dots in the lower-left corner of the graph in Figure A1.5. The feasible space for the relaxed problem is the shaded area. The solution to the relaxed problem is found by the dotted line for the objective function and is equal to $(0, 60/14)$. Rounding this solution to the nearest integer values would result in $(0, 4)$. As illustrated by the bold line for the objective function, the exact solution to the integer problem is $(2, 1)$. Using a rounded solution of a relaxed version of an integer problem instead of its exact solution can thus have a dramatic impact on the values of the decision variables!

The conclusion should not be that rounding heuristics always lead to wrong solutions. The item-pool-design problems in Chapter 10 have integer variables representing the number of items for each combination of attributes needed in the pool. For these problems, upward rounding of the values in the solution of a relaxed version of them results in only a few spare items, which may be needed after all.

As already indicated, if an LP problem is integer and an exact optimal solution is required, we can no longer restrict the search for the solution to a walk along the edges and vertices of a feasible space but have to search the entire solution space. Algorithms for such searches are known as *enumeration methods*. The simplest form of enumeration would be *explicit enumeration*, in which all feasible solutions are listed and each solution is checked for optimality. Given the astronomical size of the feasible space for a typical test-assembly problem, this method is impractical.

Fortunately, we do have methods of *implicit enumeration*. These methods move from one possible solution to the next but do so intelligently, avoiding subsets that cannot contain an optimum and cutting off portions of the solution space that need not be searched. One of these methods, the well-known *branch-and-bound method*, is discussed in Section 4.2. For other methods, such as the Balas algorithm or cutting plane algorithms, see the references in the next section.

A1.6   Literature

Mathematical programming is a well-developed area of applied mathematics, and textbooks with introductions to it abound. We only refer to a small selection of books, and our choice is based on personal experience and bias.

Classical introductory texts are Wagner (1975) and Williams (1990). The former mixes a discussion of theory with numerous applications; the latter emphasizes model building. An introduction to the bare-bones essentials of linear programming is offered in Feiring (1986). Textbooks specializing in integer and combinatorial programming are Nemhauser and Wolsey (1999) and Papadimitriou and Stieglitz (1982). The former is up to date and treats the theory at an advanced level; the latter emphasizes computational aspects. A comprehensive treatment of nonlinear programming is given in Graham, Sherali, and Shetty (1993).

In Section A1.1.3 we indicated that sequential testing can be optimized using techniques from dynamic programming but did not discuss any details. Readers interested in this topic should consult Lewis and Sheehan (1990) or Vos (1999).

Appendix 2
Example of a Test-Assembly Problem in *OPL Studio*

OPL Studio (ILOG, Inc., 2003) is an environment for developing mathematical programming applications. It helps us to create models using its *OPL* (Optimization Programming Language) modeling language, debug models, select mathematical programming options, find solutions, and browse models, solution processes, and results. A helpful tool for IP applications is its dynamic visualization of the search tree. *OPL Studio* is available in versions for *Windows* and *UNIX* operating systems.

OPL Studio includes *OPLScript*, a scripting language for dealing with sequences of models or problems that require interactive input of data and/or instructions. For example, this language enables us to find solutions for problems that require the output of a previous model as the input of the next model. Possible applications of *OPLScript* in test design are multiple-test-assembly problems that require the use of the big-shadow-test method (Section 6.3) or problems with item sets for which two-stage selection of items and stimuli is necessary (Section 7.5).

A important notion in *OPL Studio* is that of a *project*, which basically is an association between a model file and one or more data files. Projects are helpful in that they separate model and data and allow us to solve the same type of problem repeatedly for different sets of data. Once a project is started, new data files can always be inserted. Obvious applications in test design are the assembly of test forms in a program with an item pool that changes over time or with tests with different specifications.

OPL allows us to establish connections to a database or a spreadsheet. When a connection has been set up, we can read from a database or spreadsheet or write to it. For the same project, connections to multiple databases or spreadsheets are possible.

The following set of test specifications for a pool of 35 items on English is used to illustrate how *OPL Studio* can be used to solve a test-assembly problem: (i) The TIF should meet a target value of $T(\theta_c) = 4.0$ at a cutoff score $\theta_c = 0$, (ii) the test length should be equal to ten items, (iii) the test should have at least four items on vocabulary, at most four items on grammar, and at least two items measuring reading comprehension, (iv) the total word count for the test should be between 600 and 700 words, (v) the test should have no items easier than $b = -1.0$, and (vi) items 7 and 16 should not be together in the test.

The problem is represented by the model

$$\text{minimize} \sum_{i=1}^{35} I_i(0)x_i \quad \text{(objective)} \tag{A2.18}$$

subject to

$$\sum_{i=1}^{35} I_i(0)x_i \geq 4, \quad \text{(target value for TIF)} \tag{A2.19}$$

$$\sum_{i=1}^{35} x_i = 10, \quad \text{(test length)} \tag{A2.20}$$

$$\sum_{i \in V_V} x_i \geq 4, \quad \text{(vocabulary)} \tag{A2.21}$$

$$\sum_{i \in V_G} x_i \leq 4, \quad \text{(grammar)} \tag{A2.22}$$

$$\sum_{i \in V_{RC}} x_i \geq 2, \quad \text{(reading comprehension)} \tag{A2.23}$$

$$\sum_{i=1}^{35} w_i x_i \leq 750, \quad \text{(word count)} \tag{A2.24}$$

$$\sum_{i=1}^{35} w_i x_i \geq 700, \quad \text{(word count)} \tag{A2.25}$$

$$b_i x_i \geq -1, \quad \text{for } i = 1, ..., 35, \quad \text{(item difficulty)} \tag{A2.26}$$

$$x_7 + x_{16} \leq 1, \quad \text{(enemies)} \tag{A2.27}$$

$$x_i \in \{0,1\}, \quad \text{for } i = 1, ..., 35. \quad \text{(range of variables)} \tag{A2.28}$$

A model in the *OPL* language and the data set for the problem in (A2.1)–(A2.11) are given in Table A2.1 and A2.2.

The *OPL* model for this problem consists of three different sections: (i) Instructions 1–13 declare all constants, integer ranges, and variables in the model, (ii) instructions 14–25 represent the objective and constraints, and (iii) instructions 26 and 27 create the output of the model.

```
1.    int PoolSize = ...;
2.    int VocalLB = ...;
3.    int VocalUB = ...;
4.    int GrammLB = ...;
5.    int GrammUB = ...;
6.    int ReadCompLB = ...;
7.    int ReadCompUB = ...;
8.    range ID [1..PoolSize];
9.    float Information[ID] = ...;
10.   float Difficulty[ID] = ...;
11.   int WordCount[ID] = ...;
12.   range ZeroOne 0..1;
13.   var ZeroOne Item[ID];
14.   minimize
15.      sum(i in ID) Information[i] * Item[i]
16.   subject to {
17.      sum(i in ID) Information[i] * Item[i] >= 1;
18.      sum(i in ID) Item[i] = 10;
19.      sum(i in Vocabulary) Item[i] >= 0;
20.      sum(i in Grammar) Item[i] <= 10;
21.      sum(i in ReadingComprehension) Item[i] >= 0;
22.      sum(i in ID) WordCount[i] * Item[i] <= 1,000;
23.      sum(i in ID) WordCount[i] * Item[i] >= 0;
24.      forall(i in ID) Difficulty[i] * Item[i] >= -1.0;
25.      Item[7] + Item [16] <= 1; };
26.   {ID} Test = {i|i in ID : Item[i] = 1};
27.   display Test;
```

TABLE A2.1. Example of an *OPL* model for the test-assembly problem in (A2.1)–(A2.11).

More specifically, instructions 1–7 declare integer constants to represent the size of the item pool and the ranks of the first and last items in the sections on Vocabulary, Grammar, and Reading Comprehension in the pool, respectively. The data for these constants are given in the first seven lines of Table A.2.2. Instruction 8 declares the integer range that indexes the items in the pool. Real numbers for $I_i(\theta_0)$ and the difficulty parameter b_i of the items as well as integers for their word counts are declared in instructions 9–11. The data for these item attributes are given in the remaining portion of Table A2.2. Next, instruction 12 declares a range ZeroOne, which is used in the declaration of the variables required to formulate the objective and constraints in the next instruction.

```
PoolSize = 35;
VocalLB = 1;
VocalUB = 15;
GrammLB = 16;
GrammUB = 25;
ReadCompLB = 25;
ReadCompUB = 35;
Information =
    [0.55, 0.38, 0.61, 0.44, 0.51, 0.29, 0.66,
     0.48, 0.47, 0.62, 0.33, 0.58, 0.37, 0.19,
     0.56, 0.31, 0.44, 0.47, 0.59, 0.59, 0.38,
     0.46, 0.65, 0.52, 0.18, 0.33, 0.57, 0.56,
     0.64, 0.41, 0.35, 0.45, 0.53, 0.46, 0.29];
Difficulty =
    [0.22, -0.05, -0.08, -0.25, -0.11, -1.34, -0.04,
     0.25, -0.06, -0.08, -0.11, -0.07, -0.21, -1.18,
     -0.12, -0.38, -0.09, -0.06, -0.00, -0.12, -0.22,
     0.23, -0.11, -0.15, -1.93, -1.02, -0.33, -0.24,
     0.07, -0.09, -0.16, -0.33, -0.13, -0.04, -1.24];
WordCount =
    [98, 56, 33, 79, 82, 66, 78,
     89, 57, 64, 88, 51, 77, 64,
     57, 86, 57, 29, 54, 56, 76,
     86, 57, 92, 57, 56, 67, 81,
     71, 69, 62, 58, 89, 77, 63];
```

TABLE A2.2. Data set associated with *OPL* model in Table A2.1.

The objective function and constraints are formulated in instructions 14–25. They follow the model in (A2.1)–(A2.11) line by line and have a format that is easy to comprehend. Instruction 24 collects the indices of the items selected by the program in a set called *Test*, where the last line instructs the program to display *Test* as the output of the problem. If these last two instructions in the model are omitted, the output is just a sequence of zeroes and ones for all item variables.

A run of the model for the data set in Table A2.2 yielded the following output:

Optimal solution with objective value: 4.000.
Test = {2, 11, 13, 15, 16, 21, 30, 31, 32, 34}.

From the data in Table A2.2, it is easy to verify (i) that the sum of $I_i(\theta_c)$ for the items selected is equal to 4.00, (ii) four items in the test are on Vocabulary, two on Grammar, and four on Reading Comprehension,

(iii) the total word count is 706, (iv) items 6 and 25, which had b_i values smaller than -1.00, were not selected, and (v) item 16 is in the test but item 7 is not.

This example did not fully exploit the possibilities of separating the model and data. For example, it would also have been possible to declare formal constants for the bounds in the constraints in (A2.2)–(A2.10), use these in the formulation of the objective and constraints, and specify their data for the current application in the data file as well. Likewise, we could have separated the constraint on enemy sets from the membership of items of these sets. These and other options would allow us to reuse the model for data files representing alternative item pools and/or bounds in the specifications.

Answers to Exercises

Chapter 1

1.1 The distribution would be bimodal with one half of the scores equal to $X = 0$ and the other half equal to $X = n$.

It would be meaningless to use this test to evaluate learning in school; the score distribution would already be known prior to administering the test. If the test were used for selection or admission decisions, half of the test takers would be selected or admitted.

In practice, these ultimate consequences of the classical goal of test assembly are not visible because we have never been able to construct tests with $\rho_{iX} = 1$ for the items.

1.2 Substituting the parameter values into (1.16) results in a probability equal to .50 for a test taker with $\theta = 1.0$.

If c_i increases, the probability of .50 is realized at $\theta < 1.0$, the reason being a nonzero probability of guessing the item correctly.

1.3 The probabilities at $\theta = .8$ and $\theta = 1.2$ are approximately equal to .45 and .55. Because $c_i = 0$, the probabilities are symmetric about .50.

If a_i increases, the two probabilities move away from .50, showing the effect of increased discrimination by the item. For example, for $a_i = 1.8$, they are approximately equal to .41 and .59.

1.4 From probability calculus, it follows that Pr(correct)=Pr(correct|knowing)Pr(knowing)+ Pr(correct|not knowing)Pr(not knowing). The probability of correct given knowing is equal to 1, the probability of knowing is equal to $e^{-a_i(\theta - b_i)}/[1 + e^{-a_i(\theta - b_i)}]$, and the probability of correct given not knowing is equal to c_i. Substituting these probabilities and rewriting the result gives the model in (1.16).

1.5 It generally holds that $a^x = b^{\frac{\ln a}{\ln b}x}$. Thus, if we change the base of the powers in (1.16) from e to 10, the exponent has to be multiplied by a constant $\ln e / \ln 10 = (\ln 10)^{-1}$. The effect is only a change of unit of scale.

1.6 The version of the model with a guessing parameter is

$$p_i(\theta_1, \theta_2) = c_i + (1 - c_i)\frac{e^{a_{1i}\theta_1 + a_{2i}\theta_2 - b_i}}{1 + e^{a_{1i}\theta_1 + a_{2i}\theta_2 - b_i}}.$$

The probability of guessing correctly does not depend on the test taker's abilities; only the probability of knowing does. We therefore need only one (dimensionless) guessing parameter.

Introducing separate difficulty parameters, b_{1i} and b_{2i}, for each dimension would lead to a model with b_i replaced by $b_{1i} + b_{2i}$. But this model would not be identified; that is, although we could estimate the sum of these two parameters, we would not be able to estimate their individual values. Alternatively, in the two-dimensional model, parameter b_i can be viewed as a parameter that already captures the joint effect of the difficulties of the item along the two dimensions.

1.7 If $c_i = 0$, the expression for the IIF in (1.21) reduces to $I_i(\theta) = a_i^2 p_i(\theta)[1 - p_i(\theta)]$. At $\theta = 1.0$, the probability of a correct response is equal to .50 and $I_i(1.0) = .9^2 \times .50 \times .50 \approx .20$.

For the probabilities at $\theta = .8$ and $\theta = 1.2$, see Exercise 1.3. At these two values, $I_i(\theta)$ is only slightly smaller than at $\theta = 1.0$. See Exercise 1.3 for the probabilities for $a_i = 1.8$. At $\theta = 1.0$, $I_i(1.0) = 1.8^2 \times .50 \times .50 \approx .81$, while $I_i(.8)$ and $I_i(1.2)$ are still only slightly smaller.

The differences between the information-function values show their dependence on a_i. They also show that the IIF hardly changes for small deviations from $\theta = b_i$; an item informative at b_i remains so in its neighborhood.

If $c_i = .2$, the values of the IIF have to be calculated using (1.21). For example, if $a_i = .9$, the value at $\theta = b_i = 1.0$ is no longer equal to .20 but to .11. At all θ values, an item with $c_i = .2$ is less informative than an item with $c_i = 0$ due to guessing.

1.8 In Exercise 1.7, we saw that, for $c_i = 0$, the expression in (1.21) reduces to $I_i(\theta) = a_i^2 p_i(\theta)[1 - p_i(\theta)]$. The maximum value of $p_i(\theta)[1 - p_i(\theta)]$ is .25, which is reached at $\theta = b_i$. Thus, the maximum value of $I_i(\theta)$ is .25a_i^2.

1.9 From Exercise 1.8, it follows that a lower bound on the number of items required to get a TIF larger than $\mathcal{T}(\theta)$ is $4\mathcal{T}(\theta)/a_i^2$.
If a_i increases, the item becomes more informative and the bound becomes smaller. If c_i increases, the item becomes less informative and the bound becomes greater.

1.10 The number of different sets of n items from a pool of size I is equal to $\binom{I}{n}$. For $n = 10$, the choice of $I = 48$ gives us 6,540,715,896 different sets. Thus, a pool of 48 items is already large enough to give every living person a different test of 10 items!

1.11 The tests have to satisfy a constraint both on the number of multiple-choice items and the number of constructed response items. Since we have $I/2$ items in the pool of each type, the total number of different tests possible from a pool of I items is equal to the product of $\binom{I/2}{n_{MC}} \times \binom{I/2}{n_{CR}}$.

1.12 In Exercise 1.10, we already saw that a pool of 48 items enables us to assemble approximately 6.5×10^9 different tests of 10 items. The number of tests that satisfy the specifications is equal to 13×10^3. The probability that a random set of ten items from the pool satisfies the specifications is therefore approximately equal to 2×10^{-6}; that is, just 0.0002%.

1.13 The test should have a minimum of ten knowledge and ten application items. Because the subsets of items in the pool with these formats are disjoint, the solution has a minimum of 20 items.
The actual size of the test calculated by the model depends on the target values $T(\theta_k)$ imposed as lower bounds on the TIF and the values of the IIFs at θ_k for the items in the pool. If the average value of a_i is equal to 1.5, the expression derived as a general lower bound in Exercise 1.9 suggests an expected minimum test length equal to $4\mathcal{T}(0)/1.5^2 \approx 1.78\mathcal{T}(0)$ (assuming the conditional distributions of a_i given the two formats do not differ too much).

Chapter 2

2.1 The attributes in Table 2.1 are: (1) test length (categorical/test level), (2) applications (categorical/test level), (3) reliability (quantitative/test level), (4) graphics (categorical/test level), (5) multiple-choice format (categorical/test level), (6) gender orientation and minority orientation (categorical/test level), (7) nervous system (categorical/test level), (8) bias against males and bias against females (categorical/test level), (9) p-value (quantitative/item level), (10) test information (quantitative/test level), (11) set size (categorical/item-set

level), (12) response time (quantitative/test level), (13) enemy relation (logical/item level), (14) nervous system and blood vessels (cat-
egorical/test level), (15) number of words (quantitative/item level),
(16) test length (categorical/test level), and (17) addition, subtraction (categorical/test level).

For a discussion of why such attributes as in specifications 1 and 2
are classified as categorical, see the Discussion at the end of Section
3.2.1.

2.2 Specifications 3, 6, 10, and 16 are objectives; the others imply constraints.

2.3 The specifications in Table 2.1 can be reformulated as:

(1a)–(1b) The test length should be larger than or equal to 20; the
test length should be smaller than or equal to 24.

(2) The number of items on applications should be equal to 24.

(3) Maximize the reliability of the test.

(4) The number of items with graphics should be smaller than or
equal to 10.

(5) The number of multiple-choice items should be smaller than or
equal to half the test length.

(6a)–(6b) Minimize the number of items with gender orientation; minimize the number of items with minority orientation.

(7) The number of items on the nervous system should be smaller
than 5.

(8) The number of items biased against males should be equal to the
number biased against females.

(9a)–(9b) All item p-values should be larger than or equal to .40; all
item p-values should be smaller than or equal to .60.

(10) Minimize the differences between the TIF and its target function.

(11a)–(11b) The number of items in sets with a common passage
should be larger than or equal to 4; the number of items in sets with
a common passage should be smaller than or equal to 6.

(12) The expected time required to take the test should be less than
60 minutes.

(13) Items 17 and 103 should not be in the same test.

(14a)–(14b) The number of items on nervous system and blood vessels should be larger than or equal to 10; the number of items on
nervous system and blood vessels should be smaller than or equal to
15.

(15) The number of words in all items should be smaller than or equal
to 150.

(16) Minimize the length of the test.

(17) The number of items on addition should be equal to the number
on subtraction.

2.4 The trade-offs between objectives 3 and 16 and 10 and 16 are expected
to be strongest. The trade-offs between objectives 3 and 10 and 6 and
19 are expected to be weakest.

2.5 Specification 2 is an equality constraint, and this type of constraint
easily leads to infeasibility (particularly for quantitative attributes).
If the objective is to minimize the length of the test or maximize its
reliability, the constraint should be reformulated as: The number of
items on applications should be larger than or equal to 24.
In either case, we expect the number of items for the solution to be
close to 24.

2.6 If the constraint is reformulated as an objective, we lose the possibility
of formulating another specification as an objective; for example, a
specification that would otherwise imply an equality constraint (see
Exercise 2.5). Of course, we assume that specification 4 reflects the
intentions of the test assembler correctly; especially, the upper bound
of ten should not be a hidden goal value.

2.7 If the test length is constrained to be equal to n, this specification
implies a number of items with a multiple-choice format equal to
$n/2$. To avoid a constraint of this type, it could be replaced by two
inequality constraints with bounds equal to, for instance, $n/2 - 1$ and
$n/2 + 1$. If the test length is not constrained to a fixed number of
items, the specification could be replaced by two constraints on the
difference between the number of items with and without a multiple-
choice format, for instance, constraints with bounds equal to $+1$ and
-1.

2.8 An objective with about the same effects as specification 9 is: Minimize the differences between the p-values of the items and .50. The
same type of reformulation is possible for specifications 1, 11, and 14.

2.9 The following objective function minimizes the total information at
the points θ_k:

$$\text{minimize} \sum_{i=1}^{100} \sum_{k=1}^{K} I_i(\theta_k) x_i.$$

In Section 5.1, we will also introduce an objective function that minimizes the largest deviation of the TIF from the target values at a
series of points θ_k.

2.10 The constraint is $x_{17} + x_{103} \leq 1$.
If the upper bound of 1 is relaxed, the constraint loses its effect; both
items could then be selected in the test.
Alternatively, the constraint could be replaced by the objective

$$\text{minimize } x_{17} + x_{103}.$$

But this choice implies a preference for a test with neither item 17 nor item 103. Also, the actual result may be a test that contains both items, which happens if there is no feasible test with one or none of these items, that is, when $x_{17} + x_{103} \leq 1$ cannot be satisfied.

2.11 A single constraint would be: The number of items with more than 150 words should be equal to zero.
If all of these items are removed from the pool prior to the assembly of the test, these constraints can be dropped (but we would then have to recode all items, redefine the variables, and rewrite the constraints).

2.12 Examples of these objectives are:

(a) Minimize the total number of items with auxiliary material in the set of tests (categorical/multiple-test level).

(b) Minimize the differences between the information functions of the tests in the set (quantitative/multiple-test level).

(c) Maximize the number of reading passages with newspaper clips in the test (categorical/test level).

(d) Minimize the number of printed lines in the test form (quantitative/test level).

(e) Maximize the presence of stimulus 8 in the test (categorical/stimulus level).

(f) Minimize the word count of the first stimulus in the test (quantitative/stimulus level)

(g) Minimize the simultaneous presence of stimuli 17 and 19 (logical/stimulus level).

(h) Maximize the number of items on the nineteenth century in item set 12 (categorical/item-set level).

(i) Maximize the average information at an ability estimate in the item set (for an adaptive test) (quantitative/item-set level).

(j) Minimize item overlap between item sets 12 and 22 (logical/item-set level)

(k) Minimize the presence of item 112 in the test (categorical/item level).

(l) Minimize the simultaneous presence of items 259 and 334 in the test (logical/item level).
Some of these objectives may look artificial at first sight, in particular the objectives at the item and stimulus levels, but do make sense. For example, the objective in 2.12(e) is useful when we would like stimulus 8 to be present in the test but only if it keeps the test-assembly problem feasible.

For the reason why we view the objectives in 2.12(e) and 3.12(k) as categorical, see the discussion on categorical and quantitative attributes in Section 3.2.2.

Observe that quantitative and categorical objectives at the item level have an identical effect on the presence of the item in the test. The same holds at the stimulus level. Consider for example the following quantitative objective at the item level: Maximize the discrimination index of item 112. Because item 112 is either selected or not, the objective would have the same effect as the objective in 2.12(k).

For the interpretation of the objectives in 3.12(g) and 3.12(l), see Exercise 2.10.

Chapter 3

3.1 Examples of a categorical and quantitative constraint at test level are

$$\sum_{s\in V_c^{\text{stim}}} n_s x_s \geq n_c^{\min} \quad \text{for all } c,$$

and

$$\sum_{s=1}^{S} q_s x_s \geq b_q^{\min},$$

where V_c^{stim} is the set of stimuli with attribute c.
Examples of constraints at the stimulus level are

$$x_s = 1, \quad s \in V_1^{\text{stim}},$$

and

$$15 x_s \leq q_s, \quad \text{for all } s,$$

where V_1^{stim} is the set of indices of the stimuli with a combination of attributes required in the test. The second set of constraints requires all stimuli in the test to have an attribute value $q_s \geq 15$; compare this with (3.14).

It is only possible to formulate constraints at the item or item-set level if we have variables at the item level.

3.2 The constraints are

(a)

$$\sum_{i\in V_{MC}\cap V_V} x_i \geq 15,$$

where V_{MC} and V_V are the sets of indices of the items in the pool with a multiple-choice format and those on vocabulary.

(b)
$$\sum_{i\in V_{SA}\cap V_B} \pi_i x_i > 8,$$

where V_{SA} and V_B are the sets of indices of the items with a short-answer format and those on biology.

(c)
$$x_{i_s^*} = 0, \quad \text{for } i_s^* \in V_G \cap \overline{V}_M,$$

with V_G and V_M the sets of indices of the items on geography and with a map.

(d)
$$10x_{i_s^*} \le l_{i_s^*},$$

with i_s^* the index of the pivot item for stimulus s and $l_{i_s^*}$ the total number of lines in this stimulus.

(e)
$$\sum_{i\in V_s} x_i \le k_s x_{i_s^*}, \quad \text{for all } s,$$
$$\sum_{i\in V_s} l_i x_i \ge 35 x_{i_s^*}, \quad \text{for all } s,$$

where i_s^*, V_s, and k_s denote the index of the pivot item, the set of indices of the items, and the number of items in the pool for stimulus s, respectively. (For the reason why we need to add the first set of constraints, see Section 3.2.3 and Exercise 3.6.)

(f)
$$x_{i_{18}^*} + x_{i_{27}^*} \le 1.$$

3.3 The objectives are

(a)
$$\text{minimize } y$$

subject to
$$\sum_{i\in V_A} x_i - \sum_{i\in V_F} x_i \le y,$$
$$\sum_{i\in V_A} x_i - \sum_{i\in V_F} x_i \ge -y,$$

where V_A and V_B are the sets of indices of the items biased against or in favor of second-language test takers.

(b)
$$\text{minimize } \sum_{i\in V_A\cup V_G} x_i,$$

where V_A and V_G are the sets of indices of the items on algebra and geometry.

(c)
$$\text{minimize} \sum_{i \in V_S \cap V_V} x_i,$$

where V_S and V_V are the sets of indices of the items on spelling and vocabulary.

(d)
$$\text{minimize} \sum_{i \in V_{SS} \cap V_{ST}} x_i,$$

where V_{SS} and V_{ST} are the sets of indices of the items on social studies and social tension.

If $V_{ST} \subset V_{SS}$, the objective should be formulated as

$$\text{minimize} \sum_{i \in V_{ST}} x_i.$$

(e)
$$\text{minimize } y$$

subject to

$$\sum_{i=1}^{I} t_i x_i \le 60 + y,$$

$$\sum_{i=1}^{I} t_i x_i \ge 60 - y,$$

where t_i is the expected time on item i.

3.4 Conditional constraints of these types are not treated in this book. They can often be modeled by an appropriate choice of auxiliary 0-1 variables, but this is not necessary for the constraint in 3.4(a) and (b).

(a) The constraint is equivalent to

$$x_8 = 1 \longrightarrow \sum_{i \ne 8} t_i x_i \le 105,$$

which can be represented as

$$\sum_{i \ne 8} t_i x_i - 105 < (\sum_{i=1}^{I} t_i)(1 - x_8),$$

where $\sum_{i \ne 8}$ denotes the sum over all indices except $i = 8$.

(b) Let V_C the set of indices of the items that involve a computation. The constraint is equivalent to

$$\sum_{i \in \overline{V}_C} x_i = 0 \longrightarrow x_{39} = 0,$$

which can be represented as

$$x_{39} \leq \sum_{i \in \overline{V}_C} x_i.$$

If item 39 involves a computation, the constraint is always true and thus is redundant.

(c) The constraint is equivalent to

$$x_{i_{11}^*} + x_{i_{12}^*} = 2 \longrightarrow \sum_{s=1}^{S} x_{i_s^*} \leq 5,$$

which can be represented as

$$x_{i_{11}^*} + x_{i_{12}^*} - 1 \leq \zeta,$$

$$\sum_{s=1}^{S} x_{i_s^*} - 5 \leq S(1 - \zeta),$$

where it is assumed that the total number of stimuli is equal to S.

(d) These constraints are equivalent to

$$\sum_{i=1}^{I} x_{i1} < 30 \cap \sum_{i=1}^{I} x_{i2} < 30 \longrightarrow x_{i_1^*} + x_{i_2^*} \leq 1, \quad \text{for all } i,$$

where x_{i1} and x_{i2}, $i = 1, ..., I$, are 0-1 variables for the assignment of item i to tests 1 and 2, respectively. (For the definition of these variables, see Section 6.2.) These constraints can be represented as

$$30 - \sum_{i=1}^{I} x_{i1} < I\zeta_1,$$

$$30 - \sum_{i=1}^{I} x_{i2} < I\zeta_2,$$

$$x_{i_1^*} + x_{i_2^*} \leq 3 - \zeta_1 - \zeta_2, \quad \text{for all } i.$$

Since the condition in the conditional constraints contains a conjunction, two auxiliary variables, ζ_1 and ζ_2, are necessary.

3.5 Using 0-1 variables x_{it} for the selection of item $i = 1, ..., I$ for test $t = 1, 2$, the difference is minimal for

$$\text{minimize } y$$

subject to

$$n_1^{-1} \sum_{i=1}^{I} b_i x_{i1} - n_2^{-1} \sum_{i=1}^{I} b_i x_{i1} \leq y,$$

$$n_1^{-1} \sum_{i=1}^{I} b_i x_{i1} - n_2^{-1} \sum_{i=1}^{I} b_i x_{i1} \geq -y.$$

3.6 If no variables for the pivot items were added to the constraints on the categorical and quantitative attributes of the sets, we would select all sets with these attributes. The constraints would then be bound to become inconsistent with respect to each other and to (3.38) and (3.39), and the model would have no feasible solution.
If we used (3.39) only, $\sum_{i \in V_s} x_i$ would satisfy $n_s^{\min}$ for $i_s^* = 1$, but this expression could take any value larger than 0 for $i_s^* = 0$. This is impossible if (3.38) is present, which would then enforce $\sum_{i \in V_s} x_i = 0$. The same holds for (3.41) and (3.42) as well as (3.43) and (3.44).
If the test specifications do not involve an upper bound, a useful solution is to add a constraint to the model with an arbitrary upper bound that can never become active. For example, if only the lower bound in (3.39) is required, we could add the constraint

$$\sum_{i \in V_s} x_i \leq k_s x_{i_s^*},$$

where k_s is the size of the set for stimulus s in the pool.

3.7 The first objective implies

$$\text{maximize } \sum_{i=1}^{I} r_i x_i.$$

The second objective specifies a goal value for the average π value, which can be approximated using a model as in (3.70)–(3.73).

(a) For the weighted-objectives method, we get

$$\text{maximize } w_1 \sum_{i=1}^{I} r_i x_i - w_2 y$$

subject to

$$\sum_{i=1}^{I} \pi_i x_i \leq .5n + y,$$

$$\sum_{i=1}^{I} \pi_i x_i \geq .5n - y,$$

where both w_1 and w_2 are assumed to be positive.

(b) Goal programming is only possible if we introduce an arbitrary upper bound to the readability of any test from the pool, $r^{\max}$. The two objectives can then be combined as

$$\text{minimize } w_1 y_2 + w_2 y_2$$

subject to

$$\sum_{i=1}^{I} r_i x_i = r^{\max} - y_1,$$

$$\sum_{i=1}^{I} \pi_i x_i \leq .5n + y_2,$$

$$\sum_{i=1}^{I} \pi_i x_i \geq .5n - y_2,$$

$$y \geq 0$$

Because the two objectives are on different scales, we have to weigh the variables in the objective function.

(c) A minimax approach is used in the following model:

$$\text{minimize } y$$

subject to

$$r^{\max} - \sum_{i=1}^{I} r_i x_i \leq w_1 y,$$

$$\sum_{i=1}^{I} \pi_i x_i - .5n \leq w_2 y,$$

$$\sum_{i=1}^{I} \pi_i x_i - .5n \geq -w_2 y,$$

$$y \geq 0,$$

where we have added weights to the constraints to account for the difference in scale between the two objectives.

(d) In the sequential method, if maximum readability is the objective with the highest priority, we should first solve the problem with the objective function

$$\text{maximize } \sum_{i=1}^{I} r_i x_i.$$

The final solution is then obtained by solving

$$\text{maximize } y$$

subject to

$$\sum_{i=1}^{I} \pi_i x_i \leq .5n + y,$$

$$\sum_{i=1}^{I} \pi_i x_i \geq .5n - y,$$

$$\sum_{i=1}^{I} r_i x_i \geq b_r^* - \delta,$$

$$y \geq 0,$$

where b_r^* is the value of the objective function in the solution of the first problem and δ is a small tolerance.

The sequential method is easiest to implement (provided one of the objectives has first priority) because the task of choosing appropriate weights in the three other methods is difficult. For the application of goal programming, we also need to produce a satisfactory guess of the upper bound $r^{\max}$.

3.8

$$\text{Minimize } \sum_{i=1}^{75} x_i$$

subject to

$$\sum_{i=1}^{75} I_i(-1)x_i \leq 8,$$

$$\sum_{i=1}^{75} I_i(1)x_i \leq 8,$$

$$\sum_{i=1}^{75} I_i(-1)x_i \geq 7,$$

$$\sum_{i=1}^{75} I_i(1)x_i \geq 7,$$

$$\sum_{i=1}^{25} x_i \leq \sum_{i=26}^{75} x_i,$$

$$\sum_{i=61}^{65} x_i = 5x_{61},$$

$$x_i \in \{0,1\}, \quad \text{for } i = 1, ..., 65.$$

Chapter 5

5.1

$$\text{Maximize } \sum_{k=1}^{K} w_k \sum_{i=1}^{I} I_i(\theta_k)x_i$$

subject to

$$\sum_{i=1}^{I} I_i(\theta_k)x_i \leq \mathcal{T}_k, \quad \text{for all } k.$$

5.2 At some of the values θ_1, θ_2, and θ_3, the TIF exceeds its target by an amount of .8. At the other θ value(s), the difference is smaller than .8.

If the items have an average discrimination equal to 1.3, the maximum information in an average item is $(1.3)^2 \times .25 \approx .42$ (see Exercise 1.8). Thus, a difference of .8 is approximately the equivalent of half an item located at the θ value where it occurs, which seems a reasonable result.

5.3 The values are $\mathcal{T}(\theta_1) = 10 + .4 = 10.4$, $\mathcal{T}(\theta_2) = 15 - .5 = 14.5$, and $\mathcal{T}(\theta_3) = 10 + .7 = 10.1$.

5.4 The sign of the deviation can only be ascertained by calculating $\sum_{i=1}^{I} I_i(\theta_k)x_i$ at each θ_k for the values of the decision variables in the solution and comparing the result with $\mathcal{T}_k$.

5.5 One possible approach is

$$\text{maximize } y$$

subject to

$$\sum_{i=1}^{I} I_i(\theta_k)x_i \leq R_k y + \delta, \quad \text{for all } k,$$

$$\sum_{i=1}^{I} I_i(\theta_k)x_i \geq R_k y - \delta, \quad \text{for all } k,$$

$$y \geq 0,$$

where the size of the tolerance parameter δ should be chosen to avoid both a loose result and infeasibility. The tolerances in this approach have an absolute size. By replacing the right-hand sides of the constraints by $(R_k + \delta)y$ and $(R_k - \delta)y$, respectively, their size becomes relative to the actual height of the TIF.

5.6 Minimization of the difference between test reliability and a target value becomes possible if we define δ and ε in (5.43)–(5.46) as decision variables and add the objective function

$$\text{minimize } w_1\delta + w_2\varepsilon$$

to the model. Our motivation for (5.34)–(5.37) in Section 5.2.1 suggests a relatively larger value for w_1 than for w_2.

5.7 The result is explained by the uniformity of the weights w_k. The items are selected to compromise between the sums of first-order, second-order, and third-order powers. Because equal weight is given to the less important target values for the sums of the third-order powers, the compromise turns out to be less favorable to the sums of first-order and second-order powers.

5.8 The lower bound in (5.64) cannot be positive. As a consequence, the constraint produces outcomes for $x_{ij} = 1$ and $x_{ij} = 0$ that are both admissible. The constraint in (3.14) had a positive lower bound; as a consequence, it was false for $x_i = 0$.

5.9 This generalization requires 0-1 decision variables x_{ijk} for the assignment of items i, j, and k to the same triple. The model is

$$\text{minimize } \sum_{i=1}^{n}\sum_{j=1}^{n}\sum_{k=1}^{n} \delta_{ijk}x_{ijk}$$

subject to

$$\sum_{j,k|j\neq i,k\neq i} x_{ijk} = 1, \quad \text{for all } i,$$

$$x_{ijk} = x_{ikj}, \quad \text{for all } i, j, \text{ and } k,$$

$$x_{ijk} = x_{kij}, \quad \text{for all } i, j, \text{ and } k,$$

$$x_{ijk} = x_{kji}, \quad \text{for all } i, j, \text{ and } k,$$

$$x_{ijk} = x_{jki}, \quad \text{for all } i, j, \text{ and } k,$$

$$x_{ijk} = x_{jik}, \quad \text{for all } i, j, \text{ and } k,$$

$$\sum_{i,j,k|i=j=k} x_{ijk} = 0,$$

$$x_{ijk} \in \{0,1\}, \quad \text{for all } i, j, \text{ and } k.$$

Observe that δ_{ijk} is now a measure for the "distance" between $i, j,$ and k; for example, $\delta_{ijk} = \delta_{ij} + \delta_{ik} + \delta_{jk}$. The model can be written more parsimoniously, as in (5.79)–(5.81). (Try to formulate this version.)

5.10 For a fixed value of j the sum in (5.80) runs from the top of column j in the matrix down to its diagonal, and then over the elements in the row $i = j$ to the right of the diagonal. The sum thus contains all possible pairs with item j. Because the diagonal of the matrix is ignored, (5.70) is not needed.

5.11 The model is identical to (5.58)–(5.61) with the objective function replaced by

$$\text{minimize} \sum_{j=1}^{5} \sum_{i=1}^{I} |b_i - b_j| x_{ij}.$$

Alternatively, we could use (5.62)–(5.64) or (5.65) and (5.66) with $|b_i - b_j|$ substituted for δ_{ij}. The model does not need a constraint on the length of the test because (5.59) guarantees the same number of items as the reference test.

Chapter 6

Note: Several of the exercises in this and the following chapters ask for alternative model formulations. We give only one example for each exercise but, for some of them, other formulations are equally good.

6.1

$$\text{Maximize} \sum_{t=1}^{2} (.30x_{1t} + .85x_{2t} + .89x_{3t} + .48x_{4t})$$

subject to

$$\sum_{i \in V_1} x_{it} = 2, \quad \text{for } t = 1, 2,$$

$$\sum_{i \in V_2} x_{it} = 1, \quad \text{for } t = 1, 2,$$

$$x_{it} \in \{0,1\}, \quad \text{for } i = 1, ..., 4 \text{ and } t = 1, 2.$$

The objective function contains the total contribution by the two tests. It is assumed that the two tests are not required to be parallel with respect to their contributions to the target. (The assumption is not important, however. Since the data in Table 6.1 admit only one feasible solution, any objective would give the same result!)

6.2 Choosing 0-1 variables x_{ijt} for the decision on the selection of item i for test t to match item j in the reference test, the model becomes

$$\text{minimize} \sum_{t=1}^{T}\sum_{i=1}^{I}\sum_{j=1}^{n} \delta_{ij}x_{ijt}$$

subject to

$$\sum_{i=1}^{I} x_{ijt} = 1, \quad \text{for all } j \text{ and } t,$$

$$\sum_{j=1}^{n} x_{ijt} \leq 1, \quad \text{for all } i \text{ and } t,$$

$$x_{ijt} \in \{0,1\}, \quad \text{for all } i, j, \text{ and } t.$$

Observe that the coefficients in the objective function do not depend on t.

6.3

$$\text{Minimize } y$$

subject to

$$\sum_{i=1}^{I} I_i(\theta_k)(x_{i1} - x_{i2}) \leq y, \quad \text{for all } k,$$

$$\sum_{i=1}^{I} I_i(\theta_k)(x_{i1} - x_{i2}) \geq -y, \quad \text{for all } k,$$

$$\sum_{i=1}^{I} x_{i1} = n_1,$$

$$\sum_{i=1}^{I} x_{i2} = n_2,$$

$$x_{it} \in \{0,1\}, \quad \text{for all } i \text{ and } t.$$

6.4

$$\text{Maximize } y$$

subject to

$$\sum_{i=1}^{I} I_i(\theta_k)x_{it} \geq y, \quad \text{for } t = 1,2,3,$$

$$\sum_{i \in V_{MC} \cap V_P} x_{it} \leq 10, \quad \text{for } t = 1,2,3,$$

$$\sum_{i \in V_{CR} \cap V_{IP}} x_{it} \leq 10, \quad \text{for } t = 1,2,3,$$

$$\sum_{i \in V_{LF}} x_{it} \leq 10, \quad \text{for } t = 1,2,3,$$

$$f_i x_{it} \le 3, \quad \text{for all } i \text{ and } t = 1, 2, 3,$$

where the subscripts of the sets V represent the appropriate categorical attributes, and f_i is a counter for the number of times item i has already been administered.

We used upper bounds in the content constraints because the objective is maximization of test information.

6.5 See (6.19)–(6.23). The number of extra variables is equal to 2,100, namely 700 for every pair of tests. The number of extra constraints is 2,103, namely 700 for (6.22)–(6.23) and one for (6.20) for each pair of tests. The constraint in (6.21) can be dropped because we only have an upper bound on the size of the overlap.

6.6

$$\text{Maximize } y$$

subject to possible constraints at the following levels:

Multiple-Test Level

$$x_{i1} + x_{i2} + z_i \le 1, \quad \text{for all } i;$$

Test Level

$$\sum_{i=1}^{I} I_i(\theta_k) x_{it} \ge R_{kt} y, \quad \text{for all } k \text{ and } t = 1, 2,$$

$$\sum_{i=1}^{I} I_i(\theta_k) z_i \ge \sum_{t=3}^{T} R_{kt} y, \quad \text{for all } k,$$

$$\sum_{i=1}^{I} x_{it} \gtreqless n_t, \quad \text{for } t = 1, 2,$$

$$\sum_{i=1}^{I} z_i = \sum_{t=3}^{T} n_t, \quad \text{for } t = 1, 2,$$

$$\sum_{i \in V_c} x_{it} \gtreqless n_{ct}, \quad \text{for all } c \text{ and } t = 1, 2,$$

$$\sum_{i \in V_c} z_i \gtreqless \sum_{t=3}^{T} n_{ct}, \quad \text{for all } c,$$

$$\sum_{i=1}^{I} q_i x_{it} \gtreqless b_{qt}, \quad \text{for } t = 1, 2,$$

$$\sum_{i=1}^{I} q_i z_i \gtreqless \sum_{t=3}^{T} b_{qt};$$

Definition of Variables

$$x_{it} \in \{0, 1\}, \quad \text{for all } i \text{ and } t = 1, 2,$$

$$z_i \in \{0, 1\}, \quad \text{for } i.$$

6.7 See Section 4.3 or A1.4 for network-flow programming. One possible approach (Armstrong, Jones, & Wu, 1992) is to define a reference test with items $j = 1, ..., n$ with a TIF equal to the target that has to be met. These items can be used as demand nodes, while items $i = 1, ..., I$ in the pool are the supply nodes. In addition, we define δ_{ij} as the "distance" between the information function of item i and reference item j (for example, the sum of distances at the points θ_k, or the largest distance at these points). Suppose each test is required to have n_c items with categorical attribute c, where the number of items with these attributes available in the pool is equal to N_c. The decision variable for the assignment of item i to reference item j is x_{ij}. In addition to the demand nodes $j = 1, ..., n$, we define a dummy node to which all unused items are assigned. The variable for the decision on the assignment of item i to the dummy node is denoted as z_i.

The model is

$$\text{minimize} \sum_{i=1}^{I} \sum_{j=1}^{n} \delta_{ij} x_{ij}$$

subject to

$$\sum_{j=1}^{n} x_{ij} = 1, \quad \text{for all } i,$$

$$\sum_{i=1}^{I} x_{ij} = T, \quad \text{for all } j,$$

$$\sum_{i \in V_c} z_i = N_c - n_c T, \quad \text{for all } c,$$

$$x_{ij} \in \{0, 1\}, \quad \text{for all } i \text{ and } j,$$

$$z_i \in \{0, 1\}, \quad \text{for all } i.$$

The model assigns T items to each demand node. The categorical constraints guarantee that $n_c T$ of the total number of items assigned to the demand nodes are for attribute c.

The second stage of this approach consists of the assignment of all items to T individual tests (e.g., using the simultaneous model in (6.3)–(6.13) or a heuristic).

It is impossible to add a quantitative constraint to the problem without destroying the network-flow nature of the model. But an approximation is to categorize q, define sets V_{cq} for all possible combinations of c and categories of q, and redefine all constraints using bounds on the number n_{cq} for the combination of categories c and q. The constraints to be added to the model are

$$\sum_{i \in V_{cq}} z_i = N_{cq} - n_{cq} T, \quad \text{for all } c \text{ and categories of } q.$$

An alternative approach is Lagrangian relaxation (Section 4.3). Constraints on enemy items cannot be added to the model for the same reason. They should be imposed during the second stage, when the items at the demand nodes are assigned to the T tests.

6.8 Continuing the notation in Section 6.5, and adding variables x_{jklb} for the decision on the selection of triple (j, k, l) to booklet b, the constraints are

$$\sum_{j=1}^{N} x_{jb} \leq 4, \quad \text{for all } b,$$

$$\sum_{j=1}^{N} x_{jb} \geq 3, \quad \text{for all } b,$$

$$\sum_{b=1}^{B} x_{jb} \geq 5, \quad \text{for all } j,$$

$$\sum_{b=1}^{B} z_{jklb} \geq 1, \quad \text{for all } j < k < l,$$

$$3z_{jklb} \leq x_{jb} + x_{kb} + x_{lb}, \quad \text{for all } b \text{ and } j < k < l,$$

$$z_{jklb} \geq x_{jb} + x_{kb} + x_{lb} - 2, \quad \text{for all } b \text{ and } j < k < l,$$

$$x_{jb} \in \{0, 1\}, \quad \text{for all } b \text{ and } j,$$

$$z_{jklb} \in \{0, 1\}, \quad \text{for all } j < k < l.$$

6.9 The test for the first stage was selected using

$$\text{minimize } y$$

subject to

$$\sum_{i=1}^{I} I_i(-1.2)x_i \geq y,$$

$$\sum_{i=1}^{I} I_i(0)x_i \geq y,$$

$$\sum_{i=1}^{I} I_i(1.2)x_i \geq y.$$

The three tests for the second and third stages were selected with the same objective function but the following constraints:

$$\sum_{i=1}^{I} I_i(-1.2)x_{i1} \geq y,$$

$$\sum_{i=1}^{I} I_i(-1.2)x_{i2} \geq y,$$

$$\sum_{i=1}^{I} I_i(-1.2)x_{i3} \geq y.$$

Chapter 7

7.1 The constraints can be reformulated as

(a)

$$z_s = 0, \quad \text{for all } s \in V_G \cap \overline{V}_M.$$

(b)

$$10z_s \leq l_s.$$

(c)

$$\sum_{i=1}^{I_s} x_{i_s} \leq k_s z_s, \quad \text{for all } s.$$

$$\sum_{i=1}^{I_s} l_{i_s} x_{i_s} \geq 35 z_s, \quad \text{for all } s.$$

(d)

$$z_{18} + z_{27} \leq 1.$$

(e) The constraint in Exercise 3.4(c) is equivalent to

$$z_{11} + z_{12} = 2 \rightarrow \sum_{s=1}^{S} z_s \leq 5,$$

with S the number of stimuli in the pool. Using an auxiliary 0-1 variable ζ, it can be represented as

$$z_{11} + z_{12} - 1 \leq \zeta,$$

$$\sum_{s=1}^{S} z_s - n \leq S(1 - \zeta).$$

7.2 The constraints can be formulated as:

(a)

$$\sum_{i_s \in V_{DD}} x_{i_s} \leq 2z_s, \quad \text{for all } s,$$

with V_{DD} the set of indices of the items in the pool with a data display.

(b)
$$z_s = 1, \quad \text{for all } s \in V_{NC},$$

with V_{NC} the set of indices of the stimuli in the pool with a newspaper clip.

(c)
$$\sum_{i_s=1}^{I_s} b_i x_i \le b^{\max} z_s, \quad \text{for all } s,$$

$$\sum_{i_s=1}^{I_s} b_i x_i \ge 1.5 z_s, \quad \text{for all } s,$$

where $b^{\max}$ is the maximum value of the item-difficulty parameter in the pool. (See Exercise 3.6.) It is assumed that the size of the sets is fixed in other item-set level constraints.

(d)
$$\sum_{s=5}^{9} \sum_{i_s \in V_O} x_i \le 2,$$

with V_O the set of indices of the items in the pool on optics. (This constraint implies the selection of some of the stimuli 5–9.)

(e)
$$z_7 = z_8.$$

(f)
$$z_{22} + x_{8_{27}} \le 1.$$

7.3 The objectives can be reformulated as:

(a)
$$\text{Minimize } y$$

subject to
$$\sum_{s=1}^{S} w_s z_s \le 750 + y,$$

$$\sum_{s=1}^{S} w_s z_s \ge 750 - y,$$

with S the number of stimuli in the pool and w_s the number of words in stimulus s.

(b)
$$\text{Minimize } y$$

$$\sum_{i_s=1}^{I_s} r_{i_s} x_{i_s} \le r_s + y, \quad \text{for all } s,$$

$$\sum_{i_s=1}^{I_s} r_{i_s} x_{i_s} \geq r_s - y, \quad \text{for all } s,$$

with r_{i_s} and r_s the readability of item i_s and stimulus s.

(c)

$$\text{Minimize } \sum_{s=1}^{S} f_s z_s,$$

with S the number of stimuli in the pool and f_s a counter for the number of times stimulus s has already been exposed.

(d)

$$\text{Maximize } \sum_{s \in V_5} z_s,$$

with V_5 the set of indices of the stimuli with an upper bound equal to five on the size of their item set.

(e)

$$\text{Minimize } y$$

subject to

$$\sum_{s=1}^{S-1} \sum_{i_s=1}^{I_s} x_{i_s} - \sum_{i_S=1}^{I_S} x_{i_S} \leq y,$$

$$\sum_{s=1}^{S-1} \sum_{i_s=1}^{I_s} x_{i_s} - \sum_{i_S=1}^{I_S} x_{i_S} \geq -y,$$

with $S - 1$ the number of stimuli in the pool and S a dummy stimulus for the set of discrete items.

7.4 The constraints can be formulated as follows:

(a) Let V_8 and V_{14} be the sets of indices of the items for stimuli 8 and 14, respectively, and k_8 the number of items in V_8. The constraint is equivalent to

$$z_8 + z_{14} = 2 \rightarrow \sum_{i_8 \in V_8 \cap V_{18}} x_i \leq 3,$$

which can be represented as

$$z_8 + z_{14} - 1 \leq \zeta,$$

$$\sum_{i \in V_8 \cap V_{18}} x_{i_8} - 3 \leq k_8(1 - \zeta).$$

(b) Let V_{MC} and V_{CR} be the sets of indices of the items with a multiple-choice and a constructed response format and k_s is the number of items in the pool available for stimulus s. The constraint is equivalent to

$$\sum_{i_s \in V_{CR}} x_{i_s} - \sum_{i_s \in V_{MC}} x_{i_s} > 0 \to z_s = 1,$$

with the additional requirement that at least ten item sets satisfy the condition in this implication. This case can be represented as

$$\sum_{s=1}^{S-1} \zeta_s \geq 10.$$

$$\sum_{i_s \in V_{CR}} x_{i_s} - \sum_{i_s \in V_{MC}} x_{i_s} > -k_s(1 - \zeta_s)$$

$$\sum_{i_s \in V_{CR}} x_{i_s} - \sum_{i_s \in V_{MC}} x_{i_s} < k_s z_s, \quad \text{for all } s,$$

(c) Let V_{Ma} and V_{Mi} be the sets of indices of the items with a majority and minority orientation and k_s the number of items available in the pool for stimulus s. The specification is equivalent to

$$\sum_{i_s \in V_{Ma} \cup V_{Mi}} x_{i_s} > 1 \to \sum_{i_s \in V_{Ma}} x_{i_s} - \sum_{i_s \in V_{Mi}} x_{i_s} = 0,$$

which can be represented as

$$\sum_{i_s \in V_{Ma} \cup V_{Mi}} x_{i_s} - 1 < k_s \zeta,$$

$$\sum_{i_s \in V_{Ma}} z_{i_s} - \sum_{i_s \in V_{Mi}} z_{i_s} \leq k_s(1 - \zeta_s), \quad \text{for all } s,$$

$$\sum_{i_s \in V_{Ma}} z_{i_s} - \sum_{i_s \in V_{Mi}} z_{i_s} \geq -k_s(1 - \zeta_s), \quad \text{for all } s.$$

Observe, however, that the problem has a hidden implication: If $\sum_{i_s \in V_{Ma} \cup V_{Mi}} x_{i_s} = 0$, it also holds that $\sum_{i_s \in V_{Ma}} x_{i_s} = 0$ and $\sum_{i_s \in V_{Ma}} x_{i_s} = 0$. It is therefore possible to use a much simpler unconditional representation

$$\sum_{i_s \in V_{Ma}} z_{i_s} - \sum_{i_s \in V_{Mi}} z_{i_s} = 0.$$

7.5 In stage 1, we average the quantitative item attributes because the actual size of the sets in the test is unknown. In stage 2, we constrain the size of the set and therefore are able to formulate regular quantitative constraints at the set level.

Chapter 8

8.1 Suppose θ_1 is the intentional ability and θ_2 is a nuisance ability. If we constrain the expression in (8.10) by an upper bound, we restrict the set of feasible solutions and may be forced to select a test from the pool that is less than optimal for the measurement of θ_1 (Sections 2.4.2. and 4.2). For the case of an objective function with respect to the nuisance ability, see the analysis of trade-off between (8.10) and (8.11) in the discussion of (8.9)-(8.11).

8.2 The best approach is to set $w_{1kl} = 1$ for all points (k, l) for the first variance function. For the second function, we can set $w_{2kl} = 1$ for $k = l$ and $w_{2kl} = 0$ for $k \neq l$. Setting a weight equal to zero effectively removes its constraint from the model.

8.3 Draw a graph to prove that if

$$\xi_1 = \lambda\theta_1 + (1 - \lambda)\theta_2$$

represents the first dimension, the dimension orthogonal to it is represented by

$$\xi_2 = -(1 - \lambda)\theta_1 + \lambda\theta_2.$$

The transformation we seek is a mapping from the old discrimination parameters a_1 and a_2 to new parameters a_1^* and a_2^*. Since the probabilities in (1.17) are invariant under the transformation, they have to satisfy

$$\begin{aligned} a_1\theta_1 + a_2\theta_2 &= a_1^* [\lambda\theta_1 + (1 - \lambda)\theta_2] \\ &\quad + a_2^* [-(1 - \lambda)\theta_1 + \lambda\theta_2]. \end{aligned}$$

Solving for a_1^* and a_2^* gives

$$a_1^* = \frac{\lambda}{\lambda^2 + (1 - \lambda)^2} a_1 + \frac{(1 - \lambda)}{\lambda^2 + (1 - \lambda)^2} a_2,$$

$$a_2^* = -\frac{1 - \lambda}{\lambda^2 + (1 - \lambda)^2} a_1 + \frac{\lambda}{\lambda^2 + (1 - \lambda)^2} a_2.$$

Since the orientation of the ability space depends only on the portion of the parameter structure that contains θ_1 and θ_2, the reparameterization does not involve any change of b_i.

For $\lambda = .5$, it holds that $\xi_1 = .5\theta_1 + .5\theta_2$ and $\xi_2 = -.5\theta_1 + .5\theta_2$, where the parameter transformation simplifies to

$$a_1^* = a_1 + a_2,$$

$$a_2^* = -a_1 + a_2.$$

Chapter 9

9.1 Because we now have a minimum level of accuracy for the ability estimates instead of a fixed test length, we make the following assumptions:

(a) Each test taker should be guaranteed a test with information minimally equal to $\mathcal{T}$ at his or her true ability level.

(b) A minimum test length $n^{\min}$ is derived from the distribution of the item-parameter values in the pool (e.g., the minimum length necessary to satisfy $\mathcal{T}$ if the test starts at the test taker's true ability θ for any possible value of θ).

(c) The categorical test-level constraints in (9.13) can be expressed using the proportions of items in the test with attribute c, p_c.

(d) The same holds for the item-level constraints on desired combinations of categorical attributes in (9.16).

(e) All bounds b_q in the quantitative test-level constraints in (9.14) are specified for the minimum test length, $n^{\min}$.

(f) Tolerances δ, ε, and γ are specified to guarantee feasibility of the models for the selection of the items $g = 1, \dots$.
   The model can then be formulated as

$$\text{minimize } \sum_{i=1}^{I} I_i(\widehat{\theta}^{(g-1)}) x_i \quad \text{(objective)}$$

subject to possible constraints at the following levels:

Test Level

$$\sum_{i=1}^{I} I_i(\widehat{\theta}^{(g-1)}) x_i \geq \mathcal{T}, \quad \text{(test information)}$$

$$\sum_{i=1}^{I} x_i \geq n^{\min}, \quad \text{(minimal test length)}$$

$$\sum_{i \in V_c} x_i \leq p_c \sum_{i=1}^{I} x_i + \delta, \quad \text{for all } c, \quad \text{(categorical attributes)}$$

$$\sum_{i \in V_c} x_i \geq p_c \sum_{i=1}^{I} x_i - \delta, \quad \text{for all } c, \quad \text{(categorical attributes)}$$

$$\sum_{i=1}^{I} q_i x_i \leq \left(b_q / n^{\min} + \varepsilon\right) \sum_{i=1}^{I} x_i, \quad \text{(quantitative attributes)}$$

$$\sum_{i=1}^{I} q_i x_i \geq \left(b_q / n^{\min} - \varepsilon\right) \sum_{i=1}^{I} x_i; \quad \text{(quantitative attributes)}$$

Subtest Level

$$\sum_{i \in R_g} x_i = g - 1; \quad \text{(previous items)}$$

Item Level

$$\sum_{i \in V_1} x_i \leq p_1 \sum_{i=1}^{I} x_i + \gamma, \quad \text{(categorical attributes)}$$

$$\sum_{i \in V_1} x_i \geq p_1 \sum_{i=1}^{I} x_i - \gamma, \quad \text{(categorical attributes)}$$

$$\sum_{i \in V_0} x_i = 0, \quad \text{(categorical attributes)}$$

$$q_i x_i \leq b_q^{\max}, \quad \text{for all } i, \quad \text{(quantitative attributes)}$$

$$b_q^{\min} x_i \leq q_i, \quad \text{for all } i, \quad \text{(quantitative attributes)}$$

$$\sum_{i \in V_e} x_i \leq 1, \quad \text{for all } e; \quad \text{(enemies)}$$

Definition of Variables

$$x_i \in \{0,1\}, \quad \text{for all } i. \quad \text{(range of variables)}$$

9.2 The alternative criterion is sensitive to changes in the composition of the shadow test after the first item for a new stimulus has been selected, whereas the criterion proposed in Section 9.3 is sensitive to outliers (i.e., single items in sets with extremely large information at $\hat{\theta}^{(g-1)}$). It is therefore not possible to formulate a general preference for one of these criteria.

9.3 Let $j = 1, ..., J$ be an arbitrary population of test takers and η_{ij} an indicator variable equal to one if item $i = 1, ..., I$ has been exposed to test taker j and zero otherwise. The sum of the exposure rates is equal to

$$\sum_{i=1}^{I} \left(\sum_{j=1}^{J} \eta_{ij}/J \right) = \sum_{j=1}^{J} \left(\sum_{i=1}^{I} \eta_{ij} \right) /J = n,$$

where the last transition holds because each test taker j is exposed to n items; that is, $\sum_{i=1}^{I} \eta_{ij} = n$ for all j.
Since the sum of the exposure rates is fixed, lowering the rate of one item results in an increase of the sum of the rates for all other items by the same amount.
The average exposure rate for a 15-item test from a pool of 350 items is equal to $15/350=.04$. A minimum bound of .05 for the rates of all items is therefore impossible.

9.4 If $P^t(S_i \mid \theta) > r^{\max}$, it holds that

$$
\begin{aligned}
P^{(t+1)}(A_i \mid \theta) &= P^{(t+1)}(A_i \mid S_i, \theta) P^t(S_i \mid \theta) \\
&= \left(r^{\max}/P^t(S_i \mid \theta)\right) r^{\max} \\
&= r^{\max}.
\end{aligned}
$$

Thus, the adjustment has been chosen to yield a predicted exposure rate at $t+1$ equal to $r^{\max}$. (However, the prediction is based on the assumption that $P^t(S_i \mid \theta)$ remains constant, which is not true because the new selection rate of an item depends on the joint effect of the preceding adjustments for all items.)
The adjustment for $P^t(S_i \mid \theta) \le r^{\max}$ does not make much sense if the control parameter is already lower than 1. It therefore seems safer to set $P^{(t+1)}(A_i \mid S_i, \theta) = P^{(t)}(A_i \mid S_i, \theta)$ in this case or to base the adjustment rule on the criterion of $P^t(A_i \mid \theta) \le r^{\max}$ instead of $P^t(S_i \mid \theta) \le r^{\max}$.

9.5 From (9.45), it follows that

$$
\begin{aligned}
P(E_i \cup \overline{F} \mid \theta) &\le \frac{r^{\max}}{P(A_i \mid E_i \cup \overline{F} \mid \theta)} \\
&= \frac{r^{\max} P(E_i \cup \overline{F} \mid \theta)}{P(A_i \cap (E_i \cup \overline{F}) \mid \theta)} \\
&= \frac{r^{\max} P(E_i \cup \overline{F} \mid \theta)}{P(A_i \mid \theta)}.
\end{aligned}
$$

But

$$
\begin{aligned}
P(E_i \cup \overline{F} \mid \theta) &= 1 - P(\overline{E}_i \cap F \mid \theta) \\
&= 1 - P(\overline{E}_i \mid \theta) P(F \mid \theta) \\
&= 1 - (1 - P(E_i \mid \theta)) P(F \mid \theta) \\
&= 1 - P(F \mid \theta) + P(F \mid \theta) P(E_i \mid \theta),
\end{aligned}
$$

where the independence assumption makes the second transition possible. Substituting the last result in the preceding expression and simplifying gives (9.46).
The independence assumption is reasonable for a professionally designed item pool. Typically, such pools are 8–10 times as large as the test and have multiple items with each of the combinations of attributes required for the shadow test. If so, the probability of a feasible solution does not depend on the ineligibility of a small subset of items in the pool. In fact, if $P(F \mid \theta) = 1$, which invariably has been the case in our simulation studies, it follows that $P(E_i \cap F \mid \theta) = P(E_i \mid \theta)$, and independence holds trivially.

9.6 If $P^{(e)}(F \mid \theta) = 1$, it also holds that $P^{(e)}(E_i \cup F \mid \theta) = P^{(e)}(E_i \mid \theta)$. Therefore, from (9.46),

$$P^{(e+1)}(E_i \mid \theta) < P^{(e)}(E_i \mid \theta) \text{ if } P^{(e)}(A_i \mid \theta) > r^{\max},$$

$$P^{(e+1)}(E_i \mid \theta) = P^{(e)}(E_i \mid \theta) \text{ if } P^{(e)}(A_i \mid \theta) = r^{\max},$$

$$P^{(e+1)}(E_i \mid \theta) > P^{(e)}(E_i \mid \theta) \text{ if } P^{(e)}(A_i \mid \theta) < r^{\max},$$

which shows the adaptation for test taker $e + 1$ based on the result for test taker e.

9.7 Because of (9.49), it holds for an average test taker in the population that $\tau = 0$. As a result, β_i is the expected logtime for a test taker on item i, and $\sum_{i=1}^{T} \exp(\beta_i)x_i$ is the expected total time on the test. If t_{tot} has been set well for the population of test takers, they can thus be expected to finish in time.

9.8 For n random variables with a common standard deviation σ, the standard deviation of their sum can be approximated as $\sigma/\sqrt{n}$. A useful estimate of the standard deviation of the total time on a test from this pool is therefore 5 seconds.

9.9 The choice of the 50th percentile implies a constraint on the total time for an average test taker (see Exercise 9.7). This choice makes sense for a longer test (see Exercise 9.8). However, if we approach the end of the test, the variance of the total time on the remaining items becomes more sensitive to the variances of the individual items, and the move to the 95th percentile guarantees better protection of the test taker against running out of time.

9.10 The determinant of the covariance matrix was given in (8.4) as

$$|I(\theta_1, \theta_2)| = \left(\sum_{i=1}^{n} a_{1i}^2 p_i q_i \right) \left(\sum_{i=1}^{n} a_{2i}^2 p_i q_i \right) - \left(\sum_{i=1}^{n} a_{1i} a_{2i} p_i q_i \right)^2.$$

The item with the best projection for the determinant is item i with the minimal value for

$$\left(\sum_{j \in \overline{R}_g \cup \{i\}} a_{1j}^2 p_j^{(g-1)} q_j^{(g-1)} \right) \left(\sum_{j \in \overline{R}_g \cup \{i\}} a_{2j}^2 p_j^{(g-1)} q_j^{(g-1)} \right)$$
$$- \left(\sum_{j \in \overline{R}_g \cup \{i\}} a_{1j} a_{2j} p_j^{(g-1)} q_j^{(g-1)} \right)^2.$$

Chapter 10

10.1 The design space for the test specifications in Exercise 3.8 is the Cartesian product of the following attributes: (i) content (arithmetic; graphs; use of pocket calculator); (ii) item-difficulty parameter; (iii) item-discrimination parameter; and (iv) guessing parameter. Item information is calculated from the values of the item parameters at each design point. We can ignore the expected response time because it is approximately constant for each item and test taker.

If we choose ten values each for the difficulty and discrimination parameters, and three values for the guessing parameter, the design space contains $3 \times 10 \times 10 \times 3 = 900$ points.

It is not necessary to reduce a space of this size, but if it were required, we could reduce the number of points to 300 by assuming a common value for the guessing parameter (e.g., the reciprocal of the number of response alternatives).

10.2

$$\text{Minimize } \sum_{i=1}^{900} \varphi_d x_d$$

subject to

$$\sum_{d=1}^{900} I_d(-1)x_d \le 9,$$

$$\sum_{d=1}^{900} I_d(1)x_d \le 9,$$

$$\sum_{d=1}^{900} I_d(-1)x_d \ge 7,$$

$$\sum_{d=1}^{900} I_d(1)x_d \ge 7,$$

$$\sum_{d=1}^{900} x_d = 30,$$

$$\sum_{d \in V_A} x_d \le \sum_{d \in V_G \cup V_{PC}} x_d,$$

$$x_d \in \{0, 1, ...\}, \quad \text{for } d = 1, ..., 900,$$

where V_A, V_G, and V_{PC} are the sets of the design points with the content categories arithmetic, graphs, and use of pocket calculator. The constraint on items 61–65 can be ignored because it is a logical constraint at the item level.

10.3 For this extension, a model with variables x_{dt}, $t = 1, 2$, is required:

$$\text{minimize} \sum_{i=1}^{900} \varphi_d x_{dt}$$

subject to

$$\sum_{d=1}^{900} I_d(-1)x_{d1} \leq 9,$$

$$\sum_{d=1}^{900} I_d(1)x_{d1} \leq 9,$$

$$\sum_{d=1}^{900} I_d(0)x_{d2} \leq 9,$$

$$\sum_{d=1}^{900} I_d(2)x_{d2} \leq 9,$$

$$\sum_{d=1}^{900} I_d(-1)x_{d1} \geq 7,$$

$$\sum_{d=1}^{900} I_d(1)x_{d1} \geq 7,$$

$$\sum_{d=1}^{900} I_d(0)x_{d2} \geq 7,$$

$$\sum_{d=1}^{900} I_d(2)x_{d2} \geq 7,$$

$$\sum_{d=1}^{900} x_{dt} = 30, \quad \text{for } t = 1, 2,$$

$$\sum_{d \in V_A} x_{dt} \leq \sum_{d \in V_G \cup V_{PC}} x_{dt}, \quad \text{for } t = 1, 2,$$

$$x_{dt} \in \{0, 1, ...\}, \quad \text{for } d = 1, ..., 900 \text{ and } t = 1, 2.$$

10.4 The aggregation of the test length is straightforward. We do not have to aggregate the constraint on the relation between the numbers of items on arithmetic, graphs, and the use of a pocket calculator. Because the TIFs of the two tests are constrained at different points θ_k, an additional assumption with respect to the choice of target values is necessary; for instance, we could assume that it is necessary to constrain both TIFs at all four points $\theta = -1, 0, 1$, and 2, with aggregated bounds equal to 14 and 18.

10.5 The changes required for the model in the preceding answer are: (i) substitution of $x_{d1} + z_{d12}$ for x_{d1} and $x_{d2} + z_{d12}$ for x_{d2}, and (ii) the addition of the constraints

$$\sum_{d=1}^{900} z_{d12} \leq 8,$$

$$\sum_{d=1}^{900} z_{d12} \geq 4.$$

10.6 Let V_{SE}, V_M, V_{CE}, V_L, and V_E be the sets of stimulus points with the attributes static electricity, magnetism, current electricity, light, and description of an experiment, respectively, and V_C, V_{PL}, V_{KC}, and V_{KP} the sets of item points with the attributes computational activity, use of a physical law, knowledge of a concept, and knowledge of a principle.

The model is

$$\text{minimize} \sum_{e=1}^{E} \sum_{d=1}^{D} \varphi_{d_e} x_{d_e} + \sum_{e=1}^{E} \varphi_e z_e$$

subject to

$$\sum_{d=1}^{D} x_{d_e} = 40,$$

$$\sum_{d \in V_C^{\text{item}}} x_{d_e} \leq 18,$$

$$\sum_{e \in V_{SE}^{\text{stim}}} z_e = 2,$$

$$\sum_{e \in V_M^{\text{stim}}} z_e = 2,$$

$$\sum_{e \in V_{CE}^{\text{stim}}} z_e = 2,$$

$$\sum_{e \in V_L^{\text{stim}}} z_e = 2,$$

$$\sum_{e \in V_E^{\text{stim}}} z_e \leq 4,$$

$$\sum_{d=1}^{D} x_{d_e} \leq 6z_e, \quad \text{for all } e,$$

$$\sum_{d=1}^{D} x_{d_e} \geq 4z_e, \quad \text{for all } e,$$

$$\sum_{d \in V_{PL}^{\text{item}}} x_{d_e} > \sum_{d \in V_{KC}^{\text{item}} \cup V_{KP}^{\text{item}}} x_{d_e}, \quad \text{for all } e,$$

$$x_{d_e}, z_e \in \{0, 1\}, \quad \text{for all } d \text{ and } e.$$

10.7 In the first stage, the stimuli are selected using

$$\text{minimize} \sum_{e=1}^{E} \varphi_e z_e$$

subject to

$$\sum_{e \in V_{SE}^{\text{stim}}} z_e = 2,$$

$$\sum_{e \in V_M^{\text{stim}}} z_e = 2,$$

$$\sum_{e \in V_{CE}^{\text{stim}}} z_e = 2,$$

$$\sum_{e \in V_L^{\text{stim}}} z_e = 2,$$

$$\sum_{e \in V_E^{\text{stim}}} z_e \leq 4,$$

$$z_e \in \{0, 1\}, \quad \text{for all } e.$$

In the second stage, the items are selected using

$$\text{minimize} \sum_{d=1}^{D} \varphi_d x_d$$

subject to

$$\sum_{d=1}^{D} x_d = 40,$$

$$\sum_{d \in V_C^{\text{item}}} x_d \leq 18,$$

$$\sum_{d \in V_{PL}^{\text{item}}} x_d > \sum_{d \in V_{KC}^{\text{item}} \cup V_{KP}^{\text{item}}} x_d,$$

$$x_d \in \{0, 1\}, \quad \text{for all } d.$$

In the third stage, we use indices $s_e = 1, ..., S_e$ to denote the individual stimuli required at stimulus point $e \in \mathcal{E}$ according to the solution for the stimulus model calculated in the second stage. In addition, we have variables y_{ds_e} for the assignment of the items at the points d to the stimuli s_e. The items are assigned to the stimuli using

$$\sum_{e=1}^{E} \sum_{s=1}^{S_e} \sum_{d=1}^{D} \varphi_{d_e} y_{ds_e}$$

subject to

$$\sum_{e=1}^{E} \sum_{s=1}^{S_e} y_{ds_e} = x_d^*, \quad \text{for all } d,$$

$$\sum_{d=1}^{D} y_{ds_e} \leq 6, \quad \text{for all } s \text{ and } e,$$

$$\sum_{d=1}^{D} y_{ds_e} \geq 4, \quad \text{for all } s \text{ and } e,$$

$$y_{ds_e} \in \{0, 1\}, \quad \text{for all } d, \ s, \text{ and } e,$$

where φ_{d_e} is the cost of writing an item at d for a stimulus at e and x_d^* is the value of decision variable x_d in the solution for the item model calculated in the first stage. Observe that the model has supply constraints and item-set level constraints only. All other test specifications have already been realized in stage one or two.

Chapter 11

11.1 Ignoring the rounding operation in (11.18), the number of items required at d is equal to

$$\frac{\eta_d}{J r^{\max}}.$$

The total number of items required in the pool is equal to

$$I^* = \frac{\sum_{d=1}^{D} \eta_d}{J r^{\max}}.$$

As the item pool is required to be minimally equal to $I^{\min}$, the minimum number of items needed at d is

$$\frac{\eta_d I^{\min}}{J r^{\max} I^*} = \frac{\eta_d I^{\min}}{\sum_{d=1}^{D} \eta_d}.$$

Upward rounding gives

$$N_d = \mathrm{int}\left(\frac{\eta_d I^{\min}}{\displaystyle\sum_{d=1}^{D} \eta_d}\right).$$

Likewise, for the case of conditional exposure control, we have

$$N_d = \mathrm{int}\left(\max_k \left\{\frac{\eta_d^{(k)} I^{\min}}{\displaystyle\sum_{d=1}^{D} \eta_d^{(k)}}\right\}\right).$$

11.2 Analogous to (11.19),

$$N_e = \mathrm{int}\left(\max_k \left\{\frac{\mu_e^{(k)}}{J^{(k)} r^{\max}}\right\}\right).$$

Hence,

$$N_{d_e} = \mathrm{int}\left(\max_k \left\{\frac{(1 + \varepsilon_e)\eta_{d_e}^{(k)}}{J^{(k)} r^{\max}}\right\}\right),$$

with ε_e in (11.42) defined for the conditional version of (11.41).

11.3 The model is identical to (11.47)–(11.50) with the following exceptions: (i) the attribute space $\mathcal{D}$ is a one-dimensional space defined by
a set of discrete values of discrimination parameter a; (ii) the distance
measure δ_{id} is defined as the absolute difference between a_i and a_d;
and (iii) the following types of constraints added to the model:

$$\sum_{i \in V_\beta} x_{id} \gtrless n_{d_\beta}, \quad \text{for all } d \text{ and } \beta,$$

where $\beta = 1, ..., B$ is a partition of the range of values for difficulty
parameter b, V_β is the set of indices of the items with a value in interval β, and n_{d_β} are bounds on the number of items assigned to d
from interval β.
Although the new distance measure is simpler, a serious problem
with this alternative model is the risk of infeasibility due to the new
constraints on the distributions of the values for the difficulty parameter. The original model, however, always has a solution for each set
of values for the bounds n_d in (11.49) with $\sum_{d=1}^{D} n_d = I$.

11.4 The values of θ_t are the midpoints of the intervals with 10% of the
probability mass. They can be found by solving $\Phi(\theta_t) = .10t$ for
θ_i using a conventional table for the standard normal cumulative
distribution function $\Phi(.)$.

11.5 Let $i_d = 1, ..., I_d$ be the index of the ith item at design point $d \in W$, where W is the subset of points in $\mathcal{D}$ for which the pool has at least H items. The following model uses variables $x_{i_d h}$ for the decision on the assignment of item i at point d to item pool $h = 1, ..., H$:

$$\text{minimize } y$$

subject to

$$\sum_{d=1}^{W} \sum_{i_d=1}^{I_d} I_{i_d}(\theta_k)(x_{i_d h'} - x_{i_d h''}) \le y, \quad \text{for all } k \text{ and } h' \ne h'' = 1, ..., H,$$

$$\sum_{d=1}^{W} \sum_{i_d=1}^{I_d} I_{i_d}(\theta_k)(x_{i_d h'} - x_{i_d h''}) \le y, \quad \text{for all } k \text{ and } h' \ne h'' = 1, ..., H,$$

$$\sum_{i_d=1}^{I_d} x_{i_p h} = m_d/H, \quad \text{for all } d \in W, \text{ and } h,$$

$$\sum_{h=1}^{2} x_{i_d h} = 1, \quad \text{for all } i \text{ and } d \in W,$$

$$x_{i_d h} \in \{0, 1\}, \quad \text{for all } i, d \in W, \text{ and } h,$$

where m_d is the number of items available at d, and it is assumed that m_d/H is an integer (possibly after previous editing of the master pool).

The two-stage procedure is a heuristic, and its solutions can never be better than those for the model above. But the model above entails an extremely large number of variables and constraints for a master pool of realistic size.

Bibliography

This bibliography contains all literature on test design known to the author along with the other publications referred to in this book.

Aarts, E. H. L., & Korst, J. H. M., & van Laarhoven, P. J. M. (2003). Simulated annealing. In E. Aarts & J. K. Lenstra, (Eds.), *Local Search in Combinatorial Optimization.* Princeton, NJ: Princeton University Press.

Aarts, E. H. L., & Lenstra, J. K. (Eds.) (2003). *Local Search in Combinatorial Optimization.* Princeton, NJ: Princeton University Press.

Ackerman, T. (1989). *An Alternative Methodology for Creating Parallel Test Forms Using the IRT Information Function.* Paper presented at the annual meeting of the National Council on Measurement in Education, San Francisco, CA.

Adema, J. J. (1990a). *Models and Algorithms for the Construction of Achievement Tests.* Unpublished doctoral dissertation, University of Twente, Enschede, The Netherlands.

Adema, J. J. (1990b). The construction of customized two-staged tests. *Journal of Educational Measurement, 27,* 241–253.

Adema, J. J. (1992a). Methods and models for the construction of weakly parallel tests. *Applied Psychological Measurement, 16,* 53–63.

Adema, J. J. (1992b). Implementations of the branch-and-bound method for test construction. *Methodika, 6,* 99–117.

Adema, J. J., Boekkooi-Timminga, E. & Gademan, A. J. R. M. (1992). Computerized test construction. In M. Wilson (Ed.), *Objective measurement: Theory into Practice* (Vol. 1) (pp. 261–273). Norwood, NJ: Ablex.

Adema, J. J., Boekkooi-Timminga, E., & van der Linden, W. J. (1991). Achievement test construction using 0-1 linear programming. *European Journal of Operations Research, 55,* 103–111.

Adema, J. J. & van der Linden, W. J. (1989). Algorithms for computerized test construction using classical item parameters. *Journal of Educational Statistics, 14,* 279–290.

Ariel, A., van der Linden, W. J., & Veldkamp, B. P. (in press). A strategy for optimizing item-pool management. *Journal of Educational Measurement.*

Ariel, A., Veldkamp, B. P., & van der Linden, W. J. (2004). Constructing rotating item pools for constrained adaptive testing. *Journal of Educational Measurement, 41,* 345–359.

Armstrong, R. D., & Jones, D. H. (1992). Polynomial algorithms for item matching. *Applied Psychological Measurement, 16,* 365–373.

Armstrong, R. D., Jones, D. H., & Kunce, C. S. (1998). IRT test assembly using network-flow programming. *Applied Psychological Measurement, 22,* 237–246.

Armstrong, R. D., Jones, D. H., Li, X., & Wu, I.-L. (1996). A study of network-flow a algorithm and a noncorrecting algorithm for test assembly. *Applied Psychological Measurement, 20,* 89–98.

Armstrong, R. D., Jones, D. H., & Wang, Z. (1994). Automated parallel test construction using classical test theory. *Journal of Educational Statistics, 19,* 73–90.

Armstrong, R. D., Jones, D. H., & Wang, Z. (1995). Network optimization in constrained standardized test construction. In K. D. Lawrence (Ed.), *Applications of Management Science: Network Optimization Applications* (Vol. 8) (pp. 189–212). Greenwich, CT: JAI Press.

Armstrong, R. D., Jones, D. H., & Wang, Z. (1998). Optimization of classical reliability in test construction. *Journal of Educational and Behavioral Statistics, 23,* 1–17.

Armstrong, R. D., Jones, D. H., & Wu, I.-L. (1992). An automated test development of parallel tests. *Psychometrika, 57,* 271–288.

Armstrong, R. D., & Little, J. (2003). *The Assembly of Multiple-Form Structures.* Paper presented at the Annual Meeting of the National Council on Measurement in Education, Chicago, IL.

Atkinson, A. C. (1982). Developments in the design of experiments. *International Statistical Review, 50,* 161–177.

Baker, F. B., Cohen, A. S., & Barmish, B. R. (1988). Item characteristics of tests constructed by linear programming. *Applied Psychological Measurement, 12,* 189–200.

Béguin, A. A., & Glas, C. A. W. (2001). MCMC estimation and some model-fit analyses of multidimensional IRT models. *Psychometrika, 66,* 541–562.

Berger, M. P. F. (1994). A general approach to algorithmic design of fixed-form tests, adaptive tests, and testlets. *Applied Psychological Measurement, 18*, 141–153.

Berger, M. P. F. (1997). Optimal designs for latent variable models: A review. In J. Rost & R. Langeheine (Eds.), *Applications of Latent Trait and Latent Class Models in the Social Sciences* (pp. 71–79). Münster, Germany: Waxmann.

Berger, M. P. F. (1998). Optimal design of tests with items with dichotomous and polytomous response formats. *Applied Psychological Measurement, 22*, 248–258.

Berger, M. P. F., & Mathijssen, E. (1997). Optimal test designs for polytomously scored items. *British Journal of Mathematical and Statistical Psychology, 50*, 127–141.

Berger, M. P. F., & van der Linden, W. J. (1992). Optimality of sampling design in item response theory models. In M. Wilson (Ed.), *Objective measurement: Theory into Practice* (Vol. 1) (pp. 274–288). Norwood, NJ: Ablex.

Berger, M. P. F., & van der Linden, W. J. (1995). Het optimaal ontwerpen van tests met verschillende optimaliteitscriteria [Designing educational tests with different criteria of optimality]. *Tijdschrift voor Onderwijsresearch, 20*, 79–92.

Berger, M. P. F., & Veerkamp, W. J. J. (1996). A review of selection methods for optimal test design. In G. Engelhard, Jr. & M. Wilson (Eds.), *Objective Measurement: Theory into Practice* (Vol. 3) (pp. 437–456). Norwood, NJ: Ablex.

Binet, A., & Simon, Th. (1905). Méthode nouvelles pour le diagnostic du niveau intellectual des anormaux. *L'Anneé Psychologique, 11*, 191–244.

Birnbaum, A. (1968). Some latent trait models and their use in inferring an examinee's ability. In F. M. Lord & M. R. Novick, *Statistical Theories of Mental Test Scores* (pp. 397–479). Reading, MA: Addison-Wesley.

Bloom, B. S., Hastings, J. T., & Madaus, G. F. (1971). *Handbook on Formative and Summative Evaluation of Student Learning*. New York: McGraw-Hill.

Boekkooi-Timminga, E. (1987). Simultaneous test construction by zero-one programming. *Methodika, 1*, 1101–112.

Boekkooi-Timminga, E. (1989). *Models for Computerized Test Construction*. Unpublished doctoral dissertation, University of Twente, Enschede, The Netherlands.

Boekkooi-Timminga, E. (1990a). The construction of parallel tests from IRT-based item banks. *Journal of Educational Statistics, 15*, 129–145.

Boekkooi-Timminga, E. (1990b). A cluster-based method for test construction. *Applied Psychological Measurement, 15*, 129–145.

Boekkooi-Timminga, E. (1991). *A Method for Designing Rasch Model Based Item Banks*. Paper presented at the Annual Meeting of the Psychometric Society, Princeton, NJ.

Boekkooi-Timminga, E. (1993). Computer-assisted test construction. *Social Science Computer Review, 11*, 292–300.

Boekkooi-Timminga, E., & Sun, L. (1991). CONTEST: A computerized test construction system. In J. Hoogstraten & W. J. van der Linden (Eds.), *Methodologie* (pp. 69–76). Amsterdam, The Netherlands: SCO.

Boekkooi-Timminga, E., & van der Linden, W. J. (1988). Algorithms for automated test design. In F. J. Maarse, L. J. M. Mulder, W. P. B. Sjouw, & A. E. Akkerman (Eds.), *Computers in Psychology: Methods, Instrumentation, and Psychodiagnosis* (pp. 171–176). Berwyn, PA: Swets Publishing.

Boomsma, Y. (1986). *Item Selection by Mathematical Programming*. Unpublished master's thesis, University of Twente, Enschede, The Netherlands.

Butterfield, E. C., Nielsen, D., Tangen, K. L., & Richardson, M. B. (1985). Theoretically based psychometric measures of inductive reasoning. In S. E. Embretson (Ed.), *Test design: Developments in Psychology and Psychometrics*. Orlando, FL: Academic Press.

Chang, H., & van der Linden, W. J. (2003). Optimal stratification of item pools in alpha-stratified adaptive testing. *Applied Psychological Measurement, 27*, 262–274.

Chang, H., & Ying, Z. (1996). A global information approach to computerized adaptive testing. *Applied Psychological Measurement, 20*, 213–229.

Chang, H., & Ying, Z. (1999). a-stratified multistage computerized adaptive testing. *Applied Psychological Measurement, 23*, 211–222.

Claassen, A. (1997). *Optimal Test Design: Assembling Tests Using a Genetic Algorithm* (Internal report). Arnhem, The Netherlands: Cito.

Cronbach, L. J. (1970). *Essentials of Psychological Testing* (3rd ed.). New York: Harper & Row.

de Gruijter, D. N. M. (1990). Test construction by means of linear programming. *Applied Psychological Measurement, 14*, 175–181.

DuBois, P. H. (1970). *A History of Psychological Testing*. Boston: Allyn & Bacon.

Fan, M. (1997). *A Comparison of Computerized Test Assembly Programs for Constructing Parallel Test Forms*. Paper presented at the Annual Meeting of the Psychometric Society, Gatlinburg, TN.

Fedorov, V. V. (1972). *Theory of Optimal Experiments*. New York: Academic Press.

Feiring, L. (1986). *Linear Programming: An Introduction*. Thousand Oaks, CA: Sage Publications.

Feuerman, F., & Weiss, H. (1973). A mathematical programming model for test construction and scoring. *Management Science, 19*, 961–966.

Fleishman, E. A., & Quaintance, M. K. (1984). *Taxonomy of Human Performance: The Description of Human Tasks*. Orlando, FL: Academic Press.

Gademan, A. J. R. M. (1987). *Item Selection Using Multi-objective Programming* (OIS Report No. 1). Arnhem, The Netherlands: Cito.

Glas, C. A. W. (1988). Psychometric aspects of maintaining standards of examinations. *Educational Psychology, 8*, 257–270.

Graham, M. S., Sherali, H. D., & Shetty, C. M. (1993). *Nonlinear Programming: Theory and Algorithms* (2nd ed.). New York: Wiley.

Gulliksen, H. (1950). *Theory of Mental Tests.* New York: Wiley. [Reprinted in 1987 by Erlbaum, Hillsdale, NJ]

Haladyna, T. M. (1994). *Developing and Validating Multiple-Choice Questions.* Hillsdale, NJ: Erlbaum.

Hambleton, R. K., & Swaminathan, H. (1985). *Item Response Theory: Principles and Applications.* Boston, MA: Kluwer-Nijhoff.

Hambleton, R. K., Swaminathan, H., & Rogers, H. J. (1991). *Fundamentals of Item Response Theory.* Newbury Park, CA: Sage Publications.

Hastie, T., Tibshirani, R., & Friedman, J. (2001). *The Elements of Statistical Learning.* New York: Springer.

Hertz, A., Taillard, E., & de Werra, D. (2003). Tabu search. In E. Aarts & J. K. Lenstra (Eds.), *Local Search in Combinatorial Optimization.* Princeton, NJ: Princeton University Press.

Hetter, R. D., & Sympson, J. B. (1997). Item exposure control in CAT-ASVAB. In W. A. Sands, B. K. Waters, & J. R. McBride (Eds.), *Computerized Adaptive Testing: From Inquiry to Operation* (pp. 141–144). Washington, D.C.: American Psychological Association.

Huitzing, H. A. (2003). *Infeasibility in Automatic Test Assembly: Analysis, Causes and Solutions.* Unpublished doctoral dissertation, University of Groningen, The Netherlands.

Huitzing, H. A. (2004). Using set covering with item sampling to analyze the infeasibility of linear programming test assembly models. *Applied Psychological Measurement, 28*, 355–375.

Huitzing, H. A. (2004). An interactive method to solve infeasibility in linear programming test assembly models. *Journal of Educational Measurement, 41*, 175–192.

Huitzing, H. A., Veldkamp, B. P., & Verschoor, A. J. (2005). Infeasibility in automatic test assembly models: A comparison study of different methods. *Journal of Educational Measurement, 42*, 223–244.

ILOG, Inc. (2003). *CPLEX 9.0.* Incline Village, NV: ILOG, Inc. [URL: www.ilog.com]

ILOG, Inc. (2003). *OPL Suite 3.7.* Incline Village, NV: ILOG, Inc. [URL: www.ilog.com]

Irvine, S. H., & Kyllonen, P. C. (Eds.) (2002). *Item Generation for Test Development.* Mahwah, NJ: Erlbaum.

Johnson, E. G. (1992). The design of the national assessment of educational progress. *Journal of Educational Measurement, 29*, 95–110.

Kelderman, H. (1987). Some procedures to assess target information functions. In W. J. van der Linden (Ed.), *IRT-Based Test Construction* (Research Report 87-2). Enschede, The Netherlands: University of Twente, Department of Educational Measurement and Data Analysis.

Kester, J. G. (1988). *Various Mathematical Programming Approaches toward Item Selection* (OIS Project Report No. 3). Arnhem, The Netherlands: Cito.

Lewis, C., & Sheehan, K. (1990). Using Bayesian decision theory to design a computerized mastery test. *Applied Psychological Measurement, 14,* 367–386.

Li, Y. H. (2002). *Multidimensional Computerized Adaptive Testing with Shadow-Test and Item-Exposure Constraints.* Paper presented at the annual meeting of the American Educational Research Association, New Orleans, LA.

Li, Y. H., & Schafer, W. D. (2003). *Increasing the Homogeneity of CAT's Item-Exposure Rates by Minimizing or Maximizing Varied Target Functions while Assembling Shadow Tests.* Paper presented at the Annual Meeting of the National Council on Measurement in Education, Chicago, IL.

LINDO Systems, Inc. (2003). *LINDO 6.1.* Chicago, IL: LINDO Systems, Inc. [URL: www.lindo.com]

Lord, F. M. (1970). Some test theory for tailored testing. In W. H. Holtzmann (Ed.), *Computer-Assisted Instruction, Testing, and Guidance.* New York: Harper and Row.

Lord, F. M. (1971). Robbins-Monro procedures for tailored testing. *Educational and Psychological Measurement, 31,* 2–31.

Lord, F. M. (1980). *Applications of Item Response Theory to Practical Testing Problems.* Hillsdale, NJ: Erlbaum.

Lord, F. M., & Novick, M. R. (1968). *Statistical Theories of Mental Test Scores.* Reading, MA: Addison-Wesley.

Lord, F. M., & Wingersky, M. S. (1984). Comparison of IRT true-score and equipercentile observed-score "equatings." *Applied Psychological Measurement, 8,* 452–461.

Luecht, R. M. (1996). Multidimensional computerized adaptive testing in a certification or licensure context. *Applied Psychological Measurement, 20,* 389–404.

Luecht, R. M. (1998). Computer-assisted test assembly using optimization heuristics. *Applied Psychological Measurement, 22,* 224–236.

Luecht, R. M., & Hirsch, T. M. (1992). Computerized test construction using average growth approximation of target information functions. *Applied Psychological Measurement, 16,* 41–52.

McKinley, R. L., & Reckase, M. D. (1983). *An Extension of the Two-Parameter Logistic Model to the Multidimensional Latent Space* (Research Report ONR 83-2). Iowa City, IA: American College Testing.

Miyaji, I., Nakagawa, Y., & Ohno, K. (1995). Decision support system for composition of the examination problem. *European Journal of Operational Research, 80,* 130–138.

Mühlenbein, H. (2003). Genetic algorithms. In E. Aarts & J. K. Lenstra (Eds.), *Local Search in Combinatorial Optimization.* Princeton, NJ: Princeton University Press.

Nemhauser, G. L., & Wolsey, L. A. (1999). *Integer and Combinatorial Optimization.* New York: Wiley.

Papadimitriou, C. H., & Stieglitz, K. (1982). *Combinatorial Optimization: Algorithms and Complexity.* Englewood Cliffs, NJ: Prentice-Hall.

Paragon Decision Technology (2004). *AIMMS 3.5.* Haarlem, The Netherlands: Paragon Decision Technology. [URL: www.aimms.com]

Parshall, C. G., Spray, J. A., Kalohn, J. C., & Davey, T. (2002). *Practical Considerations in Computer-Based Testing.* New York: Springer.

Pellegrino, J. W., Mumaw, R. J., & Shute, V. J. (1985). Analysis of spatial aptitude and expertise. In S. E. Embretson (Ed.), *Test Design: Developments in Psychology and Psychometrics.* Orlando, FL: Academic Press.

Peterson, C., & Söderberg, B. (2003). Artificial neural networks. In E. Aarts & J. K. Lenstra (Eds.), *Local Search in Combinatorial Optimization.* Princeton, NJ: Princeton University Press.

Popham, W. J. (1978). *Criterion-Referenced Measurement.* Englewood Cliffs, NJ: Prentice-Hall.

Razoux Schultz, A. F. (1987). *Item Selection Using Heuristics* (IOS Report No. 2). Arnhem, The Netherlands: Cito.

Reckase, M. D. (1985). The difficulty of test items that measure more than one ability. *Applied Psychological Measurement, 9,* 401–412.

Reckase, M. D. (1997). A linear logistic multidimensional model for dichotomous item response data. In W. J. van der Linden & R. K. Hambleton (Eds.), *Handbook of Modern Item Response Theory.* New York: Springer.

Robin, F., van der Linden, W. J., Eignor, D. R., Steffen, M., & Stocking, M. L. (2004). *A Comparison of Two Procedures for Constrained Adaptive Test Construction* (Research Report RR-04-39). Princeton, NJ: Educational Testing Service.

Sanders, P. F., & Verschoor, A. J. (1998). Parallel test construction using classical item parameters. *Applied Psychological Measurement, 22,* 212–223.

Segall, D. O. (1996). Multidimensional adaptive testing. *Psychometrika, 61,* 331–354.

Segall, D. O. (2000). Principles of multidimensional adaptive testing. In W. J. van der Linden & C. A. W. Glas (Eds.), *Computerized Adaptive Testing: Theory and Practice* (pp. 53–73). Boston, MA: Kluwer Academic Publishers.

Segall, D. O. (in preparation). Methods of improving item security in adaptive testing. In W. J. van der Linden & C. A. W. Glas (Eds.), *Elements of Adaptive Testing.* New York: Springer.

Silvey, S. D. (1980). *Optimal Design.* London: Chapman & Hall.

Spearman, C. (1904). The proof and measurement of association between two things. *American Journal of Psychology, 15,* 72–101.

Sternberg, R. J., & McNamara, T. P. (1985). The representation and processing of information in real-time verbal comprehension. In S. E. Embretson (Ed.), *Test Design: Developments in Psychology and Psychometrics*. Orlando, FL: Academic Press.

Stocking, M. L. & Lewis, C. (1998). Controlling item exposure conditional on ability in computerized adaptive testing. *Journal of Educational and Behavioral Statistics, 23*, 57–75.

Stocking, M. L., & Swanson, L. (1993). A method for severely constrained item selection in adaptive testing. *Applied Psychological Measurement, 17*, 277–292.

Stocking, M. L., & Swanson, L. (1998). Optimal design of item banks for computerized adaptive testing. *Applied Psychological Measurement, 22*, 271–279.

Stocking, M. L., Swanson, L., & Pearlman, M. (1993). Application of an automated item selection method to real data. *Applied Psychological Measurement, 17*, 167–176.

Sun, K. T. (1999). Applying AI technique to construct a desired test. In G. Cumming, T. Okamoto, & L. Gomez (Eds.), *Advanced Research in Computers and Communication in Education*. Amsterdam, The Netherlands: IOS Press.

Swanson, L., & Stocking, M. L. (1993). A model and heuristic for solving very large item selection problems. *Applied Psychological Measurement, 17*, 151–166.

Sympson, J. B., & Hetter, R. D. (1985). Controlling item-exposure rates in computerized adaptive testing. *Proceedings of the 27th Annual Meeting of the Military Testing Association* (pp. 973–977). San Diego, CA: Navy Personnel Research and Development Center.

Theunissen, T. J. J. M. (1985). Binary programming and test design. *Psychometrika, 50*, 411–420.

Theunissen, T. J. J. M. (1986). Optimization algorithms in test design. *Applied Psychological Measurement, 10*, 381–389.

Theunissen, T. J. J. M. (1996). *Combinatorial Issues in Test Construction*. Unpublished doctoral dissertation, University of Amsterdam, The Netherlands.

Theunissen, T. J. J. M., & Verstralen, H. H. F. M. (1986). Algoritmen voor het samenstellen van toetsen [Algorithms for test assembly]. In W. J. van der Linden (Ed.), *Moderne Methoden van Toetsconstructie- en Gebruik* (pp. 32–39). Amsterdam, The Netherlands: Swets & Zeitlinger.

Timminga, E. (1985). *Geautomatiseerd Toetsontwerk: Itemselectie met Behulp van Binair programmeren* [Automated Test Design: Item Selection Using Binary Programming]. Unpublished master's thesis, University of Twente, Enschede, The Netherlands.

Timminga, E. (1998). Solving infeasibility problems in computerized test assembly. *Applied Psychological Measurement, 22*, 280–291.

Timminga, E., & Adema, J. J. (1995). Test construction from item banks. In G. H. Fischer & I. W. Molenaar (Eds.), *The Rasch Model: Founda-*

tions, Recent Developments, and Applications (pp. 111–127). New York: Springer.

Timminga, E., & Adema, J. J. (1996). An interactive approach to modifying infeasible 0-1 linear programming models for test construction. In G. Engelhard, Jr. & M. Wilson (Eds.), *Objective Measurement: Theory into Practice* (Vol. 3) (pp. 419–436). Norwood, NJ: Ablex.

Timminga, E., van der Linden, W. J., & Schweizer, D. A. (1996). *ConTEST 2.0: A Decision Support System for Item Banking and Optimal Test Assembly* (Computer software and manual). Groningen, The Netherlands: iec ProGAMMA.

Timminga, E., van der Linden, W. J., & Schweizer, D. A. (1997). *ConTEST 2.0 Modules: A Decision Support System for Item Banking and Optimal Test Assembly* (Computer software and manual). Groningen, The Netherlands: iec ProGAMMA.

van der Linden, W. J. (1986). The changing conception of testing in education and psychology. *Applied Psychological Measurement, 10*, 325–332.

van der Linden, W. J. (1987a). Automated test construction using minimax programming. In W. J. van der Linden (Ed.), *IRT-Based Test Construction* (Research Report 87-2). Enschede, The Netherlands: University of Twente, Department of Educational Measurement and Data Analysis.

van der Linden, W. J. (1987b). Models for use in computerized test systems. In J. Moonen & T. Plomp (Eds.), *Developments in Educational Software and Courseware* (pp. 299–307). Oxford: Pergamon Press.

van der Linden, W. J. (1989). Optimaliseringsmodellen voor klassieke toetsconstructie uit een gecalibreerde itembank [Optimization models for classical test construction from a calibrated item bank]. In W. J. van der Linden & L. J. Th. van der Kamp (Eds.), *Meetmethoden en Data-Analyse* (pp. 33–42). Amsterdam, The Netherlands: Swets & Zeitlinger.

van der Linden, W. J. (1991). Toetsconstructie als een voorbeeldig ontwerpprobleem [Test construction as an example of a design problem]. In S. Dijkstra, H. P. M. Krammer, & J. M. Pieters (Eds.), *De Onderwijskundig Ontwerper* (pp. 61-70). Amsterdam, The Netherlands: Swets & Zeitlinger. (In Dutch)

van der Linden, W. J. (1992). *Selecting Passage-Based Items for Achievement Tests* (Internal report). Iowa City, IA: American College Testing.

van der Linden, W. J. (1994a). Optimum design in item response theory: Applications to test assembly and item calibration. In G. H. Fischer & D. Laming (Eds.), *Contributions to Mathematical Psychology, Psychometrics, and Methodology* (pp. 308–318). New York: Springer.

van der Linden W. J. (1994b). Computerized educational measurement. In T. Husen and T. N. Postlethwaite (Eds.). *International Encyclopedia of Education* (2nd ed.) (pp. 992–998). Oxford: Pergamon Press.

van der Linden, W. J. (1995). Advances in computer applications. In T. Oakland & R. K. Hambleton (Eds.), *International Perspectives on Academic Assessment* (pp. 105–124). Boston: Kluwer-Nijhof.

van der Linden, W. J. (1996). Assembling tests for the measurement of multiple traits. *Applied Psychological Measurement, 20*, 373–388.

van der Linden, W. J. (1998a). Optimal assembly of psychological and educational tests. *Applied Psychological Measurement, 22*, 195–211.

van der Linden, W. J. (1998b). Optimal test assembly [Special Issue]. *Applied Psychological Measurement, 22(3)*.

van der Linden, W. J. (1998c). Assembling test forms for use in large-scale assessments. In M. L. Bourque (Ed.), *Proceedings of Achievement Levels Workshop* (pp. 24–43). Washington, DC: National Assessment Governing Board.

van der Linden, W. J. (1998d). Bayesian item-selection criteria for adaptive testing. *Psychometrika, 63*, 201–216.

van der Linden, W. J. (1999a). Empirical initialization of the ability estimator in adaptive testing. *Applied Psychological Measurement, 23*, 21–29 (Corrigenda *23*, 248).

van der Linden, W. J. (1999b). Multidimensional adaptive testing with a minimum error-variance criterion. *Journal of Educational and Behavioral Statistics, 24*, 398–412.

van der Linden, W. J. (2000a). Constrained adaptive testing with shadow tests. In W. J. van der Linden & C. A. W. Glas (Eds.), *Computerized Adaptive Testing: Theory and Practice* (pp. 27–52). Boston, MA: Kluwer Academic Publishers.

van der Linden, W. J. (2000b). Optimal assembly of tests with item sets. *Applied Psychological Measurement, 24*, 225–240.

van der Linden, W. J. (2000c). A test-theoretic approach to observed-score equating. *Psychometrika, 65*, 437–456.

van der Linden, W. J. (2001a). Computerized adaptive testing with equated number-correct scoring. *Applied Psychological Measurement, 25*, 343–355.

van der Linden, W. J. (2001b). Computerized test construction. In N. J. Smelser & P. B. Baltes (Eds.), *International Encyclopedia of Social and Behavioral Sciences* (Vol. 4) (pp. 2477–2480). Oxford: Elsevier Science Ltd.

van der Linden, W. J. (2002). Automated test assembly systems. In R. Fernandéz-Ballasteros (Ed.), *Encyclopedia of Psychological Assessment* (Vol. 1) (pp. 123–128). Newbury Park, CA: Sage.

van der Linden, W. J. (2003). Some alternatives to Sympson-Hetter item-exposure control in computerized adaptive testing. *Journal of Educational and Behavioral Statistics, 28*, 249–265.

van der Linden, W. J. (2005a). A lognormal model for response times on test items. *Journal of Educational and Behavioral Statistics, 30*. In press.

van der Linden, W. J. (2005b). Classical test theory. In K. Kempf-Leonard (Ed.), *Encyclopedia of Social Measurement* (Vol. 1) (pp. 301–307). San Diego, CA: Academic Press.

van der Linden, W. J. (2005c). Item response theory. In K. Kempf-Leonard (Ed.), *Encyclopedia of Social Measurement* (Vol. 2) (pp. 379–387). San Diego, CA: Academic Press.

van der Linden, W. J. (2005d). A comparison of item-selection methods for adaptive tests with content constraints. *Journal of Education Measurement, 42*, 283-302.

van der Linden, W. J. (2005e). Evaluating equating error in observed-score equating. *Applied Psychological Measurement, 28*. In press.

van der Linden, W. J. (submitted). Assembling tests with optimal predictive validity.

van der Linden, W. J. (in preparation). Using response times to improve adaptive testing. In W. J. van der Linden & C. A. W. Glas (Eds.), *Elements of Adaptive Testing*. New York: Springer.

van der Linden, W. J., & Adema, J. J. (1998). Simultaneous assembly of multiple test forms. *Journal of Educational Measurement, 35*, 185–198 (Addendum *36*, 90–91).

van der Linden, W. J., Ariel, A., & Veldkamp, B. P. (2005). Assembling a CAT item pool as a set of linear test forms. *Journal of Educational and Behavioral Statistics, 29*. In press.

van der Linden, W. J., & Boekkooi-Timminga, E. (1988). A zero-one programming approach to Gulliksen's matched random subsets method. *Applied Psychological Measurement, 12*, 201–209.

van der Linden, W. J., & Boekkooi-Timminga, E. (1989). A maximin model for test design with practical constraints. *Psychometrika, 54*, 237–247.

van der Linden, W. J., & Chang, H. (2003). Implementing content constraints in alpha-stratified adaptive testing using a shadow test approach. *Applied Psychological Measurement, 27*, 107–120.

van der Linden, W. J., & Glas, C. A. W. (Eds.) (2000), *Computerized Adaptive Testing: Theory and Practice*. Boston, MA: Kluwer Academic Publishers.

van der Linden, W. J., & Glas, C. A. W. (Eds.) (in preparation). *Elements of Adaptive Testing*. New York: Springer.

van der Linden, W. J. & Hambleton, R. K. (1997). *Handbook of Modern Test Theory*. New York: Springer.

van der Linden, W. J., & Luecht, R. M. (1996). An optimization model for test assembly to match observed-score distributions. In G. Engelhard, Jr. & M. Wilson (Eds.), *Objective Measurement: Theory into Practice* (Vol. 3) (pp. 405–418). Norwood, NJ: Ablex.

van der Linden, W. J., & Luecht, R. M. (1998). Observed-score equating as a test assembly problem. *Psychometrika, 63*, 401–418.

van der Linden, W. J., & Pashley, P. J. (2000). Item selection and ability estimation in adaptive testing. In W. J. van der Linden & C. A. W. Glas (Eds.), *Computerized Adaptive Testing: Theory and Practice* (pp. 1–25). Boston, MA: Kluwer Academic Publishers.

van der Linden, W. J., & Reese, L. M. (1998). A model for optimal con-strained adaptive testing. *Applied Psychological Measurement, 22*, 259–270.

van der Linden, W. J., Scrams, D. J., & Schnipke, D. L. (1999). Us-ing response-time constraints to control for differential speededness in computerized adaptive testing. *Applied Psychological Measurement, 23*, 195–210.

van der Linden, W. J., & Veldkamp, B. P. (2004). Constraining item-exposure rates in computerized adaptive testing with shadow tests. *Jour-nal of Educational and Behavioral Statistics, 29*, 273–291.

van der Linden, W. J., & Veldkamp, B. P. (submitted). Conditional item-exposure control in adaptive testing using item-ineligibility probabilities.

van der Linden, W. J., Veldkamp, B. P., & Carlson, J. E. (2004). Optimizing incomplete block designs for large-scale educational assessments. *Applied Psychological Measurement, 28, 317–331.*

van der Linden, W. J., Veldkamp, B. P., & Reese, L. M. (2000). An in-teger programming approach to item pool design. *Applied Psychological Measurement, 24,* 139–150.

van der Linden, W. J., & Zwarts, M. A. (1989). Some procedures for com-puterized ability testing. *International Journal of Educational Research, 13,* 175–187.

Veldkamp, B. P. (1999). Multiple objective test assembly problems. *Journal of Educational Measurement, 36,* 253–266.

Veldkamp, B. P. (2001). *Principles and Methods of Constrained Test As-sembly.* Unpublished doctoral dissertation, University of Twente, En-schede, The Netherlands.

Veldkamp, B. P. (2002). Constrained multidimensional test assembly. *Ap-plied Psychological Measurement, 26,* 133–146.

Veldkamp, B. P. (2005). Optimal test construction. In K. Kempf-Leonard (Ed.), *Encyclopedia of Social Measurement* (Vol. 2) (pp. 933–941). San Diego, CA: Academic Press.

Veldkamp, B. P., & van der Linden, W. J. (2000). Designing item pools for computerized adaptive testing. In W. J. van der Linden & C. A. W. Glas (Eds.), *Computerized Adaptive Testing: Theory and Practice* (pp. 149–162). Boston, MA: Kluwer Academic Publishers.

Veldkamp, B. P., & van der Linden, W. J. (2002). Multidimensional adap-tive testing with constraints on test content. *Psychometrika, 67,* 575–588.

Veldkamp, B. P., & van der Linden, W. J. (in preparation). Designing item pools for computerized adaptive testing. In W. J. van der Linden & C. A. W. Glas (Eds.), *Elements of Adaptive Testing.* New York: Springer.

Veldkamp, B. P., van der Linden, W. J., & Ariel, A. (2003). Mathematical-programming approaches to test-item pool design. In S. P. Shohov (Ed.), *Advances in Psychology Research* (Vol. 19) (pp. 93–108) . New York: Nova Science Publishers.

Verschoor, A. (1991). *OTD: Optimal Test Design* (Computer software and manual). Arnhem, The Netherlands: Cito.

Verschoor, A. (2004). *IRT Test Assembly Using Genetic Algorithms* (Unpublished manuscript). Arnhem, The Netherlands: Cito.

Vos, H. J. (1999). Applications of Bayesian decision theory to sequential mastery testing. *Journal of Educational and Behavioral Statistics, 24*, 271–292.

Votaw, D. F. (1952). Methods of solving some personnel classification problems. *Psychometrika, 17*, 255–266.

Wagner, H. M. (1975). *Principles of Operational Research, with Applications to Managerial Decisions.* London: Prentice-Hall.

Wainer, H. (2000). *Computerized Adaptive Testing: A Primer.* Mahwah, NJ: Erlbaum.

Wang, C.-S., & Ackerman, T. A. (1998). *Two Item Selection Algorithms for Creating Parallel Test Forms* (Unpublished manuscript). Urbana-Champaign, IL: University of Illinois, Department of Educational Psychology.

Way, W. D. (1998). Protecting the integrity of computerized testing item pools. *Educational Measurement: Issues and Practice, 1*, 17–27.

Way, W. D., Steffen, M., & Anderson, G. S. (1998). Developing, maintaining, and renewing the item inventory to support computer-based testing. In C. N. Mills, M. Potenza, J. J. Fremer, & W. Ward (Eds.), *Computer-Based Testing: Building the Foundation for Future Assessments* (pp. 89–102). Hillsdale, NJ: Lawrence Erlbaum Associates.

Way, W. D., Swanson, L., Steffen, M., & Stocking, M. L. (2001). *Refining a System for Computerized Adaptive Testing Pool Creation* (Research Report 01-18). Princeton, NJ: Educational Testing Service.

Weiss, D. J. (Ed.) (1982). *New Horizons in Testing: Latent Trait Theory and Computerized Adaptive Testing.* New York: Academic Press.

Wigdor, A. K., & Green, Jr., B. F. (Eds.) (1991). *Performance Assessment for the Workplace* (Vol. 1). Washington, DC: National Academy Press.

Wightman, L. F. (1998). Practical issues in computerized test assembly. *Applied Psychological Measurement, 22*, 292–302.

Williams, H. P. (1990). *Model Building in Mathematical Programming.* New York: Wiley

Wu, I.-L. (2001). A new computer algorithm for simultaneous test construction of two-stage and multistage testing. *Journal of Educational and Behavioral Statistics, 26*, 180–198.

Yen, W. M. (1983). Use of the three-parameter model in the development of standardized achievement tests. In R. K. Hambleton (Ed.), *Applications of Item Response Theory.* Vancouver: Educational Research Institute of British Columbia.

Index

 Springer
the language of science

springeronline.com

The Kernel Method of Test Equating

A.A. von Davier, P.W. Holland, and D.T. Thayer

Kernel Equating is based on a flexible family of equipercentile-like equating functions and contains the linear equating function as a special case. This book will be an important reference for (a) Statisticians and others interested in the theory behind equating methods and the use of model-based statistical methods for data smoothing in applied work; (b) Practitioners who need to equate tests—including those with these responsibilities in testing companies, state testing agencies and school districts; and (c) Instructors in psychometric and measurement programs.

2004. 229 p. (Statistics for Social Science and Public Policy) Hardcover
ISBN 0-387-01985-5

Explanatory Item Response Models

P. De Boeck and M. Wilson

This volume gives a new and integrated introduction to item response models from the viewpoint of the statistical theory of generalized linear and nonlinear mixed models. This new framework allows the domain of item response models to be co-ordinated and broadened to emphasize their *explanatory* uses beyond their standard *descriptive* uses.

2004. 382 p. (Statistics for Social Science and Public Policy) Hardcover
ISBN 0-387-40275-6

Test Equating, Scaling, and Linking
Second Edition

M.J. Kolen and R.L. Brennan

This second edition adds chapters on test scaling and test linking. The themes of the second edition include * the purposes of equating, scaling and linking and their practical context; data collection designs; statistical methodology; designing reasonable and useful equating, scaling, and linking studies; importance of test development and quality control processes to equating; and equating error, and the underlying statistical assumptions for equating

2004. 548 p. (Statistics for Social Science and Public Policy) Hardcover
ISBN 0-387-40086-9

Easy Ways to Order ▶ Call: Toll-Free 1-800-SPRINGER • E-mail: orders-ny@springer.sbm.com • Write: Springer, Dept. S8113, PO Box 2485, Secaucus, NJ 07096-2485 • Visit: Your local scientific bookstore or urge your librarian to order.